Politics in German Literature

Studies in German Literature, Linguistics, and Culture

Edited by James Hardin
(*South Carolina*)

Essays in Memory of Frank G. Ryder

Frank G. Ryder

Politics in German Literature

Edited by
Beth Bjorklund and Mark E. Cory

CAMDEN HOUSE

Copyright © 1998 Beth Bjorklund and Mark E. Cory

All Rights Reserved. Except as permitted under current legislation, no part of this work may be photocopied, stored in a retrieval system, published, performed in public, adapted, broadcast, transmitted, recorded, or reproduced in any form or by any means, without the prior permission of the copyright owner.

First published 1998
Camden House
Drawer 2025
Columbia, SC 29202–2025 USA

Camden House is an imprint of Boydell & Brewer Inc.
PO Box 41026, Rochester, NY 14604–4126 USA
and of Boydell & Brewer Limited
PO Box 9, Woodbridge, Suffolk IP12 3DF, UK

ISBN: 1–57113–082–9

Library of Congress Cataloging-in-Publication Data

Politics in German literature / edited by Beth Bjorklund and Mark E. Cory.
    p.   cm. – (Studies in German literature, linguistics, and culture)
  "Essays in memory of Frank G. Ryder"—Half t.p.
  Includes bibliographical references and index.
  ISBN 1–57113–082–9 (alk. paper)
  1. German literature – History and criticism. 2. Politics and literature—Germany—History. I. Bjorklund, Beth. II. Cory, Mark E. III. Series: Studies in German literature, linguistics, and culture (Unnumbered)
PT134.S75P68 1998
830.9'358—dc21
                                                      97–31383
                                                        CIP

This publication is printed on acid-free paper.
Printed in the United States of America

Contents

	Acknowledgments	ix
1	Introduction *Mark E. Cory and Beth Bjorklund*	1
2	Goethe's *Iphigenie auf Tauris* and the First Amendment *Horst Lange*	8
3	The American European Karl Postl/ Charles Sealsfield on the US and Europe in the 1820s *Paul Michael Lützeler*	27
4	The (Mis)Fortune of Commerce–Economic Transformation in Adalbert Stifter's *Bergkristall* *Richard T. Gray*	36
5	The Personal Is Political–The Political Becomes Personal: Fanny Lewald's Early Travel Literature *Margaret E. Ward*	60
6	The German Farmer Confronts the Modern World: An Analysis of Wilhelm von Polenz's *Der Büttnerbauer* *Ronald Horwege*	83
7	The "Raw" and the "Cooked" in *fin-de-siècle* Vienna *Beth Bjorklund*	103

8 Early German Literary Cabaret and 117
   Modernism in Berlin
   David Chisholm

9 Of Weimar's First and Last Things: 132
   Montage, Revolution, and Fascism in
   Alfred Döblin's *November 1918* and
   Berlin Alexanderplatz
   Michael W. Jennings

10 "Wo gehörten sie hin?" The Berlin 153
   Autobiographies of Stephan Hermlin and
   Ludwig Greve
   David Scrase

11 *Excalibur:* Film Reception and Political 166
   Distance
   Ray Wakefield

12 *Ein weites Feld:* The Aestheticization of 177
   German Unification in Recent Works by
   Günter Grass
   Mark E. Cory

13 Contemporary Theory and the German 195
   Tradition: Some Stages in the Emergence of
   Critical Realism
   Michael Morton

14 Afterword 216
   Beth Bjorklund and Mark E. Cory

   Publications of Frank G. Ryder 219

   List of Contributors 224

   Index 227

Acknowledgments

The editors and contributors wish to acknowledge the encouragement and generous financial support towards the production of this volume received from many friends and former colleagues of Frank Ryder. In particular, we are grateful to the Department of Germanic Studies at Indiana University (Terence Thayer, Chair) and the Department of Germanic Languages and Literatures (William McDonald, Chair) and the Graduate School (Stephen Schnatterly, Vice-Provost) at the University of Virginia. We are grateful also to the following individuals: Francis Gentry, Thomas Heine, Sidney Johnson, Breon Mitchell, Kathleen O'Connor, Henry H. H. Remak, Walter Sokel, and Carl Ziegler. Thanks are also due William Plail for his expert and dedicated attention to preparation of copy. Finally, we acknowledge with thanks and affection the assistance throughout of Shirley Ryder.

Introduction

Mark E. Cory and Beth Bjorklund

The twelve original essays presented here invite reflection upon a considerable sweep of German literature, with representation from medieval, eighteenth, nineteenth, and twentieth-century subjects. This eclecticism is at once a tribute to the scholarly breadth of Frank G. Ryder, teacher, mentor, and friend to all the contributors, and at the same time an interesting commentary on the practice of German studies in America today. More so than perhaps in some other cultures, American scholars are often obliged to teach across a wide spectrum, which in turn seems to nurture an adventuresome spirit of intellectual inquiry. The editors hope this spirit proves both transparent and infectious.

The expectation of readers intrigued by a title such as *Politics in German Literature* is for fresh insight into authors whose lives and works were shaped by political events or who, by their works, themselves contributed to the politics of their day. Issues of power, of national identity, of personal freedom in tension with social progress—these are some of the themes which course through the individual essays in this volume. The editors did not attempt, however, to forge an initial consensus on what constitutes the "political," what the "literary." Almost every literary form has been accused at some point of an inherent bias favoring entrenched social power, and indeed all language can be characterized as biased toward the *is*, rather than the *ought*. But apart from that conservative bias, these essays share no common ideology, only the unspoken undercurrent of curiosity towards the way German-language authors have participated in the shaping of a fascinating culture.

All the contributors to this volume are aware that literature and politics use language differently, sometimes have different goals, can in fact exist in considerable tension. This tension, as well as the eclectic spirit mentioned at the outset, makes the arrangement of these essays something of a challenge. Ray Wakefield's reflections on the curious lack of resonance in Germany for John Boorman's 1981 film *Excalibur* engages both Arthurian and contemporary issues. Michael Morton's elucidation of a theory of critical realism juxtaposes Leibniz and Derrida. Horst Lange's reconsideration of religious violence in Goethe's *Iphigenie auf Tauris* has implications for headline stories in both German and American newspapers of today. Consequently, any of these might have initiated or concluded the collection. The solution arrived at seeks a reasonable compromise between the logic of chronology and the meditative spirit which informs many of the contributions.

In the lead article, Horst Lange extends and corrects the provocative argument made originally in 1977 by Wolfdietrich Rasch, by which we are forced to reconsider whether Goethe's *Iphigenie* is satisfactorily understood as the *summa* of German Classicism, independent of the shaping forces still active from the Enlightenment. In a close reading of the text typical of the Ryder approach, Lange asks whether it is not really Goethe's concern to focus our attention on the ways we construe the words of mortal priests and oracles to meet our competing political and personal agendas. Reading the drama as a clash of competing "hermeneutics of divine signs," Lange shows how easily this competition escalates into a "hermeneutics of suspicion," which culminates in physical violence and the threat of general chaos. Goethe's play, as an allegory then of the dangers of religious intolerance, gains resonance both backwards in time to the Enlightenment debates regarding the issue of church and state and forwards to the consequences of the different political solutions adopted in Germany after the Religious Peace of Augsburg and in the United States. In conclusion, Lange honors Goethe's preference for art as a pedagogical tool superior to either constitutional solution, but reminds us that even Goethe's majesty proved inadequate in the face of the political failure to stem the religious intolerance of rampant anti-Semitism in Germany's recent past.

Similarly intrigued by contrasting political approaches on the American and European continents, Paul Michael Lützeler invites us to evaluate the American experiment with democracy after a modest fifty years, as seen through the eyes of the Austrian novelist and essayist, Karl Postl (Charles Sealsfield). In almost seamless fashion, Lützeler picks up on Lange's discussion of the American rejection of Hobbes's views on political absolutism as guarantor of social stability and shows how Sealsfield celebrated American successes in maximizing individual liberty without succumbing to anarchy. Praising George Washington and the Austrian emperor Joseph II, Sealsfield attacks John Quincy Adams and Austria's then chancellor Clemens von Metternich with equal vigor. In America, Sealsfield saw reason for sustained optimism, especially in the 1828 candidacy of Andrew Jackson. For Europe, Sealsfield's hope lay in the rise of a stronger middle class, rather than in an American-style revolution. Neither of Sealsfield's two major essays, *Austria as it is* and *Die Vereinigten Staaten von Nordamerika, nach ihren politischen, religiösen und gesellschaftlichen Verhältnissen betrachtet*, argues for the adoption of a united states of Europe as solution to the lack of social, religious, political, and artistic freedom on the European continent. Lützeler concludes by speculating on how Postl/Sealsfield would view progress toward individual liberty on his favorite continents in the shrinking world at the close of our millenium.

Richard T. Gray reminds us how deeply unsettling the revolution, which Sealsfield did not foresee, but which nevertheless came in 1848, was for Sealsfield's fellow Austrian, Adalbert Stifter. Famous for pastoral idylls that seem deliberately to resist the kind of industrial expansion and social progress that fascinated Sealsfield, Stifter is most often invoked as an example of the way threatening forces of modernity could be dampened and gently assimilated into more durable and ultimately more humane values. Gray challenges this conventional image of Stifter by a close reading of *Bergkristall*, and especially of the revisions undertaken for publication in *Bunte Steine*, a reading that shows how a seemingly simple village tale brings two rival value systems into conflict, one system consciously venerating the stability of the past, the other unconsciously preparing the way for the enormous transition of economic power to the commercial middle class that was to happen despite the failed political Revolution of 1848. By arguing that a grudging acceptance of commerce and a new economics of exchange function as the "unacknowledged ghostwriter" of *Bergkristall*, Gray discovers an entire new layer of significance in Stifter, one that makes the already rich imagery of his fictional landscape more potent, denser, and remarkably modern. The preservation of political order and stability, Stifter's highest value, becomes in this reading not only a function of his famous "sanftes Gesetz," but of a willingness to embrace new habits of work and a new pattern of economic exchange.

If fictional travel from village to village is a kind of code for Stifter's mid-nineteenth-century ambivalence towards modern commerce, the real travel of women authors at this same time accompanied and stimulated far-reaching social and political change. Observing that "for women, the act of traveling itself could have an emancipatory effect," Margaret E. Ward concentrates on the neglected early travel literature of a writer whose novels and diaries have richly rewarded recent efforts to pay attention to some of the less often heard voices in German literature. Fanny Lewald had enjoyed enough support for her literary aspirations to have published three novels (anonymously at her father's insistence) by the time she left her parental home in Königsberg, but it was her trip to Italy in 1846 that gave her the physical, intellectual, and emotional distance required for genuine independence. Ward describes this journey, and its extension to France and England, as a complicated and simultaneous double voyage of discovery without and within. Drawing upon Lewald's letters, essays and diaries, she develops these two strands in such a way that the encounters with other, perhaps more emancipated women such as Ottilie von Goethe and Adele Schopenhauer, her reactions to art, her love for the married Adolf Stahr, and her increasingly sophisticated observations on the events leading up to and following the Revolution of 1848 trace much more than the modest original goal of producing a guide for fellow women travelers. In the way the internal emancipatory journey through this period of staggering social and political change for women is contained beneath the surface of works ostensibly devoted to travel, we are led to appreciate the way the personal becomes political and the political highly personal.

Change is again the theme of Ronald Horwege's analysis of the once popular novelist Wilhelm von Polenz. Drawing upon the best seller *Der Büttnerbauer*, Horwege reveals Polenz to be an acute observer of the decline of the German agrarian class, while elucidating the pervasive *völkisch* aesthetic responsible for the novel's widespread popularity at the turn of the century and its subsequent disappearance from the German literary horizon. Land reform, the emancipation of the peasant class, and the increasing mechanization of farming throughout the course of the nineteenth century collide powerfully with stubbornly held convictions about the sanctity of the venerable relationship between the land, God, and the tillers of the soil. Those, like the novel's protagonist, who fail to adapt cannot survive, while even those who can are subverted by the greed of capitalists. Horwege traces the various ways the tensions in the novel have been understood over time, each chapter in the reception revealing as much about its own age as about Polenz. Noting that at one level this is a novel about people attempting to cope with massive systemic changes, with new economic forces that defy orthodox behaviors and lead to the demonization of convenient "enemies," Horwege concludes with the question of whether the reissuing of *Der Büttnerbauer* in 1994, together with two other novellas and a flurry of critical attention in East European countries, might signal a new audience for Polenz and, if so, what this might portend.

Part of the tension in Polenz's novel stems from the conversion during the nineteenth century of the German peasantry into a proletarian class. The next three essays deal with the way that proletariat begins to compete with established cultural elites in cities like Berlin and Vienna to define new social issues and ultimately a new aesthetic. Beth Bjorklund focuses on Vienna with a contrast between the "raw" works of proletarian author Alfons Petzold and the delicately nuanced and fashionably "cooked" work of contemporaries such as Stefan Zweig, Arthur Schnitzler, Hugo von Hofmannsthal, and Rainer Maria Rilke. Drawing on autobiography, novels, and poetry, Bjorklund teases out of starkly contrasting lives abundant examples of the way privilege and poverty shape divergent reservoirs of language, theme, and significance in writers otherwise so closely identified. Noting that despite a considerable body of work, Alfons Petzold has all but disappeared from German literary history, she moves to questions of literary reception and to the dilemma of how the proletarian writer can or should compete in forms so strongly associated with bourgeois literary culture.

David Chisholm shifts our attention from Vienna to Berlin, but keeps our focus on the proletariat. In contradistinction to the more famous literary cabaret of Weimar Germany, Berlin's earliest experiments with "Tingeltangel" were relatively simple affairs, "raw" in Bjorklund's terms. By 1900, however, interest in raising the artistic level of performance and in attracting a more sophisticated audience began pushing the German working-class variety theaters in the direction of high art, while still consciously striving to preserve the earthy vitality absent from most turn-of-the-century bourgeois theater. Chisholm positions this effort in terms of the larger intellectual tensions engendered by modernism, as the early German cabaret movement struggled to contribute to social and aesthetic progress in keeping with progress made in technological and economic terms. He details the extent to which sensitivity of the Prussian state and the resulting censorship both constrained and stimulated performances in such early cabarets as Ernst von Wolzogen's Buntes Theater genannt Überbrettl and Max Reinhardt's Schall und Rauch, as well as the increasing tendency for these early cabarets to orient themselves toward the literary *avant-garde*. Ultimately, the growing nationalism in the decade before World War I silenced political satire, and the quality of performances diminished, only to flower again after the war, now nurtured by freedom from political censorship in the heady days of Weimar culture.

The triumph of modernism is Michael Jennings's focus in his essay on montage, revolution, and fascism in two works by Alfred Döblin. Best known for his evocation of an entire culture from Berlin's colorful Alexanderplatz, Döblin was also a pioneer in the application of cinema's montage technique to literature. In describing this technique, Jennings carefully documents the juxtaposition of concrete elements from the new social space of an always fluid, sometimes chaotic metropolis that has come to characterize literary montage. Perhaps more significantly, he analyzes why, after briefly abandoning montage for conventional historical narrative, Döblin returns to distinctly modernist techniques for his massive novel of the failed revolution, *November 1918*. In both works, it is the capacity of literary montage to work productively with the detritus of human life—whether in a working-class section of a huge city or on the battlefield—that makes Döblin's fiction adequate to the bewildering constellation of events marking both revolutions and modern urban life. Jennings concludes his essay by challenging readers to see in this technique not only an aesthetic uniquely suited to the modernist expectation of greater objectivity, but a wistful political credo celebrating the pulsing and often fragmentary polyphony of many voices as an allegory of the highest form of democracy.

Döblin wrote *November 1918* in political exile from National Socialism. The totalitarian state that emerged from the collapse of democracy in Weimar affected Germany and German culture more profoundly than any political change in history. The essay of David Scrase continues the theme initiated by Michael Jennings by addressing the autobiographical writings of two German Jews who spent the early years of the Reich in Berlin. As Bjorklund was able to do for Vienna at the turn of the century, Scrase develops sharply contrasting stories, even from within the assimilated community of Berlin Jews. The celebrated poet Stephan Hermlin, born in privileged circumstances, was ironically attracted to communism, to which he remained ideologically committed until his recent death in April 1997, despite differences with the postwar GDR regime. The little-known poet Ludwig Greve, born to middle-class parents, responded to the experience of persecution not by turning to communism, but to Zionism, actually emigrating with his mother to Palestine after the war. Scrase takes us beyond these superficial differences, however, to probe the relationship between the self and the world to which unique access is afforded in the literary genre of autobiography. Looking as much to what is left out of the parallel autobiographies in question, Hermlin's *Abendlicht* and Greve's *Wo gehörte ich hin?*, Scrase traces each author back to positions remarkably similar to their respective starting points: Greve before his death in 1991 as an assimilated Jew in West Germany and Hermlin as a self-confessed bourgeois poet struggling to reconcile his art and his politics.

The legacy of National Socialism patterns in several highly predictable forms, but occasionally in ways that are as surprising as they are subtle. From his musings on the curious lack of critical response in Germany to the 1981 film *Excalibur*, Ray Wakefield postulates that the "valorization of a charismatic male leader of mythical proportions" has become simply unacceptable to contemporary German critics and audiences. Linking the release of director John Boorman's film in Germany with the fascination attending Klaus Theweleit's *Männerphantasien*, Wakefield argues that *Excalibur's* stunningly consistent visual metaphor of men as armored warriors with a vulnerable core and women as superficially pliant but internally hard objects awakened profound distrust at both the aesthetic and political levels.

Preeminent among those who have navigated the labyrinth of German letters between the collapse of National Socialism and the collapse of the Berlin Wall fifty years later, Günter Grass has charted a distinctly political course in his many novels, essays, poems, and sketches. Mark E. Cory considers the four very different works published after the fall of the Wall as a coherent whole, with the 1995 *Ein weites Feld* as its major statement. Much criticized for his failure to embrace German unification, Grass is shown to have been consistent in championing the idea of a German confederation, which would preserve a single cultural nation with two independent political states. His skepticism about unification, most pointedly articulated in the essay *Schreiben nach Auschwitz*, was rooted in the dark legacy of an excess of political power. When unification came nevertheless, Grass resurrected the figure of Theodor Fontane as a vehicle for his elaborate comment on Germany on the verge of a new millennium. Cory charts the political and social progress and setbacks recorded in what may be the most compelling aesthetization of a tumultuous century, all layered in Grass's distinctive time zone of the "Vergegenkunft."

The twelfth and final essay addresses the common theme of politics and German literature in a manner different from the preceding chapters. Rather than with literary reflections of the political revolutions of 1848 or 1918, of the wars of this or an earlier century, of political divisions or unification, Michael Morton writes about a revolution in our habits of thinking and about wars between dogmatism and skepticism in recent Western intellectual history. What makes this essay appropriate to our volume is that Morton traces the emergence of a modern critical theory back to Leibniz, in particular to his theory of universal harmony as both a metaphysical account of reality *and* as an "aspiration for the organization and conduct of human affairs in society." Morton argues that a modern critical theory developed from Leibniz, with contributions from Kant, Wittgenstein, and Habermas, can dissolve the irrational bases of epistemological skepticism and hence substitute for the empty confusion into which contemporary Derridian critical theory has fallen. Noting the recent spoof of this theory published unwittingly by the journal *Social Text,* Morton cautions that "irrationalism and obdurately maintained ignorance are not, finally, laughing matters, because in a host of ways they are corrosive, and in the end at least potentially destructive, of the edifice of civilization itself." If Michael Morton is right in believing that Leibniz was at least in part motivated by the need to substitute a rational basis of domestic and international human affairs for the irrational horror of the Thirty Years' War, then the labor of those American scholars represented here to understand and interpret German literature as it deals with politics from Goethe to Grass has abundant relevance for both continents, now and in the future. Charles Sealsfield/Karl Postl had figured that out about a century and a half ago.

Goethe's Iphigenie auf Tauris *and the First Amendment*

Horst Lange

Without being able to argue in sufficient detail for it here, I would like to claim that Wolfdietrich Rasch's *Goethes "Iphigenie auf Tauris" als Drama der Autonomie* (1977) should be regarded as a milestone in the history of Goethe scholarship, since the implications of its argument go far beyond a mere revision of our reading of the play itself. Rasch showed convincingly that Iphigenie's moral superiority, which generally was given credit for the last-minute defusing of tension between Greeks and Taurians, exists only in the minds of many of Goethe's interpreters. In so doing he disproved the previously unquestioned assumption that Goethe's first classical play was a quasireligious homage to the redemptive powers of Iphigenie's character as the epitome of humanity. Rasch thus strongly challenged the commonly held belief that Goethe's classicism centered on the concept of *Humanität*. Moreover, by arguing that Goethe instead engages in an Enlightenment-style critique of the power orthodox religion tries to exercise over mankind, he forced us to rethink Goethe's position towards this movement, making it likely that Goethe ought to be considered a participant of the Enlightenment, and not, as often has been held, a member of its opposition. All that entails, if Rasch is right, that we will eventually have to find a new way of defining what we understand under the term *Weimar Classicism*.

For Rasch, the Enlightenment's interest in religion was rooted mainly in a concern for the individual's quest for autonomy. In his argument, the gods of Goethe's play are substitutes for the cruel and irrational God of the Old Testament, who, with his demands for complete and unquestioned obedience, in turn represents the *bête noire* of the Enlightenment: the God of orthodox religion. For example, where the God of Genesis categorically and without explanation demands from Abraham the sacrifice of his son, the goddess Diana in the play orders Agamemnon in a similar fashion to sacrifice his daughter; both stories symbolize for Rasch orthodoxy's demand for unquestioning submission to authority. Since Rasch succeeds in showing that the characters refuse to rely on divine intervention for a way out of their predicament and are saved precisely because of this refusal, he feels entitled to claim Goethe's play for the Enlightenment insofar as this movement propagated the emancipation of the individual from gods like those in the play.

While this essay will follow Rasch's lead and place Goethe's play firmly in the tradition of the European Enlightenment, it will attempt a certain shift in emphasis. However deeply the Enlightenment's interest in religion might have been generated by a concern with the individual, I would like to submit that it had another, possibly even more important origin. In my view, the unprecedented series of religious wars in the wake of the Reformation cannot be underestimated as an influence on the incipient Enlightenment project. The degree of violence exhibited by these wars was stunning: possibly no war either in antiquity or the Middle Ages could measure up to the devastation the Thirty Years' War visited upon the Rhineland Palatinate or the duchy of Württemberg, where more than 80% of the population perished. Facts like these must have been a major affront to an emerging intellectual movement which not only had begun to believe in the moral progress of mankind, but formed its inchoate identity around the assumption that the human mind had the power to construct society in a way which did away with all major forms of evil. Thus, it cannot come as a surprise that in texts central to the Enlightenment canon many core Enlightenment figures—one need only think of Hobbes, Spinoza, Locke, and Madison—reflected upon the problem of religiously motivated violence and offered various precepts for its avoidance.

With that in mind, this essay tries to go a step beyond Rasch by showing that we should look at Goethe's *Iphigenie* as a part of the Enlightenment tradition precisely because it shares its concern with the origins of and possible remedies against religious violence. Since the latter invariably revolved around the problem of whether church and state should be united (as, among others, Hobbes, Spinoza, and Montesquieu proposed) or strictly separated (as Locke, Madison, and Jefferson demanded), my argument will culminate in an outline of Goethe's own original position toward the church-state relationship. It is an interesting coincidence that Goethe's work on *Iphigenie* developed to maturity in the same decade that witnessed both Jefferson's and Madison's success in realizing their dream of erecting a wall between church and state. A comparison of the features of both projects in conjunction with a reflection on their role in the development of the two nations should throw new light on both achievements.

I

If my interpretation proposes a shift in emphasis from the concept of individual autonomy to the theme of religiously motivated violence, it might be of interest to point out that such a shift can already be justified by considering an important weakness of Rasch's interpretation. As already mentioned, Rasch assumes that the motivation for mortals to try to emancipate themselves from their subordination to the gods rests in the fact that these gods are cruel, fickle, and irrational in their dealings with mortals.[1] On the face of it, this assumption certainly seems to describe the text accurately. After all, the goddess Diana asks for Iphigenie's sacrifice, only to reverse herself immediately and save the girl. But then even this rescue does not seem to be a blessing, since it only results in Iphigenie's solitary exile, a condition she considers to be "a second death" (53). The gods further seem to have cast a terrible spell on the house of Tantalus, cursing each new generation with horrible crimes and unspeakable suffering, thereby revenging Tantalus' original transgression by trying to wipe out his entire progeny. But is it not inconsistent, then, that at the end of the play the gods allow Orestes and Iphigenie to escape death, return home, and reestablish the family's rule over Mycenae? And another point: Apollo certainly seems to have sufficient pity on Orestes to tell him in an oracle how he can overcome the wrath of the Furies. But why does he formulate the oracle in such a devilishly ambiguous way that the one interpretation adopted by everybody makes war between Taurians and Greeks all but inevitable until the possibility of a second meaning is serendipitously discovered? Did he, the god of prophecy, not foresee the potential for violence inherent in his apparent demand that Orestes steal from the Taurians their dearest religious artifact? Or did he just derive sadistic pleasure out of watching mortals risk their lives because of a plausible but mistaken interpretation of his words?

A closer look at the text might, however, present a significantly different picture. For it must be said in regard to all but one of the events of the play that there is no sufficient evidence which would unquestionably link an earthly event to a god's intervention. What can, on closer examination, be said concerning these events is only that one of the characters of the play *claims* the existence of such a divine link; but, on the face of it, there exists no reason why we should take his or her word for it. Let us consider a simple example. When Iphigenie relates to Thoas the blood-chilling history of her family, she places the responsibility for all the horrendous crimes squarely on divine shoulders:

> ...es schmiedete
> Der Gott um ihre Stirn ein ehern Band.
> Rat, Mäßigung und Weisheit und Geduld
> Verbarg er ihrem scheuen düstern Blick;
> Zur Wut ward ihnen jegliche Begier,
> Und grenzenlos drang ihre Wut umher. (330–35)[2]

But it is not at all clear from this passage why we should believe Iphigenie's theory, as Rasch does (103). Since no additional evidence is cited, it might as well have been the morally fallible nature of the Tantalides which brought about all the violent horror, a fact which might be too painful for Iphigenie to admit. Similarly, it can be said of every action ascribed to the gods that they, too, just might have had a human origin. Did Diana order Agamemnon to sacrifice Iphigenie? Not necessarily; it is, strictly speaking, the priest Kalchas who does so, claiming simply to transmit Diana's wish. But he just might have erred in this determination of divine intention, or even, for whatever reason, he just might have made it up.[3] Did Apollo display a mean streak by endangering Orestes' life through the deliberate ambiguity of the oracle? Not necessarily, since the oracle could well have been the fabrication of the Delphic priests or the Pythia. It seems clear that such "demythologizing" arguments can be made in respect to every event where divine causes are asserted, with one notable exception: only a supernatural explanation can account for Iphigenie's rescue from the altar in Aulis. The fact that all the Greeks deem her dead and the Taurians are mystified about her sudden appearance on their island makes it impossible for the divine involvement in this event to be the fabrication of Iphigenie or any other character.[4]

Since the play does not give us any information about whether the gods are really behind earthly events, it is not a play about their relationship to mortals. Given the one exception just mentioned, its plot—that is, the chain of events unfolding between mortals—can be fully described without any recourse to divine interference. But, to be sure, it cannot be described without reference to numerous instances in which mortals claim to see divine intervention in earthly affairs. Such claims are central in the decision-making of the characters and are thus the real engine behind the dynamics of the plot: Orestes and Pylades come to Tauris on behalf of an oracle; Thoas reintroduces human sacrifice because he claims that it is Diana's wish; Iphigenie refuses to marry Thoas because she believes Diana still wants her to return to her homeland; and the list could easily be continued. Therefore, it seems fair to say that the play is fundamentally concerned with the claims made by its characters about the true intentions of the gods, how these claims come into existence, and, perhaps most important, what their consequences are.

Incidentally, this insight helps us understand how Rasch could come to think that the play portrays the gods as fickle and irrational. Since he takes what various characters say about the gods at face value, he cannot account for the inconsistencies among the opinions of different characters and is reduced to ascribing them to the gods themselves. Since Rasch's gods are the creation of the play's characters, the perceived fickleness of the deities is nothing but the reflection of the confusion of various mortals about divine intentions.

If all this is correct, then it has to be asked how the characters come to believe they have knowledge of divine intentions. This question is particularly important because the claim that gods did actually speak to the mortals is made just once, in the case of the oracle which sends Orestes off to Tauris; but even then, mortals in the form of the Delphic priests presumably still functioned as intermediaries. In all the other cases, the characters seem to take earthly events not just as events, but in addition as veiled signs which, if deciphered properly, allow them to determine divine intentions. The various passages that will be analyzed in the following pages will provide ample evidence for the characters' use of this *hermeneutics of divine signs*, as I would like to call it. Therefore I can limit myself at this stage of my argument to pointing out just one instance of this hermeneutics. How does Thoas know that Diana wants to reestablish human sacrifice, which, after all, was a hallowed tradition until Iphigenie, in her role as the new priestess, abolished it? How does he know that it was an "Unrecht...[Diana] die alten Opfer vor[zu]enthalten" (507f)? He knows because the fact that his last son was recently killed by his enemies can in his eyes only be read as a divine sign, as a manifestation of divine ire. Only if we assume such a hermeneutic maneuver on his part can we understand his emphatic claim that he is responsible for his son's death by allowing Iphigenie, out of a weakness for her, to abolish the sacrifice (506-19).

His reasoning seems to be wanting at best. Why should the death of his son be a sign at all and not just some accidental event? And if it is a sign, why should it have this particular meaning? In fact, the text highlights the weakness of his hermeneutic hypothesis by letting Arkas use, in a preceding conversation with Iphigenie, a different hermeneutics of divine signs to come to the opposite conclusion concerning Diana's attitude towards the human sacrifice:

> Hat nicht Diane, statt erzürnt zu sein
> Daß sie der blut'gen alten Opfer mangelt,
> Dein sanft Gebet in reichem Maß erhört?
> Umschwebt mit frohem Fluge nicht der Sieg
> Das Heer? und eilt er nicht sogar voraus? (128-32)

Where Thoas' hermeneutics chooses as its central divine sign his son's death, only to deduce Diana's ire from it, Arkas elects to take as his sign the recent military victory and infers from it the benevolent attitude of the goddess. The fact that the text itself pointedly avoids tipping the balance in favor of one or the other reading is not only further proof that the play's concern is not with the gods, but rather with the opinions mortals entertain about them. In addition, it illustrates how the text consciously casts doubts on the truth claims made by mortals about the will of the gods.

This playing off against each other of differing, if not mutually exclusive, hermeneutics is not a singular occurrence in the text; rather, it constitutes an important textual strategy. Let me discuss another example. After Orestes and Pylades have been captured by the Taurians, they try to make sense of this unexpected turn in their adventure. Orestes reads their capture as a clear sign that Apollo's "Wink" (710)—the oracle which previously promised rescue—was just a ruse by the gods to lure them into captivity and subsequent death, thereby succeeding in the full implementation of their plan to destroy the house of Tantalus:

> Mich haben sie zum Schlächter auserkoren,
> Zum Mörder meiner doch verehrten Mutter,
> Und eine Schandtat schändlich rächend, mich
> Durch ihren Wink zu Grund' gerichtet. Glaube,
> Sie haben es auf Tantals Haus gerichtet,

Und ich, der Letzte, soll nicht schuldlos, soll
Nicht ehrenvoll vergehn. (707–13)

His invariably upbeat companion Pylades, however, manages to give his reading of the same event a completely different spin.[5] According to him, he and Orestes have the honor of being chosen by the gods to realize Apollo's longstanding dream of having the statue of his sister transferred to his temple in Delphi. In addition, the obstacles both friends encounter during their quest are meant first as an atonement for earlier transgressions–Orestes' matricide–and secondly as an opportunity to prove themselves great heroes who commit great deeds, that is, as an opportunity to realize their biggest dream since early childhood:[6]

> Vielleicht reift in der Götter Rat schon lange
> Das große Werk. Diane sehnet sich
> Von diesem rauhen Ufer der Barbaren
> Und ihren blut'gen Menschenopfern weg.
> Wir waren zu der schönen Tat bestimmt,
> Uns wird sie auferlegt […]
> Zu einer schweren Tat beruft ein Gott
> Den edlen Mann, der viel verbrach, und legt
> Ihm auf was uns unmöglich scheint zu enden.
> Es siegt der Held, und büßend dienet er
> Den Göttern und der Welt, die ihn verehrt. (733–39, 744–48)

Before going on, let me quote another, very prominent example of two hermeneutics of divine signs clashing irreconcilably. Both Iphigenie and Thoas rest their respective claims that she should, or should not, give herself in marriage to the king on supposedly divine, yet mutually contradictory signs:

> *Iphigenie:* Hat nicht die Göttin, die mich rettete,
> Allein ein Recht auf mein geweihtes Leben? […]
> Vielleicht ist mir die frohe Rückkehr nah;
> Und ich, auf ihren Weg nicht achtend, hätte
> Mich wider Willen hier gefesselt?
> Ein Zeichen bat ich, wenn ich bleiben sollte.
> *Thoas:* Das Zeichen ist, daß du noch hier verweilst. (438–48)

Every hermeneutics must count as arbitrary when the definition of what constitutes a sign is so unclear that the absence of a sign for one interpreter, namely Iphigenie, can itself be taken as a sign by the other, Thoas.

If, as therefore seems to be the case, the text pointedly displays the arbitrariness of the various hermeneutics of divine signs, it will not come as a surprise to note that the characters themselves display an awareness of it. They do that, to be precise, by insinuating that not the sign's logic, but wishful thinking or even an ulterior motive on the part of the other is responsible for his or her (mis)interpretation. Witness how Thoas takes Iphigenie's claim that the gods want her to remain unmarried as a projection of her own desire, and how Iphigenie in turn accuses Thoas of letting his desire for her cloud his proper judgment:

> *Thoas:* Es spricht kein Gott; es spricht dein eignes Herz.
> *Iphigenie:* Sie reden nur durch unser Herz zu uns.
> *Thoas:* Und hab' ich, sie zu hören, nicht das Recht?
> *Iphigenie:* Es überbraust der Sturm die zarte Stimme. (493–96)

Passages like these are, if my interpretation is correct, probably best described by saying that the hermeneutics of divine signs brings forth, by its very inability to convince others, a *hermeneutics of suspicion*, which accuses the other of surreptitiously making up the things he or she claims are of divine origin.

It is important to see that the emergence of this hermeneutics of suspicion marks the place where the hermeneutics of divine signs begins to engender aggression or even violence. The tension between Iphigenie and Thoas which manifests itself in the tit-for-tat of hermeneutic suspicions I just quoted grows into a quite serious exchange of low blows as the suspicions grow deeper. Thoas starts by suspecting that behind Iphigenie's claim to understand the will of the gods better than he there stands a twofold arrogance: the cultural arrogance of the Greek towards the supposedly uncultured barbarian and the familial arrogance of a member of the Tantalide clan who claims to be descended from the gods. This is what happens when he skeptically inquires about the suggestion that the divine voice is not audible to everybody:

> *Thoas:* Die Priesterin vernimmt sie wohl allein?
> *Iphigenie:* Vor allen andern merke sie der Fürst.
> *Thoas:* Dein heilig Amt und dein geerbtes Recht
> An Jovis Tisch bringt dich den Göttern naher,
> Als einen erdgebornen Wilden. (497–501)

His is quite a serious insult, and Iphigenie, contrary to her traditional reputation of being the epitome of gentleness, retaliates in kind. She proceeds to accuse Thoas' hermeneutics of divine signs not only of misunderstanding ("mißverstehen") the gods fundamentally, but of projecting his tendencies as a bloodthirsty barbarian onto those selfsame gods:

> Der mißversteht die Himmlischen, der sie
> Blutgierig wähnt; er dichtet ihnen nur
> Die eignen grausamen Begierden an. (523–25)

It is important to realize that the transformation of a hermeneutics of divine signs into a hermeneutics of suspicion is not at all limited to this particular scene. Let me point out just two additional examples. When Pylades elaborates on the optimistic view of the divine plan I have discussed above, Orestes cannot help but comment ironically on the appearance of wishful thinking on Pylades' part:

> Mit seltner Kunst flichst du der Götter Rat
> Und deine Wünsche klug in eins zusammen. (740–41)

And when much later Iphigenie makes the claim that Diana demands a cleansing ceremony for the statue soiled by the presence of a matricide, Thoas cannot hold back his "Argwohn" (1768) that all this is part of a ruse. As the spectator familiar with Pylades' plan of deception knows, at least in this case his hermeneutics of suspicion is justified.

II

I hope I have shown sufficiently that the fundamental conflicts of the play, as well as the characters' potential to resort to violence, are deeply rooted in their religious beliefs and their distrust of the religious beliefs of others. Therefore it is natural to ask what possibly could have motivated Goethe to pay so much attention to the complexities of Greek religion. It was not only long past and could therefore only command a historical interest, but, in addition, its polytheism, its rites, its moral code, and its role in society differed so much from contemporary religion that the usefulness of a poetic exploration of its intricacies for throwing light on the present appears to have been quite limited. If Classicism was meant to be a literary endeavor which, by its sheer aesthetic power, tried to shape Goethe's fractured audience into a unified community, into a public with a common moral purpose, how then could Goethe have thought that a play dealing with such seemingly remote problems could possibly function as its showcase?

The answer is that, just as the play's dramatic form does not try to imitate Greek drama, it is not really concerned with Greek religion. Instead, Goethe merely uses the latter as an allegory. In principle, Wolfdietrich Rasch already proposed such a reading when he focused on the parallels between Agamemnon's sacrifice of Iphigenie and Abraham's sacrifice of Isaac, concluding that the Greek gods are stand-ins for the fierce God of the Old Testament and both in turn represent the God of contemporary orthodox religion. His interpretation, however, seems somewhat of a stretch, since it can hardly account for the meaning of all the other trappings of Greek religion Goethe inserted into the play. The existence of oracles as social institutions; the sisterly love between Apollo and Diana; the Furies' inexorable persecution of Orestes; the divine descent of mortals like the Tantalide family; the replacement of the Titans by the Olympians (a fact that still deeply reverberates in the play's present, as Iphigenie's *Parzenlied* demonstrates)–all these things are essential to our understanding of the play, yet difficult to integrate into Rasch's allegorical scheme. In addition, the reduction of orthodoxy's theological scope to the Old Testament's conception of God leaves out the New Testament's contribution, where at least Paul's letters are of indisputable relevance to most traditional versions of orthodox doctrine. There is more in the Bible than just episodes like Abraham's sacrifice, to which, rightly or wrongly, intolerance and orthodoxy did appeal for their purposes.

Rasch's difficulties, it seems to me, can be overcome with the help of an interpretive shift from a concern with the gods to a concern with the characters' opinions about them. If the actual details of Greek religion are, in fact, of no central importance for the understanding of contemporary Christianity, the problems originating in the uses and abuses of various hermeneutics of divine signs are. It seems reasonable to say that behind Luther's revolutionary ideas about grace and Christian freedom stood a significantly different conception of how to read Scripture, how to understand the word of God. If this is true, then it can be said that the violence erupting in the European religious wars of the sixteenth and seventeenth centuries was simply the most tangible expression of an underlying clash of different hermeneutics of divine signs. Therefore, I think it is possible to say that the war of interpretation in the play is an allegory of the war of interpretation which engulfed Europe in the wake of the Reformation, or, in other words, that the violent clashes in the play are allegories of the religious wars of that time. And insofar as Reformation history is filled with examples of unholy alliances between religious beliefs and political expediency—one need only think about the motives of Henry VIII to distance himself from Rome or about the complex relation between religion and raw power politics in the reasons why France and Sweden joined the Thirty Years' War—it can even be claimed that the concept of a hermeneutics of suspicion as presented by the play is indispensable to a true understanding of Reformation history.

If this allegorical reading is correct, then other allegorizations gain plausibility. The fierce argument between Thoas and Iphigenie over whether or not Diana demands human sacrifice might very well be taken as an allegory of one of the important points of contention during the Reformation—namely, the question of how God is to be properly worshipped; questions such as whether the congregation was allowed to share in the drinking of the wine during the Eucharist were so important to many people that already the Hussites went to war over them. In addition, the mutually exclusive claims by the Greeks and the Taurians that theirs is the sole right of possession of Diana's statue might very well be read as an allegory of the struggle over which religious persuasion really can claim to be in God's grace and truly act on God's behalf.

Let me proceed to consider how this allegorical connection between Goethe's play and the religious wars of the Reformation places the text into the context of Enlightenment discussions about religious violence.

This discussion found its proper start in the second part of Hobbes's *Leviathan*, where Hobbes leaves the first part's generally secular discussion of the structure and legitimacy of the sovereign's power in order to reflect on the danger which rival religious claims constitute for the public peace. His fundamental thesis states that Christianity is, contrary to what medieval scholastics taught, a religion whose only justification lies in the truth of divine revelation, not in the ratiocinations of philosophy. But revelation cannot take place without the mediation of individuals who transmit God's word to the people at large and interpret it for them, thereby engaging in the activity I called the hermeneutics of divine signs. These individuals Hobbes calls "lieutenants" or "prophets" (90, 272ff), and he immediately realizes that different hermeneutics of divine signs will by necessity be at odds with each other:

> That there were many more false than true prophets, appears by this, that when Ahab (1 *Kings* xxii) consulted four hundred prophets, they were all false impostors, but only one Micaiah. (283)

Therefore, Hobbes himself recommends the employment of a hermeneutics of suspicion (emphasis added):

> Men had need to be very *circumspect and wary*, in obeying the voice of man, that pretending himself to be a prophet, requires us to obey God in that way, which he in God's name telleth us to be the way of happiness. For he that pretends to teach men the way of so great felicity, pretends to govern them; that is to say, to rule and reign over them; which is a thing, that all men naturally desire, and is therefore worthy *to be suspected* of ambition and imposture; and consequently, ought to be examined and tried by every man, before he yield them obedience. (283)

It is important to note that Hobbes's suspicions about practitioners of the hermeneutics of divine signs are directed mainly towards attempts to "govern...rule and reign," towards attempts to wrest the control of political power away from the lawful sovereign. This for Hobbes is particularly perilous, since the conflicting interpretations of various prophets will always endanger the public peace; and because the sovereign's single *raison d'être* according to Hobbes is to guarantee this peace, the sovereign's ability to do so will be severely compromised if one of the agents he is supposed to hold in check can rival his power.

His solution to the problem of religious violence was simple: he declared that the sovereign be by necessity also the head of the church and determine all of its public features, such as the doctrines of the publicly confessed religion, the principles of the interpretation of scripture, and the rituals of religious worship. While Hobbes thus brought all public aspects of religion under the jurisdiction of the sovereign, he nevertheless declared the religious conscience of the individual to be free from the reach of government. The citizen was free to believe secretly whatever he chose, as long as he performed all visible rituals according to the sovereign's precepts. By thus outlawing all "prophets" but himself, the sovereign fuses the state and the church into one entity:

> Therefore a Church, such a one as is capable to command, to judge, absolve, condemn, or do any other act, is the same thing with a civil commonwealth, consisting of Christian men; and is called a *civil state*, for that the subjects of it are *men;* and a *Church*, for that the subjects thereof are *Christians*. (306)

This principle of eliminating religiously motivated violence by letting the sovereign determine the beliefs of his subjects was already in practice throughout Europe; after all, the famous clause of the Religious Peace of Augsburg, which stipulated that *cuius regio, eius religio*, commanded nothing different. Hobbes had only given philosophical depth to actual political practice, and, probably due to the clarity and incisiveness of his analysis, the demand for a unity of church and state became the standard theoretical approach to the problem: writers as different as Spinoza, Montesquieu, and even Rousseau followed in his footsteps.

The experience of history with this proposal, however, was anything but reassuring. Deeply religious people naturally saw the achievement of their redemption as the most important part of their moral agenda and were therefore apprehensive about the government telling them how they had to behave in public in order to save their souls. Far from pacifying the country by eliminating the difference between sects, the usurpation of the church's power by the sovereign soon became the occasion for civil disobedience, if not outright civil war. For what good could legal sanctions, even the threat of death, do against religious disobedience, if in the eyes of the believer obedience would lead to eternal damnation? The first major Enlightenment thinker to realize that Hobbes's recipe against religious violence just added another layer of violence to the sectarian strife already existing was John Locke. Therefore, he proposed in his *Letter Concerning Toleration* that the government should itself be neutral about matters of religion and let various sects coexist, but do everything in its power to curtail sectarian violence.

Encouraged by the example of the Netherlands, where religious toleration worked quite successfully, some of the most influential constitutional thinkers of the American Revolution, particularly Thomas Jefferson and James Madison, pushed for the incorporation of Locke's ideas into the legal foundation of their home state, Virginia, and ultimately the new nation.[7] After Jefferson's proposed "Bill for Establishing Religious Freedom" (1779) had originally failed in the Virginia Legislature, their endeavors were more successful in their opposition to a "Bill establishing a provision for Teachers of the Christian Religion" (1785).

Instrumental in the defeat of this bill, which would have provided for the salaries of Anglican clergy with taxpayers' money, was Madison's pamphlet *Memorial and Remonstrance against Religious Assessments* (1785). It is interesting in this text to see how much the memory of the European experience with religious violence and the fear that such violence was already spreading in the New World were in the back of Madison's mind:

> Torrents of blood have been spilt in the old world, by vain attempts of the secular arm to extinguish Religious discord, by proscribing all difference in Religious opinions....The very appearance of the Bill has transformed that "Christian forbearance, love and charity," which of late mutually prevailed, into animosities and jealousies, which may not soon be appeased. What mischiefs may not be dreaded should this enemy to the public quiet be armed with the force of a law? (304)

Ultimately, of course, this political stance was most influential in the framing of the U.S. Constitution, where the First Amendment erected on a federal level that wall between church and state of which Jefferson so famously spoke.

It is important to realize that Goethe was intimately familiar with these problems. Not only did he have since his childhood a stupendous knowledge of the Bible and the history of Christianity, not only did he delve deeply into constitutional law during his legal education, he must have also been intimately familiar with the intricacies of the church-state relation ever since he thoroughly studied Hobbes's most ardent disciple, Spinoza. In *Dichtung und Wahrheit* he writes:

> Die Kirchengeschichte war mir fast noch bekannter als die Weltgeschichte, und mich hatte von jeher der Konflikt, in welchem sich die Kirche, der öffentlich anerkannte Gottesdienst, nach zwei Seiten hin befindet und immer befinden wird, höchlich interessiert. Denn einmal liegt sie in ewigem Streit mit dem Staat, über den sie sich erheben, und sodann mit den Einzelnen, die sie alle zu sich versammeln will. Der Staat von seiner Seite will ihr die Oberherrschaft nicht zugestehen. (504)[8]

In fact, Goethe's interest in this subject matter was so deep that he dedicated his Strasbourg dissertation *De legislatoribus* to its exploration.[9] He clearly used a heavy dose of Spinoza, since his thesis repeats Spinoza's and Hobbes's theory of state control over all public aspects of religion in conjunction with the freedom of individual conscience:

> Ich hatte mir daher in meinem jugendlichen Sinne festgesetzt, daß der Staat, der Gesetzgeber, das Rechte habe, einen Kultus zu bestimmen, nach welchem die Geistlichkeit lehren und sich benehmen solle, die Laien hingegen sich äußerlich und öffentlich genau zu richten hätten; übrigens sollte die Frage nicht sein, was Jeder bei sich denke, fühle oder sinne. (506)

Given Goethe's extensive background, it should come as no surprise that the problem of the relation between church and state resurfaces in a text as concerned with religious violence as *Iphigenie auf Tauris*. Twice do the state, represented by Thoas or his mouthpiece Arkas, and the church, represented by Diana's high priestess Iphigenie, argue about an important public aspect of religious procedure, and twice do they claim to have sole jurisdiction over it.

The first dispute concerns the reintroduction of human sacrifice. This is not just an argument over moral principle and divine intention, it has a clear political dimension to it. Thoas claims that the reintroduction of the sacrifice is necessary because its termination has endangered the public peace. Arkas had already mentioned earlier that the king was afraid of "Verwegnen Aufstand und frühzeit'gen Tod" (163), and Thoas puts this fear of rebellion in more concrete terms: his subjects might rise up because they think that Thoas, out of his affection for Iphigenie, had put their safety at risk by alienating the protectress of their polis, Diana:

> Du hattest mir die Sinnen eingewiegt,
> Das Murren meines Volks vernahm ich nicht;
> Nun rufen sie die Schuld von meines Sohnes
> Frühzeit'gem Tode lauter über mich.
> Um deinetwillen halt' ich länger nicht
> Die Menge, die das Opfer dringend fordert. (516–21)

Whereas Thoas allows Iphigenie, at least for the time being, to be priestess in accordance with Diana's wishes ("Sei Priesterin / Der Göttin, wie sie dich erkoren hat" 504-5), he nevertheless feels entitled to claim, because of the political ramifications of the matter, that this ecclesiastical question falls squarely under his jurisdiction. He insists it was he, not the priestess, who temporarily ended the sacrifice: "*ich* [habe Diana] die alten Opfer vorenthalten" (506–8, emphasis mine), and has no qualms about bluntly ordering Iphigenie to do as he says: "Tu deine Pflicht" (531).

Iphigenie on her part certainly claims the position of what Hobbes called the "prophet." Quite effortlessly, for example, she is able to take on the role of Diana's mouthpiece in her greeting of Arkas: "Unsre Göttin sieht willkomm'nem Opfer / Von Thoas Hand mit Gnadenblick entgegen" (61–2). But as much as she maintains that the final decision about the sacrifice rests with her, she is also keenly aware that as matters stand in the kingdom of Tauris, she, the priestess, is serving at the pleasure of Thoas. Witness how she explains her predicament to the captured Greeks:

> Wie könnt ich euch
> Mit mörderischer Hand dem Tode weihen?
> Und niemand, wer es sei, darf euer Haupt,

So lang' ich Priesterin Dianens bin,
Berühren. Doch verweigr' ich jene Pflicht,
Wie sie der aufgebrachte König fordert;
So wählt er eine meiner Jungfraun mir
Zur Folgerin, und ich vermag alsdann
Mit heißem Wunsch allein euch beizustehn. (932-40)

Iphigenie does not agree, but she has to admit that Thoas, through his power as a sovereign, can exercise the privilege of clerical investiture.

The second dispute about the conflicting jurisdiction of church and state erupts on the occasion of Iphigenie's claim that a special purification rite for the statue of Diana has become necessary because of the soiling presence of the matricidal Orestes. This is, of course, a ruse devised by Pylades, who invented the necessity of this ritual in order to create an opportunity for the theft of the statue. It is interesting to see how, upon being informed about the ritual, Arkas insists that only the king has the authority to order such an undertaking, whereas Iphigenie insists that Thoas, by prohibiting it, would trespass on her rights as Diana's priestess:

Arkas: Ich melde dieses neue Hindernis
Dem Könige geschwind, beginne du
Das heil'ge Werk nicht eh' bis er's erlaubt.
Iphigenie: Dies ist allein der Priest'rin überlassen.
Arkas: Solch seltnen Fall soll auch der König wissen.
Iphigenie: Sein Rat wie sein Befehl verändert nichts. (1441-46)

Later, after Iphigenie has meekly given in to Arkas' demands, Pylades makes clear that insisting on the freedom of ecclesiastical matters from state intervention was part of his ruse. "Warum hast du nicht / Ins Priesterrecht dich weislich eingehüllt?" he asks (1580-81). Flabbergasted about her willingness to compromise, he orders her to insist absolutely on the separation of church and state the next time:

Ruhig
Erwarte du die Wiederkunft des Boten,
Und dann steh fest, er bringe was er will:
Denn solcher Weihung Feier anzuordnen
Gehört der Priesterin und nicht dem König. (1593-97)

III

It therefore can be said that in *Iphigenie auf Tauris,* Goethe, along lines characteristic for Enlightenment thought, reflects upon religious conflict and the violence it inspires. In addition, he clearly delineates the two major constitutional paradigms which the Enlightenment proposed as possible remedies. What seems different from traditional Enlightenment thought, however, is the fact that the text appears to be astonishingly noncommittal when it comes to endorsing one of these two constitutional paradigms. It rather appears as if the ability of either to prevent religiously motivated violence is seriously being questioned. When Iphigenie argues for the separation of church and state to prolong the moratorium on human sacrifice, she does so for the sake of overcoming the religious violence represented by it. But later, when she, prodded by Pylades, again insists on this separation, she does so on behalf of an act of religious violence—namely, the abduction of Diana's statue, which is after all the holiest possession of the Taurians. Here the call for a wall between church and state is not promoting peace, but rather is instrumental in bringing about the confrontation between Taurians and Greeks which approaches open warfare in the final scene. Similarly it can be said about Thoas' defense of the principle of unity between church and state that, as much as he might want to promote public peace and preserve the religious integrity of his community by defending the statue, this defense ultimately serves the purpose of killing for religious reasons everyone who is a foreigner in Tauris. It seems fair to say that nowhere does the plot of the play suggest that religious violence could be avoided by constitutional regulations of the relation between church and state.

But then again, it is indisputable that the outbreak of violence at the end of the play is contained and a reconciliation between the hostile camps achieved. Therefore it seems reasonable to assume, on the one hand, that Goethe tried in fact to present a solution to the problem of religious violence and, on the other hand, that this solution is meant to be an alternative to precepts of constitutional law. This paper is not the place to analyze Goethe's proposed solution in a reasonably thorough manner; in fact, it is my belief that a sufficient understanding of it still has to be accomplished by Goethe scholarship. A sketch of its crucial features will, however, complete the argument in the present paper and perhaps point to a larger study.[10] As Rasch has already pointed out, Iphigenie's decision to tell the truth to Thoas and expose Pylades' elaborate ploy does not in itself suffice to solve the conflict. It might be responsible for Thoas' recognition of her good intentions and his willingness to admit that Orestes is, in fact, her brother and has therefore not come to Tauris solely out of evil intent. But this in itself cannot remove the true cause of the impending war—namely, the contradictory claims made upon the statue of Diana. Thoas himself makes this point very forcefully, when he answers Iphigenie's plea for peace:

> Und hübe deine Rede jeden Zweifel
> Und bändigt' ich den Zorn in meiner Brust:
> So würden doch die Waffen zwischen uns
> Entscheiden müssen; Friede seh' ich nicht.
> Sie sind gekommen, du bekennest selbst,
> Das heil'ge Bild der Göttin mir zu rauben.
> Glaubt ihr, ich sehe dies gelassen an? (2095-101)

Clearly, there is nothing Iphigenie can do about Thoas' reasoning, because it is essentially correct. Thoas' claims to the statue are at least as sound, if not more so, than those made by the Greeks, and it is definitely not, as over a century of Goethe scholarship has maintained, his barbarian nature which is responsible for the confrontation and which therefore might be overcome by the civilizing power of Iphigenie's *Humanität*. Instead, the situation is defused by Orestes' new, ostensibly more authoritative interpretation of the oracle, which effectively removes the *casus belli*. He manages to construe the meaning of the oracle in such a way that it no longer requires them to bring the statue to Greece. In other words, religious violence in the play is overcome by a fundamental change in the hermeneutics of divine signs. These signs are now reinterpreted in a way which the allows the causes for strife between different religious factions simply to evaporate.

Although, as I mentioned, the scope of the present study does not allow for many details, it can be argued that the true and hidden plot of the play concerns the different developments in the various characters' hermeneutics of divine signs. A few words about the case of Orestes may be sufficient for the sake of my argument. He was originally the person with the gloomiest view of the gods, and his hermeneutics tended to blame them for every conceivable misfortune. It is important to see how he overcomes his theological pessimism and is once again willing "nach Lebensfreud' und großer Tat zu jagen" (1364). His vision of Hades makes it apparent that the gods are not really bent on the destruction of the Tantalides, for they live in perfect harmony, whereas Tantalus, the original transgressor, is being punished. In addition, when he subsequently experiences the liberation from the wrath of the Furies without any atonement on his part, he realizes that the gods are obviously not out to destroy him, and, thus gains the ability to employ a new hermeneutics of divine signs, one which presupposes a generally benevolent attitude of the gods. Precisely because in the final scene the demand of the oracle for war does not seem to square with his newfound belief in divine benevolence, he is able to conceive of an alternative interpretation ascribing to the gods the most peaceful of intentions, the reunion of the dispersed family of Agamemnon. With respect to Orestes, therefore, the play contains a form of education about the proper reading of divine signs, an education culminating in the ingenious and peace-making reinterpretation of the oracle.

If this interpretation is correct and the characters' revision of their hermeneutics of divine signs brings about religious peace, it seems fair to conclude that, given the play's skepticism towards both separation and unification of state and church, Goethe seemed to think that only a transformation in religious attitude, and not some feature of a state's constitution, had the power to achieve religious peace. And, it might be added, he seemed to think that only a work of art, such as his *Iphigenie auf Tauris*, can bring about such a transformation. It is interesting to note that a similar conception seems to be at the heart of Lessing's treatment of religious violence in *Nathan der Weise*. The whole point of the parable of the rings seems to be that the three brothers, who after all represent the three great monotheistic religions, can only end their strife if they change their attitude towards the rings, and that means if they change their way of thinking about the intentions of their father, God. The message of Lessing's play seems to be that our attitude towards religion and God's master-plan for the history of mankind has to be changed.

Goethe's or Lessing's distrust of the power of political solutions, such as constitutional amendments, and their concomitant reliance on the power of art to bring about public peace contrast sharply with the approach by Jefferson and Madison, where no change of religious attitudes is attempted and all trust is put in the effectiveness of constitutional regulation. History, it seems, has spoken in favor of the American approach. Especially after the Fourteenth Amendment was interpreted by the Supreme Court to mean that the guarantee of religious freedom is binding not only on the federal government, but also on the states, a multitude of religious persuasions unparalleled in its variety in the Western world has flourished in the U.S. in an atmosphere of comparative peace. Germany, however, has not been so lucky. Due to its prolonged lack of political unity, it was unable to institute a constitutional arrangement entrusted with taking care of its deep and historically painful religious divisions. When Germany finally turned from a cultural entity into a unified nation, the same man, Bismarck, who had unified the country politically, immediately divided it along religious lines by declaring the famous *Kulturkampf* of the state against the Catholic church. And the same academic culture which enshrined Goethe and Lessing in the Pantheon of German literature showed no real resistance against, and even participated in, the rise of the most insidious of religious prejudices, anti-Semitism. Germany not only failed to achieve more than a highly fragile truce between its two major denominations, it was particularly unsuccessful in making the country hospitable to religious minorities such as Jews. At the same time when Germans were secure in the belief that their cultural heritage had given them a claim to be among the most civilized of nations, with Goethe to a large extent being given credit for this achievement, the National Socialists could with impunity set out to mastermind human sacrifice on a scale far, far beyond anything Thoas could have imagined.

Goethe's approach, his belief in the redeeming power of literature, had failed. The simple fact that after two centuries of Goethe scholarship an article can argue that the centrality of religious violence in the play has gone unnoticed shows that the very strength of this play–its subtlety–has also been its downfall in practical terms. Nobody's hermeneutics of divine signs seems to have been fundamentally altered. What a contrast that is to Madison's approach, who already in 1818 could write the following to Mordecai M. Noah, a Jew whom Madison during his tenure as president had employed in his foreign service:

Sir–I have received your letter of the 6th, with the eloquent discourse delivered at the consecration of the Jewish Synagogue. Having ever regarded the freedom of religious opinions & worship as equally belonging to every sect, & the secure enjoyment of it as the best human provision for bringing all either into the same way of thinking, or into that mutual charity which is the only substitute, I observe with pleasure the view you give of the spirit in which your Sect partake of the blessings offered by our Govt and laws. (310)

One is tempted to conclude that with respect to solving fundamental problems of society, literature is, in the final analysis, powerless. Level-headed politics, however, might stand a reasonable chance.[11]

Notes

[1] Already here one might find fault with the logic of Rasch's scheme. On the fictional level of the text, as I will have opportunity to show later, the gods do exist, as Rasch assumes. But if then these existing gods are cruel and fickle, then it would not be advisable for mortals to try to gain autonomy from them, since this seems to be a foolproof way of incurring their wrath. One is reminded of the British atheist who on his deathbed was urged by a priest to forswear Satan and calmly replied: "This is not the time to make enemies."

[2] References to *Iphigenie auf Tauris* here and elsewhere throughout the essay are to line numbers in vol. 3.1 of Johann Wolfgang Goethe, *Sämtliche Werke*, edited by Norbert Miller and Hartmut Reinhardt. (See Works Cited)

[3] It is important to note that suspicions of ulterior motives are already cast upon Kalchas by Euripides in his version of *Iphigeneia in Aulis*, and that, as Rasch points out, Kalchas is portrayed as a rather sinister figure in Voltaire's version of the play.

[4] With all likelihood, this is the reason why Rasch never identifies the characters' emancipation from the gods with an emerging belief that the gods do not exist. After all, when the characters accept the alternative interpretation of the oracle in the last scene, they never doubt that it actually is the word of a god.

[5] It is interesting to note that Pylades seems to be aware, probably more so than the other characters, that an act of interpretation is involved in their claims about the gods. By using the verb "auslegen" to describe how he arrived at his take on their fate, he makes clear that a hermeneutic activity played a central role: "Ganz anders denk' ich, und nicht ungeschickt / Hab' ich das schon Gescheh'ne mit dem Künft'gen / Verbunden und im stillen ausgelegt" (730–32). He even goes so far as to formulate general principles of his hermeneutics of divine signs: "Der Götter Worte sind nicht doppelsinnig, / Wie der Gedrückte sie im Unmut wähnt" (613–14).

[6] The concepts "Held" and the "große Tat" are important themes, manifesting themselves throughout the play in the identity formation of the young Orestes and Pylades. Particularly relevant are lines 665–706 and 763–67.

[7] See, for example, Madison's assessment: "It was the belief of all sects at one time that the establishment of Religion by law, was right & necessary; that the true religion ought to be established in exclusion of every other; and that the only question to be decided was which was the true religion. The example of Holland proved that a toleration of sects, dissenting from the established sect, was safe & even useful." (Letter to Edward Livingston, 10 July 1822, in: *Madison*, p. 309)

[8] References to *Dichtung und Wahrheit* are to page number in vol. 16 of Johann Wolfgang Goethe, *Sämtliche Werke*, edited by Peter Sprengel. (See Works Cited).

[9] This text is unfortunately lost to us. It was rejected by the Strasbourg faculty, but probably not, as some scholars claim, because of its poor quality, but rather because it was politically too sensitive. Strasbourg was a Protestant university subject to the Catholic King of France, and to argue, as Goethe in effect did, that the sovereign had jurisdiction over its religious conduct, was inopportune, to say the least. See *Gerstenberg* 49f.

[10] I am currently at work on a longer study which tries to show the importance of both Enlightenment political thought and constitutional law for Goethe's major works between 1770 and 1790.

[11] I am grateful to John Carson Pettey for his helpful comments on an earlier draft of this paper.

Works Cited

Hobbes, Thomas. *Leviathan: Or the Matter, Forme and Power of a Commonwealth Ecclesiastical and Civil*. Edited by Michael Oackeshott. Oxford: Oxford UP, n.d.

Gerstenberg, Ekkehard. *Recht und Staat in Goethes "Götz von Berlichingen."* Diss. University of Würzburg, 1952.

Goethe, Johann Wolfgang. *Sämtliche Werke nach Epochen seines Schaffens*. 20 vols. Edited by Karl Richter. Munich: Carl Hanser, 1987–.

Locke, John. *A Letter Concerning Toleration*. In *John Locke's "A Letter Concerning Toleration" in Focus*, edited by John Horton and Susan Mendus. London and New York: Routledge, 1991.

Madison, James. *The Complete Madison: His Basic Writings*. Edited by Saul K. Padover. New York: Harper & Brothers, 1953.

Rasch, Wolfdietrich. *Goethes "Iphigenie auf Tauris" als Drama der Autonomie*. Munich: C.H. Beck, 1977.

The American European Karl Postl/Charles Sealsfield on the US and Europe in the 1820s

Paul Michael Lützeler

One hundred years ago a young German scholar who had studied in Berlin and Vienna arrived in St. Louis. He had emigrated to America five years earlier at the age of twenty-five. Because he was unhappy with the lack of opportunity in his own country and because he had heard about the prospering society in America, he had accepted offers to teach at schools in the eastern United States. At the age of thirty he came to Washington University in St. Louis, a university which was only ten years older than the young scholar. St. Louis—at that time the fourth largest metropolis in the United States—was growing and expanding. The city was finishing Union Station—then one of the largest railroad stations in the world—and was making plans for the third Olympic Games and the World's Fair of 1904. The young scholar who joined Washington University in the mid-1890s was the first professor of German at Washington University, the position having been endowed by Adolphus Busch, owner of the Anheuser-Busch brewery. The young man was named Professor of European Literature and later became the first Chairman of the German Department and the first Dean of the Graduate School of Arts and Sciences at Washington University. His name was Otto Heller. He is frequently referred to in David W. Detjen's comprehensive study *The Germans in Missouri 1900-1918*. Detjen mentions that in 1900 Otto Heller proudly provided the information that nearly half of the students at Washington University were enrolled in courses teaching the German language or German literature and culture. Translated into today's numbers, this would mean that the German Department at Washington University would have to cope with roughly 5,000 students: times have changed!

Some one hundred seventy-five years ago, in 1823, a young scholar who had studied in Prague came to America from Vienna. Because he was unhappy with the outlook for scholars in his home country and since he had heard of the general prosperity in the United States, he had decided to emigrate to America. He was particularly interested in the newer states of the Union, those along the Mississippi River, and his special attention was drawn to the cities of St. Louis and New Orleans. He was convinced that these two cities would soon reach the status of such metropolitan areas as New York and Philadelphia. Both St. Louis and New Orleans were situated at vital points on the Mississippi, the most important inland trade route of the country. In 1807 Robert Fulton had built the first steamboat, an event that had a tremendous impact on the commercial development of the Midwest. The young man from Prague who traveled through the United States during the 1820s was Karl Postl. In America he went by the name of Charles Sealsfield, and under that name he published numerous novels that provided his readers with a realistic portrayal of contemporary life in America. His most popular novels were *The Cabin Book*, *Frontier Life*, and *Tokeah: Or the White Rose. An Indian Tale*. He published these works in English as well as in German, and during the nineteenth century he was a widely-read author in the United States, England, and the German-speaking countries of Europe.

Charles Sealsfield had studied theology in Prague. He felt that under Metternich, during the Restoration era, the outlook for the future was bleak. His excellent teacher, the philosopher, mathematician, and theologian Bernhard Bolzano, had been expelled from the University of Prague. Bolzano was a follower of the tradition of Enlightenment that had characterized the reign of Habsburg Emperor Joseph II.

Otto Heller must have felt an affinity with Charles Sealsfield. Heller founded international Charles Sealsfield research, himself contributing a comprehensively commented bibliography, a book on Sealsfield's language, and a few essays on the author's novels. Otto Heller's students continued his work, and not too many years ago a student of one of his students, the American Germanist Karl Arndt, produced the first edition of Sealsfield's collected works.

This essay deals with the comparison of America and Europe made by Charles Sealsfield in 1826 and 1827, at the time the United States celebrated its fiftieth anniversary. After a four-year stay in the United States, Sealsfield produced two essayistic books, one on the United States of America, the other on Europe with particular emphasis on Austria. Both works voiced the sharpest criticism of the prevailing neo-absolutist monarchism. During the Napoleonic era the critical confrontation with Bonaparte's imperial aspirations had dominated the European debate among contemporary writers. Since the beginning of the Metternich regime that debate had changed along with the new political situation. The United States was held up as a model for Europe; in this regard the Frenchman Victor Hugo and the German Ludwig Börne come to mind. Of course many of the European intellectuals of that time who were preoccupied with thoughts of America had never actually been there, but nevertheless they looked to that country as a new utopia.

Sealsfield, however, had traveled extensively in the United States. His book *Die Vereinigten Staaten von Nordamerika, nach ihren politischen, religiösen und gesellschaftlichen Verhältnissen betrachtet* offered an analysis of the political conditions under President John Quincy Adams. This book had its counterpart in a study on Europe, *Austria as it is*. Both books were published in close succession and followed similar patterns of argumentation. Furthermore, both books exhibited the Enlightenment's view of progress in liberty and an anti-Restoration attitude. Whereas the volume on America provided a political analysis of the United States, the book on Austria offered a confrontation with dominant European politics. Both books were written for a European as well as an American public. The author took pains to let his readers know that what he wrote about American politics also held true for European politics, and vice versa. He stated this quite clearly in the foreword to his book on America when he wrote that the United States had put to shame all European calculations and predictions of anarchy; that the country had proven that man could be free and still live within the boundaries of law. Unlike the French Revolution, the American Revolution had not resulted in anarchy. Sealsfield believed that through its political life the United States confirmed the enlightened criticism of Hobbes's thesis, a thesis which proclaims that only an absolute government can prevent anarchy. Sealsfield felt that America's liberal constitution would affect the political culture of Europe, and that the assertion that an absolute government was essential would be disproved through the example of enlightened American politics.

Austria as it is is one of the most critical political essays on Restoration Europe under Metternich. Sealsfield analyzed Metternich's politics not only as an Austrian matter but as a phenomenon of the European continent in general. Metternich's foreign and internal policies were paradigmatic for the rest of Europe. He had planned and executed this policy within the framework of the so-called Holy Alliance.

The negative criticism in these books is balanced by positive praise. In both books two politicians of the late eighteenth century are celebrated by Sealsfield as the founding fathers of the new America and the modern Austria, respectively; both books attack the then current politics of the two countries' leading statesmen; both books express the need for politicians who could provide alternatives to the present situation; both books make freedom of the individual citizen the main criterion for judging society; and both books follow up with comparative discussions of four freedoms: freedom of religion, freedom of the press, freedom of education, and freedom of trade.

Sealsfield had the utmost respect for George Washington, the first president of the American Republic. One could imagine no one more serene, he wrote, more composed, and yet–in all his simplicity–more dignified than this man who had imprinted his character upon the politics of the United States. In the more recent Austrian history Sealsfield accorded this level of respect only to Emperor Joseph II. He felt that this ruler had brought about the liberation of the farmers in Austria, along with introducing a general code of law for the citizenry. Whenever the author mentioned Joseph II in his book on Austria, he expressed regret that the enlightened politics of this monarch had not been continued. The actions of contemporary American and Austrian politicians were measured against the accomplishments of George Washington and Joseph II. This comparison resulted in a devastating condemnation of John Quincy Adams, then president of the United States, and of Clemens von Metternich, the Austrian chancellor. Sealsfield claimed that Adams had achieved his presidency through utterly undemocratic means; his clever dealings– not the election–had put him in the seat of power. The author accused Adams of aspirations to the monarchy. Sealsfield especially despised in Adams his tendency toward political manipulation. Repeatedly he likened the president's actions to the diplomatic intrigues at the courts of St. Petersburg, Paris, and London.

Sealsfield stated that with his monarchist ambitions, Adams posed the greatest threat to the freedom of the United States. Adams, Sealsfield argued, could not represent monarchical interests more strongly if the Holy Alliance itself had dispatched him. The author was certain, however, that the American people were well aware of Adams's leanings, which accounted for the fact that he was a highly unpopular president and would most assuredly lose the 1828 elections.

Sealsfield's polemics against undemocratic policies were even less restrained in his characterization of the goals and practices of Metternich or of the Austrian Emperor Franz I. He stressed the ideological brotherhood of Emperor and Chancellor and stated that Franz I had found in Metternich a man after his own heart, a man who was not in the least burdened by such considerations as religion, morals, or principles. Like John Quincy Adams, Metternich–according to Sealsfield–showed no particular talents, and when it came down to more than tricks or manipulation, his genius would desert him. Although Metternich had managed to prevent the aristocracy from exerting its influence, he had not succeeded in recruiting the aristocracy to his own domestic politics. Basically the Restoration was supported by the civil servants. According to Sealsfield, Metternich had turned his government officials into blindly obedient machines, having quelled in them any feeling of honor or decency.

Nor did Sealsfield mince words when it came to criticizing Metternich's foreign policy. Like an enormous spider, the author wrote, Metternich had covered Europe with his web, with spies in every capital. Sealsfield asserted that no civilized country had ever been subjected to such utterly cunning absolutism as Austria under Metternich.

But where in the United States or in Europe could one find alternatives to the politics of John Quincy Adams and Clemens von Metternich? The book on America presented a strong endorsement of Andrew Jackson, the 1828 presidential candidate. Jackson owed his popularity to his success as a general, notably the victory over the English in the decisive battle of New Orleans in 1815. Since then the general had basked in the glory of being the nation's champion of liberty. Sealsfield pointed to the importance of the New Orleans victory for the United States by comparing it to famous European campaigns, such as the battle against Napoleon at Leipzig. As a liberal, Jackson impressed Sealsfield as a second George Washington. He perceived Jackson as the fitting antidote to Adams and his monarchist party. But both Sealsfield's criticism of Adams and his praise of Jackson were exaggerated. Jackson was no second Washington, and Adams was no second Louis XIV. It was the graphic juxtaposition of absolute and democratic principles that was important.

Under Metternich's regime, Austrians looked in vain for a new Joseph II. In the oppressive climate of the Restoration period there was no hope for the enlightened thinking and political traditions of Joseph's reign. In contrast to America, Austria knew no politician who might have mounted a serious challenge to Metternich. Sealsfield showed that whereas political situations in the United States could be adjusted by means of regularly held elections, in Restoration Europe the only imaginable alternative to the existing regime was revolution. A few years earlier Joseph Görres had dealt with this European dilemma in his essay *Europe and the Revolution*, a work with which Sealsfield was probably familiar.

Critics of society and culture love to argue in the form of binary oppositions. Among the contrasts with which Sealsfield worked were America's independence and Europe's dependence, American freedom and European restraint, the American constitution and the lack of constitutions among the European states. Sealsfield pointed out that in the history of the world there existed no other example of a country having made such gigantic progress in the short time span of fifty years as had the United States of America. The country had grown from three million people at the end of the Revolution to eleven million, from thirteen states to twenty-four; revenue had more than quadrupled. At the same time, American politics had reached global dimensions: in 1823 President Monroe had declared that Europe's intervention in the affairs of the American continent would no longer be tolerated. Referring to the Monroe Doctrine, Sealsfield felt compelled to remark that the childhood of the United States was now over, that the nation had come of age.

Sealsfield commented on America's global importance not only as a political analyst but also as philosopher of history. He considered the Revolution of 1776 mankind's victory over tyranny, superstition, and prejudice. The United States had the course of events on its side, that is, the law of history that a person's individual freedom tends to increase. Sealsfield felt that the spirit of civilization was moving toward the West, that good fortune had fallen on America, and that the spirit of Europe would now flee to the banks of the mighty Mississippi. We can only speculate how he might have reacted to later and more skeptical views on the dialectics of Enlightenment, let alone to postmodern doubts regarding the metanarrative of progressive freedom of mankind. He did, however, recognize some of the contradictions inherent in American society, especially slavery. The fact that slavery was legal in a number of Union states was hardly reconcilable with a picture of freedom for all. Sealsfield considered himself an enemy of any kind of slavery. More than a quarter of a century before the Civil War he predicted that the North American union would come apart over this struggle.

Nevertheless, Sealsfield considered the social atmosphere in continental Europe more explosive than that in the United States. He also foresaw the European revolutions that would occur later in the century. Everywhere on the Continent one was confronted with the contrast between rural poverty and the wealth of the aristocracy. Sealsfield's remark about the royal castle in Stuttgart was representative of that contrast: he admitted that it was the most beautiful royal residence in Germany, but at the same time he complained that the Swabian towns and villages were in deplorable condition. He also criticized the French for having adopted an all-too-pious attitude since the Restoration of 1815, an attitude hardly befitting the country of Montesquieu and Rousseau. In Europe, he considered England the last refuge of freedom, praising this country for its liberal constitution. When would Germany, the fatherland of Herder, Schiller, and Goethe, finally find its way to its own freedom, following in the footsteps of England, which had fought for its rights after Shakespeare and Milton had enlightened their fellow countrymen? As Heinrich Heine would later in *French Conditions*, Sealsfield explored the idea-deed model for democratization. Yet in contrast to Heine, Sealsfield felt that it was not France but England that stood for *political* progress. Like Heine, however, Sealsfield believed that Germany represented the *spiritual* progress of Europe. As the Glorious Revolution with its Bill of Rights had followed upon the English literary and philosophical era of the seventeenth century, so too—Sealsfield hoped—might there begin in Germany a period of political and social action after an era of classical literature and idealistic philosophy had laid a progressive conceptual framework. It goes almost without saying that Sealsfield thought very highly of the democratically organized confederacy of Switzerland where he was to spend the last three decades of his life.

But Sealsfield had little short-term hope for moving towards the deeds of freedom when he contemplated the contemporary political realities of the continental states. The people's ideas for enhanced political freedom could not be realized, since every constitution would meet with Metternich's strictest opposition. Sealsfield's longer-range hope lay in the development of a future European middle class. He cited the example of England, which had been unable to put its excellent constitution to lasting use until the aristocracy's hold had been broken and a strong middle class had developed. In other words, the fight for a constitution was useful only if it went hand-in-hand with the emergence of a middle class. Consequently, the establishment of constitutions in Germany and Austria would require an appropriate redistribution of property and educational reform. With the aid of reforms in the style of Emperor Joseph II or Freiherr vom Stein, such a middle class might have been possible. Since the politicians of the Restoration period had blocked such reforms, however, revolution was seen as the only option.

The hoped-for constitutions would have guaranteed religious freedom, freedom of the press, freedom of education, and freedom of trade. It was these four freedoms that Sealsfield discussed specifically in his comparison of America and Europe. In Austria, especially, the influence exerted on the Church by the emperor was far too great. By comparison, the power of the kings of France and England in clerical affairs was minimal. In the Danubian monarchy, even the Pope wielded little authority over his church. Sealsfield approved of the legally sanctioned separation of Church and State in America. He considered it a cultural achievement that, in contrast to most European countries, the United States had no ruling religion and that the clergymen were not paid by the State.

The most striking evidence of freedom in the United States was the position enjoyed by the press. What would be considered a crime in Europe, unfettered public scrutiny of the government by the press, was considered a duty by American citizens, Sealsfield noted. Consequently, respect for public opinion was very high in the United States. The contrast to the Austrian system could hardly be greater. Under Metternich, censorship, rather than freedom of the press, was the rule. In Austria everyone was surrounded by a circle of spies, intended to snuff out even the smallest flame of political dissent. Sealsfield claimed that the far-reaching influence of the Austrian secret police surpassed all imagination. If one believes Sealsfield, even the despised East German Stasi could have taken lessons from Metternich, whose network of spies covered the entire empire, touching the farmer's hut, the citizen's home, the landlord's pub, and the nobleman's castle.

As to the American educational system, Sealsfield was particularly impressed with primary education in the United States. In his opinion the country owed its high degree of enlightenment and education to its excellent grammar schools. In a comparison of the American and European university systems Sealsfield pointed out the advantages and disadvantages of education in the United States. He wrote that the educated American did not possess the well-rounded education of the Englishman, nor did he share the systematic studiousness of the German, but that in the art of extracting the practical and applying this knowledge to life, the Americans would put the Europeans to shame. Sealsfield also pointed to the educational possibilities for women as a particularly American phenomenon, saying that no other country paid so much attention to the education of the female sex as did the United States.

According to Sealsfield, the picture of education in Austria was pitiful. He complained that the politics of Metternich were forcing the Austrian people into mental darkness. Visits to the university library or the royal library were painful because, although these collections were among the richest of Europe, the best parts of their holdings were inaccessible. It was impossible for professors to work and research freely—indeed, they were forbidden to do so. The influence of Metternich's censorship on literature and theater was catastrophic. Sealsfield stated that an Austrian writer was probably the most tortured being on earth because he was not allowed to think freely, to philosophize, or to be humorous; in short, he was not permitted to be anything distinctive. The Burgtheater in Vienna at that time had one of the greatest German-speaking authors in Franz Grillparzer. His *Sappho* (1818), written shortly after the Restoration began, was rightfully praised as one of the most beautiful current tragedies. According to Sealsfield, however, Grillparzer's later *Medea* (1822) featured a rather boring, tame heroine in whom one could recognize the fear of Austrian censorship. Such a development was as appalling as it was inevitable, given the conditions in Austria during that time.

Sealsfield hastened to add that the situation in Germany was not much different. What might the Germans—basically a well-educated people—

achieve, he mused, if they were granted freedom? Censorship had turned German scholars into dreamy idealists far removed from reality. Sealsfield contended that concentrating on medieval texts, such as the Siegfried Saga, helped make them forget their restricted lives and their sorrows. German scholars were able to provide exact descriptions of the political systems of China, Japan, or Thailand, but overlooked their own political misery. Here Sealsfield was expressing what Madame de Staël and Heinrich Heine had critically and satirically stated earlier about contemporary German scholarship.

When Sealsfield compared trade practices, the United States naturally fared better than continental Europe. The author asserted that the American's favorite occupation was that of doing business. For entrepreneurs, the United States was undoubtedly the best country in the world, since in America the sanctity of private property was assured, as were a firm and liberal government and the unlimited freedom to trade with any nation on the globe. In central Europe, however, governments put up barriers to free trade. The author sneered that they were turning their small countries into a sort of Japan where the markets could offer only what had been produced domestically.

Like Görres and Heine, Sealsfield belonged to those authors who continued the discourse on Europe during the time of the Restoration between 1815 and 1830. Their argument centered on the idea of personal freedom and its guarantee through liberal basic laws in the framework of constitutional monarchies. Freedom of religion, freedom of the press, and the right to an education, as well as to free trade, were central to these demands. Consequently they attacked Metternich's restorative politics. In his demand for a liberal constitution, Sealsfield was closer to Görres than to Heine. Heine's adoration of Napoleon was alien to him. Like Görres, Sealsfield saw in Bonaparte's politics the endangering rather than the enhancement of citizens' liberties. While there was appreciation for the progressive achievement of Napoleon's *Code Civil*, the French Emperor drew criticism because of his censorship, his warmongery, and his opposition to free trade. But what most distinguishes Sealsfield's critical strategies is the juxtaposition of American and European conditions. America played no role at all in Görres's considerations and only a marginal one in Heine's. Sealsfield did not make his comparisons simply to suggest America as the ideal for Europe. In contrast to other European strategists among the writers, neither did Sealsfield use his references to America in order to suggest a unification of the continent after the American model; European unity was not a topic for Sealsfield. Pointing to America was rather intended to provide a constant incentive for the Europeans. The author wanted to demonstrate that the practice of freedom was able to produce success in the everyday life of a society. Even before Tocqueville, Sealsfield predicted that America would outrank Europe on account of its liberties and that it would achieve the status of a world power.

What would attract Sealsfield's attention if he were to visit America today, one hundred and seventy-five years later? Since he was so concerned with the practical side of freedom, one could imagine that he would take notice of the new multiculturalism in the United States. While the cultural climate in Europe today is influenced by new nationalisms, while ethnic conflict, civil war, and cultural demarcation are rampant there, the United States (like Australia and Canada), is working on its transformation to a multicultural society. The image of the rainbow denotes the ethnic and cultural diversity of the country. The rainbow presents the spectrum of colors in their individual splendor and offers an alternative to the melting-pot image. Spurred on by the civil rights and feminist movements, there is a growing awareness in the United States that one can live most freely in a pluralistic, multi-ethnic, and multicultural society. As in Australia and in Canada, a common legal system is seen as the necessary framework for social cooperation; a common judicial bond as the basis on which a multifaceted culture can thrive. This vision, imperfect though it remains at the close of the present century, is likely to be prominent in North America's lessons for Europe in the new millenium.

* This essay is a shortened, revised version of my article "Karl Postls frühe Amerika- und Europa-Essayistik."

Works Cited

Detjen, David W. *The Germans in Missouri, 1900–1918: Prohibition, Neutrality, and Assimilation.* Columbia: U of Missouri P, 1985.

Görres, Joseph von. *Europa und die Revolution.* Stuttgart: Metzler, 1821.

Heine, Heinrich. *Reisebilder, mit den Briefen aus Berlin und dem Bericht über Polen.* Munich: Goldmann, 1982.

Heller, Otto. *Charles Sealsfield: Bibliography of His Writings.* St. Louis: Washington UP, 1939.

_____. *The Language of Charles Sealsfield.* St. Louis: Washington UP, 1941.

Lützeler, Paul Michael. "Karl Postls frühe Amerika- und Europa-Essayistik." In *Literatur und Erfahrungswandel 1789–1830,* edited by Rainer Schöwerling, Hartmut Steinecke, and Günter Tiggesbäumker, 147–67. Munich: Fink, 1996.

Sealsfield, Charles [Karl Postl]. *Die Vereinigten Staaten von Nordamerika, nach ihren politischen, religiösen und gesellschaftlichen Verhältnissen betrachtet.* 2 vols. Stuttgart und Tübingen: Cotta, 1827. Vol. 1 of *Sämtliche Werke von Charles Sealsfield.* Edited by Karl J. R. Arndt. Hildesheim and New York: Olms, 1972.

_____. *Austria as it is: or Sketches of continental courts, by an eye-witness.* London: Simpkin and Marshall, 1828. Vol. 3 of *Sämtliche Werke von Charles Sealsfield.* Edited by Karl J. R. Arndt. Hildesheim and New York: Olms, 1972.

The (Mis)Fortune of Commerce: Economic Transformation in Adalbert Stifter's Bergkristall

Richard T. Gray

One of the most characteristic traits of Adalbert Stifter's fictional world is its evocation of a premodernist historical period with an aura of invariability and permanence. Although he spent over twenty years of his formative life in Vienna, an international metropolis destined to become the intellectual crucible of modernism, few elements of the industrial world, with its hustle and bustle, its impersonality, its emphasis on competition, monetary gain, and proprietary relations, find their way into his fiction. This is perhaps nowhere so true as for the novella *Bergkristall*, which tells of the inhabitants of Gschaid, a small village all but cut off from the rest of the world by mountainous terrain. Indeed, this story explicitly thematizes the constancy and invariance of this village and its inhabitants, of whom it is said:

> Sie sind sehr stettig und es bleibt immer beim Alten. Wenn ein Stein aus einer Mauer fällt, wird derselbe wieder hineingesezt, die neuen Häuser werden wie die alten gebaut, die schadhaften Dächer werden mit gleichen Schindeln ausgebessert, und wenn in einem Hause schekige Kühe sind, so werden immer solche Kälber aufgezogen, und die Farbe bleibt bei dem Hause. (187)

Just as the inanimate objects of the village always remain self-identical, the same fallen stone being placed back in the wall, the roof repaired with the same kind of shingle, and even the house paint never changing color, the animate world of the village—the cows, and presumably the people, as well—continually draws on the same gene-pool, so that identical characteristics recur from generation to generation. Yet despite this assertion of the nearly absolute isolation of the village—no major roads pass through it, the inhabitants form "eine eigene Welt" and possess their own language, "die von der der Ebene draußen abweicht" (186)—on the level of plot *Bergkristall* is concerned with fundamental transgressions of this law of constancy and autonomy. The shoemaker of Gschaid has imported a foreign element into the gene-pool by marrying the daughter of the wealthy dyer from Millsdorf, a commercial center in the adjacent valley. The shoemaker himself has a somewhat checkered past: he left the village in his youth and returned with a *habitus* and with habits out of keeping with the norms of Gschaid (195). And the offspring of his marriage, the children Konrad and Sanna, become by village standards veritable world travelers by constantly making the trip across the mountain pass to the town of Millsdorf in order to visit their grandparents. The entire life of this family that stands in the center of the narrated events, then, is marked by transgressions of the isolation and constancy of life in the village. One of the principal questions raised by the text thus becomes whether these deviations from the law of invariance are ultimately reigned in and drawn into the circle of historical sameness, or whether they disrupt the closed circle of Gschaid by introducing change and expanding the horizon of the village. Critics have tended to defend the first line of argumentation, interpreting *Bergkristall* as a story about the integration of the foreign, the acceptance of the dyer's daughter and her children into the community of Gschaid, and the shoemaker's embracing of the interpersonal values of the village.[1] My interpretation will follow the second line, arguing that the shoemaker and his family represent a major transformation in the living and working conditions in Gschaid, a change that is essentially of an economic and commercial nature.

If Stifter's texts in general invoke bucolic idylls apparently untainted by modern commercialism, they also contain–by its very absence, as it were–an implicit critique of the economic reality in which Stifter and his contemporaries lived. This reality was one of burgeoning industrialization, expansion of the market economy, the rise of the monied bourgeoisie, and a parallel decline of the petite bourgeoisie and the independent craftsperson. In fact, Stifter's own family was adversely affected by this economic development. His father, Johann Stifter, was forced to abandon his trade as a linen weaver, turning instead to the flax trade and agriculture to win his livelihood when cheap imports from English factories displaced higher-priced handmade linen throughout Europe (Naumann 1).

Stifter scholarship has traditionally been dominated by critics whose attitudes are those of the antiquarian historian as described by Friedrich Nietzsche in the second of his "Unzeitgemäße Betrachtungen," *Vom Nutzen und Nachtheil der Historie für das Leben.* The antiquarian outlook, according to Nietzsche, is one marked by unquestioning veneration of the past, by a sense of piety toward its symbols and the desire to preserve and possess them. In this sense Stifter's critics have tended to emulate his own antiquarian views. But to treat Stifter and his utopias in such an uncritical manner, as Horst Albert Glaser has argued, is to take his utopianism at its word, without recognizing that it is created *ex negativo*, as it were, in explicit opposition to the prevailing reality of Stifter's day (viii). For Glaser, as for other left-oriented critics,[2] the industrial world is conspicuous in Stifter's fiction by its very absence: it is the missing, unidentified center that structures Stifter's pastoral vision. By definition, however, such structural centers can never remain completely unarticulated: they find their way secretly and inconspicuously into the narratives they create. As this essay will attempt to demonstrate, nascent commercialism and the economics of exchange function as the unacknowledged ghostwriter of Stifter's *Bergkristall*–a ghostwriter whose signature can yet be detected in the palimpsest of the text.

Like all but one of the stories collected in the volume *Bunte Steine*, *Bergkristall* has a compositional history that encompasses Stifter's experience of the 1848 revolution. First published in 1845 under the title *Der heilige Abend,* this story was revised in the wake of the revolution for inclusion in *Bunte Steine,* which appeared in 1852. It is well known that the revolution was far and away the most cataclysmic event Stifter ever experienced, initiating several major transitions in his life and thought. One of these was his move from Vienna to Linz immediately following the revolution. Another was his newfound pedagogical mission, his sense that the role of intellectuals must be one of positive intervention in the general education of the masses, teaching them to rely on reason for the control of their otherwise unrestrained instincts. The conception of *Bunte Steine* as a book for young people, of course, is evidence for this pedagogical purpose, as are Stifter's collaboration on a humanistic reader for the public schools and his assumption of the duties of school superintendent in Linz. But the most concrete testimony to the fluctuation Stifter's thought was undergoing at this time can be found in the profusion of cultural-political essays he wrote in the months subsequent to the revolution. Ultimately, witnessing the chaos and violence of the events of 1848 transformed Stifter from a radical democrat who advanced the issues of political change into an archconservative who, skeptical of the ability of human beings to liberate themselves from their own egotistical drives, argued for the necessity of a repressive social and political order much like that represented in the antiquated Habsburg monarchy.[3] Thus in the essay "Die oktroyierte Verfassung," written in March 1849, he explicitly turns against the idea of grassroots democracy and justifies acceptance of the constitution handed down from above by the Habsburg emperor. His primary argument against democracy is that the masses of commoners are not yet mature enough for self-rule, that they are far too driven by effects and egoistic desires to be entrusted with the freedom to decide their own political fate. Even more significant, perhaps, is that Stifter condemns the disorder and uncertainty caused by the revolutionary events almost solely on economic grounds. In this same essay he writes:

> Das Land ist im Zustande des Überganges, jeder hält in seinen Unternehmungen soviel als möglich zurück, bis er in den Zustand der Gewißheit kommt, Handel, Gewerbe, Künste stocken, die Verarmung geht in einem erschreckenden Grade vorwärts, dieser Zustand muß geändert werden, und es muß ein Vertrauen erweckender [Zustand], der der bestimmten Gesetze eintreten. (40)

This appeal to a stable order and the trust it engenders as the *sine qua non* for economic prosperity is one of the most prominent leitmotifs of the essays of this period. It is articulated most forcefully in a central passage from "Der Staat," Stifter's defense of the political state as the guarantor of security:

> Die festbegründete Ordnung gibt jedem einzelnen das Gefühl der Sicherheit, und mit diesem Gefühle setzt er sich mit andern in Verkehr, daß sie wechselweise durch Geschäfte das bekommen, was jeder

braucht.... Je geordneter die Verhältnisse sind, desto mehr brauchen die Menschen, weil sie auch Verdienst haben, desto mehr kann der Handwerker hervorbringen, desto mehr kann er auch wieder Arbeiter beschäftigen. Der Kaufmann macht im Gefühle der Sicherheit Bestellungen in entfernten Ländern, er führt die Produkte derselben herbei und sendet die unsrigen dahin. (23f)

The entire system of trade, from the most rudimentary exchange between two individuals to the circulation of goods in the worldwide market, relies, according to Stifter, on the political stability afforded by the well-founded state. The needs of human beings are tied directly to their incomes, and an increase in the latter, brought on by expanding commerce, in turn stimulates production and raises income levels. Stifter's description reads like a textbook example of the co-dependence between overriding market forces and individual needs and actions, and he recognizes that this entire spiral with its concomitant prosperity is founded on the psychological qualities of confidence and faith. He stresses this psychological factor in economic affairs when he turns his example around and enumerates the debilitating consequences of political insecurity: the withholding of agricultural products and manufactured goods from the market, a shortage of money in circulation, the eventual collapse of many businesses, and the impoverishment and suffering of the masses. All this leads Stifter to the assertion that the most sacred duty of every citizen is the preservation of the political order (24).

If we compare the orderliness and inherent rationality of this postrevolutionary portrayal of the market economy with Stifter's prerevolutionary view, articulated in the essay "Waarenauslagen und Ankündigungen" from the 1844 collection *Wien und die Wiener in Bildern aus dem Leben*, we get a sense of how dramatically the experience of the revolution alters Stifter's economic thinking. In this earlier work it is an irrational "Kauflust," the obsessive desire to buy experienced by every individual, that drives the expanding consumer market. Stifter sets about explaining the sudden proliferation of showcases for the display and advertisement of commodities on the streets of Vienna. His reaction manifests a degree of critical insight into the subtle mechanisms of the consumer mentality that one would not expect to find until a century later.[4] Stifter begins his examination with the simple remark that these display cases have the obvious purpose of advertising—and hence of selling—specific commodities. But he immediately recognizes "daß diese Auslagen und Ankündigungen nicht nur den Zweck haben, daß der kaufe, der will, sondern vielmehr und eigentlich den, daß der kaufe, der nicht will" (167). Stifter elucidates this with a comparison drawn from the Bible: the first skilled salesperson to seduce an unwilling consumer into buying something he or she did not want was the snake in paradise, and Eve was his first victim. Now, this comparison is significant, because what it implies is that the semblance and deceit of such salesmanship is the root of all evil, the underlying reason for the banishment of human beings from paradise. But the snake does not bear sole responsibility for this situation: it is able to prey on the instinctual "Kauflust," the lust to buy, that is "ein altes Erbübel des menschlichen Geschlechtes" (168). Thus the seductive salesperson, the modern snake, recognizes that the sale of his or her goods ultimately depends solely on the superficialities of external packaging, not on the usefulness or even the quality of the item itself. Indeed, the buying public, according to Stifter, has bought so completely into the conventions of commodity aesthetics that it refuses to buy whenever these conventions are not upheld (175). Clearly, it is a long way from these critical, even cynical remarks on nascent consumerism to the valorization of the market economy as the ultimate good elicited by a stable political apparatus, the position Stifter upholds in his postrevolution essays. This shift from the condemnation of commerce in the guise of consumerism and its glorification as the basis of all economic advancement and prosperity is inscribed into the novella *Bergkristall*, itself a product of this transitional period of Stifter's life.

The claim that *Bergkristall* thematizes economic and commercial issues can scarcely help but call forth resistance, if not indignation. Is not this novella, after all, just a simple story about two children who, surprised by a sudden snowstorm as they traverse a mountain pass on Christmas Eve in order to return home from a visit to their grandparents, are kept from falling asleep and freezing to death by the grandeur and mercy of nature? Is not this story the veritable prototype of Stifter's "sanftes Gesetz," the gentle law articulated in his theoretical preface to *Bunte Steine*, which claims that even the most insignificant natural phenomena are the manifestations of higher laws, and that these laws of nature—the merciful rescue of two children, for example—have their parallels in the moral world of human nature? Where could this narrative of childish innocence, natural disaster, and grand rescue possibly be tainted by questions of commerce, consumerism, and economic exchange? This is the question I will attempt to answer.

Etymologically the name "Gschaid" derives from a German word meaning "divergence," with the specific significance of "watershed." Geographically, the village of Gschaid lies on one side of a watershed, the ridge that separates it from the town of Millsdorf in the next valley, and this is certainly one of the relevant meanings of the name. But in historical terms the village of Gschaid also passes through a watershed transition in the course of the events Stifter's novella relates: it undergoes an economic paradigm shift from a self-sufficient, predominantly land-based, agricultural economy to one increasingly dependent on the production of manmade commodities, the influx and circulation of money, and trade with other commercial centers. In his "Die deutsche Ideologie," written in 1845–46 at approximately the same time Stifter drafted the first version of *Bergkristall*, Karl Marx describes this transformation, which he ties to the emergence of the bourgeoisie as the ruling economic class.

> Hier tritt also der Unterschied zwischen den naturwüchsigen und den durch die Zivilisation geschaffenen Produktionsinstrumenten hervor.

Der *Acker* (das Wasser etc.) kann als naturwüchsiges Produktionsinstrument betrachtet werden. Im ersten Fall, beim naturwüchsigen Produktionsinstrument, werden die Individuen unter die Natur subsumiert, im zweiten Falle unter ein Produkt der Arbeit. Im ersten Falle erscheint daher auch das Eigentum (Grundeigentum) als unmittelbare, naturwüchsige Herrschaft, im zweiten als Herrschaft der Arbeit, speziell der akkumulierten Arbeit, des Kapitals. Der erste Fall setzt voraus, daß die Individuen durch irgendein Band, sei es Familie, Stamm, der Boden selbst etc. etc., zusammengehören; der zweite Fall, daß sie unabhängig voneinander sind und nur durch den Austausch zusammengehalten werden.... Im ersten Falle kann die Herrschaft des Eigentümers über die Nichteigentümer auf persönlichen Verhältnissen, auf einer Art von Gemeinwesen beruhen, im zweiten Falle muß sie in einem dritten, dem Gelde, eine dingliche Gestalt angenommen haben. (378f)

In general, the villagers of Gschaid conform to what Marx terms the natural, or immediate economy. They view themselves primarily as the subordinates of nature, which they venerate almost to the point of deification. Similarly, nature appears to them to be the source and basis of all their personal wealth. This reliance on nature is concretized in their relationship to the "Gars," the snow-capped mountain that looms far above the village. Stifter's narrator explicitly cites the mountain as the basis of the villagers' livelihoods: it is the source of water that drives their mills, waters their fields, and quenches their thirst; it provides the wood to build and heat their homes (189). But beyond these practical necessities, the Gars also serves as a source of infinite pride, and the villagers identify so closely with it that they often feel "als hätten sie ihn selber gemacht" (187). The mountain is, as Marx says of the natural economy, the foundation of the villagers' conception of personal property. Moreover, as the distinguishing trait of the village, the mountain also symbolizes the villagers' communal bond. "Als das Auffallendste, was sie in ihrer Umgebung haben, ist der Berg der Gegenstand der Betrachtung der Bewohner, und er ist der Mittelpunkt vieler Geschichten geworden" (187). Community in *Bergkristall*, as so often in Stifter's works, is explicitly defined in terms of narrative interchange.[5] As the primary subject of narrative for the people of Gschaid, the Gars represents their tacit communal bond. Manifest in their relationship to the mountain, then, is the natural economy that provides the villagers with their subsistence.

Given the symbolic significance of the Gars for the natural economy of Gschaid, it is especially telling that it also becomes a commercial resource for the villagers. For among its utilitarian aspects, mention is also made of its touristic value.

Der Berg gibt den Bewohnern außerdem, daß er ihre Merkwürdigkeit ist, auch wirklichen Nutzen; denn wenn eine Gesellschaft von Gebirgsreisenden herein kömmt, um von dem Thale aus den Berg zu besteigen, so dienen die Bewohner des Dorfes als Führer, und einmal Führer gewesen zu sein, dieses und jenes erlebt zu haben, diese und jene

Stelle zu kennen, ist eine Auszeichnung, die jeder gerne von sich darlegt. (187)

What Stifter describes here is a rudimentary form of something that takes place today on a much grander scale: ecotourism, the commercialization of those final outposts of untrammeled nature, a nature not yet touched by commercial exploitation, industrialization, and metropolitanization. Although the villagers venerate their mountain for its natural qualities, it is these same qualities, ironically, that make it exploitable for commercial tourism, a phenomenon that will ultimately strip it of its natural mystique.[6] Prerequisite for this touristic exploitation of the Gars, of course, is a strict delineation between "nature" and the rural communities it supports on the one hand, and the industrialized city on the other; and this same segregation, according to Marx, signals the split between the natural and the commercial economies (Marx 379). This division is thematized in *Bergkristall* as the juxtaposition between Millsdorf, the "Marktflecken," or commercial center (192), and Gschaid, the rural, predominantly agricultural community. The possibility of exploiting the Gars for the purposes of tourism gives a first indication that the "Millsdorfization"—the commercialization and modernization—of Gschaid is already underway in the narrated time of Stifter's story. Ecotourism represents an important shift in the lifestyle of the villagers away from a reliance on nature for immediate sustenance to an indirect dependence based on its value to others. This is symbolized in the monetary compensation, the "Lohn" (187) they receive for their duties as tour guides. Moreover, Stifter's language hints at the priority of this monetary exploitation of the mountain over its more immediate, natural uses when he refers to the former as "genuine utility"—as opposed, we must presume, to merely apparent, or at least lesser, utility. This touristic exploitation of the Gars thus provides an important interface between Gschaid and the external, commercial world. The Gars attracts well-to-do city-slickers for whom the experience of unblemished nature represents an uncommon adventure; but this ecotourism thereby breaches the autonomy and self-sufficiency of the village, importing not only the adventure-hungry tourists, but also their economic system.

In the person of the shoemaker, the father of Stifter's children-protagonists, the avatar of commerce and progressive economics has, in fact, already infiltrated the village of Gschaid and its economic attitudes. As the main producer of "Kunsterzeugnisse," man-made commodities (185), he conforms to those characteristics Marx identifies in the modern commercial economy: he is subordinate not to nature, but to his own labor; he is an accumulator of landed possessions and capital; his relations to others are not communally based, but grounded rather in business relations and exchange; and he is explicitly associated with a monetary economy. Beyond this, however, he is the only villager who cultivates business relations that extend beyond the perimeter of Gschaid itself, and in this sense he is the representative of a commercialism that ruptures the apparent autonomy and self-sufficiency of the village.[7]

To be sure, the shoemaker is not the sole representative of modern commerce in this story; the model he emulates, the text suggests, is that of his father-in-law, the dyer in Millsdorf. In both versions of the story, Millsdorf, the more flourishing of the two towns, is expressly associated with trade and commercial activity. In *Der heilige Abend* it is described as having commerce, "Verkehr," with outlying areas (144); and in *Bergkristall* it is said to maintain city-like trades and livelihood ("städtische Gewerbe und Nahrung" 193). Moreover, the dyer himself is one of the wealthiest, commercially most successful citizens of Millsdorf, someone who owns large parcels of agricultural land and understands how to improve his economic situation, as we read in the first version of the text, by employing trade and exchange ("Handel und Tausch" 150). In the second version this connection to industrialization is drawn out even more: the dyer has "ein sehr ansehnliches Gewerbe...mit vielen Leuten und sogar, was im Thale etwas Unerhörtes war, mit Maschinen" (195). More important than his factory-like business and his commercial success, however, are the personal characteristics he displays. His paramount virtues are productivity and profitability: "Der Färber war ein thätiger und unternehmender Mann, der aus seinen Angelegenheiten gerne Alles herauszog, was herauszuziehen war, und nicht leiden konnte, wenn eine Minute entweder bei ihm oder bei andern ohne Arbeit vorüber streichen mußte" (*Der heilige Abend* 149). Indeed, his devotion to his business enterprise is so total that he rarely has time for his grandchildren when they cross the pass to visit, and he is so obsessively concerned with the accumulation of wealth that he even refuses to give them the most meager present: "Denn obwol er nur die einzige Tochter hatte und einmal Alles an sie fallen mußte, gab er doch jetzt nicht die kleinste Kleinigkeit weg, weil Alles zur Gedeihung und Führung seines Geschäftes, das seine Freude war, als Grundstük dienen und mitarbeiten mußte" (*Der heilige Abend* 150). The dyer, in other words, is the paragon of what C. B. Macpherson has called "possessive individualism," a political and economic philosophy that stresses ownership, acquisition, and property as the foundation of personal worth and sociopolitical power (3). He is not avaricious for the sake of avarice, but simply for the sake of good business sense: he is, in short, a consummate capitalist.

Now, it is certainly tempting to see the dyer as a negative example who, by exerting nefarious pressure on his son-in-law, the shoemaker in Gschaid, can be held responsible for the latter's corruption, his exclusive commitment to his occupation, and his subsequent estrangement from family and community. But such an interpretation ignores the fact that in the years following the Revolution of 1848, Stifter himself became an advocate of precisely that possessive individualism manifested in the characters of the dyer and the shoemaker. We have already examined the motive of economic prosperity as the tenor that dominates Stifter's sociopolitical thinking in the essays from the postrevolutionary period. But the radical imbrication of power and economic status in Stifter's political and social thought can perhaps best be seen in the essay "Der Zensus," published in May 1849. At issue in this essay are the characteristics that qualify individuals to stand for election as democratic representatives. Stifter's first impulse, true to the Enlightenment tradition, is to cite education. But, he then counters, education, especially practical experience, is difficult, if not impossible, to document. What trait, then, can be taken as an unmistakable sign of leadership ability? Stifter's answer is as simple as it is astonishing: accumulated personal property, wealth. It is worth examining in some detail the logic and language with which he justifies this assertion.

> Wer wenig Mittel hat, kann gewöhnlich auch wenig lernen, er beschäftigt sich in einem kleinen Kreise von Menschen, in einem Dorfe, in einer Stadt und lernt nicht andere Dinge kennen, die in dem Staate Einfluß haben; wo sollte es z. B. der Taglöhner, der Handlanger und dergleichen wissen, der nie über die Grenze seiner kleinen Beschäftigung hinausgekommen ist: aber der, der größere Mittel besitzt, kann sich eine größere Bildung erwerben, er hat ein größeres Geschäft, das führt in manche Länder und Gegenden, und er lernt die Verhältnisse im Großen und, wie sie im Staate eingreifen, erkennen; überdies ist er durch seinen Besitz an die Dauer des Staates und seines Glückes gebunden, daß er sich nicht leicht an zerstörende Versuche wagt, die für den Staat schlecht ausfallen könnten, was aber der Besitzlose sehr gerne tut, weil er bei Veränderung zu gewinnen hofft. (*Kulturpolitische Aufsätze* 56f)

The upshot of this argument is that the propertied elite, because they have everything to lose and little to gain from political change, will be the best managers of the state's affairs and the best defenders of the status quo; the propertyless or impoverished workers, by contrast, have everything to gain and little to lose from political change, and hence are more likely to wager on political upheaval and radical transformation. Most shocking, perhaps, is Stifter's claim that personal property and possessions are the precondition not for education, but for *educatability*, the ability or desire to learn as such. His assumption here seems to be that anyone who can manage great assets with success will by definition also have the managerial skills to oversee the functions of the state. More to the point, however, is his critique of the worker or villager who can never extricate himself from local issues and hence can acquire no broad perspective on matters of the state. This stands in crass opposition to the glorification of rural life so common in Stifter's fictional writings, including *Bergkristall*. What seems clear, at any rate, is that at the time in which he revised *Bergkristall* for inclusion in *Bunte Steine*, the possessive individualism manifest in the Millsdorf dyer and, by extension, in the Gschaid shoemaker would scarcely have been an object of Stifter's unmitigated reprehension.

Ultimately it is the shoemaker who imports new commercial practices and the values of possessive individualism into the self-sufficient natural economy of Gschaid. In fact, the shoemaker so resembles the dyer in his personal and business traits that he could be his clone. In the second version of the story, Stifter motivates this similarity by hinting that the shoemaker has entered into a veiled competition with the dyer to see if he can outdo the latter's economic success. The dyer himself, of course, incites this competition when he baldly asserts to his son-in-law that economic success is the sole measure of personal worth. "Ein rechter Mensch," he states following the marriage of the shoemaker with his daughter, "müsse sein Gewerbe treiben, daß es blühe und vorwärts komme, er müsse daher sein Weib seine Kinder sich und sein Gesinde ernähren, Hof und Haus im Stande des Glanzes halten, und sich noch ein Erkleckliches erübrigen, welches Letzere doch allein im Stande sei, ihm Ansehen und Ehre in der Welt zu geben" (198). It is not enough simply to run one's business so that it maintains a steady state; it must "flourish"–the same word, not coincidentally, that was used to describe the "flourishing" town of Millsdorf–and grow. Furthermore, according to the philosophy of possessive individualism defended by the dyer, *superabundant* wealth, property that exceeds what is necessary for mere subsistence, capital, is the only thing that can provide one with dignity and prestige.

With this statement the dyer gives the shoemaker sufficient grounds on which to legitimate the drive for luxury and extravagance that are integral to his personality. Even before his unexpected self-reformation into a successful businessman, the shoemaker's distinguishing traits had been the unconventional exorbitance of his dress, his desire for pleasure, and his need for recognition, as expressed in his irrational obsession with the winning of hunting trophies (195). Stifter's text draws an implicit connection between the drive for recognition concretized in these hunting prizes and the shoemaker's subsequent economic pursuits. "Der Preis [awarded at these hunting competitions] bestand meistens aus Münzen, die künstlich gefaßt waren, und zu deren Gewinnung der Schuster mehr gleiche Münzen ausgeben mußte, als der Preis enthielt, besonders, da er wenig haushälterisch mit dem Gelde war" (195). Stifter makes a point of indicating that the basic weakness of the shoemaker prior to his reform is one of the cardinal sins against possessive individualism: the failure to budget his money wisely and subordinate his personal desires to his long-term economic well-being. Nonetheless, his prizes, the mounted coins he collects, contain an open reference to the commercial principles he will later uphold. Indeed, his error, this passage suggests, is that he displays an irrational preference for coins set in mountings, that is, for coins that do not circulate and whose value hence is purely symbolic. In fact, he is willing to lay out many coins that are valid currency in order to acquire a single noncirculating coin that simply serves as a symbol of his prowess as a hunter.

The lesson the shoemaker must assimilate, in other words, is the fundamental lesson of capitalism: he must learn to defer gratification, to subordinate his immediate desires for prestige and accomplishment by diverting them into strategies for long-term economic planning and accumulation of wealth. The shoemaker, who had always distinguished himself in school (195), turns out to be a model student in the school of (economic) life as well, even outdoing his teacher, the dyer. By successfully channeling his previously unbridled desires completely into his occupational endeavors, the shoemaker establishes himself as one of the leading citizens of Gschaid—second only to the preacher and the schoolteacher, whose shoes he makes (194)—and an entrepreneur whose recognition extends well beyond the village. "Einige Zeit nach dem Tode seiner Eltern...änderte sich der Schuster gänzlich. So wie er früher getollt hatte, so saß er jezt in seiner Stube, und hämmerte Tag und Nacht an seinen Sohlen. Er sezte prahlend einen Preis darauf, wenn es jemand gäbe, der bessere Schuhe und Fußbekleidungen machen könne" (196). The relationship with his father-in-law, then, reinforces his inclination toward ostentation, but helps harness and funnel it in more "productive" and economically profitable directions. The transformation of the shoemaker from an eccentric boaster to a model—if yet boastful—businessman thus represents a classic case of Freudian sublimation: his prior obsessions do not become any less obsessive, they are simply transferred to a new aim, to the accumulation of wealth, an aim that, under the conditions of possessive individualism, now brings him precisely the kind of recognition he desires. What it does not bring him, of course, is acceptance among his fellow villagers: he remains, so to speak, the odd man out, but for different reasons. Instead of playing the part of the village idiot, the social eccentric, he has assumed the role of the village plutocrat, the economic outsider whose commercialism and wealth set him apart from all the other citizens of Gschaid, who still rely mainly on nature and the natural economy rather than on commerce.

One of the major changes Stifter introduces into this story when revising it for inclusion in *Bunte Steine* is an expansion of the history of the shoemaker and his family, in particular an elaboration on his commercial operations. Whereas this section supplying personal background encompasses only six pages in *Der heilige Abend* (144–50), it occupies ten pages in *Bergkristall* (193–203).[8] In the revised version, Stifter seems intent on rescuing the shoemaker from the relatively negative picture painted of him in *Der heilige Abend*. For example, whereas in the first version he is called, prior to his remarkable conversion, a "Gemsedieb" (146), a chamois poacher who is clearly involved in illicit activities, in *Bergkristall* he is simply referred to as a "Gemsewaldschütze" (195), an expert chamois huntsman. The detailed exposition of the ways he organizes and manages his business would also seem to be a redeeming factor. However, viewed from the perspective I am outlining here, the structures he introduces appear as nothing other than measures for rationalizing his shoemaking industry, making it more efficient, increasing his customer base, and turning a better profit. Although in *Der heilige Abend* the shoemaker seems merely to be running a cottage industry, himself manager, laborer, and salesperson all in one, in *Bergkristall* he occupies several workers. Moreover, he is extremely selective about those he employs: "Er nahm keine andern Arbeiter als die besten, und trillte sie noch sehr herum, wenn sie in seiner Werkstätte arbeiteten, daß sie ihm folgten, und die Sache so einrichteten, wie er befahl" (196). The shoemaker, in short, is a veritable taskmaster—the verb "trillen" is associated in particular with military drills—perhaps even a tyrant, who expects from his workers the very same discipline he demands of himself. Since we can assume that his pool of employees is drawn from Gschaid itself, his shoe business becomes the center from which the techniques of rationalization and the commercial practices of a protoindustrial economy are disseminated in the village. The rationalization of production develops to such an extent, in fact, that the shoemaker creates a ledger, assigns each pair of shoes a serial number, and keeps records of each sale and the customer's level of satisfaction (197). He even installs a showroom in his house with windows to the outside, and the "shining" shoes and boots put out on display–reminiscent of the display cases Stifter describes in "Waarenauslagen und Ankündigungen"–attract the attention and awaken the "Kauflust" of people throughout the valley, who come to stare longingly at these shoes through the glass (196–97).

The proof of the pudding is in the eating; but the proof of prosperity is in the earning. In this respect, as well, the shoemaker can take pride in his success. His roomy, well-kept, and comfortably furnished house stands on the main square in Gschaid, alongside all the better homes (193). Whereas previously even the people of Gschaid had had their shoes made outside the village, not only they but the inhabitants of the entire valley now order their shoes from the shoemaker in Gschaid. Indeed, ultimately even some people from Millsdorf and from other valleys begin to buy his superior quality work (196). Finally, because among his economic strategies is specialization in hiking boots, his reputation even reaches into the flatlands: "Sogar in die Ebene hinaus verbreitete sich sein Ruhm, daß manche, die in die Gebirge gehen wollten, sich die Schuhe dazu von ihm machen ließen" (196). As a result, the shoemaker can afford the kind of luxury that, as he learned from his father-in-law, is the sole measure of honor and prestige, and he even accumulates some savings (193). But honor and prestige have their price. In the shoemaker's case, the price is such fanatical devotion to his work that he almost completely neglects his family. His wife, after all, suspects "daß er die Kinder nicht so liebe, wie sie sich vorstellte, daß es sein solle" (199), and on the Christmas Eve when the children set off to trek across the pass to Millsdorf, he is so preoccupied with customers that he scarcely takes notice of their plan (203).

Stifter clearly did not see the shoemaker's exaggerated work ethic as negatively as most critics would have us believe.[9] To be sure, the shoemaker's commercial tactics are so aggressive as to eliminate most of his competition. But Stifter invests considerable effort in playing down this potentially unsavory trait by stressing, especially in the second version of the story, the kindness and generosity with which the shoemaker treats his village competitor, old Tobias.

> Die kleine Ausnahme [to the statement that there is only one shoemaker in Gschaid], deren oben Erwähnung geschah, und die Nebenbuhlerschaft der Alleinherrlichkeit des Schusters ist ein anderer Schuster, der alte Tobias, der aber eigentlich kein Nebenbuhler ist, weil er nur mehr flikt, hierin viel zu thun hat, und es sich nicht im Entferntesten beikommen läßt, mit dem vornehmen Plazschuster in einen Wettstreit einzuge-

hen, insbesondere, da der Plazschuster ihn häufig mit Lederfleken Sohlenabschnitten und dergleichen Dingen unentgeldlich versieht. (194)

This passage is significant because it bears witness to Stifter's own ambivalence with regard to the commercial success of the "shoemaker on the square." Especially interesting is the way in which Stifter first introduces Tobias as an occupational rival to the shoemaker, but then retracts this designation, since Tobias has been reduced merely to repairing, not manufacturing shoes. Implicit in the formulation "nur mehr flikt" is the notion that Tobias had formerly made shoes, as well, and Stifter leaves open whether he has ceased this activity because of old age or because he has been forced out of business by the expansion of his more accomplished "rival" on the square. And when Stifter invokes the concept of free-market competition, he does so only to assert openly that this notion cannot be used to describe the relationship between the shoemaker and Tobias. As if the tensions created by this dialectic of assertion for the sake of retraction were not enough to suggest a deep-seated equivocation on Stifter's part, the manner in which he justifies his assertion that the relationship between the shoemakers is not a competitive one also cuts two ways. On the one hand, the shoemaker's generosity in giving Tobias his leather scraps can be taken as an act of uncommon kindness, especially since he is thereby supporting a "rival." However, since, as Stifter emphasizes, this action motivates Tobias not to consider the shoemaker his competitor, it could also be interpreted as an especially sly, even devious business strategy: by supplying him gratis with materials sufficient for the repair, but not the manufacture of shoes, he not only encourages Tobias to engage in noncompetitive pursuits, but also wins him over with an ostensible act of kindness.

The aim of this exposition of the shoemaker and the modern commercialism and capitalist rationalization he represents has been to indicate just how intimately the thematics of possessive individualism and economic transformation are woven into the fabric of Stifter's *Bergkristall*.[10] The next step will be to show the relevance of this problematic for the primary plot line of the story, the children's traverse of the pass on Christmas Eve and the threat they face and ultimately overcome. I will argue that we should read this story line allegorically. Not, however, as an allegory of the grandiosity and mercy of nature, nor of reintegration into family and community, but rather as an allegory of successful economic exchange, of a prosperous commercialism that dares to break down traditional barriers to trade and ultimately ushers in a new prosperity. Here we should recall that the Christmas story, which provides both a temporal and an ideational backdrop for *Bergkristall*, is not a tale that confirms the past, but instead one that affirms a changing future. In the Christian West, the birth of Christ is the paradigm for the beginning of a new era, the demarcation point between the old chronology and the new. My thesis will be that the children's successful crossing of the pass to Millsdorf and back, like the commercial success of their father, marks a new age in the economic development of Gschaid, an era of exchange, of profitable commerce with the outside world, of protoindustrial prosperity. Nothing could be further, of course, from the traditional reading of this text as a—to be sure, nostalgic—glorification of human harmony with nature and the aggrandizement of a community held together by interpersonal commitment and moral values. My interpretation will demonstrate that this discourse of "family values" is, in fact, a mere ideological disguise for a symbolic narrative that advocates the embracing of commerce as a sophisticated strategy for mastery of nature and for economic productivity and prosperity.

Taken even on the most superficial level, the children's journeys across the pass from Gschaid to Millsdorf and back represent a rudimentary form of commerce. As a rule, they carry nothing with them to Millsdorf, but on their return home they are laden with food, gifts, and sometimes even money. Now the dyer, we recall, had strictly refused to provide his daughter and the shoemaker with any financial assistance, even in the form of a dowry; but his wife does not feel herself obliged to adhere to this rule:

> Sie gab den Kindern nicht allein während ihrer Anwesenheit allerlei, worunter nicht selten ein Münzstük und zuweilen gar von ansehnlichem Werthe war, sondern sie band ihnen auch immer zwei Bündelchen zusammen, in denen sich Dinge befanden, von denen sie glaubte, daß sie nothwendig wären, oder daß sie den Kindern Freude machen könnten. Und wenn oft die nehmlichen Dinge im Schusterhause in Gschaid ohnedem in aller Trefflichkeit vorhanden waren, so gab sie die Großmutter in der Freude des Gebens doch, und die Kinder trugen sie als etwas Besonderes nach Hause. (202)

It is important that coins, the symbolic mediators of commerce, are specifically mentioned here. Indeed, the children themselves, in their circulation between Millsdorf and Gschaid, function as a kind of symbolic mediator, a medium of exchange between village and town. A monetary economy is, of course, the cornerstone of modern commercial expansion: money, in the words of David Hume, is an "oil which renders the motion of the wheels [of trade] more smooth and easy" (309). And the ambitions of the children's father, the shoemaker, are also directly associated with his desire to collect certain coins, as we have seen. In the passage from *Bergkristall* just cited, the ambivalence of commerce is inscribed in the differing perspectives the narrator presents on the items the children transport: whereas to the grandmother they appear to be necessities, they are in fact revealed to be superfluous luxuries since they are already available in abundance in the children's home. It is only in the children's Christmas traverse that the utility of these articles—and hence the grandmother's perspective—will ultimately be affirmed, for they give the children the sustenance they need to survive the frigid night in their mountain cave. This is just one respect in which the story underwrites the usefulness of commerce, and we will examine the implications of this in more detail below.

For the moment I would like to pursue a brief biographical excursus that underscores the connection between the children and acts of exchange. In a letter to Emil Kuh from August 1871 (reprinted with *Bergkristall* in the *Historisch-kritische Gesamtausgabe* 2/4: 65–67), Stifter's friend Friedrich Simony, an alpine researcher and geographer, relates an incident he experienced with Stifter in the summer of 1845 that provided the immediate impetus to the composition of *Der heilige Abend.* Hiking together in the Alps, Stifter and Simony were surprised by a violent thunderstorm. Shortly thereafter they encountered two children, drenched to the bone, who approached them on the same trail. The children spoke to Stifter and Simony, offering to sell them strawberries they had picked along the path. Stifter agreed to the purchase, under the condition that the children themselves eat the strawberries and in exchange tell the two men about their travels and how they took shelter during the thunderstorm. Simony goes on to relate how he later showed Stifter drawings of an ice cave, and how the writer remarked to him about the stark contrast between the vitality of the children they had met and the desolation of this cave. The details of how Stifter transformed these associations into the plot of *Bergkristall* do not interest us here.[11] What does interest us, however, is the centrality of commerce and exchange in the encounter with the children. The children in this incident appear, as it were, in the role of entrepreneurs: they sell the wild strawberries they have picked along their hike. Scholars who have drawn on this biographical incident for examinations of *Bergkristall* have without exception ignored this commercial transaction. Yet it is, in fact, central to an understanding of the way in which Konrad and Sanna in Stifter's narrative are connected to the issues of trade and commerce raised by the activities of their father and grandfather. The moment of commercial exchange in the biographical incident reinforces the idea that the children in *Bergkristall* embody the commercial exchange between the protoindustrial economy of Millsdorf and the natural economy that as yet is still dominant–if threatened–in Gschaid.

The biographical incident described by Simony has its most concrete manifestation in the central symbol of *Bergkristall*: the red "Unglüksäule" (190), the memorial to the baker who died trying to cross the pass between Millsdorf and Gschaid.

> Auf dem Halse, der den Schneeberg mit einem gegenüberliegenden großen Gebirgszuge verbindet, ist lauter Tannenwald. Etwa auf der größten Erhöhung desselben, wo nach und nach sich der Weg in das jenseitige Thal hinab zu senken beginnt, steht eine sogenannte Unglüksäule. Es ist einmal ein Bäker, welcher Brod in seinem Korbe über den Hals trug, an jener Stelle todt gefunden worden. Man hat den todten Bäker mit dem Korbe und mit den umringenden Tannenbäumen auf ein Bild gemalt, darunter eine Erklärung und eine Bitte um ein Gebet geschrieben, das Bild auf eine roth angestrichene hölzerne Säule gethan, und die Säule an der Stelle des Unglükes aufgerichtet. (189–90)

The incident Simony relates and the memorial to the baker are connected by two attributes: superficially by the red color of the memorial itself, which harks back to the red strawberries the children sold to Stifter; more substantially by the commercial connection to the baker who perishes while involved in an explicitly commercial enterprise, the transport of his wares across the pass. The relevance for the children Konrad and Sanna, who likewise carry goods over the pass, is self-evident. Indeed, among the articles the grandmother places in their packs on the day of their fateful traverse is bread (207).[12]

The importance of the "Unglüksäule" as symbol is indicated by the increased frequency of its occurrence in *Bergkristall* over against the first version of the story. In *Der heilige Abend* it is mentioned only five times and is called, curiously, a "Martersäule,"[13] whereas in the final version the "Unglüksäule" appears no less than fourteen times (Sinka 2). Even more significant, perhaps, is its precise geographical location: it stands at the highest point of the pass between Millsdorf and Gschaid, and as such it marks the barrier that separates the two villages as well as the threshold that joins them together. This equivocation is important, because for the baker the pass is indeed a barrier, and he pays for his attempt to transgress it with his life. For the children, however, it is—and although imposing and threatening, ultimately remains—a juncture. Not only does the "Unglüksäule" mark this geographical and thematic seam, it functions as the symbolic nodal point in the text in general. As we will see, most lines of signification in *Bergkristall* eventually lead back to this object and the incident, the "misfortune" it represents.

The death of the baker is, of course, itself symbolic: his misfortune stands in for a greater, more abstract misfortune: the misfortune of commerce. It is probably no coincidence that bread is the commodity he is transporting. It is, to cite a passage from Stifter's novella *Zwei Schwestern,* "das einfachste aller Dinge, das weltverbreitetste...das Symbol und das Zeichen aller Nahrung der Menschen" (1099). Indeed, bread is the one commodity that every village would be expected to produce on its own, presumably in each individual household, and hence would not need to be imported. Taking bread to Gschaid would be much like taking owls to Athens.[14] Moreover, the baker's commercial enterprise fails to take account of that famous paradox of economic value first articulated by Adam Smith: namely, that the most abundant and requisite articles, those with the greatest use-value, have little or no exchange-value.[15] The baker is, in short, a misguided entrepreneur. But that is precisely why his action can function in the text as a kind of symbol for the aberrations of modern commerce, for an economic strategy gauged not toward the satisfaction of existential needs, but instead motivated solely by commercial expansion and profit-taking. The baker's action ultimately represents the division of labor, the displacement of an activity accomplished by all, the baking of bread, by a commercial practice that introduces specialization. In this sense the baker is directly connected to the shoemaker of Gschaid, who also introduces division of labor, specialization, and commerce. But the baker, unlike the shoemaker—and unlike his children in their commercial traverse of the pass—pays with his life for this attempt to inject commercialism and modern economic practices into the self-sufficient, natural economy of Gschaid. As long as the "Unglüksäule," the memorial to the misfortune of commerce and of modern economic practices, remains standing, it admonishes all who see it or know about it that modern economics is unwelcome here: for the baker and his ilk, the pass is an absolute, impenetrable barrier. But the "Unglüksäule" falls, and its fall spells the end of a shared narrative, a "mythology," that relates the inherent misfortune of commerce.[16]

The "Unglüksäule" serves a double function: on the one hand it is a marker that warns against entrance into the commercial age; but it also serves, on the other hand, as a waysign. It indicates the place where the paths that connect the two valleys join and are intersected by a third path that leads up to the lifeless desolation of the glaciers. *Bergkristall* is structured in such a way that the traverse of the children parallels that of the baker—with the significant difference, of course, that they survive their ordeal. They do so despite—or perhaps precisely because of—the fact that the memorial to the baker, which serves both as an admonition against frivolous commerce and as a waysign, has mysteriously fallen down. The absence of the post as waysign, of course, is what causes the children to stray onto the glacier: in this sense its disappearance is prerequisite for the possibility that the children will experience the baker's unenviable fate. Yet when the "Unglüksäule" is read symbolically as a warning against the dangers of modern commerce, its fall represents the lifting of this ban and hence already portends the children's rescue. The unfortunate crossing of the baker and the more fortunate one of the children thus mark two differing perspectives on the modern commercial economy. The former view, roughly that held by Stifter prior to the Revolution of 1848 and manifest in the critique of commodity aesthetics voiced in "Waarenauslagen und Ankündigungen," condemns commercialism as a transgression of the self-sufficient natural economy. The latter view, that assumed by Stifter following the revolution and expressed in the possessive individualism of his cultural-political essays, embraces modern commerce as the source of all prosperity and political stability. While both of these perspectives are present in *Bergkristall*, the latter one has the final word: since the children are symbols and mediators of commercial exchange, their rescue is also the rescue of (monetary) mediation and commerce. Thus Stifter's text ultimately valorizes modern economic principles. What *Bergkristall* relates is a historical paradigm shift in the evaluation of the modern industrial economy and its division of labor from one of misfortune to one of fortune—in both senses of the word. The mysterious, unexpected conversion of the shoemaker from profligate, intemperate dandy to hardworking, dedicated, successful entrepreneur is emblematic of this overarching historical change. That neither of these transformations is motivated in the narrative even in the slightest way, but is marked instead by a break or a logical gap, is a fact the significance of which we will discuss in a moment.

The text brings considerable evidence in support of this theory of a historical mutation. We have already examined some of it in the analysis of the economic attitudes represented by the dyer and the shoemaker. But there are at least two more levels on which the story confirms this hypothesis. The most obvious is the change that follows upon the rescue of the children. At the conclusion of the tale, Stifter's narrator explicitly addresses the role of this event as a turning point in the history of Gschaid:

> Das Ereigniß hat einen Abschnitt in die Geschichte von Gschaid gebracht, es hat auf lange den Stoff zu Gesprächen gegeben, und man wird noch nach Jahren davon reden, wenn man den Berg an heitern Tagen besonders deutlich sieht, oder wenn man den Fremden von seinen Merkwürdigkeiten erzählt. (239)

The rescue of the children opens up a new chapter in the history of Gschaid. The story of the children has become a new narrative, one shared by the community, that replaces an old narrative, the story of the baker. The mythology of the villagers, in other words, has undergone a principal shift: it is no longer structured around a tale that signifies the misfortune of commerce, but around one that tells of its miraculous, unexpected success. If the shoemaker has altered the de facto economic practices of the village, his children have reshaped its economic ideology by becoming the subjects of a new narrative, of a new history. That this new history is one which embraces commerce and possessive individualism is signalled in the language with which the children's integration into the village is described. Whereas in *Der heilige Abend* the concluding paragraph of the text begins, "Die Kinder waren von nun an, da sie von den Gschaidern gerettet wurden, erst rechte Eingeborne des Dorfes" (175), in *Bergkristall* the parallel passage runs, "Die Kinder waren von dem Tage an erst recht *das Eigenthum* des Dorfes geworden, sie wurden von nun an nicht mehr als Auswärtige sondern als Eingeborne betrachtet" (239; emphasis added). While in the first version the children have merely become true natives, in the final version they must first become *possessions* in order to be recognized as natives. This explains the transformation in the feelings of the shoemaker toward his children, as well. Far from abandoning the ethics of possessive individualism and recognizing the errors of his protocapitalist economic strategies, he learns to love his children only when he can subordinate them to this ethic, viewing them as possessions among others. Property, its accumulation, and its protection, have the final say in *Bergkristall.*

We can arrive at this same conclusion by tracing a specific set of symbolic exchanges that occur in the text. These can be identified by following the associative connections between the red "Unglüksäule" and the red flag that signals the rescue of the children and is planted on the Krebsstein once they have been found (238). This flag has a special history: "Es ist die rothe Fahne, welche der fremde Herr, der mit dem jungen Eschenjäger den Gars bestiegen hatte, auf dem Gipfel aufpflanzte, daß sie der Herr Pfarrer mit dem Fernrohre sähe, was als Zeichen gälte, daß sie oben seien, und welche Fahne damals der fremde Herr dem Herrn Pfarrer geschenkt hat" (233–34). Via the young Eschenjäger, who served as a mountain guide for the stranger, this pennant is connected to the ecotourism that is just one symptom of the breakdown of the natural economy in Gschaid. Moreover, it is significant that it is none other than the young Eschenjäger who is associated with this commercial tourism. Aside from the baker, the only other narrative of misfortune and death on the mountain that the children know is the story of the old Eschenjäger, presumably the father of the young mountain guide. It is the image of the old Eschenjäger, who fell asleep and froze to death up on the mountain, that motivates Konrad and Sanna to stay awake during their ordeal (225, 227). This admonishing vision of death, as much as the coffee extract and the wonders of nature, is what keeps the children alive. The historical transformation that takes place between the misfortune of the baker and the fortune of the children, then, is paralleled by the misfortune of the elder Eschenjäger and the fortune—good fortune and tourism-derived wealth—of the young Eschenjäger. The shift in narratives represented by this generational change is concretized in the fall of the red "Unglüksäule" at the pass and its replacement by the red flag on the Krebsstein. If the former marked the misfortune of commerce and warned against the demise of the self-sufficient natural economy, the latter symbolizes the embracing of exchange and modern commerce as the only road to prosperity and fortune. It marks off a geographical and symbolic terrain that is higher and more visible than the pass at which the memorial to the baker and to the misfortune of commerce stood.

Throughout Stifter's works matters of economics tend to be banished to a vague realm of contingency and chance, "Zufall." Wealth is often acquired as if by magic, and it often disappears just as mysteriously. One example of this can be found in the autobiographical story related by the preacher in the novella *Kalkstein*. His great-grandfather, he tells us, was a foundling who acquired substantial wealth simply by buying raw materials at a low price and selling them at a profit. That is all we are ever told about his economic rise, as if profit-taking entailed no risks and were as easy as buying low and selling high. Even more obscure is the way in which the preacher's brother loses this fortune: again, we are told nothing concrete about his business dealings, merely that "etwas Furchtbares" happened and that he was forced to declare bankruptcy (116). In the aforementioned novella *Zwei Schwestern*, written at approximately the same time as *Der heilige Abend*, this contingency of economic boom and bust is directly thematized. The narrator of the tale, Otto Falkhaus, introduces himself as a "ein Kind des Zufalles." But the main coincidence in his life is his acquisition of wealth, which his narrative motivates with nothing other than the vague assertion that he had come into this fortune "durch außerordentliche Tätigkeit und durch sehr geschickte Berechnungen" (994,

996). His friend Rikar experiences the opposite fate: he forfeits almost his entire fortune and property as a result of an unspecified lawsuit that he loses for unknown or at least unstated reasons. Moreover, precisely why Rikar is able to retain one ramshackle, infertile property remains unknown even to him. Contingency as the driving force behind the entire narrative in *Zwei Schwestern* stands in for the role of chance where economic fortune and misfortune are concerned in all of Stifter's works. Throughout his writing, the economic structures that bring financial gain or disaster are marked only by narrative gaps, by coincidences, or by miracles. Thus economics appears on the surface to be nothing but a matter of fate. This is true for *Bergkristall* as well. Indeed, this story thematizes the contingency of economics as a contingency in nature: the historical transformation that Gschaid is undergoing, due primarily to the change in economic principles introduced by the shoemaker (following the model of the dyer), is disguised as a wonder of nature (or of religious faith). The rescue of the children is possible, the dyer reminds his son-in-law and us, because, contrary to the norm under such weather conditions, the snowstorm that stranded the children was not accompanied by wind (238). *Bergkristall* thus manifests in paradigmatic fashion what Walter Benjamin criticizes as Stifter's inability to distinguish between nature and fate.[17] But nature and fate both stand in for something else in Stifter, namely for the interventions of human beings in their own economic history. This human component, self-responsibility for one's (economic) fate, is invariably repressed in Stifter, marked by narrative discontinuities that are papered over by appeals to coincidence, nature, chance. What lurks incessantly behind the laws of nature in Stifter is then not the "gentle law" of human morality touted in his preface to *Bunte Steine*, but rather the iron law of modern economics.[18] What we are able to discern in our reading of *Bergkristall* is the return of this repressed element both on the narrative plane, in the story of the shoemaker's economic rise, and on the symbolic level, in the transmutation of the "Unglüksäule" from a symptom of the misfortune of commerce to a sign of the fortune modern economic practices can produce. The rescue of the children is thus actually only an epiphenomenal manifestation, or a symbolic rendering, of a deep-seated economic transformation, the shift from a natural economy of self-sufficiency to a commercial economy of rationalized labor, trade with the outside world, and the use of monetary instruments. Commerce is the modern Christ child whose birth brings salvation.

Stifter, like so many middle-class intellectuals of his age, harbored profoundly equivocal feelings toward the market economy. The fatalism and contingency associated throughout his writing with economic success and failure is just one aspect of this. In *Bergkristall* this equivocation manifests itself as the tension between glorification of the autonomy of rural community and valorization of the commercialism and prosperity of the shoemaker. Stifter's ideal is probably a fusion of these two economic models: capitalism with a human face, as it were. If *Bergkristall* does indeed conclude on a utopian note, then that utopia is one of a Gschaid that has successfully fused the interpersonal trust and community values of the natural economy with the economic principles and prosperity of protoindustrial capitalism. But this reading is probably too positive. A more cynical view would be that the discourse of "family values" in Stifter is nothing but a veneer that hides a narrative about economic growth and prosperity for the propertied elite. If this rings similar to the strategies pursued by political conservatives even today, then that, at least, is no coincidence. What my analysis has sought to demonstrate is that *Bergkristall* cannot simply be read as the exaltation of nature and rural community that critics have traditionally discovered here. On the contrary, the deep-structural message of this text is the affirmation of a capitalist economic transformation that reduces nature to an exploitable resource: the myth of commerce as misfortune is banished and replaced by a narrative that views commerce as the necessary prerequisite for all fortune and prosperity—but not necessarily for the fortune and prosperity of all.

Notes

[1] For interpretations that stress this integrative element, see Doppler 13; Kauf 58–9; and Stopp, esp. 174–75.

[2] Theodor Adorno formulates this discrepancy in Stifter's narratives in terms of an ideologically motivated denial of capitalist society that is so exaggerated as to revert to nonideological truth. See Adorno 346. On the critique of the capitalist lifestyle implicit in its very banishment from Stifter's works, see also Hans Höller.

[3] In this sense Stifter's cultural-political essays form a countermodel to the political agitation he found so distasteful in the authors of Young Germany. Indeed, in a letter to his publisher Gustav Heckenast of October 1849, Stifter goes so far as to blame the "Frasenthume der Afterlitteratur" for the excesses of the revolution (*Sämtliche Werke* 18: 15).

[4] Stifter's remarks anticipate in many respects the profound critique of the city and of modern commodities voiced by Walter Benjamin in the 1935 essay "Paris, die Hauptstadt des XIX. Jahrhunderts," *Gesammelte Schriften* 5/1: 45–59. Cf. in the same volume Benjamin's notes under the heading "Ausstellungswesen, Reklame, Grandville" 232–68.

[5] On the importance of narrative in Stifter, its role of preserving the past and securing the future, see Geulen 10.

[6] On this contradictory attitude of the villagers to the Gars, see Oswald 78.

[7] The shoemaker, the narrator tells us, "kaufte…mit erübrigten Summen nach und nach immer mehr Grundstüke so ein, daß er einen tüchtigen Besiz beisammen hatte" (198). Oswald notes that the shoemaker is constantly occupied with his customers, even on Christmas Eve when the children ask permission to cross the pass to visit their grandparents; see his *Das dritte Auge* 75.

[8] Franz Egerer and Adolf Raschner's claim that Stifter introduces no significant changes to the text from the first to the second version thus cannot be upheld; see their "Einleitung" to volume 5 of Stifter's *Sämtliche Werke* VII–XCV, here pp. lix–lx.

[9] See especially Oswald 75, who accuses the shoemaker of "hubris." In general, the traditional interpretive line, which views the threat to the children as atonement for their father's sins against the community, is founded on the assumption that the shoemaker's zeal is a thoroughly negative trait. See Doppler 13, Kauf 59f, and Stopp 172–75.

[10] Erika Swales's remarks about the centrality of property in *Bergkristall* are coherent with the possessive individualism of the shoemaker and the dyer; see 40.

[11] Hugo Schmidt has developed these connections; see 323–25.

[12] The connection between the bread carried by the baker and that transported by Konrad and Sanna has been noted by at least two critics, but both fail to read this as a sign of changing attitudes on the role of commerce in the village. See Sinka 12 and Stopp 172.

[13] The term "Martersäule," with its allusion to martyrdom, raises a new set of questions about the text. Since the column is erected in memory of the baker, it would seem that he–not the children–is the martyr. But a martyr to what? To commerce? If so, that would confirm the arguments pursued here, since the baker would have perished for the sake of an as yet unacknowledged and unaccepted economic endeavor. But the notion of martyrdom leads to various other associations in the text, especially to the Christmas story. It may also be significant that the shoemaker, although mentioned by name only once (236), bears the name of a Christian martyr, Sebastian. Is the implication that he, too, is a martyr for commerce? Is his martyrdom somehow connected to the mysterious head wound he is supposed to have received in his days as a chamois hunter (195)? These issues can only be raised as provocative questions, for they would lead us too far away from the primary line of argumentation pursued here.

[14] It is significant to recall, however, that this quality of superfluity is present in the commerce of the children, as well, who only "import" to Gschaid things already present there in abundance. Thus the baker's commercial enterprise is not condemned for its superfluity, but for some other reason.

[15] On this economic paradox, see Andrew Skinner's introduction to Adam Smith's *The Wealth of Nations* (Harmondsworth: Penguin, 1974), 11–97, here p. 47.

[16] It is thus impossible to uphold Hilde D. Cohn's surprising claim that the story of the "Unglüksäule" is nothing but a cultural anecdote in Stifter's text and has no relation to the primary narrative; see 259.

[17] Walter Benjamin, "Stifter," *Gesammelte Schriften* 2/2: 608–10. A related claim is that of Paul Requadt, who maintains that Stifter fails to distinguish between na-

ture and history; see his "Stifters 'Bunte Steine' als Zeugnis der Revolution und als zyklisches Kunstwerk" 155.

[18] On this larger claim that Stifter's "gentle law" is an ideological disguise for the hard realities of capitalist economics, see Tielke 9–13, 108–09.

Works Cited

Adorno, Theodor. *Ästhetische Theorie*. Edited by Gretel Adorno and Rolf Tiedemann. 9th ed. Frankfurt: Suhrkamp, 1989.

Benjamin, Walter. *Gesammelte Schriften*. Edited by Rolf Tiedemann and Hermann Schweppenhäuser. 12 vols. Frankfurt: Suhrkamp, 1972–.

Cohn, Hilde D. "Symbole in Adalbert Stifters 'Studien' und 'Bunten Steinen.'" *Monatshefte* 33 (1941): 241–64.

Doppler, Alfred. "Schrecklich schöne Welt? Stifters fragwürdige Analogie von Natur- und Sittengesetz." In *Acta Austriaca-Belgica: Adalbert Stifters schrecklich schöne Welt: Beiträge des internationalen Kolloquiums zur Adalbert Stifter-Ausstellung,* edited by Roland Duhamel, Johann Lachinger, Clemens Ruthner, and Petra Göllner, 9–15. Linz: Adalbert-Stifter-Institut des Landes Oberösterreich, 1994.

Geulen, Eva. *Worthörig wider Willen: Darstellungsproblematik und Sprachreflexion in der Prosa Adalbert Stifters*. Munich: Iudicum, 1992.

Glaser, Horst Albert. *Die Restauration des Schönen: Stifters* Nachsommer. Stuttgart: Metzler, 1965.

Hume, David. "Of Money." *The Philosophical Works.* 4 vols. 3: 309–23. Boston: Little, Brown, 1854.

Kauf, Robert. "Interpretation und 'Relevanz.' Am Beispiel von *Ritter Gluck, Bergkristall* und *Der blonde Eckbert.*" *Die Unterrichtspraxis* 5 (1972): 56–65.

Macpherson, C. B. *The Political Theory of Possessive Individualism: Hobbes to Locke*. Oxford: Oxford UP, 1962.

Marx, Karl. "Die deutsche Ideologie." *Die Frühschriften*. Edited by Siegfried Landshut, 339–485. Stuttgart: Kröner, 1971.

Naumann, Ursula. *Adalbert Stifter*. Stuttgart: Metzler, 1979.

Nietzsche, Friedrich. *Vom Nutzen und Nachtheil der Historie für das Leben*. In *Sämtliche Werke: Kritische Studienausgabe,* edited by Giorgio Colli and Mazzino Montinari. 15 vols. 1: 265–70. Munich: Deutscher Taschenbuch Verlag, 1988.

Oswald, Marcel. *Das dritte Auge: Zur gegenständlichen Gestaltung der Wahrnehmung in Adalbert Stifters Wegerzählungen*. Bern: Lang, 1988.

Requadt, Paul. "Stifters 'Bunte Steine' als Zeugnis der Revolution und als zyklisches Kunstwerk." In *Adalbert Stifter: Studien und Interpretationen,* edited by Lothar Stiehm, 139–68. Heidelberg: Lothar Stiehm, 1968.

Schmidt, Hugo. "Eishöhle und Steinhäuschen: Zur Weihnachtssymbolik in Stifters 'Bergkristall.'" *Monatshefte* 56 (1964): 321–35.

Sinka, Margit M. "Unappreciated Symbol: The *Unglücksäule* in Stifter's *Bergkristall.*" *Modern Austrian Literature* 16 (1983): 1–17.

Stifter, Adalbert. *Bergkristall.* In *Werke und Briefe: Historisch-kritische Gesamtausgabe.* Edited by Alfred Doppler and Wolfgang Frühwald. II/2: 181–240. Stuttgart: Kohlhammer, 1978–.

_____. "Die oktroyierte Verfassung." In *Kulturpolitische Aufsätze.* Edited by Willi Reich, 37–42. Einsiedeln: Benziger, 1948.

_____. "Der Staat." In *Kulturpolitische Aufsätze.* Edited by Willi Reich, 23–33. Einsiedeln: Benziger, 1948.

_____. *Kalkstein.* In *Werke und Briefe: Historisch-kritische Gesamtausgabe.* Edited by Alfred Doppler and Wolfgang Frühwald. II/2: 61–132. Stuttgart: Kohlhammer, 1978–.

_____. *Sämtliche Werke.* Edited by August Sauer et al. 25 vols. Prague: Tempsky, Calve 1901ff.; Reichenberg: F. Kraus, 1908–.

_____. "Waarenauslagen und Ankündigungen." In *Sämtliche Werke.* Edited by August Sauer et al. 15: 167–80. Prague: Tempsky, Calve 1901–; Reichenberg: F. Kraus, 1908–.

_____. *Zwei Schwestern: Studien.* Edited by Fritz Krökel and Karl Pörnbacher, 975–1122. Munich: Winckler, 1950.

Stopp, Frederick. "Die Symbolik in Stifters *Bunten Steinen.*" *DVjs* 28 (1954): 165–93.

Swales, Erika. "The Doubly Woven Text: Reflections on Stifter's Narrative Mode." In *Adalbert Stifter heute: Londoner Symposium 1983,* edited by Johann Lachinger, Alexander Stillmark, and Martin Swales, 37–43. Linz: Adalbert Stifter Institut, 1985.

Tielke, Martin. *Sanftes Gesetz und historische Notwendigkeit: Adalbert Stifter zwischen Restauration und Revolution.* Frankfurt: Lang, 1979.

The Personal Is Political—The Political Becomes Personal: Fanny Lewald's Early Travel Literature

Margaret E. Ward

In the past decade, a number of critics have turned their attention to how travel has transformed women's view of the world and themselves, and how women writers have shaped both the content and form of travel literature. Elke Frederiksen, for example, argues convincingly that gender is a significant variable in this genre, especially in the eighteenth and early nineteenth centuries when few women traveled and only exceptional ones wrote about it for a wider audience (107). For women, the act of traveling itself could have an emancipatory effect. It was often experienced as a key factor in their personal liberation from familial and societal expectations. The attention to personal transformation, what Annegret Pelz calls the "auto-geographical," in the travel literature of key women writers has characterized much of feminist criticism on this subject. Fanny Lewald (1811–1889) is often cited by Frederiksen and others as an example of the way travel could provide a means of breaking out of traditional female role-expectations in the middle of the nineteenth century. But in her early works of travel literature she actually gives scant attention to that inner journey by comparison to others, for example Ida Hahn-Hahn, who is held up by some as a model (Cf. Bäumer, Felden 69, and Frederiksen 121).

Lewald's entire *oeuvre* is characterized by what Catherine Stimpson terms a "double-voiced discourse" that complicates the relationship between the individual woman writer, culture, and society. Lewald thus simultaneously participates in the dominant male discourse of the outer political and social world, and a muted one which involves the search for self as a woman and a writer. In her early travel literature her observations of the people and places she is visiting are closely intertwined with this inner journey. For her, the personal is political, and the political becomes personal. This article explores that complex intertwining of the journey without and within. In the spirit of a "gynocentric criticism" it tries to untangle the threads of a complicated relationship in order "to plot the precise cultural locus of female literary identity and to describe the forces that intersect an individual woman writer's cultural field" (Showalter quoted in Abel 31–32).

It was a trip to Italy in 1845–46 that finally enabled Lewald to make a decisive break with the strictures of her upbringing as the eldest child in an assimilated Jewish merchant family in Königsberg. Her father had sent her to the same Pietist private school as her two younger brothers but then expected the dutiful daughter to come back into the house at thirteen and follow her mother's model of domesticity. The brothers were allowed to pursue further education and required to convert in order to assure their upward mobility in Prussian society. Lewald, on the other hand, was expressly told she need not take this step. Although the family was not observant, Lewald herself felt deeply ambivalent about her eventual conversion and thematized this repeatedly in her fiction, in which Jewish daughters are often the only figures able to achieve her ideal of an androgynous model of human wholeness.

Even though Lewald had begun the process of emancipation by refusing an arranged marriage of convenience in 1836, she still felt that she required her father's permission to begin publishing essays and tendentious novels in the 1840s. David Lewald continued to exercise considerable authority over her, even after her mother's death a few years later. He insisted, for example, that she continue to publish anonymously, ostensibly to avoid embarrassment to the family and thereby ensure that her younger sisters would remain marriageable. Even though at least one woman mentor tried to convince her this would be detrimental to the writing career she had begun to imagine for herself, Lewald complied with her father's wishes until after her third novel, *Eine Lebensfrage* (1844). In the spring of 1845 she achieved a modicum of independence by moving from an aunt's house to a room of her own in Berlin, and she garnered her father's approval for a first trip without an accompanying family member. One should note that her decision to go to Italy rather than France, however, was largely due to her father's lifelong wish to visit the former country and his admiration for Goethe. It is also significant that Lewald found herself postponing the departure for several months while she advertised for a traveling companion, a precaution her father insisted upon. The daughter of an artisan, a woman only slightly more seasoned as a traveler than Lewald herself, was evidently considered suitable (*Meine Lebensgeschichte* 3: 315–16, 389).

Lewald had expected to expand her cultural horizon and deepen her appreciation of the classical and the modern world on this trip to Italy, but not to precipitate a radical break with familial expectations. However, in Rome she became acquainted with a number of freer spirits: Ottilie von Goethe, Adele Schopenhauer, the artist Elisabeth Baumann, and the recently divorced archaeologist Sibylle Mertens-Schaafhausen. Each of these women served as a model of female independence, whereas she recognized in two childhood friends who were living in Rome the kind of female dependence from which she now wished to free herself. By spring 1846 Lewald had begun to shed some of the internalized values of her middle-class upbringing. One outward sign of her new independence was that she deliberately parted company with her chaperone. To keep this companion *in loco parentis* any longer would have been a mockery, since she had already stepped beyond the bounds of what her father would have approved by falling passionately in love with a married man. By the time Adolf Stahr returned to his family and his teaching post in Oldenburg in April, Lewald had decided that this relationship was so vital to her that she would risk her father's rejection in order to preserve it. But she was spared what would surely have been a painful confrontation with him, since he died rather unexpectedly a month later.

Because this first Italian sojourn played such a vital role in Lewald's personal process of emancipation, her first-person account of this Roman romance has been the focus of considerable critical attention. However, Konstanze Bäumer disparagingly characterizes the *Römisches Tagebuch* as "Inszenierung eines gehobenen Selbstwertgefühls im Goetheschen Stil" (153). And Frederiksen mistakenly identifies it as Lewald's first work of travel literature (120). This so-called diary was not actually written until 1865, two decades after the events it portrays. It was conceived as a continuation of Lewald's autobiography, *Meine Lebensgeschichte* (1860–61), which narrates her life up to 1845 as a novel of development. This account of her trip to Italy, especially the love affair with Stahr, like the first three volumes of the life, was written largely from memory. When Lewald presented it to her then husband of ten years as a gift, he urged immediate publication. But she refused to share this most intimate chapter of her life-journey with a wider audience, for she felt it was too personal. After Stahr's death in 1876, she drew some solace from reworking the manuscript, but she confided in a close friend that she was still reluctant to publish it. Only in 1897, nearly a decade after her death, did it appear in a journal under the title "Neues Leben, Neues Lieben" and thirty years thereafter in the shortened version edited by Heinrich Spiero.[1] The interest which this text has elicited among feminist scholars may be due to the fact that it is more overtly "auto-geographical" than her actual travel literature of the earlier period: *Italienisches Bilderbuch* (1847), *Erinnerungen aus dem Jahre 1848* (1849), and *England und Schottland* (1851).[2]

While Lewald was in Italy she was already anticipating the writing of her first work of travel literature because she hoped it would provide her with a good source of income. Instead of keeping a personal travel journal, she compiled long, diary-like letters which she sent home bimonthly. She later used them as the primary source for her first work in this genre, *Italienisches Bilderbuch*, which was only written after her return to Berlin. Since her family was the initial audience for these letters, Lewald exercised self-censorship from the outset. She thus appears to concentrate almost exclusively on Italy and its people, giving the reader only an inkling of the personal, emancipatory journey which was also underway–encouraged both by Stahr and by her new group of women friends. But only in *Römisches Tagebuch*, with twenty years' hindsight, can she view the entire Italian sojourn as the culminating chapter in a linear emancipatory narrative. By contrast, the reader must be attentive to every nuance of form and content to find the signposts of the personal journey in *Italienisches Bilderbuch*. They are most often couched covertly in intercalated tales or revealed indirectly through metaphors of the self.

Being a newcomer to this genre, Lewald had, in fact, quite modest goals. She claims to want to provide a useful guide for other travelers. She thus delights in offering practical advice on transportation, food, and lodging. However, she is also convinced that she can dispel some of the prejudices other Northerners–less adaptable than herself–had unfairly spread about Italian life and manners (154). The book certainly lacks the self-consciousness of *Römisches Tagebuch*, and it is remarkably free of references to famous men like Goethe or Byron who had preceded her. From the outset Lewald expresses her firm determination to experience Italy in her own way. By contrast to Fanny Mendelssohn, who–on a similar trip earlier in the decade–repeatedly referred her correspondents to specific passages in their well-worn copies of Goethe's *Italienische Reise*, Lewald offers her own judgments about both works of art and ordinary people (Mendelssohn 45, 47, 70, 77). It is Lewald's genuine interest in the conditions of daily life which provides the most striking feature of this work, giving it a distinctly political tone. Every appreciation of Italy's cultural heritage and the poetry of its present is tempered by her realistic assessment of the woeful economic conditions of ordinary people. She is especially critical of the Catholic Church's complicity in this and even risks dire predictions about the inevitability of future political upheaval.

Lewald saves her most personal barbs for those occasions when she observes or experiences discrimination directed against women or Jews. During her stay in Florence, for example, she had heard of uprisings in the Romagna and of a young monk in the Dominican cloister of San Marco who was advocating a united, free Italy based on a more enlightened religion and social reform. Lewald admits she would have liked to meet this modern-day Savonarola, but women were barred as visitors to the monastery. She registers a rather sarcastic response: "In einem Lande, in welchem man den Kultus der Jungfrau hat, müßten sich aber vor den Frauen Türen und Tore öffnen, wenn man uns nicht so eitel machen will zu glauben, unser bloßer, flüchtiger Anblick könne den Seelenfrieden der frommen Brüder stören" (112).

Lewald's consciousness of class as well as gender issues sometimes comes rather unexpectedly to the fore as she describes her personal reactions to works of art. The best example is her description of the Scythian Knife Sharpener, a famous statue in the Uffizi's Tribuna in Florence. Her interpretation of this crouched figure looking up to await Apollo's orders before slaying Marsyas removes him entirely from the mythic and places him squarely in a contemporary, political context: "Der Typus des Proletariers ist es, dessen Menschennatur nicht zur Arbeitsmaschine zu entwürdigen ist; es ist der Arbeiter auch unserer Tage" (100). Lewald imagines that he is asking a question of heaven–why his labor should be exploited by another. One day he may answer this himself, she speculates, by turning the well-honed blade on his master. It is noteworthy that here a rather personal reaction to a work of classical sculpture becomes the vehicle to express her emerging view of the inevitability of social and political revolution in Europe in her own day. The source of Lewald's keenest insights with reference to political and social life is often personal conversations she initiates, like that with a young Franciscan monk she meets in a stagecoach, or with a hotel owner she challenges to defend the high price of the breakfast he has just served her. He explains how the people are being crushed under a burden of taxes (124–29).

Lewald often narrates her travelogue using the first person plural. With this pronoun she is referring to a number of actual companions: at first her chaperone or friends made along the way, and once the liaison with the teacher from Oldenburg has begun, Adolf Stahr. However, the journey within is more often revealed when Lewald narrates in the third person, for it is only within the fictional framework of intercalated tales that she can really reveal her deepest personal concerns and private longings. Lewald's impressions of the Roman carnival, for example, are filtered through a love story set against the backdrop of this folk festival. The rather unusual choice of a fictional love plot as the centerpiece of an otherwise nonfictional work allowed Lewald to draw on her personal experiences without subjecting her love affair to public scrutiny (218–58).

It is also at the beginning of this tale, "Aus dem Karneval," that Lewald vents her visceral reaction to the festival's opening ritual, in which representatives of the Jewish populace bring the yearly tribute exacted by the Roman Senate: "Das beginnt in Stille mit der sich ewig wiederholenden Kränkung der unglücklichen Bewohner des Ghetto" (218–19). During Holy Week, shortly before Stahr's departure from Rome, the two had attended the baptism of converts in the Lateran Cathedral. In Lewald's account of this event, she shows how strongly she identified with the one Jewish young man who presented himself. She is especially incensed that he is required to forsake his Jewish family in order to become a member of the Catholic Church, a fact she calls a travesty. "Hörte denn Christus auf, Jude zu sein?" she asks pointedly (280). Here, too, where her personal feelings are most closely intertwined with her political views of the matter, she crosses the border into fiction, weaving a tale in which she imagines the painful isolation of the new convert who now has the right to damn his own people, as well as the extreme sorrow of his family, whom she pictures seated at a Seder meal in their ghetto home. Lewald even switches briefly to the first person singular as she registers her reactions to the actual conversion ritual: "Ein Zug von Stumpfheit lag schwer auf den scharfen, jüdisch klugen Zügen seines Gesichtes. Er tat mir sehr leid" (280). Lewald may very well have been remembering her own ambivalence at the time of her conversion in 1830, which she had portrayed in her second novel, *Jenny* (1843; cf. *Meine Lebensgeschichte* 1: 324–27).

Another expression of deep personal feeling is placed near the end of her carnival tale in which Lewald compares the festival itself to a flaming love affair which must end in full flower, the lovers to be parted forever (254). But this metaphor seems strangely out of place since the fictional lovers are neither separated nor deprived, but rather assisted by the carnival atmosphere and their friends so that the girl's family is won over, and they can be happily united at the end. The narrator's exclamation is thus only a thinly disguised personal cry which actually reflects Lewald's sense of despair as her lover prepared to return to his family.

Other subtle signs of the journey within take the form of recurring metaphors of the self. In describing her first views of Italy in the *Bilderbuch,* Lewald uses vegetative images. She draws attention to the vast difference between the northern and southern climate. Despite the use of the third person, the following passage is a first indicator of what will become a key metaphor of the self in this and later works: "Pflanzen, die bei uns kümmerlich im Schutz der Gewächshäuser gedeihen, blühten hier kräftig unter freiem Himmel..., weil man der Natur hier größere Freiheit gegönnt hatte, sich in ihrem Reichtum zu entfalten" (15). In Italy Lewald had finally been released from the hothouse environment of her extended family. She was able to blossom as she had greater freedom to open herself up to new experiences, choose her own friends and develop vigorous new roots for her future development. Variations on this same metaphor of the self are used repeatedly in the autobiography and made most explicit with reference to the Italian sojourn in the *Römisches Tagebuch*:

> Wenn ein junger Baum Bewußtsein hätte, der lange in einem dürftigen, ihn zurückhaltenden Erdreich gestanden und urplötzlich in den ihm zusagenden Boden verpflanzt würde, so müßte ihm so zumute sein, wie mir in jenen Tagen. Ich fühlte mich förmlich wachsen. Ich empfand es, wie ich in jeder Stunde Neues, Schönes in mich aufnahm, wie es mir zu eigen ward, wie meine Seele sich aufschloß, sich erweiterte und befreite. (28)

After Stahr's departure, Lewald visited the grotto of Egeria outside Rome. Legend tells that this water nymph consorted with King Numa Pompilius and healed him through her selfless caring. In Lewald's retelling of this story she creates another metaphor of the self, here by means of the intercalated tale. The nymph Egeria is a figure who can stand for the kind of renunciatory love which Lewald thought she would now need to emulate in her relationship to Stahr. The fame and happiness of the loved one are Egeria's only ambition; she cares nothing for the judgment of others. Lewald thus describes her visit to the grotto in the first person singular as a kind of pilgrimage. But she seems to have realized that this place—seemingly made for lovers in its solitary beauty—is, like the story of the nymph, only the stuff of fantasy. In reality, she had to worry quite concretely about an uncertain future in both the personal and political realms.

After the Italian interlude and her father's death, Lewald's life entered a phase which can best be described by the German concept of *Wanderjahre.* It was literally a period in which she seemed to be constantly on the move, but it also served the purpose that ideally a journeyman's *Wanderjahr* did after a period of apprenticeship and before settling down to life as a master craftsman. Lewald's horizons widened to encompass the political and social landscape of Europe as a whole. She thus began to draw comparative conclusions about herself and Germany. The next decade marks a period in which she began to establish herself as a self-supporting, independent person, a woman writer with a mind of her own. Indeed it was during these years that she developed the political ideas which she later worked out more systematically in her major essays on women's education and right to work, *Osterbriefe für die Frauen* (1863) and *Für und wider die Frauen* (1870). It is during this period that Lewald was able to stake out the new terrain on which her future personal, social, political, and literary life would rest, and her travel experiences played a decisive role in that process of self-definition.

Stahr had confessed his love for Lewald to his wife as soon as he returned to Oldenburg, and it was he who first rejected renunciation as unrealistic. But nearly ten years passed before a divorce could be finalized and the two married in February 1855. Although Lewald and Stahr wrote each other nearly daily and tried to find every opportunity to meet, there was no sign at first that either spouse was willing to consider divorce. Not only the emotional ties to his wife and their five children, but an inability to imagine a way of supporting himself outside of Oldenburg left Stahr virtually paralyzed. He dreamed at first of establishing a *ménage à trois*, but that, in turn, was not acceptable to Lewald. She was determined not to let go, yet it was not easy for her to imagine that she would ever marry this man whom she adored.

Returning to Berlin from Italy in the summer of 1846, Lewald had faced many uncertainties. Although she already had a modest reputation as a writer of novels and short stories and was finally willing to publish using her own name, she was not sure that she could support herself and several younger sisters—who had become her charges—in this way. She was still experimenting with a variety of literary genres and styles. She admired the writers of the *Vormärz*, especially Heinrich Heine, but she looked primarily to other women novelists as models. It was during these next few years that she began to reassess the novels of George Sand, a writer whom she greatly admired. She also rather vehemently rejected the novels of the Countess Ida Hahn-Hahn, while promoting those of Charlotte Brontë, Elizabeth Gaskell, and George Eliot. While she clearly sought Stahr's advice as she wrote to him about her various writing projects, it would be a simplification to say that he had taken her father's place. Stahr's role before their marriage should not be overstated. Their correspondence reveals that Lewald was the stronger personality, as well as the driving force in the relationship. She also had very strong opinions about both politics and literature. It was she who finally persuaded Stahr to share her admiration for Heine, whom they visited in Paris together in 1850. Lewald only very gradually shifted her allegiance to Goethe under Stahr's tutelage. More importantly, Lewald continued to rely on female mentors and friends to guide and sustain her.[3]

A consideration of Lewald's two other works of travel literature written during these years reveals some striking similarities to the *Italienisches Bilderbuch*. Although the journey without continues to predominate in the text, there are still some signposts of the journey within, especially in *Erinnerungen*, again most often revealed by means of intercalated tales and metaphorical language. Frederiksen and Felden have rightly pointed to the contradictory aspects of Lewald's early travelogues and to the fact that they tend to be less open in form and more ambivalent in their rejection of traditional female role-expectations than the travel literature of other women, most notably Ida Hahn-Hahn. But this criticism tends to privilege a certain kind of female "auto-geographical" travel-writing and thus fails to appreciate the peculiar "double-voiced discourse" of these texts. The observations of the people and places she was visiting become increasingly intertwined with the personal. It was in fact Lewald's keen observations of women in these countries which helped her to reconsider the German political, social, and literary scene and to examine her own personal choices as a woman and as a woman writer.

When Lewald first returned to Berlin she felt totally estranged from her family. Most of her psychic energy was now devoted to fostering the relationship to Stahr, since renunciation no longer seemed to be an option worthy of consideration. Financial exigency dictated that she must quickly prepare the *Bilderbuch* for publication and begin a series of new literary projects. But her writing also gave her a real sense of direction and purpose, an identity no longer tied to family or place. Berlin was little more than a base of operations. Lewald constantly changed her lodgings as she could not afford to pay for them while she traveled. The city only became home in October 1852, when she moved to an apartment on Leipzigerplatz, after which Stahr—finally separated but not yet divorced—also moved there permanently.

Lewald first met Stahr's wife, Marie, in Berlin in May 1847. The following winter she spent the holidays in Oldenburg with the Stahr family. Then in February she set out for Paris with her friend, Therese von Bacheracht. In the few days between 22 and 24 February, the monarchy of Louis Philippe had been toppled. The women arrived in Paris on 10 March. Lewald later heavily edited her long letters—sent this time primarily to Stahr—for *Erinnerungen aus dem Jahre 1848*. She dedicated the book to Therese von Lützow, by then divorced and remarried to a distant cousin.[4] Recently social historians have begun to recover women's forgotten or misjudged role in the revolutionary upheavals of 1848. Being an observer, rather than one of the more colorful female participants like Mathilde Franziska Anneke or Louise Aston, Lewald has not been scrutinized very carefully as to her political views. Some analyses draw the conclusion that even among the more active women, noted either for their journalistic and/or charitable efforts, like Louise Otto and Kathinka Zitz-Halein, or as the wives of revolutionaries like Amalie Struve, Emma Herwegh, and Johanna Kinkel, radical political views were not necessarily linked to feminist consciousness in 1848. With the exception of Aston, German women advocated the limitation of women's political activity to family and cultural affairs.[5]

It is difficult to place Lewald within the wide spectrum of nascent political positions from moderately liberal to social democratic which characterized the fragmented efforts of 1848. She did have connections to some of the German radicals in Paris and visited Georg and Emma Herwegh, for example. Lewald praised the latter, but found the former's thinking unclear. She worried about his tendency toward anarchy and a latent desire for martyrdom. While she was certainly aware of the legitimate social discontents of the time and even sympathetic to Herwegh's socialist goals, she did not think social reform could be swiftly accomplished (*Erinnerungen* 2: 130). Lewald also visited with the Duchess Marie d'Agoult, who had published an *Essai sur la liberté* under her pseudonym, Daniel Stern. But Lewald most wanted to meet George Sand and Heinrich Heine. The former was at her country estate in Berry, so Lewald collected copies of her *Lettres au peuple* and even toyed with the idea of translating them into German. She considered the visit with Heine the high point of her Parisian stay.[6]

Lewald was particularly alert to the role of women in the French upheavals. When she attended a meeting of the *Club central des republicains* on March 16, Lewald specifically noted the number of working women who attended. The following day she was an eyewitness to street demonstrations. Although many other visitors were leaving Paris because of the increasing threat of violence, Lewald reassures her correspondent that she has encountered no difficulties while walking through the streets. In fact, she seems to have enjoyed that extraordinary freedom of movement, along with the opportunity it afforded to be a critical observer. Lewald probably acquired the numerous handbills and sheet music with the latest revolutionary lyrics from street hawkers at this time. She liked the "Marseillaise" and regretted that the Germans had no such stirring anthem (1: 72–73; 181–82).

Lewald was evidently well enough known in some French circles to have been contacted by Eugene Niboyet, the publisher of *Les voix des femmes,* a self-described "socialist and political journal, organ of the interests of all women" (quoted in Moses 128). The first issue had appeared on 19 March. Niboyet appealed to Lewald as a "sister" in the cause of peace and humanity, and Lewald responded in a friendly way. Lewald saved the fourth issue of this journal in which an article by Bettina von Arnim had appeared, but she noted that even George Sand, while reprinted therein, was not willing to become a regular contributor. Lewald found much of interest in it, but she also thought Niboyet's tone somewhat exaggerated. She may have been referring more to Niboyet's language, which still showed the influence of her earlier Saint-Simonian and Fourerist ties, rather than to any of her specific demands. One wishes Lewald had been more specific. Certainly her own concerns were not that far from those of the *Voix des femmes* group, and she probably liked their appeal to women's international solidarity in the cause of peace. She already supported their insistence on equality in marriage, the right to divorce, to education, and to work for women. The demand that women have the right to run for office or to vote was not put forward by this group until after Lewald's departure from Paris, and after the April election brought a conservative majority to power, the journal folded. Nothing more came from this brief contact to early French feminism (*Erinnerungen* 1: 132–135).[7]

By 19 March Lewald had heard of the revolt in Vienna and Metternich's ouster. She also began to suspect that French developments were going to take an anarchic turn, as ever more radical factions spoke out in clubs around the city. As long as the people remain uneducated, she warns, the past is doomed to repeat itself. The misuse of freedom will ultimately result in the return to dictatorship. For Lewald, general education of the people to enlightened citizenship was a prerequisite for a truly lasting republic. The French, in her view, were closer to this ideal than the people in various German lands. It is important to note that her vision of this educated citizenry always included women as well as men, and that was one reason for her consistent advocacy on behalf of women's education.

The metaphor Lewald uses in writing to Stahr on 22 March 1848, when she first hears the news of the 18-19 March uprising in Berlin, provides a striking signpost of the journey within. As she wonders about the political future of central Europe, she likens the relationship between the German rulers and their people to a marriage irreparably broken from within. Her insistence on this metaphor, which she used again in a letter to the Archduke of Saxony-Weimar, Carl Alexander, a year later, puts into high relief the way in which the personal and the political were intertwined in her thought throughout this chaotic period. For even while focusing on the dramatic and crucial political events of the moment, she was clearly alluding to Stahr's failed marriage, and no doubt hinting to him that this broken relationship could only be violently overthrown, not repaired: "Eine wirkliche Aussöhnung zwischen unserem mittelalterlich monarchischen Könige und der Idee der Volksfreiheit ist so unmöglich, wie die Herstellung einer innerlich zerstörten Ehe" (Cf. *Erinnerungen* 1: 206; Göhler 1: 23-24).

As the first news from Berlin reached Lewald a few days later, her anxiety about German developments predominates. But her correspondence still includes some interesting observations from her last days in Paris. In one anecdote she approvingly mentions seeing a procession of seamstresses, "welche Verbesserung ihrer Lage verlangten, wie man sie den männlichen Kleiderarbeitern bewilligt hatte: höhern Lohn und kürzere Arbeitszeit" (1: 217). But Lewald also notes that only she and Therese take any special notice of this procession of women. Evidently the French were more used to such female participation in public. While Lewald does not say so directly, one can infer that she was quite impressed by this example which gave living proof to the thesis put forward in Niboyet's journal: "It is a mistake to believe that by improving the lot of men, that by that fact alone, the lot of women is improved" (quoted in Moses 128).

On her return to Berlin in late March, Lewald was struck by the many contrasts to French conditions. In Prussia there had been only a modest rejection of absolutism, not a true revolution. She was dismayed to find that neither the tendency of the people to subservience, nor the bureaucratic caste system had been broken. Interestingly, when her brother asks her what she herself most hoped for from a republic, Lewald emphasizes her own goal of personal autonomy.[8] As a writer she also welcomed the new freedom from censorship. She can now openly criticize the Camphausen government for its willingness to compromise with the crown at a moment when she felt it should be demanding more concessions. On the other hand, she praises the Berlin citizens, who disprove the accusation that democrats are just a mob of anarchists when they participate in a peaceful demonstration to the gravesite of the men and women who had died in the March uprising. It is in this context that Lewald remarks—almost as an aside—about a group of women, the wives and daughters of members of the Democratic Club. She notes first that the crowd—not she—finds their participation in the demonstration distasteful (2: 44–45). Well aware of cultural differences from one country to the next and the power of public opinion, Lewald suggests that in German-speaking countries such public displays by women might hinder their just demand for equality. Gerlinde Hummel-Hassis takes this passage completely out of context, interpreting it as an antifeminist statement (10). She thus overlooks the way in which Lewald tailors her remarks to her German audience as she considers the immediate Prussian situation. Lewald herself had clearly taken no offense at women's open participation in meetings and demonstrations in Paris. The statement is also very carefully couched in the impersonal third person (one) which conveys no sense of personal affront. It is the kind of tactically cautious argument, geared to the specific stage of each country's political development, which is so characteristic of Lewald and which she will make again, for example, in the 1870s with regard to women's right to vote (Cf. "Die Frauen und das allgemeine Wahlrecht").

By late June 1848 Lewald was discouraged, despite the fact that a German parliament had convened in Frankfurt am Main and the Prussian National Assembly in Berlin. She admitted to Stahr that she found little to reassure her in the turn of events at home or abroad and that his love was her only refuge. She regretted the increasingly strident debates caused by the polarization of right and left, and she doubted that the new Prussian government under Auerswald and Hansemann could improve the situation. The shutting down of the national workshops by the French government, the workers' uprising in Paris, and the bloody street fighting 23–26 June depressed her. Lewald spent much of the summer at von Bacheracht's in Hamburg where she could more easily meet her lover. In fact, she was increasingly preoccupied with their personal affairs. She was willing to put aside her political reservations about the Prussian government when it was a matter of securing what she thought of as her life's happiness, since she was actively exploring the possibility of a post for Stahr in the ministry of education. Twice in a letter of 16 August 1848 to her longtime friend, Johann Jacoby, now a member of the Frankfurt parliament, she emphasizes the importance of these private concerns over the political (Silbener 1: 485).

In the second volume of *Erinnerungen* we find under the title "Aus dem Leben eines Malers" a revealing intercalated tale which confirms this renewed emphasis on the personal. In Hamburg she had visited the atelier of Rudolph Lehmann. She retells his experiences during the June uprising in Paris. While ostensibly a recounting of actual events, this doubly-distanced account simultaneously reveals the journey within. Lewald casts the French revolt as a class conflict between the bourgeois government and the proletariat. Those who had nothing to lose and who considered themselves abandoned by their former allies had naturally turned to violence. The high point of the story is a scene in which a young woman, who had already lost everything—husband, child, and home—in the street fighting, rushes headlong onto the barricades with the red flag in her hand and is brutally shot down by the advancing government troops. Lehmann, dismayed by what he has just witnessed, returns to his studio and searches in his memory for some image to help him regain his equilibrium so he can finish a painting of Saint Sebastian. Instead of returning to the scene he has just witnessed, he conjures up a memory of two Italian women whom he had seen while on Capri the year before. They come to symbolize for him grief, longing, and yet salvation and hope. This story had great appeal for Lewald. She clearly identifies with the artist-bystander, not with the woman on the barricades. The need to sustain a sense of personal equilibrium in order to continue writing was paramount. Furthermore, like Lehmann, she relied on her memories of Italy as a refuge from the struggles of the present and the prospect of a future full of "Blut und Jammer." Her personal memories of Italy, like Lehmann's, can provide "die Befreiung des Künstlers von schmerzvoller Erregung" (2: 162–66; 173).

Nevertheless Lewald found a return to the political scene irresistible. She thus spent part of the fall in Frankfurt am Main, listening to the parliamentary debates. In her reports to Stahr she often mocks the men of the Paulskirche for their petty factionalism, using the following metaphor for what she sees as their inability to give birth to the republic: "Da ist doch jede junge Frau, die mit dem Blick auf ihre Mutter und Großmutter in ihr Wochenbette geht, muthiger und verständiger als diese Männer" (2: 247). By the time Lewald hurried back to Berlin in November, Vienna had been occupied, the parliament there disbanded, and her friends, Moritz Hartmann and Julius Fröbel, arrested along with Robert Blum. In Berlin von Brandenburg had formed a new government, but everyone was expecting a coup. Perhaps recalling Therese von Bacheracht's recent personal rejection at the hands of her lover, Karl Gutzkow, and fearing she herself might be faced eventually with the same in the torturous relationship with Stahr, Lewald once again chooses an unusual, gender-specific image to describe the current political situation:

> Dieses Gouvernement kommt mir vor wie ein treuloser Liebhaber, der schlecht genug, treulos zu sein, nicht den Muth besitzt, seinen Verrath zu gestehen, sondern seine Geliebte durch Martern dazu zwingen möchte, das scheidende, trennende Wort zuerst auszusprechen. (2: 310)

Once martial law had been declared, Lewald's mood became even more somber. She finds the political atmosphere in Berlin as personally stifling, "als hätten sie ein eisernes Netz über uns ausgespannt, als wäre uns selbst der Anblick des Himmels entzogen. Die Thore sind offen, die Straßen sind frei–aber man hat dennoch das Gefühl, sich in einem Gefängnisse zu befinden" (2: 323). By the end of December the Prussian National Assembly had been dismissed and the king had imposed a constitution from above. Franz Joseph had been installed as the new emperor of Austria, and Louis Napoleon had become prince-president of France. The proclamation of the rights of the German people by the Frankfurt parliament on 28 December seemed only a sign of its impotence in the face of counterrevolution. Lewald thought there was little prospect that any concrete democratic gains would be made in the near future, and she feared the forces of reaction. She admired Jacoby's calm hopefulness, and from him she borrowed the Biblical image of Moses in order to end her memoirs on a somewhat affirmative note. Lewald herself seems to have realized that this image did not fit her own situation, however. It was more appropriate for a man like Jacoby, who had at least been an actor in the revolutionary drama. While she shared with him the belief in the progressive development of society which projected that a promised land of freedom would eventually be reached, her apocalyptic vision of the bloody catastrophe which would eventually be visited on Europe because of the current victory of reaction gives the close of her memoirs a characteristic note of ambivalence. She even correctly predicts that her political views–especially this warning–will be easily disregarded because it is uttered by a woman, "weil ein Weib ihn ausgestossen hat" (2: 348–49).[9]

Even more revealing is a statement in a personal letter Lewald sent to Jacoby less than a month later. It gives an accurate measure of disillusionment with the political situation and her frustration at women's restricted influence on the political stage:

> Auch hier sieht es schlecht aus, glauben Sie mir. Ich habe für die nächste Zukunft nur den Wunsch, daß man keine neuen Versuche machen, nicht auf das Volk zählen möge, solange man nicht sicher darauf rechnen kann. Es geht mir oft wie Madame Roland; ich möchte sagen: il me fallait une autre ame, un autre sexe ou un autre siecle! Was hilft es denn, daß *wir* glauben, weil wir wissen–wenn die ganze Welt umher wie blind ist und so taub, daß die das ferne Rollen des nahenden Donners nicht hört? (Silbener 1: 549–51)

A year later, matters in the by now overlapping personal and political spheres seemed even bleaker to Lewald. Her closest woman friend, Therese von Lützow, had departed for Java after her remarriage. Stahr had once again returned to Oldenburg; the possibility that he would obtain a legal separation from his wife seemed remoter than ever. An invitation from Amely Bölte, who had been working in England as a governess since 1839, to return there with her, suddenly held great appeal for Lewald.[10] While she had already drawn some conclusions about the English from her contact with them in Italy and from her reading of English literature and history, she had come to appreciate the importance of basing one's opinions on personal experience. She probably also speculated that such a tour could provide the material for another travelogue. She had no major new writing projects to keep her in Berlin. The historical novel, *Prinz Louis Ferdinand,* completed in 1848, had finally been published to mixed reviews. The next major novel, *Wandlungen,* was only beginning to take shape, and the *Erinnerungen* were nearly completed. She probably also concluded that placing the Channel between herself and Stahr, herself and the whole dismal political situation on the Continent, could only be positive.

Because she was still working on the 1848 memoirs in December, however, Lewald was unable to accompany Bölte back to England as originally anticipated. The new year began altogether badly. In addition to the pressure of the immediate writing deadline, several weeks had passed without a single word from Stahr. In desperation—convinced that he must be seriously ill—she wrote his wife, pleading for her to send some word or have the children write if she or Stahr could not. Matters were made worse by the fact that she had to go daily to nurse her brother, Otto, who was recuperating only slowly from a nervous fever. But she still found time to prepare for the anticipated journey by reading Macaulay's *History of England* and novels by Thackeray and Dickens.[11] By the time Lewald left Berlin in April 1849, she had received a long letter from Therese von Lützow, written after her arrival in Batavia (Djakarta). Her friend extolled the separation from family and friends as a way to achieve clarity about oneself and one's homeland. Lewald was certainly at a juncture where she needed to do both. As she had confided to her diary already in March, for her, the one depended on the other: "'Mit sich fertig zu werden,' das ist eigentlich alles. Ist man das, aber ganz und gar, so ist man gefeit wie der hörnerne Siegfried und wird auch mit den Menschen und mit der Welt fertig" (*Gefühltes und Gedachtes* 9). England, of course, was not nearly so far away, nor as exotic a place as Java from which to come to terms with oneself or to make cultural comparisons, but Lewald found it could serve both these purposes.

Lewald first spent a few seeks with Stahr and some other friends in Bonn, not arriving in London until mid-May. For three months she made this her base, with only brief excursions into the countryside. Then she visited Robert Chambers, a freethinker and popularizer of pre-Darwinian scientific theories, in Edinburgh and made a two-week tour to the Scottish highlands and the Hebrides. The month of August was spent with a new friend, the writer Geraldine Jewsbury in Manchester, after which Lewald returned briefly to London and from there back to the Continent, this time meeting Stahr in Paris and visiting Heine before returning to Berlin.

Lewald was not entirely dependent on Bölte for contacts. The latter was able to introduce her to Thomas and Jane Carlyle, but the two German women soon had a falling out. Lewald may well have been disappointed to find that a governess had virtually no access to society. Three undated letters from Bölte to Lewald–probably from this period–refer vaguely to wrongful accusations and misunderstandings, as Bölte complains in a curious trilingual sentence: "Après tout sind wir ihnen doch immer zwei foreigners."[12] The way Lewald was "lionizing in London" probably further strained what was not a close friendship to begin with (Jane Carlyle quoted in Ashton 277). A further complication was surely Bölte's embitterment over her recent loss of a position with the banker, Sir Isaac Goldsmid, after his son-in-law, Count D'Avigdor, had made amorous advances. It was the Countess D'Avigdor, who had translated *Italienisches Bilderbuch*, so Lewald already counted this family among her few English acquaintances. And she admired Sir Isaac as one of the founders of University College and an agitator in the 1820s for Jewish emancipation (*England und Schottland* 1:67–68; 292; Cf. Ashton 215). Lewald also had a way of opening her own doors. Even Therese von Bacheracht had complained to Gutzkow of Lewald's "Dampfmaschinenart" in such social situations (Vortriede 85). After Lewald had met Thackeray and Geraldine Jewsbury at a breakfast, she quickly became friends with the latter and accepted her invitation to Manchester. Bölte evidently disparaged Jewsbury as "a woman who smokes, and falls passionately in love with one man after another," calling her book, *The Half-Sisters*, "immoral" (quoted in Ashton 213). Lewald, on the other hand, rather admired Jewsbury's unpretentiousness and even recommended this novel to her readers (2: 308).

The two-volume *England und Schottland*, simply subtitled *Reisetagebuch*, much like the *Bilderbuch* and the *Erinnerungen*, was based on the long diary-like letters Lewald wrote during her travels. These were now sent exclusively to Stahr, and the tone is much more personal, since he often appears directly as the addressee *(Du)*. The book purports to have the same kind of guidebook purpose as *Italienisches Bilderbuch*. In the preface Lewald maintains that the four-month sojourn had provided her with some "Belehrung," which served as a corrective to her previous views of England and Scotland, as it would for anyone willing to travel "mit offener Seele und mit offnem Auge" (viii). But Lewald's intent was not in fact as modest as it had been for *Bilderbuch*. She has a more didactic purpose, although–as Felden notes–the disingenuous apologia in the preface is typical of women's travel literature (41–42). In keeping with its stated intention to serve as a guidebook, it does contain a great deal of standard fare: descriptions of the Tower of London, the treasures of the British Museum, and the obligatory visit to the House of Commons, for example. It also abounds with often witty or touching portraits of the people Lewald met, from Macaulay, Thackeray, and Carlyle to beggars and prostitutes. Signposts of the journey within seem to have almost disappeared, with the possible exception of the long passage on Mary, Queen of Scots. This could be interpreted as an extended intercalated tale, in which Lewald identifies with qualities she attributes to Mary, and which therefore serves as an extended metaphor of the self. Felden makes this argument, and she treats the ambivalences to be found in this text within the text in some detail. She ignores the fact, however, that Lewald was not its author. She was merely passing on her notes of a biography by Henry Glasford Bell, *Life of Queen Mary,* that she thought would be of interest to Stahr and to her readers (2: 333). This long manuscript was intended to tide him over while Lewald went off to the Hebrides since she anticipated that she would not be able to send letters with any regularity from there.

What is of primary interest in this last of Lewald's three early works of travel literature, however, is the way the journey without dominates, especially its most political aspects. It has apparently totally eclipsed any references to the journey within because they have by now become fully intertwined. Not only is the personal seen to be political, but the political has become very personal. We cannot ignore the fact that Lewald's comments on the English way of life and its social institutions often dwell on the lot of women and children. Her concern for them as a group forms a recurring theme here, and she by now feels confident of her own opinions in such matters to wish to persuade her readers of their value. As Felden shows, this does not mean Lewald has left behind her socialization. Her descriptions sometimes rely heavily on metaphors which refer to the housewifely and familial sphere. But Felden also suggests—quite rightly, I think—that some of these ambivalences in the use of language suggest a conscious strategy to win over her middle-class German women readers, emphasizing that she was one of them, so that they would more willingly accept some of her more radical suggestions for improving their lot (Felden 59–63). It is certainly a strategy which was well-developed in Lewald's later essays on women.

Lewald seems to have been particularly sensitive to nuances of similarity and difference between women's lives in England and Germany and what she and her German readers could learn from these. She felt, for example, that Germans ought to observe the way the utilitarian British attacked the concrete social problems of a more advanced industrial society. Thus it was England that provided the source for some of the practical ideas which Lewald later promoted. While her contacts were primarily with middle-class English families and progressive writers, Lewald does not exclude the poor from her frame of reference. She boldly draws the attention of her readers to the abject poverty of the prostitutes she has seen on the streets of London, for example, emphasizing the way in which she identifies with them as women. Lewald places the blame squarely on society, whose laws and institutions allow this degradation to exist (1: 55).

Lewald was particularly eager to learn more about a number of projects initiated by members of the Unitarian church, Countess D'Avigdor and Miss Anna Stanwick—the translator of Goethe's and Schiller's dramas—among them. They provided continuing education courses for women, low-cost housing, and bathing and laundry facilities to poor families (1: 67–68). Lewald also comments at length on any aspect of middle-class family life which in her view ameliorated women's experience in comparison to Germany. In a rather amusing passage, she evaluates the absence of men from the home all day while at work in the city as contributing to happiness in marriage, rather than as a dangerous further separation of spheres of activity. She thinks of it as a relief to the wife to be able to carry out her daily tasks without interference from the husband. She also applauds many aspects of English child care and nutrition. Lewald is less sanguine when it comes to assessing the charity which the Church of England and other Protestant groups offered to remedy social inequities. She points out that such measures can only be considered stopgap, until the socialistic idea can reorganize social structures in such a way that general prosperity will make alms unnecessary (1: 235). Lewald's ambivalence on this point can be seen more clearly in a short story, "Sarah," inspired by this trip and set in London, which she included in her next collection of stories, *Dünen und Berggeschichten* (1851). It gives quite a negative picture of the English missionary zeal that requires a poor Jewish emigrant family to convert in order to be eligible for the assistance they so desperately need. Only the heroic efforts of the eldest daughter, Sarah, help avert what would have been a family tragedy—having to deny their faith in order to eat. Sarah manages to eke out an existence selling matches in front of the Stock Exchange and later opens up a small tobacco shop, thus rescuing the family from the clutches of these well-meaning, but misguided missionaries (2: 50–86).

In many areas of life affecting women, Lewald appreciates the English willingness to be satisfied with small beginnings, rather than waiting for major transformations to bring about a truly egalitarian society. She sees the creation of Queens College for women as one such positive example, a clear step in the right direction until a real university for women could be created or women given full access to male institutions of higher learning. She emphasizes the practicality of the effort and praises the principle of free association as a way of meeting immediate social needs. In her effort to convince her readers, Lewald betrays her frustration with the kind of factionalism which had so recently prevented the men of the German parliament from succeeding. In Germany, she complains, speculative theories are developed to their final consequences without any attempt to work things out practically. In England, on the other hand, she admires "die Energie der That" that translates into patient and tireless pursuit of a goal, one step at a time (1: 289–91). This was, in fact, the kind of energetic but patient determination in pursuit of a single, well-defined goal which characterized Lewald's dogged effort to join her life to Stahr's.

The relative independence of both women and children in England also made a deep impression on Lewald. She claims to have found no trace of "künstliche Unmündigkeit und absichtlich verlängerte Kindlichkeit" in women which, in Germany, one generally favored in the middle-class, and against which she herself had rebelled (1: 320–21). She was struck by the British lack of information about German women, however, which led many to have a particularly bad opinion of them. Lewald found that she frequently had to dispel the misinformation which had been circulated about women's participation in the 1848 revolutions, for example. Lewald seems almost amused by the question as to whether all women with socialist views wore men's clothing, spoke in public meetings, and took part in orgies. Lewald reassures the English ladies that she knows of only two German women who had worn men's clothing, one in order to participate with her husband in battle, the other "aus mißverstandenen Emancipationsideen" (1: 323-34). In her contacts with English men and women she often had to explain and defend the 1848 revolutionaries. While tolerant and secure enough to allow the political exiles refuge in their country, she comments that the English apparently have little appreciation for the republican impulse. But she refrains from using the pejorative term, "amazons," which others regularly called German women participants. She also refrains from naming any women, but she is probably referring specifically to Mathilde Anneke and Louise Aston. She is also careful to criticize the latter only for an outward show, not for her emancipatory goals which Lewald shared.

Lewald was particularly intrigued by the way in which the English system of clubs recognized the greater efficiency of taking care of basic daily needs within cooperative associations rather than individual homes. What interested her were not the private male bastions of the aristocracy but the cooperatively run cafeterias, laundries, and bathhouses for the lower classes which she visited. She grasped immediately that such facilities, if made more widely available, could also positively alter the lot of middle-class women, freeing them for other productive tasks and intellectual pursuits. She felt she had to go to some lengths to make her German readers appreciate that institutions of this kind would be beneficial rather than detrimental to family life. In order to confront even minor prejudices, she humorously compares a bowl of steamed potatoes served at home, with the same food prepared at a cooperative restaurant, claiming the latter was even better. She describes in minute detail the laundromat she visited with Jewsbury in London, which was intended to enable poor families to do their own laundry (1: 455-56).

Lewald was interested in any facility which had a practical potential to unburden housewives or families, whatever their class. She gives a detailed report of a model lodging house, which was available for weekly rentals, pointing out how important it is to meet the needs of homeless families, not just single men. She especially admires the simplicity of design in this instance. Lewald then tells the personal story of one woman she met there, a grandmother with three children in her care. The daughter had been abandoned by her husband and must support the whole family as a seamstress. Lewald explains that the lodging house has an elementary school attached to it and a library, with plans to build a bath and laundry facility in the same building. The children even have a protected play area (1: 456-65). Later in Spitalfields Lewald also visited a model lodging house for single men, and in Manchester a cotton spinnery where she also showed interest in the various provisions made for workers' housing. Lewald attributed the opposition even of English women to the expansion of such facilities to the middle-class to an unfounded fear that socialism would break up the traditional family (1: 383-84). Lewald clearly believed that the principles of socialism were the only ones which could bring about a solution to the social problems of the day, but she obviously interprets these in a broadly practical, rather than systematic way. Her admiration for the English free associations was no doubt the source of her later advocacy in the 1860s and 1870s of communal kitchens and cooperative educational programs for women in Germany.

The writer also saw herself as a literary intermediary. She discovered, for instance, that the German literature of the *Vormärz*, which she so admired, was practically unknown in England (1: 316–17). In turn, Lewald wanted her German readers to broaden their acquaintance with English novels, especially by women writers. She mentions the Brontë sisters. In addition, she recommends both the works of Geraldine Jewsbury and Elizabeth Gaskell. In the former she praises her naturalness and clarity of mind, her powers of observation combined with a spiritual freedom and lack of prejudice (2: 309). But Lewald is particularly impressed by the realism of Gaskell's *Mary Barton* (1848), with its depiction of Lancashire factory workers. As the wife of a Unitarian minister in Manchester, Gaskell had firsthand knowledge of the conditions of life in working-class families in that industrial center. Lewald attributes the strength of the novel to this, as well as Gaskell's seriousness of purpose and lack of sentimentality. Lewald views its realism quite favorably by comparison with the romantic novels of George Sand, which she had previously admired. But she no doubt has the weaknesses of her own tendentious novels of the *Vormärz* in mind when she praises the way Gaskell makes her points entirely by means of character and plot, not by didactic reflections of the narrator (2: 305–7). Felden quite rightly points to parts of this passage as examples of the way Lewald continued to think in traditional categories, as she calls Gaskell's writing more manly than that of Jewsbury and suggests that women especially have difficulty writing about the working class without a trace of sentimentality. But the passage also gives one the sense that Lewald was at that very moment changing her perception of what kind of lives women could lead and how they could write. She was also trying to sort out in her own mind what kind of novels and stories she herself wished to write.

By the end of August Lewald had to admit that she had gotten to like England rather well and had found friends there (Göhler 1:67). The only lasting friendships were with English freethinkers like Chambers, who shared her anticlerical stance, rather than with the Unitarian women, no matter how interesting she found their projects. Toward the end of her stay she also met G. H. Lewes, who was just beginning to publish a new journal, *The Leader*. Lewald provided an article about Gottfried Kinkel's imprisonment for the issue of 2 September 1850, just before his sensational prison escape, thus contributing directly to his becoming something of a cult figure in England. The contact with Lewes was renewed briefly when he and Maryann Evans (George Eliot) came to Berlin in 1854. Geraldine Jewsbury proved to be Lewald's closest English friend, however, since she had embraced the German writer as a kind of soulmate. But the effusiveness of Jewsbury's early letters, in which she tells all about her love life, soon gives way to a more generally affectionate tone. Lewald did arrange for her youngest sister, Henriette, to translate one of Jewsbury's novels into German, and as late as 1863, Jewsbury felt she could turn to Lewald on behalf of a young woman sculptor, demonstrating the way travel helped to foster women's networks from one European country to another.[13]

England never seriously competed in Lewald's affections with Italy or France, and unlike those two countries, she never visited again. But she continued to be interested in English literature and criticism. One can find many quotations from Charlotte Brontë, Thomas Carlyle, Bulwer Lytton, and J. S. Mill in her book of excerpts *(Excerptenbuch)* in her unpublished papers. As late as 1874 Lewald evidently planned to use a lengthy quotation from a Bulwer novel in responding to a request by the journal, *Frauenanwalt*, for another article on women's education. The manuscript, in the form of a letter, was evidently never completed–perhaps because of Stahr's illness and death. Only a fragmentary draft dated Berlin, 5 February 1874, remains.[14] But it at least indicates the lasting importance of this English connection for Lewald's later political writing. As Lewald contemplated her imminent departure from England and the brief reunion she anticipated with Stahr in Paris, she wrote rather wistfully: "Ich muß mich oft zwingen, nicht das Erreichbare von mir zu weisen, weil ich eben nicht alles erreichen kann, was ich erreichen möchte" (2: 311). No doubt she was thinking of the still open-ended personal and political journey on which she had embarked as a woman and a writer when she finally had the courage to emancipate herself by leaving her father's house (Cf. "Im Vaterhaus" in *Meine Lebensgeschichte* I).

Notes

[1] "Lebenserinnerungen von Fanny Lewald: Neues Leben, neues Lieben: Das Buch Adolf," *Westermanns Monatshefte* 52 (1887): 270ff. and 370ff. For her objections to its publication: Fanny Lewald, letter to Hermann Althof, 7 December 1876. Lewald-Stahr Nachlaß, Deutsche Staatsbibliothek, Berlin (hereafter *Nachlaß*). The idea of seeing something so deeply felt appear in print seems to have been offensive to Lewald. See Fanny Lewald, "To Karl Gutzkow," 23 May 1848 (Vordtriede 96).

[2] In addition Lewald later wrote with Stahr *Ein Winter in Rom* (1869); and she herself published *Sommer und Winter am Genfer See* (1869), *Reisebriefe aus Deutschland, Italien und Frankreich* (1880), and *Vom Sund zum Posilipp: Briefe aus den Jahren 1879–81* (1883). These last two collections of travel letters she had first published in newspapers and journals.

[3] On the relationship to George Sand, see Ward and Storz. During this period Lewald published an anonymous satire of Hahn-Hahn's novels, *Diogena, Roman von Iduna Gräfin H...H.* (1847).

[4] Lewald had met Bacheracht in Berlin in the spring of 1845. She knew of her as the author of a travel diary, *Briefe aus dem Süden,* but the attraction was a very

personal one. Lewald cultivated the friendship after her return from Italy and played a key role in the break-up of Therese's unhappy liaison with the author, Karl Gutzkow. The Gutzkow–von Bacheracht correspondence (ed. Vordtriede) sheds a less rosy light on this friendship than Lewald's autobiography.

[5] See Stanley Zucker, "Female Political Oppositions in Pre-1848 Germany: The Role of Kathinka Zitz-Halein," and Lia Secci, "German Women Writers and the Revolution of 1848," in Fout, ed. *German Women in the Nineteenth Century.* Gerlinde Hummel-Haasis has compiled an impressive set of documents, but the single quotation from Lewald is taken out of context; see 10, 15.

[6] See *Nachlaß* for folder with Lewald's souvenirs of 1848, including newspaper clippings, handbills, and eighteen songsheets. Lewald's copies of Sand's first and second letters, dated Paris, 7 and 19 March are also here. Lewald explained that she found it impossible to translate these texts she admired because of the vast differences in political culture reflected in the two languages. For the visit with Heine see Lewald, *Zwölf Bilder nach dem Leben* (1888).

[7] The letter addressed by Niboyet to Lewald is in the *Nachlaß*. Its tone is quite familiar. Niboyet calls her "mon bon ange" [my dear angel] as well as sister. She introduces Lewald to the journal and invites her participation. She hopes to meet her, emphasizing the need for international solidarity among women. One issue of the journal (1.4, 24 March 1848) containing the second part of von Arnim's article, "La Misere en Allemagne," is also in the *Nachlaß*. In April Niboyet advocated the election of George Sand to the National Assembly, but Sand rejected any further association with this group (Moses 140).

[8] Fanny Lewald, letter to Adolf Stahr, 25 June 1848, *Nachlaß*.

[9] Lewald later crowed to Jacoby that her publisher, Vieweg, had accepted the manuscript without ever reading it and now found himself compromised by her democratic book. Fanny Lewald to Johann Jacoby, 15 February 1850, *Nachlaß*. In the *Nachlaß* one also finds a very negative review of the book. The reviewer was angered that this Jewish woman would dare to criticize Germany!

[10] Lewald evidently got to know Bölte through her aunt, the writer Fanny Tarnow. Bölte was a translator and later also wrote novels and stories.

[11] Fanny Lewald, letter to Adolf and Marie Stahr, 13 January 1850, *Nachlaß*. Also Göhler 1: 45, 53–54, 57–58.

[12] Undated letters of Bölte to Lewald are in Sammlung Adam, Chapter 52, Staatsbibliothek Preußischer Kulturbesitz, Berlin.

[13] See Ashton 151, 277 for attribution of this article to Lewald. Confirmation is found in Jewsbury's letters to Lewald, *Nachlaß*. Of the eight letters, three date from Lewald's August 1850 stay; two shortly after her departure in fall 1850; the remainder are widely spaced: May 1851, 15 November 1857, and 12 August 1863. No letters from Lewald to Jewsbury are in the *Nachlaß*. Visits by Lewes and Evans to Lewald's Monday evening salon in Berlin are recorded in Lewald's *Privat-journal* 1847–56, *Nachlaß*.

[14] See Manuscript no. 23, *Nachlaß*. The only article Lewald published in this journal, edited by Jenny Hirsch, was the lead article in the very first issue, "Und was nun?" (1871), 1.

Works Cited

Abel, Elizabeth, ed. *Writing and Sexual Difference*. Chicago: U of Chicago P, 1982.

Ashton, Rosemary. *Little Germany: Exile and Asylum in Victorian England*. Oxford: Oxford UP, 1986.

Bäumer, Konstanze. "Reisen als Moment der Erinnerung: Fanny Lewalds (1811–1889) 'Lehr-und Wanderjahre.'" In *Out of Line/Ausgefallen: The Paradox of Marginality in the Writings of Nineteenth-Century Women*, edited by Ruth-Ellen Boetcher Joeres and Marianne Burkhard, 137–57. Amsterdam: Rodopi, 1989.

Felden, Tamara. *Frauen Reisen: Zur literarischen Repräsentation weiblicher Geschlechterrollenerfahrung im 19. Jahrhundert*. North American Studies in Ninteenth-century German Literature 13. New York: Peter Lang, 1993.

Fout, John C., ed. *German Women in the Nineteenth Century*. New York: Holmes and Meier, 1984.

Frederiksen, Elke. "Blick in die Ferne, Zur Reiseliteratur von Frauen." In *Frauen Literatur Geschichte: Schreibende Frauen vom Mittelalter bis zur Gegenwart*, edited by Hiltrud Gnüg and Renate Möhrmann, 104–22. Stuttgart: Metzler, 1985.

Göhler, Rudolf, ed. *Großherzog Carl Alexander und Fanny Lewald-Stahr in ihren Briefen 1848–1889*. 2 vols. Berlin: E. S. Mittler, 1932.

Hummel-Haasis, Gerlinde, ed. *Schwestern zerreißt eure Ketten*. Munich: Deutscher Taschenbuch Verlag, 1982.

Lewald, Fanny. *Dünen-und Berggeschichten*. 2 vols. 2: 50–86. Braunschweig, 1851.

———. *England und Schottland: Reisetagebuch*. 2nd ed. 2 vols. Berlin, 1864.

———. *Erinnerungen aus dem Jahre 1848*. 2 vols. Braunschweig, 1850.

———. "Die Frauen und das allgemeine Wahlrecht," *Westermanns Monatshefte* 28 (1870): 97–103.

———. *Gefühltes und Gedachtes, 1838–1888*. Edited by Ludwig Geiger. Dresden, 1900.

———. *Italienisches Bilderbuch*. 1847. Reprint. Edited by Therese Erler. Berlin: Rütten & Loening, 1983.

———. *Meine Lebensgeschichte 1860–61*. 2nd ed. Vol. 1–3 of *Gesammelte Werke*. Berlin, 1871.

———. *Römisches Tagebuch 1845/46*. Edited by Heinrich Spiero. Leipzig: Klinkhardt & Biermann, 1927.

Mendelssohn, Fanny. *Italienisches Tagebuch*. Edited by Eva Weissweiler. Darmstadt: Luchterhand, 1985.

Moses, Claire Goldberg. *French Feminism in the Nineteenth Century*. Albany: SUNY P, 1984.

Pelz, Annegret. *Reisen durch die eigene Fremde: Reiseliteratur von Frauen als autogeographische Schriften*. Literatur-Kultur-Geschlecht 2. Cologne: Böhlau, 1993.

Silberner, Edmund, ed. *Johann Jacoby Briefwechsel*. 2 vols. Hannover: Fackelträger, 1974.

Vordtriede, Werner, ed. *Unveröffentlichte Briefe (1842–1849) von Therese von Bacheracht und Karl Gutzkow*. Munich: Kösel, 1971.

Ward, Margaret E., and Karen Storz. "Fanny Lewald and George Sand: *Eine Lebensfrage* and *Indiana*." In *The World of George Sand*, edited by Natalie Datloff, Jeanne Fuchs, and David A. Powell, 263–70. Westport, CT: Greenwood Press, 1991.

The German Farmer Confronts the Modern World: An Analysis of Wilhelm von Polenz's Der Büttnerbauer

Ronald Horwege

> Der Bauer hat in unserem Vaterlande ein politisches Gewicht wie in wenig anderen Ländern Europas; der Bauer ist die Zukunft der deutschen Nation.
> —Wilhelm Heinrich Riehl, *Die bürgerliche Gesellschaft*

In looking at German literature and its relationship to German political and cultural developments, one inevitably encounters writers who at one time or another had an influence on German life but who are now largely ignored or forgotten. Among those are many who from a present-day perspective are considered to have played a role in the development and dissemination of ideas embraced by the National Socialists and thus fell into disrepute after 1945. These include not only writers who were active during the period of the Third Reich but also many who preceded them as advocates of *völkisch* thought or even as members of the *völkisch* movements. Precisely because *völkisch* thought had such disastrous consequences, it is important to understand its origins.

The *völkisch* movement, with its roots in the Romantic ideology of the early nineteenth century, was fueled by the social, political, and economic upheavals accompanying and following the French Revolution and the Napoleonic Wars, as well as by the developments brought about by the industrial revolution. It came to be viewed as a counterweight to the other great movements of the period, Socialism and Marxism. Instead of looking to the proletariat of the cities, as Marxist thinkers did, *völkisch* thinkers emphasized the individual and his relationship to the *Volk* and to the cosmos through his continuing relationship to nature. They thus resisted the impending industrialization and growth of large cities because they saw these developments as the cause for the uprooting of the individual, the loss of individual identity and ultimately the loss of unity with the cosmos. Like the Romantics before them, *völkisch* thinkers looked back nostalgically to the Middle Ages, only to stress the endurance of the peasant populace throughout history as preserver and defender of the true German *Volk* in the past and for the future.

In his four-volume *Naturgeschichte des deutschen Volkes als Grundlage einer deutschen Sozialpolitik* (1851–1869), Wilhelm Heinrich Riehl analyzed the different social groups in Germany in relation to the landscape in which they lived. He contrasted a peasant culture rooted in nature with the artificiality of industrialized cities, and in the natural contrast between field and forest he found justification for the preservation of what he considered to be natural divisions between social classes. He desired as an ideal society one that was hierarchical and modeled on medieval estates. Peasants and nobility were the two classes which still lived according to prescribed rules and thus were still an integral part of the landscape from which they earned their living. The bourgeoisie he saw as a disruptive element because it was composed mainly of industrialists and merchants who possessed no close relationship with nature and were thus uprooted. He saw a possibility for these to become rooted again, but only through the exercise of their traditional roles in small towns as they developed in the Middle Ages. Those who were transformed into a type of artisan living on a small piece of land to enhance their contact with nature were acceptable as a part of the *völkisch* order.

The embodiment of the evil forces attacking the rootedness of the peasant for *völkisch* thinkers was the Jew. Consistent with the traditional role of moneylenders which they had been obliged to fill since the Middle Ages, Jews often had positions as middlemen in agricultural regions in Germany, and peasants were frequently indebted to them. Then, too, Jews in the Diaspora were considered to be rootless, that is, they were without connection to the soil and thus to the cosmos. Finally, they were looked upon as being materialistic. Thus in the nineteenth century the Jew was identified with the worst aspects of the growing industrial capitalist society and hence was regarded as the enemy of the true German peasant.

In German literature of the nineteenth century, peasants and farmers came to play an increasingly important role. Annette von Droste-Hülshoff drew characters from the Westphalian heath, Adalbert Stifter from the rural solitude of the Bohemian mountains, and Gottfried Keller from the Swiss peasantry. Among naturalistic writers at the end of the nineteenth century Gerhart Hauptmann stands out, especially for his portrayal of displaced and corrupted peasants in his drama *Vor Sonnenaufgang.*

One has to look very carefully in current literary histories, however, to find mention of Wilhelm von Polenz and his best-known work, *Der Büttnerbauer* (1893).[1] Yet at the turn of the century, Polenz was a genuine best seller, known throughout Germany and considered in foreign countries to be a leading representative of German literature (Kaszynski 71). Named besides Zola, Ganghofer, Rosegger, and Clara Viebig among the ten most popular writers in the years 1900, 1901, and 1902 (Kummer 693f), Polenz was also reputedly among the favorite authors of Tolstoy and Lenin (Kindler 288).

As is often the case with popular writers, Polenz received mixed coverage in contemporary literary histories. For example, in their 1928 *Geschichte der deutschen Literatur* Wilhelm Scherer and Oskar Walzel do not mention either Polenz or his works. Friederich Kummer, on the other hand, gives Polenz two pages in the 1922 edition of his *Deutsche Literaturgeschichte des 19. und 20. Jahrhunderts.* He finds Polenz a little overrated, but in his wholesomeness and sincerity, and in the simplicity and stout strength of his characters, Kummer judges him one of the most likable authors of the decade after 1890. In one of two early biographies of Polenz, Heinrich Ilgenstein places him beside Thomas Mann as one of

Germany's really promising novel writers. He notes that *Der Büttnerbauer* was judged by many critics as the most meaningful German story since the death of Gottfried Keller and Theodor Fontane (3).

The second biography, written five years later by Adolf Bartels in 1909, is the more interesting of the two because it clearly traces Polenz's reception among *völkisch* thinkers. Bartels was a prolific writer, an ardent advocate of *Heimatkunst*, an outspoken nationalist, an anti-Semite, and an advocate of *völkisch* thought who achieved prominence under the National Socialists (Garland 61). Bartels, who also edited Polenz's collected works, considered him to be one of the greatest writers of his time, equaled only by Detlev von Liliencron and Gerhart Hauptmann (Mach 335). He credits Polenz for giving impetus to the development of *Heimatkunst* and compares *Der Büttnerbauer* to Gustav Freytag's *Soll und Haben* because Jews play a similar role in both (Bartels 13, 43). Bartels regards the final scene in the novel, in which the farmer commits suicide, as one of the greatest poetic accomplishments in the entire body of more recent German literature and predicts that the main effect of the work still lies ahead (54).

Bartels's prediction was accurate. In literary histories appearing between 1933 and 1945 Polenz received a thoroughly enthusiastic evaluation. For example, in their 1940 *Die deutsche Literatur: Geschichte und Hauptwerke in den Grundzügen,* Erich Schulz and Hans Henning present a lengthy evaluation of Polenz and of *Der Büttnerbauer*. They stress that Polenz belonged to the writers of social realism who kept away from naturalistic tendencies and that he was animated by a warm love for the *Volk*. They find the characterization of the farmer, the Büttnerbauer, to be powerful, the individual scenes to be unforgettable and the distinctive depictions of city and country to be authentic (46). Walter Linden's 1942 *Geschichte der deutschen Literatur von den Anfängen bis zur Gegenwart* calls *Der Büttnerbauer* Polenz's lasting accomplishment and stresses that the farm is put at the mercy of Jewish speculators after the farmer is overburdened by selfish members of his family who claim his inheritance. He calls the novel "ein trauriges Bild zerflatternder Volkskraft" and points out that as the young men leave their family farms to earn their keep elsewhere, the farmers are all too easily transformed into "halbindustrielle Landwirte" who greedily reach out for the few remaining small farms. He praises the novel as "ein Zeitroman von ungewöhnlich scharfem Blick" and notes that in the freely chosen death of the farmer on his last remaining field it approaches "die mythische Tiefe echten Bauerntums" (440f). Other highly favorable treatments are found in Josef Nadler (1938) and Helmuth Langenbucher (1940). It is also interesting to note that although *Der Büttnerbauer* had already been published in eleven editions by 1909, during the Third Reich it appeared in at least three additional editions, each with a different publisher.[2] Finally, George Mosse reports that the work had an influence on Adolf Hitler himself (27). Since Polenz has so often been celebrated among the works of *völkisch* writers, and since in the last few years he has once again been given some attention by scholars and by publishers,[3] interesting questions arise about the appeal of a work like *Der*

Büttnerbauer in the post-Cold War world. These questions can best be dealt with by first taking a closer look at the novel itself.

Der Büttnerbauer takes place in the Lausitz region of Saxony and depicts the downfall and ruin of the farmer Traugott Büttner at the hands of capitalist profiteers. This downfall is developed in the novel in three stages. In the first stage the farmer is forced into debt, in the second he sinks more deeply into debt and is finally forced to auction off his land, and in the third he is driven to suicide when his home is sold to the manager of the brick factory being built on the property he has lost.

The plot and character development in the novel provide an analysis of the decline of the German agrarian class. Polenz sees the beginning of this decline in the freeing of the peasants and land reforms at the beginning of the nineteenth century. Traugott's grandfather had experienced hereditary servitude and compulsory labor under the landed gentry, the family of Count Saland. With the freeing of the peasants at the beginning of the nineteenth century, the farmer suddenly had become his own master with his own farm. Polenz notes that the idea of freedom had been foreign to most of the peasants and that they would have been just as happy to remain under the protection of the nobility: "Gar manchen fröstelte da in der neugeschenkten Freiheit, und er wünschte sich in das Joch der Hörigkeit zurück" (142). Polenz does not fail to mention the difficult times brought about by the French, who plundered the region twice, and then by the Cossacks, who had come as allies but did more damage than the enemy. Then followed a drought which caused many farmers to leave their lands. As a result, the nobles were able to increase their holdings and Traugott's grandfather himself was relieved to give over one-third of his holdings to his neighbor, Count Saland. Polenz notes that with the freeing of the peasants, the nobility, which had traditionally protected the peasants, became one of their competitors.

Out of a sense of responsibility towards his son Leberecht (whose name suggests that he lives correctly) the grandfather resisted being forced completely from his land. Polenz characterizes Leberecht as a "Sohn der neuen Zeit" (143) because he was quick to take advantage of new agricultural techniques: "Leberecht Büttner war im rechten Augenblick geboren, das war sein Glück; daß er den Augenblick zu nützen verstand, war sein Verdienst. Er durfte zu einer Zeit wirken und schaffen, wo der Landmann, wenn er seinen Beruf verstand, Gold im Acker finden konnte" (144). He expanded the holdings and developed them into one of the best-kept farms in the region. His sudden and unexpected death served as a principal cause of the problems which were to develop with the son Traugott, however, for Leberecht neglected to leave a last will and testament.

Polenz constructs a mixed legacy for Traugott. Leberecht's caution becomes Traugott's mistrust, and whereas the father was thrifty and economical the son tends to be miserly and petty. The conservative mind of the old man degenerates in the son to narrow-mindedness, and energy turns to defiance and obstinacy. The one thing which did not pass from the father to the son in any form was good fortune. Traugott's unwillingness to make use of new farming and marketing techniques and his hatred for the present-day situation cause him to become increasingly alienated from the world around him and to withdraw more and more into himself as he is overtaken by modern developments.

Despite these character flaws, Traugott is the principal window through which Polenz displays the *völkisch* idea of the threefold unity of individual, land, and cosmos. The farmer's religious beliefs would appear pagan to orthodox theologians. His relationship to God is a sort of treaty based on an utilitarian agreement by which the farmer would bring his offerings to God so that God would give him good weather and see that his crops flourish. Heaven for him is a continuation of the reality in which he now lives: "Was er hier gewesen, was er auf dieser Welt geschaffen und gewollt, sollte ewigen Bestand haben" (148). His land is, in essence, his heaven, and the loss of the land would be for him the same as the loss of eternal heavenly happiness. After the death of his wife in Book Three, Traugott breaks completely with the Church, which had never been the locus of his religious feeling.

> Seine Religiosität war niemals über eine äußerliche Kirchlichkeit hinausgekommen. Nun er nicht mehr zur Kirche ging, kam das Heidentum zum Vorschein, das tief in der Natur des deutschen Bauern steckt. Was kümmerten ihn die überirdischen Dinge; von denen wußte man nichts! Der Boden, auf dem er stand, die Pflanzen, die er hervorbrachte, die Tiere, die er nährte, der Himmel über ihm mit seinen Gestirnen, Wolken und Winden, das waren seine Götter. Jene anderen, morgenländischen, hatten doch etwas mehr oder weniger Fremdartiges für ihn. (288)

As his land is being auctioned off at the end of the second part of the novel, the farmer stubbornly continues to plow his fields and to contemplate the reasons for his loss. He surmises that perhaps the reason lies in the conditions under which he took over the farm. Had Leberecht undertaken too much expansion without first looking after the development of the land he already possessed? Or perhaps the reasons could be found in earlier history, in the great war, presumably the Thirty Years' War, which had destroyed the farmland and made beggars out the German people. Or perhaps it was the treatment of the peasants before this war which had led to the Peasants' War in the sixteenth century. The deepest reason, however, lies for him much further back in history with the arrival of Roman law, which Polenz refers to as *der Romanismus*. The peasant had originally been a free man, bound only by the laws of the *Markgenossenschaft*. Whoever worked the land possessed it, and each new generation had to prove itself anew in order to keep the land. Under Roman law, however, a law which Polenz refers to as "ein fremder Geist von jenseits der Alpen" (245), one can own land without ever setting foot on it or working it. Ownership can be established by recording it in books, and land becomes a commodity which can be bought and sold. The fact that Leberecht

Büttner left no will leaves Traugott especially vulnerable under this alien, Roman law.

Besides Traugott there are four other siblings in the family. One of them, a younger brother Karl Leberecht, had left the farm as somewhat of a good-for-nothing, and all contact with him had been lost. Later he reappears as a married man and the owner of a grocery business in a midsized city in the province. One sister, now deceased, had married a foreigner named Kaschel, the owner of a pub in Halbenau. Another brother had emigrated to Austria and the second sister had married and moved away from Halbenau. Because each sibling had a claim to a share of the inheritance, the farmer was forced to buy the farm with mortgages to each of them. Under such conditions the farmer can only hope to retain his land if he retains the good will of his siblings. Polenz notes that the family has lost the public spirit which it still possessed in the farmer's youth: "Aber der alte hatte da mit einer Gesinnung gerechnet, die wohl in seiner Jugend noch die Familie beherrscht hatte: dem Gemeinsinn, der aber dem neuen Geschlecht abhanden gekommen war" (43).

The first crisis occurs early in the story when the farmer receives a letter from his brother Karl Leberecht, in which the brother demands full payment of the mortgage owed him by the beginning of July of that year. Traugott's brother-in-law Ernst Kaschel is willing to assume the mortgage, but at an interest rate of 6.5 percent, which the farmer finds to be exorbitant. When a few days later Kaschel offers the farmer the money at an interest rate of five percent under the condition that Kaschel's own mortgage also should receive five percent instead of the four percent already being paid, the farmer becomes angry and almost runs Kaschel down with his horse. At this point the farmer has his first meeting with the man who is to play a major role in bringing about his downfall, Samuel Harrassowitz. Depicted as a sly, conniving capitalist, Harrassowitz convinces Traugott to take out a loan from one of his business associates, Isidor Schönberger, who runs a "Kredit- und Vermittlungsbüro." With little hesitation Schönberger adds up the amounts owed to all of the siblings and agrees to loan the farmer the money he needs to pay off his brother, but with an interest rate of five percent. The farmer is at first very happy because of his seemingly good fortune in covering his debt, but the reader is left with a foreboding that this happiness will not last.

Although it is not made explicit until later in the narrative, the reader is immediately aware of the Jewish identity of this pair by their names and descriptions. Schönberger is described as "ein fetter Mann, kahlköpfig, mit dunklen, großen Augen, die ihm, aus tiefen Höhlen über die gebogene Nase hinwegspähend, etwas von einer großen Eule gaben" (47–48). The nose, the dark, deep-set eyes, and the fat body all fit the stereotypical looks given to the Jew, and the comparison with the owl is not only unflattering but also serves to lower him to the level of an animal. Harrassowitz's physical characteristics include his short, crooked legs, which are compared with the legs of a badger, his ugly mouth, which is not adequately covered by his red beard, his hands covered with red hair, and his obesity, as well as "die versteckte Lüsternheit seines Wesens" (85). In addition it is noted that his shirt collar is not very clean and that there are grease spots on his bright vest. It becomes clear to the reader long before it dawns on Traugott that in taking on this mortgage the farmer is in league with the devil. The materialistic graspings of the Jew were contrary to the allegedly inherent spiritual nature of the German peasant. In steering Traugott into this business deal that will ultimately bring about the loss of his farm and thus the loss of the farmer's union with nature and the cosmos, Harrassowitz and Schönberger play the role of the Tempter.

The farmer's relationship to the local nobility, the Salands, is also important. Soon after the farmer has taken out his loan from Harrassowitz he is visited by Hauptmann Schroff, who manages the Saland holdings in the absence of the family, now residing in Berlin. Schroff visits Büttner in order to buy a parcel of unused forest land which lies between two pieces of Count Saland's property. Such a sale would obviously benefit both parties in light of the farmer's financial situation, but here his stubbornness stands in the way. He has been having conflicts with the Salands because of wild animals coming from the woods and trampling his fields, but even the offer by Schroff to solve this conflict by building a fence to protect his fields is not enough for the farmer, who would rather cut off a finger than give up one field from his inherited property.

Schroff then suggests that a small parcel of useful land is better than a large one that one cannot fully use and warns him that he will face certain ruin if he does not agree to sell the land now. This, of course, causes the farmer to lose his patience completely, and he gives vent to his long-standing dispute with the Salands: "Auf uns Pauern hackt a alles ei, de Beamten wie der Edelmann. No solln mer och noch's latze Bissel hergahn do me hoan. Vun Haus und Hof mechten se uns rungertreiba, alles mechten se schlucken, bis mer gar an Bettelstabe sein" (65).

After Schroff's depiction of how he himself has lost his own land, his warning against letting one's debts pile too high and a final piece of advice that the farmer should sell the forest in order to pay a portion of his huge debt, the farmer calms down and explains that in his present situation his creditor would never allow the property to be divided. Thinking that the mortgage only involves the family members, Schroff still encourages him to go through with the deal. But at the mention of Schönberger as the holder of the mortgage, Schroff exclaims: "Mann! Wie kommen Sie zu so einem" (68). It is clear that Schroff does not like or trust Schönberger, but he still holds out hope that he can deal with the farmer's brother-in-law Kaschel, who holds the main mortgage.

When Schroff returns later after having been unable to make a deal with Kaschel, he has only one solution to the farmer's problem: the farmer should sell everything to the Salands and then lease his farmhouse and fields for life from them. The farmer reacts angrily to this suggestion, stating that he would rather die in the manure pile than give up his farm: "Sahn se den Misthaufen durte? Lieber durt druffe verrecken, aber's Gutt gah ich nich har!" (71).

It soon becomes clear why Kaschel is unwilling to deal with Schroff. He and Harrassowitz are allied in their dealings with the farmers in the area. When Harrassowitz informs him about the loan made to Büttner and asks whether he is prepared to help his brother-in-law in his difficulties, Kaschel gives him a look which serves as reassurance that Harrassowitz can depend on Kaschel not to interfere. After all, there would now seem to exist for Kaschel the possibility of eventually getting his money and at the same time having the opportunity to watch his brother-in-law lose everything.

In Polenz's description of Kaschel, the reader gains further insight into the differences between this foreigner who has married his way into the farmer's family and the healthy peasant stock which otherwise makes up the family, differences which connect him to the likes of Harrassowitz and Schönberger. He is described as a small man with a reddish, shining, thin face. From his moist rolling eyes one can see his love of alcoholic drinks, and with his bald, pointed head, his receding chin, and what is left of his jutting teeth in his beardless mouth, he resembles nothing so much as a rat.[4]

After talking with Kaschel, Harrassowitz proceeds to the Büttner farm, where the farmer has just received a registered letter in which Kaschel is calling in his mortgage, a sum of seventeen hundred marks. Once again Harrassowitz offers a loan to cover the critical debts, and he suggests that they can discuss the mortgage later. With his wife's encouragement, the farmer accepts four hundred marks as a loan to be paid back after the harvest in October and hesitantly puts his signature on the loan document.

The proceeds for the harvest are barely enough to provide subsistence for the farmer's family, let alone pay off his loan. When the farmer goes to Harrassowitz to ask for an extension, he is only able to speak with an unfriendly young man named Edmund Schmeiß, who does the dirty work for both Rosenberger and Harrassowitz, as well as for other businesses. After first refusing to extend the loan, Schmeiß visits the farm where, after ignoring the farmer's continued pleas, he takes all the cash the farmer has on hand, extends the rest of the loan for three months at an exorbitant interest rate of ten percent, and then further increases the farmer's indebtedness by selling him some artificial fertilizer which the farmer does not want, but which he feels compelled to accept in light of the present circumstances.

The summer passes, and with some unfortunate weather, difficulties with community officials, and a lot of hard work to bring in the various harvests, the farmer is increasingly plagued by feelings of guilt and uneasiness. In the household there is also little harmony. The deal that the farmer has made with Harrassowitz is more and more clearly identified as a pact with the devil: "Es war, als ob der Teufel den alten Mann geblendet hätte. Die Bäuerin hatte nicht so ganz unrecht mit ihrer Klage, daß der Bauer behext worden sein müsse" (113).

Whereas the central character in Book One is Traugott Büttner, whose personal quirks make him especially vulnerable to the machinations of Jews and outsiders, Books Two and Three focus on the farmer's second son, Gustav. Gustav is introduced when on leave from the military and learning to face responsibilities to his family and to the girlfriend he has left behind, Pauline Kaschner. After seeing the world and knowing many women, he does not at first want to return to his drab peasant roots, and indeed he does not have much of a future in Halbenau anyway, since his older brother Karl is in line to inherit the Büttner farm. In the course of his visit, however, he comes to the decision to give up his military career and to return to the family farm, where he not only is reunited with Pauline and his infant son, but also assumes the responsibility of organizing the harvest and attempting to deal with his father's overwhelming financial difficulties.

With Gustav's return the farmer's mood changes, for he sees in his second son the same qualities which his father Leberecht had possessed. Gustav immediately pays a visit to his Uncle Ernst to attempt to get an extension on the loan payment, but the long-standing hatred which has existed on both sides breaks out into the open and all possibility of dealing with Kaschel is lost. Gustav sees the light, namely that Kaschel and Harrassowitz are working together, and informs his uncle that he will never set foot in his place again: "Nu weeß ich's aber wie's steht. Ihr steckt mit dem Harrassowitz unter einer Decke. Na Ihr seid eene schöne Sorte Verwandte. Ich komme über Eure Schwelle nicht mehr, davon seid'r sicher. Pfui, Luder über solches Pack!" (155–156).

Gustav then pays a visit to Karl Leberecht in the city. He hopes to reawaken in this biological uncle the family loyalty which Karl Leberecht seemingly has given up. Gustav has reason to be pessimistic in light of this uncle's recent calling in of his own mortgage, and this pessimism proves to be well-founded. Karl Leberecht bows to the wishes of his wife, who does not want to have anything to do with her husband's country relatives and he refuses to help his brother. He justifies this refusal by arguing that he cannot take so much money out of his business to invest in a lost cause: "Wir können es nicht verantworten, so viel Geld aus dem Geschäft zu ziehen und in einer verlorenen Sache anzulegen" (165).

At this point Gustav comes to the conclusion that his father's farm cannot be saved and starts to concentrate on taking care of his own family. As preparations are being made for his wedding, he begins to search for work to support Pauline and his son. He hears that the Salands are looking for a coachman, and although this information proves to be false, he has a chance to speak with Hauptmann Schroff and thus to discuss his father's problems.

At first Hauptmann Schroff sees no hope of gaining help from Count Saland for the farmer because the farmer's land is not worth the debts owed on it. But when Gustav mentions a rumor he has heard about Harrassowitz's intentions to erect a brick factory on the Büttner land, the Hauptmann's interest is suddenly aroused because such a factory would compete with a brick factory which the Count has recently had built on his own land. He reacts violently to this news and then lets out his venom against the scoundrel Harrassowitz, who smells everything out, underbids everything, destroys prices, drives away customers, and spoils the whole population. He laments how industrialization will spread and eventually destroy agriculture and take away the Count's land. Schroff then reveals his own sentiments concerning Harrassowitz by asking Gustav whether his old father is really going to lose his land to a Jew: "Soll denn nun wirklich Ihr alter Vater vom Gute runter und der Jude rein?" (171). With this, the Hauptmann promises to write to the Count in Berlin and to recommend that he come to the aid of the farmer. Gustav's hopes are rekindled, though he sees that the real intentions of the Count are self-interest and have nothing to do with a desire to help his father.

Gustav's uncle Ernst Kaschel reveals to Harrassowitz that the Count is interested in paying his mortgage and helping the farmer get back onto his feet. Harrassowitz cannot allow such a thing to happen because that would spoil all of his plans. Harrassowitz thus dispatches Edmund Schmeiß, who visits the Count at his Berlin residence.

It is important to make some closer observations on the emerging relationship of the nobility to the neighboring farmers. Count Saland could be looked at as a representative of the new nobility. As the city has drawn many former farmers into its grasp, it has also found attraction for the nobility. Count Saland is a *Rittmeister* in the military and lives in Berlin, leaving the management of his estate in the hands of Hauptmann Schroff. He only spends a few weeks in the summer and fall on his estate. He understands little about agriculture and thus leaves all the responsibilities to his employees. The only thing important to him is the money the estate brings in.

Harrassowitz, who does not think much of the nobles, also understands that he himself would not be the right man for the job of dealing with Count Saland. He does not admit to himself directly that nobles do not like Jews, but one might assume that this is the reason he chooses Schmeiß for the job rather than pursuing the matter himself. And Edmund Schmeiß lives up to Harrassowitz's expectations. He convinces the Count that Büttner is a poor farmer and a drinker, whose sons are still worse and whose daughter has borne a child out of wedlock. In addition he informs the Count that the farmer is up to his ears in debt. Schmeiß adds that the farmer's own brother-in-law has sued him. He makes it clear that the Count will have to spend much more than a few thousand marks in order to save Büttner. With this argument the Count is convinced, sealing Traugott's fate.

But at the same time the fate of the nobility is also sealed. Unknowingly, the Count has also been duped by the capitalists. When he is finally able to buy his forest from Harrassowitz after the auctioning off of the farmer's land, he must pay a much higher price for it. In addition the brick factory and the other industrial developments which will surely follow will help to bring about the eventual ruin of the Count's own livelihood. The implication is that things would have been much different if the Count, acting as representative of the new and citified gentry, had not lost contact with the affairs of his own estate and with his own rural heritage and tradition.

At this point there enters a new agent of the modern industrialized society, the *Aufseheragent* Zittwitz, who is recruiting migrant workers to work in the sugar beet districts in the West. These farms are run according to the American model, which according to his assessment is also the model for the German farms of the future: "Diese Art des Arbeitskontraktes und der Arbeiteranwerbung überhaupt, das ist die moderne Wirtschaftsweise. So wird's in Amerika gemacht, auf den Plantagen und Farmen. Und in Zukunft wird's bei uns überall so werden. Das ist die moderne rationelle Wirtschaftsweise" (216).

Zittwitz is a fast-talking salesman. He ultimately talks Gustav into leaving his family farm to take charge of one crew from Halbenau, with the promise of a bonus at the end of the summer if his crew does its work well. Gustav's big shock comes a little later when the agent reveals to him the nature of modern business practices based on money, in short, the capitalist way of conducting business: "Heutzutage ist alles Geldgeschäft. Pro Kopf des Arbeiters–ob Mädel oder Kerl ist eins–bekomme ich von Ihnen fünf Mark. Das ist die Taxe" (224). Though Gustav feels he has been tricked into this agreement, he nonetheless follows through with it, for to break a contract could have serious consequences, and unlike his new capitalist business associates he remains a man of his word. Book Two concludes with Gustav's wedding, immediately after which he sets forth on this new adventure with Pauline and his son at his side.

Book Three begins with the adventures of these "*Sachsengänger*" upon their arrival in western Saxony. The first thing noted by the migrant workers is the changed landscape. Every available piece of land is being used for agriculture. At the same time there are no wild trees, no bushes, no weeds, no rocks, and no forest areas. There are only endless rows of sugar beets.

Moreover, industrialization has revolutionized agriculture. Instead of hand labor there are now threshing machines and drilling machines. The cattle are fed with cut-up beets, and instead of dairy cattle, beef cattle are kept, though only transported in for fattening and then mainly for the manure. The villages are more like towns with barren, whitewashed houses with tile roofs strung together in long rows. There are no *Fachwerk* houses, no wooden galleries, no straw roofs. Also there are no manure piles, no pigeon coops, no grass, and no duck ponds. The people own no cows, no chickens, and no pigs. The people, however, do not seem poor and wear city-dweller clothing. The migrant workers are also quite astonished by the fact that the children are not barefoot!

The few farmers, or rather now, landowners, live like nobles in large fancy houses and send their children to schools in the city. They are formal with each other, using the "Sie" instead of the less formal "du," and none of them sits at the same table with the workers. There are no mountains, few trees, and small unimpressive church towers. The only things which really catch one's eye are the smokestacks from a sugar factory, a brickwork, and a distillery. The farm consists of many new one-storied buildings with shiny whitewashed walls and bright red tile roofs among green beet fields which extend over to the buildings. The various parts of the large farm are connected by a railroad, which also connects all the beet farms with the sugar factory, a corporation belonging to the landowners.

The living and working conditions on the large farm are anything but pleasant. The workers are lodged in one-story barracks with one large room for the men and one for the women. The overseer's apartment is between the two large rooms. The work is hard, and the hours are long. Gustav has many responsibilities, supervising all the workers and resolving the problems that arise from time to time, while Pauline is in charge of preparing the meals for Gustav's crew. Naturally, the private life of the newlyweds suffers under the pressure. Gustav leaves early in the morning, often does not come to lunch, and upon returning late in the evening goes directly to bed. The only food supplied by the farm is potatoes, and the workers are responsible for providing the rest. A sort of company store run by a watchman in the front plant offers only poor quality wares at high prices.

In order to prevent the workers from becoming heavily indebted to this company store, Gustav's friend Häschke, an old army buddy who appeared shortly before Gustav's deal with Zittwitz and who has chosen to accompany his friend to western Saxony, comes to the rescue by taking some time off from work in the fields to scout around the area for better quality and better prices. Häschke, who is a sort of socialist revolutionary, is quick to criticize the existing social order, and helps in the course of the summer to educate Gustav about the existing conditions and to introduce him to socialist ideas.

The theme of mistrust of foreigners reappears when a Polish worker named Rogalla, the only foreigner in the group, sneaks away after the first few weeks, taking with him clothing and food stolen from his fellow workers. It is rumored that he has gone to join some fellow Poles on another beet farm, but Gustav chooses not to try to find him and bring him back. He was a problematic and lazy worker whose presence contributed little to the efforts of the group: "Möchte er bei seinesgleichen bleiben!" (255). This unreliable foreigner provides a clear contrast to the dependable and hardworking Germans accompanying Gustav to Saxony.

The owner of the farm is a Herr Hallstädt, who reputedly has made millions from beet farming and sugar manufacturing. He is said to be miserly, but his sons, who are reserve officers, make sure that their father's money is distributed to the people working for him. All communication with the owner is carried on through an inspector, who himself only communicates with the workers through his overseer. The work is done as piecework to encourage the workers to accomplish as much as possible. Gustav only sees Herr Hallstädt from a distance. This remote relationship between the employer and the employees is pointed out by Zittwitz: "Der eine gibt die Goldstücke, der andere seine Kräfte. Das ist ein Geschäft, klar und einfach. Alles wird auf Geld zurückgeführt. Das nennt man das moderne Wirtschaftssystem" (253).

As the beet harvest approaches, the workers are shocked by the news that they will now be paid by the day instead of by their production. They are also to work from sunrise to sunset. This arouses the workers, who under the leadership of Häschke refuse to work overtime without pay. Gustav must speak with the inspector, who in turn threatens to dock the pay of all who do not appear for work at four in the morning. The workers react by going on strike.

When Gustav is called in by the inspector to discuss the strike, he is received in a much more friendly manner than before. The inspector, however, reveals to him his own relationship with the farm owner: "Herr Hallstädt sei völlig unzugänglich und habe ein für allemal verboten, daß die Arbeiter direkt mit ihm verhandelten" (269). At this point, Gustav still carries the conservative views characteristic of his family background and is left cold by Häschke's political principles. He is skeptical of Häschke's conviction that it is time to show society that the worker at the end of the nineteenth century is no longer a serf and time for the little man to get some of the fat that has been skimmed off until now by the privileged. Interested only in getting that to which his workers are entitled, Gustav does not yet realize the extent to which his intentions approach the revolutionary ideas of his friend.

When at the end of the harvest Gustav is offered a position with Hallstädt for the following summer, he decides against accepting it. As a result, he does not receive the bonus that was promised to him if his workers performed well, in spite of the fact that it is a part of his contract. Because Gustav does not wish to return the next year, the farm owner finds no reason to honor that part of the contract, and Gustav cannot complain to the owner because Hallstädt has gone south. This shabby treatment by his employer has seemingly a strong effect on Gustav, and he no longer protests Häschke's complaints about the rich and their treatment of the workers. This experience leaves Gustav open for what follows, as he accompanies Häschke on a long, fourteen-day trip home. During this trip Gustav comes to know and understand the plight of the many people who have been displaced by modern, capitalist industrial society. They set out on foot, sleeping outdoors with other "Wanderburschen." Following a ride in the fourth-class section in the train with Poles, Russians, and others from the lower classes, they visit a large industrial city where Häschke has friends.

Up to this point, Gustav had refused to hear about Häschke's *Rote,* let alone to read Häschke's catechism, the words of Karl Marx. Gustav was raised with a profound dislike of politics. In fact, his father never got a newspaper and never voted. As a farmer, Traugott also despised all party activity. But after his experiences in the West, Gustav becomes acquainted with a completely new economic reality involving different working conditions, a much looser relationship between workers and employers with money as the only thing binding them, the substitution of machines for human hands, and ultimately a lack of any significant contact between landowner and his land.

On his trip with Häschke, Gustav is shocked to learn that most of the underclass, the homeless, those tossed away by society, are descendants of farmers. Who would have thought that the freeing of the farmers at the start of the nineteenth century would lead to this? He adds a comment about the tragic loss of the connection of these people to the land: "Allen war das eine gemeinsam: die Heimatlosigkeit. Von der Scholle waren sie getrennt, deren mütterliche nährende Kraft nichts ersetzen kann. Das waren die wirklich Enterbten, denn sie hatten nicht, worauf jeder von Geburts wegen Anspruch hat, ein Stück Erde, darauf er seine Füße ausruhen, auf der er leben und sterben darf " (315).

After finding lodging in the city in an attic room of a factory worker's apartment, the two friends go to a pub in the workers' district. Häschke learns that the employment situation is bad. Employers are taking advantage of the situation to lay off workers and lower wages. Unemployment is very high, and there have been many demonstrations and rallies.

At one of these rallies on the same evening they hear speeches describing the misery and the hopelessness of the workers' situation, and Gustav starts to understand these people and their misery. They simply want what he wants, a betterment of their situation. By the time he runs out of money and must go home, he knows he now has something to live for. Only in the big city is life worth living, where every moment brings new experiences: "Jetzt erst, schien es ihm, wisse er, wozu er überhaupt lebe. Bis dahin hatte er hingedämmert ohne Sinn und Verstand. Er sah auf einmal die Welt mit ganz anderen Augen an. Hier allein in der großen Stadt war das Leben des Lebens wert, wo jeder Augenblick neue Erlebnisse, neue Erfahrungen, brachte" (323).

Meanwhile Traugott's land has been auctioned off. Harrassowitz has allowed the farmer to stay on his farm, demanding no rent but insisting that the old man work the land in order to pay off some of the debt still owed him. But he makes many changes, taking away the oxen, leaving the farmer only the cows with which to pull his plow. He also removes the old apple trees which the farmer's grandfather had planted and which had provided apples for generations.

Two of the farmer's four children have not fared much better. Gustav's sister Toni has been forced to leave the farm and take a position as a nanny with Harrassowitz's daughter in Berlin. Her own child is given to Therese, the wife of Gustav's older brother Karl, who was to inherit the family farm. Therese begins to make life even harder for Karl with her continual haranguing. In his frustration Karl begins to drink heavily. Harrassowitz gives him a position in Wörmsbach on a run-down piece of land with a house on the verge of collapse and fields that have not been cultivated in many years. In order to enable Karl to acquire cattle, seed, and supplies, Harrassovitz is of course willing to lend him money, thus bringing Karl, too, into this new form of servitude.

Soon thereafter Harrassowitz takes another step by dividing the old farm and auctioning off the various portions to the Halbenau villagers. Kaschel reveals that he has bought this part of the farm from Harrassowitz and offers the old farmer a job harvesting the corn which now belongs to him. The farmer is shocked and beside himself with anger. This is an indication of what is to become of all the farms in Halbenau. Because there would be too much work for the former owner of the Büttner farm to do by himself on the parts of the farm now owned by others, Harrassowitz sends in people from the village as helpers. Then he sends wagons to haul the sheaves to Wörmsbach where he owns still more land and also a threshing machine. The threshed grain is then transported to his own granaries. Rather than being troubled with the beets, potatoes, and cabbage, he sells individual rows to the villagers, only keeping what is necessary to feed the cattle for the winter.

Through business dealings Harrassowitz is able to keep the farmers of the area constantly in his debt. He accepts payment of all kinds, from natural produce to labor and sometimes cattle, which he can sell to another of his associates. He treats the farmer now as one of his laborers, praising or scolding him according to his mood, and the farmer is by now so downtrodden that he does not resist. Traugott is held in Harrassowitz's power by the fear of being physically thrown off what had been his farm, for Harrassowitz knows that the farmer would rather have his heart torn out than be separated from the soil (292). This new type of serfdom is much worse than the serfdom under which the farmer's ancestors had to live. What is lacking in this new serfdom, he notes, is "der ausgleichende und versöhnende Kitt der Tradition" (293). Polenz calls this new serfdom "die herzlose Unterjochung unter die kalte Hand des Kapitals" (293).

Polenz consistently links this catastrophic deterioration in the circumstances of the German agrarian class to the rise of the Jews, whose parasitic qualities are exemplified in Sam Harrassowitz:

> Sam besaß das Talent seiner Rasse in hohem Maße, anderer Arbeit zu verwerten, sich in Nestern, welche fleißige Vögel mit emsiger Sorgfalt zusammengetragen, wohnlich einzurichten. Und die Natur hatte ihm eine Gemütsverfassung verliehen, die es ihm leicht machte, sich um das Geschick der fremden Eier nicht sonderlich zu grämen. (293)

The final blow comes for Traugott when Harrassowitz decides to sell off the last part of the farm and the farmhouse to the director of a brick factory. The farmer is moved to one small room in the attic of his old farmhouse and is thus forced to witness in his humiliation the final destruction of his life's work. Shortly before Gustav's return, his mother dies and the father retreats into utter isolation. Gustav's sister Ernestine announces her plans to marry Häschke and accompany him to the city. Karl has fallen victim to alcohol and becomes an invalid. Toni returns to her life as a prostitute. Thus the farmer, who is now alone and without hope, finds but one possibility left to him: he decides to commit suicide.

The suicide of the farmer at the end of the novel is perhaps the most moving scene in the book. After attending a church service for the first time since the loss of his wife and taking communion, Traugott goes to the one small room left to him in what was his home, changes into his work clothes, feeds the cattle and the pigs, and then goes into the fields. He stops and looks around one last time at his house and barn and then continues into the woods. He expresses no great bitterness against those who have driven him into this situation. He only briefly thinks about what they will say and wonders whether he will have a Christian burial, for, after all, he did attend church. He thinks of his dead wife and how much better off the dead are than the living. Finally he thinks about what is probably the main reason he must take this step: "Den Boden hatten sie ihm unter den Füßen weggerissen" (365). He does not want to be brought to the poor house. Momentarily anger flares over the destruction of his life's work, and bitterness rises against all those who did not lift a finger to help him, but he quickly overcomes these passions in the realization that the things of the world do not concern him anymore. As he swings in his dying moments at the end of the rope that he has draped over a blossoming cherry tree, he sees a vision of his father and his grandfather, and in death his eyes stare at the soil to which he has dedicated his life and soul.

Because there is no future for him in the farming region of his youth, Gustav is forced in the end to abandon his rural heritage and seek his future in the city. Although he is fortunate enough to find a position as assistant landlord in a large house in the inner city, this position is ironically symbolic of everything that he has fought against. Behind the house is a cardboard box factory, and there is also a bank and an insurance firm in the building. Although the position allows him to spend time with his family, it is noted that in this position one cannot produce anything permanent as one could do on the farm, and there is no chance for advancement. But the worst thing for him will be his separation from the life to which he had been reared, namely life on the farm. In an urban environment into which the sun does not even shine, he must separate himself completely from his past and the centuries-old tradition of his family.

Interpretations of Polenz's *Der Büttnerbauer* vary widely.[5] The most common approach is to regard it as a typical *Bauernroman* of its time and to interpret it in the context of the *Heimatkunst* movement. Among these interpreters are Tolstoy, Heuberger, Zimmermann, and Rossbacher. In this interpretation the old farmer fails not because of his own stupidity but because of the machinations of capitalism.

In contradistinction to this conservative approach, Lenin embraced the work and even spoke of a specific Prussian way in the development of capitalism in agriculture.[6] He stresses the conversion of Ernestine and Gustav into revolutionaries with the help of the proletarian Häschke. Kaszynski points out that this viewpoint is the one preserved in the German Democratic Republic (76).

But both the conservative Tolstoy and the progressive Lenin cover only certain aspects of the work and ignore the *völkisch* elements celebrated by Bartels and also by H. Krause in his 1937 dissertation and consequently embraced by the Nazis. Kascynski points out that the depiction of the destruction of an old, healthy peasant family through conditions brought from foreign origins provided splendid raw material for *völkisch* exploitation, only enhanced by the fact that the farm is butchered by a Jewish businessman from the city (53).

After 1945 there appeared the critical approach best represented by Georg Mosse and Gerhard Schweizer. In their treatments the very arguments used by Bartels and others in defense of the novel are turned against it. As we have seen, it is also at this time that Polenz and his novels disappear from most literary histories.

Kasczynski ultimately asks the reasonable question of whether the work is an abortive concoction of myth and prejudice or a realistic novel of some power whose contribution to an understanding of the times has been misunderstood. He concludes that it is in part both of these. He sees the anti-Semitism expressed in the work as a product of Polenz's own awareness of a class that saw itself in trouble because of the development of capitalism. He points out that it is no coincidence that the person who speaks out against the Jews in the book is none other than the bankrupt, but basically decent Hauptmann Schroff. But Kasczynski does not try to discount the attribution by Polenz of Harrassowitz's many negative characteristics to his race, nor the demonization of the Jew as a satanic manipulator, nor the xenophobic treatments of foreigners and outsiders. This ambivalence may ultimately be more satisfactory than the kind of naive social psychological defense represented by Günter Hartung's GDR study from 1983, according to which Polenz was not free of anti-Semitism but did not intend to give the Jews the blame for the downfall of the farmer.

The variety of responses to *Der Büttnerbauer* over the past century invites speculation as to the novel's reception in a Germany once again undergoing great changes, especially in light of the recent reissue of the work. Will the work once again be embraced in a resurgence of *völkisch* thinking, or will it speak in other ways to those who are displaced and struggling to cope with a changing German society that they may not completely comprehend? One can hope that it will be read by those who can appreciate its insights into the historical developments of the last two centuries and who can be carried away by the tragic plight of the farmer, his struggle for existence, and his ultimate downfall without at the same time embracing the negative characterizations of Jews, capitalists, and foreigners as a kind of formulaic code for the avoidance of personal responsibility, then or now.

Notes

[1] For example, in the second edition of *Deutsche Literaturgeschichte von den Anfängen bis zur Gegenwart* (Stuttgart: Metzler, 1984) he is not mentioned at all, with

only brief mention in the *Oxford Companion to German Literature* (Oxford, New York: Oxford UP, 1986), the *Annalen der deutschen Literatur* (Stuttgart: Metzler, 1971), in E.L. Stahl and W.E. Yuill's *German Literature of the 18th and 19th Centuries* (New York: Barnes and Noble, 1970), and in the twelfth edition of Fritz Martini's venerable *Deutsche Literaturgeschichte von den Anfängen bis zur Gegenwart* (Stuttgart: Kröner, 1963).

[2] The editions known to this author are noted below. Of the editions listed at least three appeared during the Nazi period. A more thorough search would presumably bring forth other editions:

> Polenz, Wilhelm von. *Der Büttnerbauer*, 11th ed. (1893; Berlin: F. Fontane, 1909).
> _____. (Leipzig: Hesse und Becker, 1900).
> _____. (Hamburg: Deutsche Hausbücherei, 1935).
> _____. (Leipzig: Buch und Volk, 1942).
> _____. (Berlin: T. Knaur Nachfolge, 1944).
> _____. (Berlin: A. Weichert, n.d.).
> _____. (English edition) *German Classics of the Nineteenth and Twentieth Centuries*, vol. 17 (1914; New York: AMS, 1969), 334–422.
> _____. (Berlin: Jugend und Volk, 1982).
> _____. (Bautzen: Lusatia, 1994). The quotations referred to in the text are from this edition.

[3] Recently two editions of his novellas have been published, *Sachsengänger* and *Luginsland*. A few articles in scholarly journals, mainly in eastern European countries, have also appeared, as well as a book by Miklós Salyámosy. As noted above, a new edition of *Der Büttnerbauer* appeared in 1994.

[4] Gerhard Schweizer notes that the comparison of Kaschel with rats is an even stronger defamation of character than the comparison of Schönberger with an owl. He connects this with Kaschel's joy in bringing harm to other people (45).

[5] Kaszynski points out five interpretative approaches (74f).

[6] Kaszynski 75. See also Lenin, *Der Kapitalismus in der Landwirtschaft* (1899) and *Die Agrarfrage und die Marxkritiker* (1901).

Works Cited

Bartels, Adolf. *Geschichte der deutschen Literatur.* 17th ed. Braunschweig: G. Westermann, 1941.

_____. *Wilhelm von Polenz.* Dresden, Leipzig: C.A. Kochs Verlagsbuchhandlung, 1909.

Garland, Henry, and Mary Garland. *The Oxford Companion to German Literature.* 2nd ed. Oxford and New York: Oxford UP, 1986.

Hartung, Günter. *Literatur und Ästhetik des deutschen Faschismus: Drei Studien*. Berlin: Akademie, 1983.

Heuberger, H. "Die Agrarfrage bei Roseggers *Jakob der letzte* und *Erdsegen*, Frenssens *Jörn Uhl* und Polenz' *Büttnerbauer*." Diss. University of Vienna, 1949.

Ilgenstein, Heinrich. *Wilhelm von Polenz: Ein Beitrag zur Literaturgeschichte der Gegenwart*. Berlin: F. Fontane, 1904.

Kindlers Literatur Lexikon, Vol. 5. Munich: Deutscher Taschenbuch Verlag, 1985.

Kaszynski, Stefan H. "Wilhelm von Polenz' *Der Büttnerbauer* Lesearten." In *Traditionen und Traditionssuche des deutschen Faschismus*, edited by H. Orlowski and G. Hartung. Vol. 3. Halle/Saale: Wissenschaftspublizistik der Martin-Luther-Universität, 1987.

Krause, H. "Wilhelm von Polenz als Erzähler." Diss. University of Munich, 1937.

Kummer, Friedrich. *Deutsche Literaturgeschichte des 19. und 20. Jahrhunderts, nach Generationen dargestellt*. 13th–16th ed. Vol. 2. Dresden: Carl Reißner, 1922.

Langenbucher, Helmuth. *Volkhafte Dichtung der Zeit*. Berlin: Junker und Dunnhaupt, 1940.

Lenin, W. I. *Der Kapitalismus in der Landwirtschaft* (1899). Vol. 4 of *Lenins Werke*. Berlin: Institut für Gesellschaftswissenschaften beim Zentralkomitee der SED, 1955.

———. *Die Agrarfrage und die Marxkritiker* (1901). Vol. 5. of *Lenins Werke*. Berlin: Institut für Gesellschaftswissenschaften beim Zentralkomitee der SED, 1955.

Linden, Walter. *Geschichte der deutschen Literatur von den Anfängen bis zur Gegenwart*. 4th ed. Leipzig: Reclam, 1942.

Mach, Edmund. "Wilhelm von Polenz." In *The German Classics: Masterpieces of German Literature Translated into English in Twenty Volumes*. Vol. 17. New York: AMS Press, 1969.

Mosse, George L. *The Crisis of German Ideology*. New York: Grosset and Dunlap, 1964.

Nadler, Josef. *Literaturgeschichte des deutschen Volkes: Dichtung und Schrifttum der deutschen Stämme und Landschaften*. Vol. 4. Berlin: Propylaen, 1938.

Polenz, Wilhelm von. *Der Büttnerbauer*. Bautzen: Lusatia, 1994.

———. *Luginsland: Dorfgeschichten*. Bautzen: Lusatia, 1993.

Riehl, Wilhelm Heinrich. *Die bürgerliche Gesellschaft.* Vol. 2 of *Naturgeschichte des deutschen Volkes als Grundlage einer deutschen Sozialpolitik.* 4 vols. 1851–1869. 9th ed. Stuttgart: Cotta, 1897.

Rossbacher, Karlheinz. *Heimatkunstbewegung und Heimatroman: Zu einer Literatursoziologie der Jahrhundertwende.* Stuttgart: Klett, 1975.

Scherer, Wilhelm, and Oskar Walzel. *Geschichte der deutschen Literatur.* 4th ed. Berlin: Askanischer Verlag, 1928.

Schulz, Erich, and Hans Henning. *Die deutsche Literatur: Geschichte und Hauptwerke in den Grundzügen.* Wittenberg: A. Ziemsen, 1940.

Schweizer, Gerhard. *Bauernroman und Faschismus: Zur Ideologiekritik einer literarischen Gattung.* Tübingen: Tübinger Vereinigung für Volkskunde, 1976.

Zimmermann, Peter. *Der Bauernroman: Antifeudalismus-Konservatismus-Faschismus.* Stuttgart: Metzler, 1975.

The "Raw" and the "Cooked" *in* fin-de-siècle *Vienna*

Beth Bjorklund

> Das Leben ist stärker als das schönste Resumé.
> —Max Winter, *Im dunkelsten Wien*

Despite his forty-some volumes of poetry and prose, the proletarian author Alfons Petzold has been all but forgotten by literary historians. One work, however, his autobiography, has recently experienced a comeback, after being reissued in 1979. First published in 1920, it is entitled *Das rauhe Leben*. If that title can be translated "Raw Life," a comparison along the lines of Lévi-Strauss's concept of "the raw and the cooked" is not inappropriate. When we compare Petzold's autobiography with records of "elite" authors, such as Zweig, Schnitzler, Hofmannsthal, and Rilke, we find mutually exclusive accounts of life in Vienna around 1900, "raw" and "cooked," so to speak.

Stefan Zweig was born in 1881, just one year before Petzold, and Zweig's autobiographical account, *Die Welt von Gestern*, forms a primary object of comparison. Arthur Schnitzler was born in 1862, two decades before Petzold; Schnitzler's autobiography, *Jugend in Wien*, can nonetheless serve as a foil for viewing Petzold's work, particularly since both writers deal with their youth, the period of identity formation. Hugo von Hofmannsthal, born in 1874, never wrote an autobiography; but societal attitudes are conveyed in his poetry, dramas, and essays. Rainer Maria Rilke was born in 1875, and his poetry treats some of the same themes as Petzold's poetry, albeit from a very different standpoint. Despite the contemporaneity of these writers, my investigation confirms Gruber's conclusion that "there are few connections between the hermetically sealed world of bourgeois high culture and...a proletarian mass counterculture" (Gruber 12).

A caveat is necessary, for first-person narratives are notoriously unreliable. Petzold calls his autobiography a "novel," which makes room for the seamless narrative that life itself never is. Despite his alleged intent, "die Wahrheit so objektiv zu schreiben, wie es mir möglich ist" (Petzold 8), human memory is fallible and selective. Zweig addresses the problem in a foreword to his autobiography: "Ich betrachte unser Gedächtnis nicht als ein das *eine* bloß zufällig behaltendes und das *andere* zufällig verlierendes Element, sondern als eine wissend ordnende und weise ausschaltende Kraft" (Zweig 13). If Zweig's problematization of the issue stands in contrast to Petzold's seemingly naive intent, that is part of the problem to be investigated. It behooves one to subject all autobiography to constant critical examination and to compare it with other kinds of evidence.

Alfons Petzold was born in Vienna in 1882 of parents who had emigrated from Saxony. His father was a craftsman, but since he died when his son was a teenager, the family's economic status declined from the level of petit bourgeoisie to that of the proletariat. Alfons, a weak, sickly child, read avidly; but he was forced to leave school at fourteen, the earliest permissible age, to help support himself and his parents. Therewith, he writes, "war meine Kindheit zu Ende" (Petzold 96). Petzold subsequently went from one job to another until ending up in the hospital with tuberculosis at age twenty-six, which forms the conclusion of his autobiography.

Petzold's mother had initially sought an apprenticeship for her fourteen-year-old, but the boy was neither physically nor emotionally equipped to meet the demands of the workplace. His attempts to learn a trade, such as that of silversmith, shoemaker, mason, baker, or waiter, resulted in failure. The apprenticeships did not offer enough money to live on, and the apprentices were treated as errand boys without being taught the trade. After two years of earning nothing and learning nothing, he gave up trying to learn a marketable skill. Thus began the working life of an unskilled laborer.

During his twelve working years, from age fourteen to the onset of illness at twenty-six, Petzold held over twenty different jobs. Some of them were factory jobs, often in small factories and family-run businesses, as was common at the time. For example, a shoe polish factory with four employees required the boiling of a chemical mixture, which led to the accidental death of the owner. That episode, like many others, is narrated with grotesque humor, and thus the tragic events never allow for the rise of sentimentality or pathos—with one exception, yet to be discussed.

The jobs illustrate the nature of work in the preindustrial and early industrial era. For example, Petzold's job in a laundry, from 6 a.m. to 7 p.m., was solely to carry water from a pump in the courtyard to the five women doing the washing on the fourth floor. In another case, a box factory in a basement was infested by rats, which the owner stalked, shot, and stuffed. The taxidermic compulsion, as revealed upon his demise, stemmed from the fact that his child had died from being bitten by a rat. Humor and self-irony is revealed in the narration of delivering cardboard boxes by means of a cart pulled by a dog. The reader can imagine how that one ended! A totally anomalous and illegal occupation, when all else failed, was catching birds and selling them to a bird dealer.

The effects of the industrial revolution were also making themselves felt, and Petzold describes the work in a bronze factory with a punch and stamp machine, where the noise was too great to allow for communication. There is no condemnation of the machine age, such as is often present in bourgeois literature; a member of the proletariat had little reason to be nostalgic for the preindustrial era. But there is a very real awareness of the danger of machines, since thoughtlessness could result in the loss of a limb, or worse.

Petzold's first encounter with a large factory was a dye plant with five hundred employees, whereby his job was to shovel coal all day. The personal misery is relativized only by the recognition of its collective aspect. Loading sacks of chocolate products that weighed up to three hundred pounds was another exhausting and monotonous job. The anonymity and uniformity in a large factory, besides the conscious exploitation and ruthlessness on the part of management, seem to have made those jobs the worst in his career. He writes, "es ergriff mich eine bittere Trostlosigkeit" (Petzold 366). That paradoxically provided the backdrop for his development of political consciousness, as he began to understand "die moralische Zersetzungsarbeit des Kapitals" (Petzold 359).

Jobs, and the search for jobs, are the primary focus of the autobiography, just as it was the main content of his life. Without exception, the jobs offered only low pay for long hours of hard work. The workday ranged from ten to fourteen hours a day, six days a week, which obviously did not leave much free time. Money is the second most frequent topic, precisely because there was so little of it. Rent and food claimed nearly the entirety of his wages, with nothing to spend at will or save for an emergency. Even a low-paying job, however, was preferable to the alternative of joblessness and consequent homelessness. Before reaching that stage, let us view the living situation.

The family moved very often, on the average of three times a year, since living conditions were directly dependent on their financial situation. The young man and his mother lived together in one-room apartments, most often in the districts of Ottakring and Hernals. The living quarters were often dark, damp, and dirty; and we get vivid descriptions of the tenement houses and the back streets of Vienna. Much research has been done on the housing situation in Vienna, and the misery is a well-documented fact (John, Winter). Petzold's mother worked as washerwoman or cleaning lady in public restrooms. For extra income they took in subtenants, the so-called "Bettgeher," to sleep in their beds during the day. Since the bed-renters had no place to go but the tavern between work and bedtime, alcoholism was a common problem.

Personal possessions are not a topic in the autobiography, for the family had so few of them. Only once, when they won in the lottery, does Petzold talk about buying clothes, and even then in a second-hand store. Food, or the lack of it, is often a topic, and they ate horse meat and used coffee grounds six times over, when necessary. Illness was frequent, since the boy was sickly from birth, and his mother aged prematurely. The lack of adequate heating in winter exacerbated the problem, and disease was usually treated with home remedies. The relationship between mother and son is the one issue in the book where Petzold does not hesitate to express himself emotionally. Family ties were strong, and many studies show "a reverence for private family virtues over public...values" (Wegs 78).

The ignominious death of his mother when Petzold was twenty years old was devastating to him, both emotionally and physically. Unemployment was high at the time, and Petzold was out of work for months, with no reserves on which to fall back. Thus his life deteriorated markedly. When he could not find work, he pawned off what was left of the furniture; and when he could not pay the rent, he went to the public asylum for a night. The description of that experience is horrendous. It was a filthy bug-infested place with sick and hungry people of both sexes and all ages sleeping virtually in a heap with no sanitary facilities.

The only alternative was to go underground, very literally, and Petzold joined the people who descended at night into the tunnels under the city. They ate and slept on the concrete floor along the underground sewage canals, where it was dark and cold and too low to stand upright, not to mention the odor and filth. In early morning they ascended to street level to look for jobs, eat in a soup kitchen, and scavenge the garbage at public markets for food. "Der Mensch als Regenwurm," in the phrase of an investigative journalist (Winter 34), was thus less of a metaphor than a real state.

When job opportunities improved, Petzold left the underground and resumed his life as a laborer. One of his last jobs was in a terra cotta factory, sanding plaster statues. The constant heavy dust in the air hastened the onslaught of tuberculosis and his subsequent hospitalization. The description of life in the public hospital puts it only one step above that of the public sleeping quarters, and Petzold nearly died. The chapter that describes his work sanding statues is entitled, with ironic quotation marks, "Wiener Kunst"; and with that we turn briefly to Petzold's experience with art and literature, as well as his views on politics, religion, and sexuality.

Given these living and working conditions, it is amazing that literature could arise at all. Petzold's writing has none of the sophistication and finesse of canonical works, but it does reveal the strength of lived experience. Although he began writing poetry early on, all of his publications came after 1910, that is, after his recovery from tuberculosis. "Recovery" is itself a wonder, and the autobiography stops just short of a fairy-tale-like ending. Petzold's poetry was "discovered" by a wealthy patron through someone who had heard him read at a coffeehouse; and that patron financed his stay in a tuberculosis sanitarium. The unusualness of that type of ending merits comment later.

Going back to that youthful poetry, which had such unexpected consequences, we see the young boy as an autodidact, reading and writing whenever time and energy and money allowed. Since reading itself was the desideratum, there seems to be little concern or even awareness of the conventionality of the reading material. Although he had few friends and no outside encouragement, he occasionally met someone with similar interests in the workplace or at the library, and once they put on an amateur theater performance. Petzold even succeeded in selling a few of his "couplets," rhymed verse for musical accompaniment. One of his stage plays was also performed at a coffeehouse; but since he could not afford the cover charge, he watched it through the garden window.

Although a victim of the social politics of the time, Petzold was politically naive until he met a colleague at work who persuaded him to join the Social Democratic Youth organization. There he learned about managerial strategies for the avoidance of workers' strikes by the prevention of solidarity among employees:

> Der Arbeiter hat bis vor kurzem Hunger gelitten, vielleicht bittere Kälte erduldet oder war obdachlos gewesen und hatte Schulden zu bezahlen, die in dieser Zeit gemacht wurden. Jetzt auszutreten? Zu streiken? Und wieder zu hungern? Ja, mein Lieber, der Hunger hat schon viele schweigen gelehrt, auszuharren, wie schwer das Joch auch war, unter das sie sich zu beugen hatten. (Petzold 363-64)

When Petzold did became politically active in a pre-election campaign, he was arrested together with other "agitators," and he lost his job because of it.

Discouraged by politics, Petzold turned to religion, although not of any institutional variety. His parents were Protestants from Saxony; and although his father had been forced to convert to Catholicism to get a bed in the hospital, such conversion was unthinkable for the young Petzold, for his experiences with the Church had been bitter. We see the mature Petzold as a critical individual, constantly questioning the values he had internalized from society. His religion seems to have been modeled on his favorite authors, and it emerged as a Tolstoian humanism. His later poetry reveals a Schillerian idealism, although it is hard to know whether that is conviction or convention.

An acquaintance once commented that his poetry lacked "Liebe"; and the topic of sexuality is conspicuous by its absence in the autobiography. The probable reason is that sexuality was taboo as a topic in working-class circles, and Petzold's occasional references to the opposite sex are harmless. We cannot know what really went on; but it seems plausible that there was very little to be concealed. He writes in another context, "daß Liebe ein Luxus ist" (Petzold 334). With working twelve hours or more a day and no adequate housing, there was perhaps no time or energy or privacy for much of a sex life. That coincides with a historian's conclusion that, contrary to popular opinion, "the majority of working-class families led sexually abstemious lives" (Wegs 125).

If "love" is a "luxury," so also is "nature," as Petzold realized one day while sitting in a public park which was subsequently taken over by wealthy patrons: "Auch diese Landschaft gehörte dem Reichtum" (Petzold 474). "Identity" was also regarded as a commodity and thus a prerogative of the affluent. How did people survive under such conditions? Even when physical needs were met, there was still little opportunity for individual expression. Although largely unspoken, we see throughout the book Petzold's search for "respectability," or dignity in a nonsuperficial sense; for "respectability was a defense against anomie, dehumanization, and disintegration of personality" (Wegs 34). Sources of self-esteem—or lack thereof—is indeed an important question, and much research remains to be done.

Turning from the "raw" to the "cooked," it is useful to consider the categories. If Lévi-Strauss deploys the concepts to characterize the dichotomy between nature and culture, my adaptation of the terms is metaphorical to an even greater extent. Lévi-Strauss worked with the myths of "primitive" societies, and he found that myths are like fires, mediating the contact between the subject and the physical world. Without fire, meat decomposes; but with too much fire, it burns. Between those two extremes, society attempts to strike a balance; the "cooked meat" is more easily digestible than the "raw meat," but it also loses some of its "naturalness."

Roland Barthes has undertaken an analogous structural analysis of the myths of developed societies. The dominant culture in the Western world today—as it was a century ago—is bourgeois, or middle class: "All that is not bourgeois is obliged to *borrow* from the bourgeoisie. Bourgeois ideology can therefore spread over everything" (Barthes 139). The form in which this "anonymous ideology" or "public philosophy" represents itself is what Barthes calls "myth." One way that myths are transmitted is by language; and language is, at its core, a problem of representation. Barthes concludes, "the wise thing would of course be to define the writer's realism as an essentially ideological problem" (Barthes 137). With Barthes, one must seek to get behind the myths.

In contrast to the insecurity of Petzold's young life, Zweig views the period as "das goldene Zeitalter der Sicherheit" (Zweig 14). Schnitzler, commenting on the climate of his youth, notes that "der Snobismus, die Weltkrankheit unserer Epoche, ausnehmend günstige Entwicklungsbedingungen vorfinden mußte" (Schnitzler 18). Both Zweig and Schnitzler were born into wealthy, professional upper-middle-class families, and each discusses his youth in terms of privilege, role-models, and leisure. Education included not only high school and the university, but also access to the theater, time and money for books, and opportunities for social events, vacations, and travel.

Childhood for Zweig and Schnitzler lasted longer than it did for Petzold. As a historian writes about adolescents in working-class families: "They were, in effect, young adults with little opportunity to engage in an adolescent culture" (Wegs 104). Since young people in wealthy families did not have to work, they could take advantage of the many opportunities available and enjoy a carefree existence to a much older age. Even as a university student, at an age when Petzold had already contracted tuberculosis from overwork, Zweig could write, "der

Tag hatte vierundzwanzig Stunden, und alle gehörten mir" (Zweig 119). It is evident that a proletarian child had virtually nothing in common with a child from a middle-class family. Nonetheless, let us view a few specific points of comparison.

One of the few things that the boys—Petzold, Zweig, and Schnitzler—had in common is their dislike of school; and it is evident that the authoritarian structures permeated all levels of society. That coincides with other reports of school as "detention centers rather than learning centers" (Wegs 15). Yet there are class differences, at least in parental attitudes if not in the children's experiences. Both Zweig and Schnitzler completed their university degrees, whereas Petzold was pulled out of school as a young teenager. That fate was regarded by the bourgeois class as bad enough to be used as a threat to a misbehaving schoolboy:

> Noch als Gymnasiast wurde uns, wenn wir eine schlechte Note in irgendeinem nebensächlichern Gegenstand nach Hause brachten, gedroht, man werde uns aus der Schule nehmen und ein Handwerk lernen lassen—die schlimmste Drohung, die es in der bürgerlichen Welt gab: der Rückfall ins Proletariat. (Zweig 52)

Another common element, not surprising among budding authors, was a love of reading, and all three of the writers mention books that impressed them as youths. Because of the availability of time and money, Zweig and Schnitzler read more widely and more of the then-contemporary literature than Petzold. Zweig elaborates on his youthful enthusiasm for the recent publications of the day, such as those by Hofmannsthal, Rilke, George, Nietzsche, Hauptmann, Strindberg, also Rimbaud, Mallarmé, Verlaine, Valéry, and Zola. None of those writers is mentioned by Petzold, whose reading material consisted of the traditional classics. Given the lack of access to newly published books, it is small wonder that proletarian poetry does not display the innovations of the *avant-garde*.

All three boys loved the theater, which, with variations, was a primary form of entertainment for all social classes except the truly indigent. Zweig talks about the "'Theatromanie' der Wiener" (Zweig 33), and he regularly attended premier performances. Schnitzler, who went on to become a dramatist, was introduced to the theater practically at birth:

> Am stärksten wurde meine Neigung zur Theaterspielerei jeder Art, bewußter und unbewußter, durch ziemlich häufigen Theaterbesuch, und dieser wieder durch die vielfachen ärztlichen und freundschaftlichen Beziehungen meines Vaters zur Theaterwelt gefördert. (Schnitzler 27)

Exposure thus began much earlier and was, above all, much more frequent for Zweig and Schnitzler than for Petzold, who had to save carefully for an occasional standing-room ticket on Monday evening.

The coffeehouse was also common to the experience of all three young men, but there were large differences among the various establishments. Whereas Petzold recounts rough and vulgar scenes in coffeehouses that provided light entertainment for working-class patrons, for Zweig the coffeehouse was a place for reading foreign-language newspapers and holding intellectual discussions: "Unsere beste Bildungsstätte für alles Neue blieb das Kaffeehaus" (Zweig 56).

Friendship is certainly a common topic, important to young people. Whereas friendships for Zweig and Schnitzler provided opportunities for bonding with like-minded people who offered mutual support, friendships for Petzold were much more restricted. He writes: "Arbeiterfreundschaften sind oft so kurz wie die Liebe der Eintagsfliegen" (Petzold 422). The long hours of work left little free time, and the constant change of jobs and residence, plus lack of transportation, nipped most friendships in the bud. Adult friendships for Zweig and Schnitzler were with prominent people, which offered opportunities for publication and recognition, of which Petzold, of course, had none.

Sexuality, while physically the same, also had very different societal restrictions and interpretations in the various social classes. Zweig articulates an attitude that is implicit in Petzold's work:

> Dieses Erwachen der Pubertät scheint nun ein durchaus privates Problem, das jeder heranwachsende Mensch auf seine eigene Weise mit sich auszukämpfen hat, und für den ersten Blick keineswegs zu öffentlicher Erörterung geeignet. (Zweig 86)

Zweig nonetheless goes on to write thirty pages on the changes in sexual mores of his time, from the Victorian morality of the nineteenth century to the greater freedom in the early twentieth. Whatever Zweig and Petzold leave out in regard to sexuality, Schnitzler seems to make up for, and he narrates his exploits with confidence and even bravado, from his first encounter with a "süßes Mädel" to "was man mit einem allzu heroischen Wort Eroberungen zu nennen pflegt" (Schnitzler 113, 143).

Zweig and Schnitzler certainly offer a broader perspective than does Petzold; but that broad view was accessible only to a very small class of people at the top of the socioeconomic spectrum. From a later perspective, Zweig comments self-critically on his sociopolitical stance around the turn of the century:

> In Wirklichkeit hatte in jenem letzten Jahrzehnt vor dem neuen Jahrhundert der Krieg aller gegen alle in Österreich schon begonnen. Wir jungen Menschen aber, völlig eingesponnen in unsere literarischen Ambitionen, merkten wenig von diesen gefährlichen Veränderungen in unserer Heimat: wir blickten nur auf Bücher und Bilder....Wir sahen nicht die feurigen Zeichen an der Wand, wir tafelten wie weiland König Belsazar unbesorgt von all den kostbaren Gerichten der Kunst. (Zweig 84)

Hofmannsthal, too, was aware of the narrow class of people of and for whom he wrote, and poems such as "Manche freilich..." have been interpreted in that light, as well as his later turn from poetry to drama. As early as 1893 Hofmannsthal expressed that awareness explicitly in the essay entitled "Gabriele d'Annunzio":

> Wir! Wir! Ich weiß ganz gut, daß ich nicht von der ganzen großen Generation rede. Ich rede von ein paar tausend Menschen, in den großen europäischen Städten verstreut. (Hofmannsthal 171)

Rilke, according to Zweig, certainly belonged to that elite group, for "alles Vulgäre war ihm unerträglich," and "bis in das Intimste und Persönlichste ging sein ästhetischer Sinn für Vollendung und Symmetrie" (Zweig 170). From that standpoint, the young Rilke often wrote about members of the lower classes, such as beggars, derelicts, and the handicapped. In such cases the poet does not pretend to be speaking from experience; rather, he impersonates a voice of someone very different from himself. Whether that stance is convincing is and was a matter of debate. Rilke's work was interpreted, even by some of his contemporaries, as an aestheticization and spiritualization of poverty. The poet defended himself against such charges by claiming "die berechtigte Unparteilichkeit des künstlerischen Ausdrucks" (Rilke 331). A modern critic writes: "Just as 'apolitical' behavior becomes of necessity 'political' in this turbulent age, so too 'impartiality' *vis-à-vis* rich and poor is in fact partiality for the rich" (Schwarz 67). Then, as now, an allegedly "apolitical" stance serves to mask conservative attitudes reinforcing the *status quo*.

My intent is not to play one type of literature off against another, for there are good reasons Petzold's poetry is not included in anthologies, nor his name in literary histories. However much his poetry may be lacking in sophistication, it does possess an "authenticity," which Hofmannsthal, among others, often found absent in refined literary discourse. The debilitating effects of consciousness and selfconsciousness are documented in Hofmannsthal's poetry and in essays such as "Age of Innocence" and the so-called "Chandos-Brief." Lack of experience with the subject matter of his poetry is one problem that Petzold did not have. His knowledge of poverty and hardship was first-hand, and his poetry reveals the strength of lived experience.

However mutually exclusive in real life, the artistry of Rilke or Hofmannsthal and the experience of Petzold seem to supplement each other for the literary critic. As Petzold himself understood, an exclusive focus on elite culture serves only to reflect the value system of the investigator:

> Ich kann nicht schmutzige Knechtschaft, Armut, Verachtung, Spott und Hohn als gerechte Weltordnung ansehen und überlasse diese

Weltansicht jenen Philosophen, die in ihr die rechtliche Anerkennung ihrer Macht über andere Menschen sehen. (Petzold 9)

The historian would certainly want to look at both sides to arrive at an accurate assessment of the time.

We know from other sources that Petzold was released from the tuberculosis sanitarium after two years, and although recovery was only partial, he lived for another twelve years. He married and had children; and he went on to write and publish prolifically. The literary recognition and financial support he received in later years made his life relatively comfortable. He died in 1923 at the age of forty. Petzold could have included that success story in his autobiography; the fact that he did not, however, is revealing.

If Petzold had cast his autobiography as a story of poor-boy-makes-good, his novel would embody the teleology of the traditional *Bildungsroman*. A rags-to-riches story would have vindicated the existing conditions and detracted from the social causes of the misery portrayed. Petzold's recovery from tuberculosis and his emancipation from the ghetto would, of course, not have been possible without assistance from mainstream society. But since such assistance is highly exceptional, Petzold chose to end his autobiography at the point where his fate was shared by many others. This emphasis on the collective aspect gives meaning to his subtitle, *Der Roman eines Menschen.*

In contrast to the *Bildungsroman*, which portrays an "exemplary" individual, a proletarian autobiography, with an essentially faceless protagonist, has been called an "antinovel":

> Solcherart gesellschaftlich gewendet, erweist sich die [Arbeiter-] Autobiographie als Antiroman. Nicht mehr durchschreitet der Held die verschiedenen Kreise einer Welt, um dadurch seine Seele zu finden und sich zur Persönlichkeit zu bilden, sondern er wird durch eine feindliche soziale Umwelt getrieben, die ihm physisch und geistig langsam vernichtet. (Witte 41)

The protagonist of such an antinovel is not an individual but rather a socioeconomic class.

Autobiography is itself a bourgeois genre, just as individualism is a bourgeois concept, stemming from the Renaissance and Reformation. Sloterdijk cites Mahrholz's "Prinzip des Individualismus" and summarizes his important conclusion: "Individualistischer Anspruch und Stil sei ein Grundzug allen bürgerlichen Lebens" (Sloterdijk 23). Proletarian society, in contrast, is organized more collectively, with work experience rather than individual interests as the cohesive factor. Sloterdijk posits a "biographical solidarity" that leads to a commonality of experience and thus also of communication:

> Der proletarische Kommunikationsmodus hat eine konkrete Gemeinsamkeit zwischen dem Autor und dem Kollektiv zur Voraus-

setzung....Der proletarische Protagonist, der für Tausende von Genossen spricht, die das gleiche erleben und erleiden, kann im Grunde nur deswegen für sie sprechen, weil er für sich selbst Typisches erlebt hat, das per se eine Übertragung gestattet. (Sloterdijk 315)

The difficulty of explicating the literary manifestations of class differences only illustrates the need for the development of criteria for viewing proletarian literature. Encapsulated in middle-class society, as many of us are, it is not easy to think beyond middle-class notions and honestly to view the "Other."

In an effort to bring Petzold up-to-date, it is instructive to view the reception of his autobiography over the past seventy-five years. The publication of *Das rauhe Leben* in 1920 elicited a positive review by a writer of no lesser renown than Hermann Broch. Aware of the simplicity of Petzold's presentation, Broch nonetheless writes, "als Dichter der gemarterten Kreatur darf er für seinen Stoff, der für sich selber spricht, Respekt fordern" (quoted in Exenberger 133). The book was, however, not well received by the Socialists and other leftists. By the 1920s, the Socialist Party had developed its own organization and hierarchy which excluded the truly impoverished elements of society. Further, the quasireligious stance that Petzold articulated in his later poetry separated him from the political activists of the time.

If Petzold was not political enough for the Socialists, he was too political for the Fascists; and with the rise of Austro-Fascism, his book was to experience a fate far worse than being ignored. A new edition of the book appeared in Graz in 1932, and it was heavily edited. Censorship continued and was intensified in the subsequent editions of the book, of which there were, surprisingly, five more (in 1940, 1941, 1947, 1948, and 1964). It was not until the 1979 edition that the original 1920 version was restored. The intent of the censorship is clear, since the book was not compatible with the then-dominant ideology. But if it was too mild for the Socialists, what exactly did the Nazis find so offensive about the work?

In comparing the various editions, Exenberger made an amazing discovery: "In den Ausgaben 1932 bis 1964 finden sich einige hundert, oft gravierende Textänderungen" (Exenberger 135). According to that report, the Nazis expunged all references not only to socialism but also to the plight of the worker. Petzold's critique of religious and educational institutions was not allowed to stand, and, of course, his antimilitaristic stance had to go as well. All favorable references to Jews, of which there are many, were obfuscated or removed. Beyond these obvious manipulations to suit Nazi ideology, a more difficult question arises.

Why did the falsified versions persist through six editions over forty-seven years before correction? A critic in 1932 made a point that remains valid in helping to explain the longevity of the falsified versions. That critic, Otto Koenig, saw the intention of censorship "als *Das*

Rauhe Leben Petzolds im Geschäftsinteresse des Verlages einem spießerisch-bürgerlichen Lesepublikum sympathischer zu machen" (quoted in Exenberger 136). In 1964, nearly two decades after the end of the war, society was still willing to accept a reprinting of the tainted version for the sake of market value.

Three decades later, in the present day, although Petzold's text has been restored, there is little reason to suppose that market interests operate any less subtly—on the contrary. At least one voice of protest has, however, arisen. The contemporary Austrian dramatist Felix Mitterer took an interest in the topic, and he wrote the screenplay for a film based on the book. The film was produced by ORF (Austrian Television) and aired in 1987.

To condense a five-hundred-page book into a ninety-minute film requires, of course, a lot of editing. Yet the film remains faithful to Petzold's text and accurately portrays the central scenes in the book. It shows the death of the father in a hospital, the brutality of the journeymen toward the young apprentices, a machine accident in a large factory, the long lines in front of a soup kitchen, the life of the men in the underground tunnels, the proletarian clientele in a coffeehouse, the protagonist's shyness in sexual matters, and the callousness of bourgeois society except for the people who stepped in to save his life. The film is very realistic—grim, one might say; and it would be unthinkable on US-American television.

If one asks why Mitterer chose to make the film, an answer might be found in his sociopolitical stance, as evidenced in his writings. Mitterer often focuses on the disenfranchised elements in contemporary society, and he portrays that world on stage, "eine Dritte Welt eigentlich, die neben uns in Europa existiert" (Mitterer Interview 302). Since his dramas often deal with present-day social conditions, I believe Mitterer is saying that socioeconomic differences—besides or beyond ethnicity, race, and gender—form the basis for the polarities in our culture today. From the film one can deduce points of intersection that Mitterer sees between the turn-of-the-(past)-century and the turn-of-the-(present)-century.

Mitterer is not the only one to make the comparison. In 1980 *The New Republic* ran a cover story entitled "The Vienna Analogy," comparing Austria to US-America. That writer sees "cultural consumerism and political passivity" as the central common elements:

> The absence of politics, a gradual social fragmentation in our nation...the retreat into the self...nostalgia, aestheticism, and a deeply passive pessimism now draw us near to *fin-de-siècle* Vienna....This smug cultural sophistication in the midst of political hopelessness, national mistrust, and boredom constitutes the real Vienna Analogy. (Botstein 27–28)

It is not a question here of registering resignation, much less retrospective moral indignation. It is rather a matter of attempting to understand our society, then and now—and acting on that insight.

Works Cited

Barthes, Roland. *Mythologies.* Translated by Annette Lavers. New York: Hill and Wang, 1972.

Botstein, Leon. "The Vienna Analogy." *The New Republic,* 20 December 1980, 26-28.

Exenberger, Herbert. "Manipulationen an der Autobiographie des Arbeiterdichters Alfons Petzold." In *Beiträge zur Geschichte der Sozialdemokratischen Arbeiterbewegung im Sudeten, Karpaten und Donauraum,* edited by Seliger Archiv Stuttgart, 130-44. Munich: Brücke, 1982.

Gruber, Helmut. *Red Vienna: Experiment in Working-Class Culture 1919-1934.* New York: Oxford UP, 1991.

Hofmannsthal, Hugo von. *Gesammelte Werke: Prosa I.* Frankfurt a.M.: Fischer, 1950.

John, Michael. "Obdachlosigkeit—Massenerscheinung und Unruheherd im Wien der Spätgründerzeit." In *Glücklich ist, wer vergißt...?* edited by Hubert Ch. Ehalt, Gernot Heiß, and Hannes Stekl, 173-94. Vienna: Böhlau, 1986.

Lévi-Strauss, Claude. *The Raw and the Cooked.* Translated by John and Doreen Weightman. Chicago: U of Chicago P, 1990.

Mitterer, Felix, adapt. *Das rauhe Leben.* By Alfons Petzold. Directed by Heidi Pils. Produced by ORF and ZDF, 1987.

———. "Interview mit Felix Mitterer," by Ursula Hassel and Deirdre McMahon. In *Das zeitgenössische deutschsprachige Volksstück,* edited by Ursula Hassel and Herbert Herzmann, 287-304. Tübingen: Stauffenburg, 1992.

Petzold, Alfons. *Das rauhe Leben: Der Roman eines Menschen.* Graz: Styria, 1979.

Rilke, Rainer Maria. *Briefe aus Muzot, 1921 bis 1926.* Leipzig: Insel, 1937.

Schnitzler, Arthur. *Jugend in Wien: Eine Autobiographie.* Vienna: Fritz Molden, 1968.

Schwarz, Egon. *Poetry and Politics in the Works of Rainer Maria Rilke.* Translated by David E. Wellbery. New York: Frederick Ungar, 1981.

Sloterdijk, Peter. *Literatur und Organisation von Lebenserfahrung: Autobiographien der Zwanziger Jahre.* Munich: Carl Hanser, 1978.

Wegs, J. Robert. *Growing up Working Class: Continuity and Change Among Viennese Youth, 1890–1938*. University Park: Pennsylvania State UP, 1989.

Winter, Max. *Das schwarze Wienerherz: Sozialreportagen aus dem frühen 20. Jahrhundert.* Edited by Helmut Strutzmann. Vienna: Österreichischer Bundesverlag, 1982.

———. *Im dunkelsten Wien*. Vienna: Wiener Verlag, 1904.

Witte, Bernd. "Paris: Arbeiterautobiographien." In *Arbeiterdichtung: Analysen–Bekenntnisse–Dokumentationen*. Edited by the Österreichische Gesellschaft für Kulturpolitik. Wuppertal: Peter Hammer, 1973.

Zweig, Stefan. *Die Welt von Gestern: Erinnerungen eines Europäers*. Stockholm: Bermann-Fischer, 1944.

Early German Literary Cabaret and Modernism in Berlin

David Chisholm

Most studies of German literary cabaret concentrate on the development of this art form after the end of the First World War, emphasizing its contributions to Weimar culture.[1] This is hardly surprising, given the talented constellation of writers, musicians, artists, actors, dancers, and singers associated with the famous literary-political cabarets of the 1920s and the great tradition of literary and political *chansons* which constituted the most important part of many of the programs. This essay, on the other hand, focuses on the earlier forms of cabaret, which helped pave the way for its further development after the First World War. Within the context of modernism, it explores some of the aesthetic, cultural, and political aspects of early German literary cabaret in Berlin. It begins toward the end of the nineteenth century with the origins of cabaret in France and the *idea* of a German cabaret, and concludes with the end of the First World War, the demise of the Wilhelmine Empire, and the chaotic beginnings of the Weimar Republic.

On the evening of 18 November 1881, Rudolphe Salis, a painter and graphic artist, opened the Chat Noir, the first French artistic cabaret, on the Boulevard Rochechouart at the foot of Montmartre in Paris. Every Friday evening writers, painters, sculptors, actors, and musicians would assemble to present their work to each other, including performances of *chansons*, recitations, and discussions of art and literature. Salis soon opened up this artists' venue to the public and began scheduling daily rather than weekly gatherings. Parisian society, curious about these Bohemian *soirées*, began to venture into Montmartre to attend the performances of these artists. The clientele gradually became more and more upper class, but this did not prevent Salis from playing tricks on the audience, including shouting insults, as individuals and groups entered or left the room. It was in the Chat Noir that the first political-satirical *chansons* were performed: Aristide Bruant, the first great *chanson* writer, and the popular *chansonnière* Yvette Guilbert performed topical, satirical texts in an entertaining manner. At about the same time *variétés* and music halls, both of which were often referred to as Tingeltangel, arose in Germany. The term "Tingeltangel," which may have been derived either from the sound sequence of military bells and cymbals in a parade or from the sound of coins dropping onto a plate, emphasized the low quality of the establishment and the performances. In contrast to the relatively exclusive French cabaret, the audience in the Tingeltangel consisted primarily of craftsmen, employees, and laborers. A variety of acts were presented, including magicians, circus numbers, ventriloquists, and jugglers, as well as *chansons* in the form of couplets, that is, stanzaic songs with topical-political or erotic content and witty, frequently recurring refrains. The couplets were not politically aggressive; rather they satirized contemporary figures and events in a light, amusing manner.

Since the early 1890s, and especially after Yvette Guilbert's tour of Germany in 1898 and the International Exhibition in Paris in 1900, lively discussions took place in artistic circles in Munich and Berlin about the possibility of a German cabaret. According to Artur Kutscher, Frank Wedekind, after his return from Paris in 1895, had already discussed plans for a German cabaret with Carl Heine, the director of the first German Ibsen Theater (Greul 93). Otto Julius Bierbaum and Ernst von Wolzogen both wanted to start a German cabaret; they realized, however, that the French cabaret style could not be transplanted to Germany without modifications, since public performances of all kinds in the Prussian city of Berlin and elsewhere in Germany were subject to strict censorship. The main concern was rather to raise the German Tingeltangel/Variété tradition to a higher *niveau*. There was much discussion at the end of the nineteenth century about reforming and artistically "ennobling" the Tingeltangel/Variété; Variété attracted a large audience, and those seriously concerned with the state of the arts in Germany hoped to break down the barriers between "high and low art" by striving for higher artistic levels in precisely those forms and genres which attracted large audiences. In 1896 Oskar Panizza expressed his views on the Variété in an essay entitled "Der Klassizismus und das Eindringen des Variété" in the monthly magazine *Die Gesellschaft*:

> Für sich betrachtet ist [das Variété] die absolute Naivität in der Anwendung der Kunstmittel; es ist die unverblümteste, weil gar nicht überdachte, Verwendung von Schminke und Puder, von Lippenrot und Wimpernschwarz, von Bauschröckchen und Trikots–ich rede bildlich– in der Kunst, und die hellste Freude, der kindliche Enthusiasmus und das reinste Entzücken über den Erfolg–komme er, woher er wolle. Das ist Variété.... Wir wollen neue Lebensflüsse, neue Nahrung für unsere Nerven, selbst auf die Gefahr des Schmerzen-Erleidens und Vergiftet-Werdens neue Blüten und Formen, Gerüche und Umrauschungen. Ist nichts anderes da als Haschisch, dann Haschisch. Ist nichts anderes da als Variété, dann Variété. (1253, 1268)

One aspect of modernism at the turn of the century was a strong desire for new stimuli and experiences, due in part to the faster pace of life engendered by industrialization, urbanization, and a rapidly increasing population in urban centers such as Berlin. In 1902 Artur Moeller van den Bruck stated in his essay "Das Variété–Eine Kulturdramaturgie" that the dynamics of modern life were leading inexorably to the rise of a variety theater in which a Europe tired of life and satiated by civilization would rejoice in a renaissance of vitality and liberated sensuality (Greul 94).

References to Tingeltangel or variety theaters appear frequently in turn-of-the-century literature, as in Heinrich Mann's 1905 novel *Professor Unrat* (the source of the 1930 film *Der blaue Engel*), in which a high school teacher falls in love with a young singer in a Tingeltangel. In Otto Julius Bierbaum's novel *Stilpe*, which appeared in 1897, the hero Willibald Stilpe starts an artistic Tingeltangel called Momus in Berlin. Typical of modernism are the effervescent enthusiasm and the high ideals which Bierbaum expresses through his main figure. Stilpe describes his new theater ecstatically:

> Was ist die Kunst jetzt? Eine bunte, ein bißchen glitzernde Spinnwebe im Winkel des Lebens. Wir wollen sie wie ein goldenes Netz über das ganze Volk, das ganze Leben werfen. Denn zu uns, ins Tingeltangel, werden Alle kommen, die Theater und Museen ebenso ängstlich fliehen, wie die Kirche. Und bei uns werden die, die bloß ein bißchen Unterhaltung suchen, das finden, was ihnen Allen fehlt: den heiteren Geist, das Leben zu verklären, die Kunst des Tanzes in Worten, Tönen, Farben, Linien, Bewegungen. Die nackte Lust am Schönen, der Humor, der die Welt am Ohr nimmt, die Phantasie, die mit den Sternen jongliert und auf des Weltgeistes Schnurrbartenden [sic] Seil tanzt, die Philosophie des harmonischen Lachens, das Jauchzen schmerzlicher Seelenbrunst....Wir werden ins Leben wirken wie die Troubadours! Wir werden eine neue Kultur herbeitanzen! Wir werden den Übermenschen auf dem Brettl gebären! Wir werden diese alberne Welt umschmeißen![2]

In September 1900 Bierbaum published his *Deutsche Chansons (Brettl-Lieder)*, and by the end of the first year had sold over 20,000 copies. Bierbaum's intention was to improve the tastes of large audiences. In contrast to Schiller's classical concept of the theater, Bierbaum saw the variety theater of the future not as a moral but rather as a purely aesthetic institution. His concept of an aesthetic variety theater has a lot in common with the tendencies of modernism and *art nouveau* at the turn of the century. His preface to the *Deutsche Chansons*, which bears the title "Ein Brief an eine Dame anstatt einer Vorrede," reveals this serious intent:

> Angewandte Lyrik,–da haben Sie unser Schlagwort. An diesem Worte kann man die ästhetischen Gesetze des Chansons, wie wir es meinen, ziehen. Es müssen Lieder sein, die gesungen werden können; das ist das erste. Das zweite und nicht minder Wesentliche aber ist, daß sie für eine Menge gesungen werden können, die nicht etwa, wie das Publikum eines Konzertsaales, darauf aus ist, 'Große Kunst' kritisch zu genießen, sondern die ganz einfach unterhalten sein will. Unsere Meinung ist nun, daß dazu die Kunst nicht zu gut ist. Wie die Freien Bühnen es dahin gebracht haben, daß der Geschmack des Theaterpublikums ein höheres Niveau erhalten hat, so wird es, denken wir, möglich sein, durch künstlerische Variétébühnen verbessernd auch auf den Geschmack der größeren Menge zu wirken.... Der heutige Stadtmensch hat, wenn Sie Gütige mir das gewagte Wort erlauben, Variéténerven; er hat nur noch selten die Fähigkeit, großen dramatischen Zusammenhängen zu folgen, sein Empfindungsleben für drei Theaterstunden auf einen Ton zu stimmen; er will Abwechslung, –Variété." (X ff.)

Wolzogen's Motley Theater

On 18 January 1901 Ernst von Wolzogen opened his Motley Theater (Buntes Theater genannt Überbrettl) in the Secessionsbühne on Alexanderplatz. Wolzogen coined the word "Überbrettl" to designate a genre that was to stand above the *Brettl*, that is, it would "ennoble" the Tingeltangel, Variété, and Music Halls. For Wolzogen, the stimulus came primarily not from Paris, but rather from Bierbaum's novel *Stilpe*, from the Danish writer Holger Drachmann, and from the philosophical-literary writings of Friedrich Nietzsche. Following Nietzsche, he demanded "ein frisches, fröhliches Niederreißen morscher alter Zäune," the "Umwertung alter verbrauchter Werte," as well as scorn for absurd excesses of authority (Rösler 61).

The première took place on the evening of the two-hundredth anniversary of the establishment of Prussia as a kingdom, which the court was celebrating with great ceremonial pomp. The lead article in the first supplement of the *Berliner Börsen-Courier* for 18 January 1901 illustrates the great importance attached to this occasion:

> Zur Feier des Krönungsjubiläums
>
> Der festliche Tag, den die preußischen Lande heute begehen, hat die Bedeutung des hohenzollernschen Staates für und in Deutschland und darüber hinaus in vollem Maße hervortreten lassen in der warmen und freudigen Antheilnahme, die sich innerhalb und außerhalb der Grenzen des Reiches unverkennbar kundgiebt. Bürgerthum und Heer, Körperschaften und Vereine, Kirchen und Schulen feiern die Erinnerung an das Ereigniß, das eine der mitbestimmenden Ursachen für das Aufsteigen Preußens zur Großmacht und zur Übernahme der Führerschaft in Deutschland war, und die höfischen Veranstaltungen, die der Weihe des Tages dienen, erhalten einen besonderen Glanz durch die Anwesenheit zahlreicher Vertreter fremder Fürstenhäuser und Staaten.

Because of this anniversary the public awaited the première of the Buntes Theater with great expectations, and the new Überbrettl was an overwhelming success. The opening program consisted of fourteen numbers:

1. "Das Lied von den lieben, süßen Mädeln" (Text: Ernst von Wolzogen; Music: James Rothstein)
2. "Rosen" (Text: Otto Julius Bierbaum; Music: Victor Hollaender)
3. "Das Laufmädel" (Text: Ernst von Wolzogen; Music: Bogumil Zepler)
4. "Das Gänschen" (Text: Robert Eysler; recited by Olga Wohlbrück)
5. "Mütter" (Text: Hugo Salus)
6. "Madame Adèle" (Text: Ernst von Wolzogen; Music: James Rothstein)
7. "Zur Dichtkunst abkommandiert" (Text: Peter Schlemihl [=Ludwig Thoma]; Music: Oscar Straus)
8. "Episode"–from Arthur Schnitzler's *Anatol*
9. "Das Mittagsmahl (Il pranzo)"–a scene by Christian Morgenstern
10. "Im Karpfenteiche"–a fable by Hanns Heinz Ewers

11. "Der lustige Ehemann" (Text: Otto Julius Bierbaum; Music: Oscar Straus)
12. Critique of Morgenstern's "Das Mittagsmahl" (supposedly by the critic Alfred Kerr, but really by Morgenstern himself.)
13. "König Ragnar Lodbrok" (ballad by Detlev von Liliencron with shadow play by Ludwig Stutz)
14. "Pierrots Tücke, Traum und Tod" (Text: Rudolf Schanzer; Music: Oscar Straus)

The sixth number, "Madame Adèle," which depicts the rise of a *Vorstadtmädel* to a *demi-mondaine* and *grande cocotte*, was the first distinctive cabaret *chanson* in the German language. The *süßes Mädel* naturally begins her song in French:

> Je suis Adèle, la reine blonde—
> On me connait, messieurs, parbleu!
> Je suis la reine, la reine de Demimonde.
> Adèle est la, faites votre jeu!
>
> O mei, o mei habs nur ka Angst—
> Ich sing auch deutsch wenns des verlangst...

The seventh number, the couplet "Zur Dichtkunst abkommandiert," turned out to be the only political fare on the program to slip past the censors. The couplet satirizes Major Josef Lauff, who had become a court poet of sorts to Kaiser Wilhelm II. Josef Lauff was the quintessential Wilhelmine poet, whose Hohenzollern dramas were parodied by Christian Morgenstern in a short drama called *Der Lauffgraf*. The performance of this couplet was particularly effective, because on the same day a festival production of Josef Lauff's *Adlerflug*, especially written for the two-hundredth anniversary of the bestowal of royal status on Prussia, was being presented both at the Royal Opera in the presence of the Kaiser and in the Royal Theater in Wiesbaden. The most successful number on the program, however, was the duet "Der lustige Ehemann" by Bierbaum and Oscar Straus, which perfectly invoked a Biedermeier atmosphere while attempting to satirize the cozy and familiar nostalgia for the past:

> Die Welt, die ist da draußen wo,
> Mag auf dem Kopf sie stehn!
> Sie intressiert uns gar nicht sehr,
> Und wenn sie nicht vorhanden wär'
> Würd's auch noch weiter geh'n.

As Jelavich points out, the Biedermeier costumes, the words, and the dance itself showed a couple totally oblivious to the outside world, but somehow the audience responded much more warmly to the nostalgia, rather than the satire: "Far from being an expression of modern times, the number represented a nostalgic looking-back to a supposedly idyllic, cozy, premetropolitan age. It did so in a distinctly antipolitical manner" (41f). In his introduction to *The Wild Stage* Lareau comments on the resulting discrepancy between the ideals which led to the founding of the Buntes Theater and the actual nature and quality of the performances:

> ["Der lustige Ehemann"] became the model for the Überbrettl *chanson*, and for many the symbol of all that was wrong with Wolzogen's theater. Although the lyrics satirize the complacency of the bourgeoisie...the audience took the parody to its heart, ignoring the irony. Capitalizing on the success, Wolzogen filled his programs with similar ornamental dancing songs in the Biedermeier style.... This theater had justified its art in opposition to the music hall's cynical commercialism but turned out to be just as commercial itself, endlessly repeating the few hit songs, tailoring its repertoire to popular demand, and paying more attention to the cash box than the literary quality. (8)

In November 1901 Wolzogen moved into his own theater which had eight hundred seats and which was decorated in *art nouveau* style. On the evening before the opening of this new theater, the following "Überlied," written by Hans Brennert, appeared in the *Berliner Tageblatt* with a dedication to Wolzogen. In these verses, Brennert unmistakably satirizes the *art nouveau* style and atmosphere of the new theater as well as Wolzogen's ambitions:

> Das Überlied
>
> Ich liebe Botticellileiber,
> Die wie Tiffanyglas so schlank;
> Ich sterbe für die Überweiber
> In Keller-Reiners Kunstausschank.
> Ich buhle gleich verliebten Pagen
> Um stilisierten Berlin W–:
> Da wohnt sie, meine Überfee!
> O Überweib, so reizerblüht,
> Dir steigt mein Lied, mein Überlied!
>
> Die stilisierte Überehe,
> Die ist mein künstlerisches Ziel!
> Mein Überweibchen schon ich sehe
> Im Überheim–im Eckmannstil!
> Von Leistikow die Wandtapeten,
> Auf Pankokläufer soll man treten;
> Um Mitternacht umfängt uns nett
> Herrn van der Veldes Überbett–
> O Überbett, auch dir steigt müd
> Mein Abendlied, mein Überlied!
>
> Und muß ich stillos einst verlassen
> die stilisierte Überwelt,
> Sollt ihr als Grabschrift mir verfassen:
> Hier ruht ein stilvergnügter Held!

> Laßt, Freunde, noch um eins mich betteln:
> Baut aus sechs kleinen Überbretteln
> Dem Leib, der meine Seele barg,
> Den stilisierten Übersarg,
> Am Übersarge, wenn ich schied,
> Singt mir mein Lied, mein Überlied. (Schutte 499f)

Following the advice of ambitious entrepreneurs, Wolzogen converted his theater to a stock company. During the second season he came into conflict with his own board of directors, who wanted to appeal to the tastes of the masses to gain a larger audience. Wolzogen was given a "leave of absence," only to leave the enterprise entirely early in 1902. At the end of the third season the theater closed for good. In the meantime, however, Überbrettl had became fashionable throughout Germany, and many imitators followed in Wolzogen's footsteps.

The infant cabaret movement in Berlin at the turn of the century can be viewed to a large extent as a product of the intellectual climate engendered by modernism. In a period of technological progress and intense economic and business activity, the gap between human and technological development, between rich and poor, urban metropolis and countryside, belief in progress and nostalgia for old traditions increased drastically. Bourgeois morals and Wilhelmine traditions stood in crass opposition to democracy and socialism and to the attempts of writers and artists to match the technological advances with intellectual, social, and cultural progress. Art was to have practical and social applications, and the concept *l'art pour l'art* was viewed as a relic of neoclassicism closely connected to bourgeois tradition and the Wilhelmine Empire. Theaters for workers were founded, and the naturalism of Henrik Ibsen and Gerhart Hauptmann—especially the plays performed in Otto Brahm's Deutsches Theater in Berlin—attempted to call attention to social inequities and the plight of the lower classes. The thought and philosophical-literary formulations of Friedrich Nietzsche, above all his endeavors to liberate the individual from the restrictions of tradition and morality, pervaded intellectual life at the turn of the century and left their mark on artists as well as intellectuals. Flowing with these currents, the early cabaret movement was searching for a rejuvenation and revitalization of art as an integral part of "modern culture." Wolzogen's pioneering effort may have foundered, but critics such as Peter Sprengel credit Wolzogen with a decisive contribution to the beginnings of cabaret in Germany as a movement which would become instrumental in overcoming the social and cultural stagnation of the Wilhelmine Empire.[3]

The First Schall und Rauch

A group under the direction of Max Reinhardt, which called itself Schall und Rauch, gave its first public performance on 23 January 1901. This cabaret was much more effective in opposing Wilhelmine values and traditions than Wolzogen's Buntes Theater. It achieved this by incorporating into its repertoire brilliant parodies of Wilhelm II's Court Theater—to such an extent that these parodies became associated with Schall und Rauch on a recurring basis. The cabaret took over two well-known figures—Serenissimus and Kindermann—from the weekly satirical magazine *Simplizissimus* and used them in place of the usual *conférencier*. As in Wilhelm II's court theater, where plays were performed for his benefit, the whole Schall und Rauch program was for the benefit of Serinissimus, who from his box seat frequently took the liberty of interrupting the performance with naive questions and comments to Kindermann.

The first performance in which Serenissimus appeared on the Schall und Rauch stage made it clear that this figure was a caricature of Wilhelm II. Schall und Rauch had already performed a parody of Hauptmann's *Die Weber* (probably written by Friedrich Kayßler), in which the social criticism and revolutionary aspects were removed: the weavers are depicted as well-dressed, well-nourished, middle-class citizens who eat roast meat, drink wine, and sing the German national anthem instead of the Weavers' Song. Before the play begins, Kindermann, the supposed author of the revised version, recites the following speech addressed to Serenissimus:

> Ew. Durchlaucht haben geruht mit Bezugnahme auf Hochdero gnädigsten Geburtstag, welchen Hochderselbe heute zu feiern die Gewogenheit haben, den Wunsch auszusprechen, ein soziales Drama kennen zu lernen. Ich habe mir unterthänigst erlaubt, zu diesem Behufe ein Machwerk neuester Litteratur in Vorschlag zu bringen, welches in dem Rufe steht, das allergefährlichste der modernen sozialen Dramen zu sein, nämlich "die Weber" von einem gewissen Gebhart [sic] Hauptmann, welcher noch heute im schlesischen Hochgebirge als Einsiedler sein Leben fristen soll. Es ist mir zu meiner großen Freude gelungen, die Schärfen des Stückes abzuschleifen, alles Grobe und Häßliche auszuscheiden, und die wenigen poetischen und moralischen Stellen zu verstärken und herauszuarbeiten, das Ganze gewissermaßen hoffähig zu gestalten, so daß Serenissimus gewissermaßen nun den Extract, das Beste daran zu sehen bekommt. Die Damen und Herren unseres herzoglichen Hoftheaters werden meinen Versuch durch ihre edle und würdevolle Darstellung auf das Angenehmste unterstützen. Geruhen Ew. Durchlaucht meine bescheidene Arbeit huldvollst in Hochdero Augenschein nehmen zu wollen. (*Schall und Rauch* 54)

In May 1901 Max Reinhardt's troupe had the opportunity to use the Deutsches Theater, in which the première of Hauptmann's *Die Weber* had taken place in 1894. Naturally, the Kaiser had his own box seat in this theater, but Wilhelm had canceled his subscription to protest Hauptmann's revolutionary drama. The troupe hit upon the idea of having Serenissimus appear personally in this same royal box, thus ingeniously associating Serenissmus with Wilhelm II!

At the end of the performance Serenissimus comes down onto the stage, strokes the actresses on their cheeks, and asks his advisor Kindermann questions which indirectly refer to Gerhart Hauptmann and to Wilhelm II's court dramatist, the retired Major Josef Lauff:

> S(erenissimus): Aber sagen Sie Kindermann, wo liegt eigentlich dieses–äh–Schlesien?
> K(indermann): Nördlich vom böhmischen Gebirge Durchlaucht.
> S: Ach so, böhmische Berge, äh–weiß schon, weiß schon–äh–danke, danke. Ja, was ich noch sagen wollte, wer war doch der Dichter des–äh–Stückes, habe vergessen–äh.
> K: Der Dichter ist Hauptmann Durchlaucht.
> S: Ach was Sie sagen. Sagen Sie ist der Mann noch aktiv?
> K: Er ist noch sehr rüstig, soviel ich weiß.
> S: Könnte doch längst Major sein, so'n Mann, was? Dieser–äh–andere–äh–vaterländische Dichter, habe den Namen vergessen, der ist doch auch Major, was, Kindermann?
> K: Jawohl Durchlaucht.
> S: Na können mich gelegentlich mal dran erinnern, werde die Sache mal gelegentlich anregen. Wer was Ordentliches kann,–äh–der soll auch–äh–was Ordentliches sein! äh! Hab ich nicht recht,–äh?
> (*Schall und Rauch* 62)

Initially Schall und Rauch performed to select, invited audiences consisting of literary and theatrical connoisseurs, but on 9 October 1901, it began giving public performances in the banquet hall of the Hotel Arnim at Unter den Linden 44. For a number of reasons, the quality of these performances was inferior to that of the earlier nonpublic programs.[4] Furthermore, a company which previously had performed only occasionally to invited audiences–on average less than once every three weeks–was now performing nightly to general audiences who did not appreciate or understand literary and theatrical parodies. Reviewers complained that the performers at Schall und Rauch were communicating only with each other rather than with the audience.

About a month after Schall und Rauch began giving public performances, another group, which called itself Die bösen Buben, was founded by Rudolf Bernauer and Carl Meinhard. Bernauer had participated in the première of Schall und Rauch, and both Bernauer and Meinhard were actors at Brahm's Deutsches Theater. On 16 November 1901, Die bösen Buben began to present their own literary, theatrical, and political parodies on an occasional basis to invited audiences in a setting and style similar to that of the early Schall und Rauch performances. The première program included different endings to Ibsen's *A Doll's House* in the style of Frank Wedekind (Nora goes to a madhouse), Maeterlinck (Nora seeks out the great door to the mystical Dark Hall, but Helmer will not give her the key), and Josef Lauff (a patriotic verse drama in which Nora and Helmer ecstatically toast the King of Scandinavia, while a bust remarkably similar to that of Wilhelm II appears on a pedestal in the background):

HELMER: Nora, kann dich wirklich nichts bewegen, bei mir zu bleiben?
NORA (blieb kalt und starr)
HELMER (sank mit verzweifeltem Aufschrei in die Knie): Nora!
(Man hörte in der Ferne den majestätischen Donner der Geschütze.)
NORA: Nichts. Es sei denn, das Wunderbarste geschähe.
(Der Geschützdonner wurde immer stärker.)
HELMER (in höchster Ekstase): Und das wäre?–Sprich!
NORA: Das unsere Prophezeiungen vom skandinavischen König eintreffen!
(Nun erhob Helmer den Regenschirm, ergriff Noras dargebotene Rechte.)
BEIDE: (richteten den mannesmutigen Blick prophetisch in die Ferne) Das walte Gott![5]

Die bösen Buben was a highly successful troupe, and they continued to perform sporadically once or twice a year to invited audiences until 1905.

In 1902 the programs of Schall und Rauch changed substantially in the direction of one-act plays consisting of both humorous sketches and serious modern plays, especially those of August Strindberg. By the end of 1902 Schall und Rauch had been transformed from a cabaret to a chamber theater (renamed Kleines Theater in 1903), whose repertoire consisted of serious dramas. In 1902–1903 Reinhardt's troupe performed Oscar Wilde's *Salome*, Hugo von Hofmannsthal's *Elektra*, and Maxim Gorky's *Nachtasyl*. On 18 February 1903 Reinhardt took over the direction of the Neues Theater (am Schiffbauerdamm), and in 1905, after a highly successful production of Shakespeare's *Midsummer Night's Dream*, he gave up the Kleines Theater. In 1906 he began directing the Deutsches Theater, where he had started his career as an actor in 1894.

The genesis of many of Reinhardt's later theatrical experiments can be traced back to the cabaret Schall und Rauch, which, along with other cabarets, served as a springboard for a rejuvenation and revitalization of German theatrical practice. In 1935 the writer Max Halbe emphasized the significance of turn-of-the-century cabaret for the development of German literature and theater:

Aber wer diese Zeit miterlebt hat, für den kann kein Zweifel sein, daß der eigentliche Umschwung zuerst weniger von oben, von der hohen Literatur, als von unten, von der Kleinkunst, vom Brettl, vom Kabarett herkam. Die auf diesem Boden erfolgende Auflockerung, ja Auflösung aller bisher gültigen literarischen und ethischen Normen war es, die dann erst die Atmosphäre für den Umschwung auch in der hohen Literatur schuf. (334)

Wolzogen's Buntes Theater (Überbrettl) and Reinhardt's Schall und Rauch inspired many other cabarets as well as so-called Kneipenbrettl or "pub-cabarets." The quality of these establishments varied greatly, and most of them did not last more than a few months, yet the best retained some of the spontaneity and improvisational character of Parisian cabaret which had been lacking in Wolzogen's theater. Two of these pub cabarets were Zum hungrigen Pegasus (1901–1902) and the Silberne Punschterrine (1901–1904). Zum hungrigen Pegasus was started on 10 October 1901 by the painter Max Tilke, and included readings and performances by Georg David Schulz, Hans Hyan, Maria Eichhorn (whose stage name was "Dolorosa"), Erich Mühsam, Peter Hille, and others. Performances took place in a small back room of Carlo Dalbelli's Italian restaurant on the Kaiserin-Augusts-Ufer near the Pottsdamer Brücke. This short-lived cabaret came to an end in the spring of 1902. On 26 November Hans Hyan started his own cabaret, the Silberne Punschterrine, in Schröder's Restaurant on Steglitzer Straße, where, following in the tradition of Aristide Bruant, he performed songs about the poor and the Berlin underworld. A former criminal himself, he sang songs in the local Berlin dialect about various types of criminals. One of his songs was based on Bruant's famous *chanson* "A la Rocquette," and, like Bruant, he frequently insulted members of his audience.

Although cabarets continued to exist in Berlin after 1905, their character changed substantially from those which opened in 1901–1902. In autumn 1907 Rudolf Nelson founded a literary cabaret (for which he borrowed the name Chat Noir) first on the Potsdamer Platz, then shortly thereafter in the "Passage" connecting Friedrichstraße with Unter den Linden. The famous *chanson* singer Gussy Holl (later greatly admired by Kurt Tucholsky) had her debut here in 1911, and the Chat Noir continued until 1914. Because of the highly patriotic atmosphere at the outbreak of the First World War, it changed its name to Schwarzer Kater, but closed the same year. A few years earlier in 1910 the so-called Neopathetisches Cabaret arose under the direction of Kurt Hiller as a venue where the early Expressionist writers of Der neue Club (Jacob van Hoddis, Ernst Blass, and Erwin Loewenson, among others) could publicly read from their works. Soon new poets joined this group, among them Georg Heym and Ferdinand Hardekopf. The Neopathetisches Cabaret thought of itself as a countermovement to the concept of *l'art pour l'art* and was closely connected with the *avant-garde* artistic and literary journals *Der Sturm* (edited by Herwarth Walden) and *Die Aktion* (edited by Franz Pfemfert).

The extreme nationalism which accompanied the outbreak of the First World War consolidated censorship in Germany under the control of the military. This made satire and parody almost impossible, and as popular entertainment became increasingly patriotic, the quality of cabaret sank to an abysmally low level. In 1921 Max Herrmann-Neisse reflected on German cabaret during the war:

> Da sank, vom Kontakt mit der europäischen Umwelt abgeschlossen, deutsches Überbrettl auf die tiefste Möglichkeit der Gattung. Nichtskönnertum legitimierte sich durch patriotische Hetzorgien, und der Ansager holte sich billigen Beifall mit dem deutschnationalen Leitartikel. So minderwertig war das künstlerische Element, daß die Tanznummern schließlich das einzige bildeten, um dessentwillen es verlohnte, hinzugehen. (110)

At the outbreak of the First World War Hugo Ball (1886–1927), who had studied with Max Reinhardt in Berlin, was engaged by the Münchner Kammerspiele. Active in theater in Munich since 1912, he had close contacts with the Blauer Reiter movement (including Franz Marc, Paul Klee, and Wassily Kandinsky) and with Frank Wedekind. In the spring of 1914 Ball had plans for an Expressionist theater of the international *avant-garde* in the Munich Künstlertheater. These plans were demolished in August 1914; Ball volunteered for military service, but his experience on the Western Front turned him into an ardent pacifist within the first few months of the war. He was released six months later because of poor health and went to Berlin. In May 1915 he emigrated with the actress and singer Emmy Hennings to Switzerland, and on 5 February 1916, they started the Cabaret Voltaire in the Meierei hotel in Zürich. Ball wrote in his diary:

> Das Lokal war überfüllt; viele konnten keinen Platz mehr finden. Gegen sechs Uhr abends, als man noch fleißig hämmerte..., erschien eine orientalisch aussehende Deputation von vier Männlein, Mappen und Bilder unterm Arm, vielmals diskret sich verbeugend. Es stellten sich vor: Marcel Janco, der Maler, Tristan Tzara, Georges Janco und ein vierter Herr, dessen Name mir entging. Arp war zufällig auch da und man verständigte sich ohne viele Worte. Bald hingen Jancos generöse 'Erzengel' bei den übrigen schönen Sachen, und Tzara las Verse älteren Stiles, die er in einer nicht unsympathischen Weise aus den Rocktaschen zusammensuchte. (cited in Greul 204)

The Cabaret Voltaire became an international center for artists from many countries. Readings from the verse of Kandinsky, Else Lasker-Schüler, Jakob van Hoddis, Christian Morgenstern, Alfred Lichtenstein, Erich Mühsam, Aristide Bruant, Max Jakob, and Franz Werfel were complemented by performances of songs and piano pieces by Claude Debussy, Alexander Scriabin, Arnold Schönberg, and others. Richard Huelsenbeck arrived from Berlin and added a distinctively polemic element. The Cabaret Voltaire saw itself at the forefront of "Art against War," as a "Noah's Ark in the storm of the raging Fatherlands" (Greul 205).

There was much disagreement regarding the origins of the term "Dada." In his diary entry of 18 April 1916, Ball wrote that he had created the word. Huelsenbeck stated that the word "Dada" was discovered by him and Ball by chance in a German-French dictionary, and Tristan Tzara proclaimed jokingly: "Ich fand das Wort am 8.2.1916, 6 Uhr nachmittags im Café de la Terrasse" (Greul 205). These are only a few of the many claims and comments about the origin of the word "Dada."

In January 1917 Richard Huelsenbeck brought Dada to Berlin. Behind closed doors, members of the Sturm group passed around scathing political caricatures by the artist George Grosz. In November 1918, when the war came to an end, revolutionary activity erupted throughout the Reich. The fall of the Bavarian Monarchy and the proclamation of the Republic by Kurt Eisner were followed two days later on 9 November by Philipp Scheidemann proclaiming the Republic in Prussia, and Karl Liebknecht (just two hours later) the Free Socialist Republic. Kaiser Wilhelm II resigned and went into exile in Holland, and Rosa Luxemburg, Liebknecht, and Kurt Eisner were assassinated early in 1919.

Already in November 1918 the Dada-movement came into the open and to the forefront: the Dadaists regarded the emperor's resignation as a major triumph; on 16 November Berlin's "Oberdada" Johannes Baader disrupted a service in the Berlin Cathedral with a "sermon" on the theme "Jesus Christus ist uns Wurst," and in the National Assembly Dadaists distributed from the balcony Baader's leaflet demanding that they take over the government. Walter Mehring joined the Berlin Dadaists, and his ludicrous "Race between a Sewing Machine and a Typewriter" in the Dada-Matinée on 7 November led to a *succès de scandale*. Baader declared: "Dada ist das Cabaret der Welt, so gut sie, die Welt, das Cabaret Dada ist" (Greul 216).

The First World War and the proclamation of the Weimar Republic in 1919 coincide with a distinct break in the development of the cabaret movement in Germany. One of the major differences is the abrupt change in the political, intellectual, and moral climate engendered by the war and its aftermath. With the abolition of preliminary police censorship and the loosening of the strict morality which had prevailed during the Wilhelmine Empire, traditional values (which had already been eroding since the turn of the century) were increasingly called into question. This new moral and political climate is expressed in many of the *chansons* written after 1918, as for example in the "Berliner Chansons und Sittengedichte" and the "Political Satires" published in 1920 by Walter Mehring in a book called *Das politische Cabaret*, as well as in the political *chansons* of Kurt Tucholsky. Mehring was actively involved in the revival of Max Reinhardt's 1901 Schall und Rauch cabaret, which reopened on 8 December 1919 in a huge beer cellar beneath the Großes Schauspielhaus. A discussion of the development of German cabaret after the First World War, however, would exceed the scope of this essay. My purpose here has been to sketch the origins of this "small art form" which later developed into one of Germany's significant contributions to Weimar culture.

Notes

*I would like to thank the Alexander von Humboldt-Stiftung, the Deutsches Literaturarchiv in Marbach, the Akademie der Künste and the Bertolt Brecht-Archiv in Berlin, and the University of Arizona in Tucson for financial and archival support of my research on German cabaret during the summer of 1996.

[1] For a recent example see Alan Lareau's excellent book, *The Wild Stage: Literary Cabarets of the Weimar Republic*.

[2] *Stilpe* 357ff. The reference to Nietzsche reflects the extent to which his influence pervaded intellectual life at the turn of the century. In the fall of 1901 a plaster cast of Max Kruse's well-known bust of Nietzsche was placed in the foyer of Wolzogen's second Überbrettl theater.

[3] "Die Idee einer modernen Kleinkunst, wie sie etwa von Ernst von Wolzogen verfochten wurde, stellte eine prinzipielle Alternative zum repräsentativen Wesen der wilhelminischen Kunst dar: die Muse kam gleichsam von Sockel herunter, im Zeichen der Unterhaltung wurde eine neue Einheit von Akteuren und Rezipienten angestrebt–grundsätzlich durfte jeder auf die Bühne, und das Bühnengeschehen war nicht ohne die lebendige Kommunikation mit dem Publikum denkbar. Zwar ist festzuhalten, daß die preußische Theatervorzensur, der auch das Kabarett unterworfen war, eine offene politische Kritik von vornherein...ausschloß. Aber...gerade durch seine Ausrichtung auf verschiedene Formen der Literatur- und Theaterparodie leistete das Kabarett der Jahrhundertwende einen entscheidenden Beitrag zu jener Emanzipation der Moderne, die sich damals auf dem Wege der Wilhelminismus-Kritik vollzog" (*Literatur im Kaiserreich* 31).

[4] One reason was that the best actors, including Reinhardt himself, were bound to contracts with Otto Brahm, the director of the Deutsches Theater.

[5] Rudolf Bernauer, *Das Theater meines Lebens* 134f. The phrase "Das walte Gott!" was a favorite of Wilhelm II.

Works Cited

Bernauer, Rudolf. *Das Theater meines Lebens: Erinnerungen.* Berlin: Lothar Blanvalet, 1955.

Bierbaum, Otto Julius. *Stilpe: Ein Roman aus der Froschperspektive.* Berlin: Schuster & Loeffler, 1897.

Greul, Heinz. *Bretter, die die Zeit bedeuten: Die Kulturgeschichte des Kabaretts.* Köln: Kiepenheuer & Witsch, 1967.

Halbe, Max. *Sämtliche Werke.* Vol. 2. Salzburg: Bergland-Buch, 1945.

Herrmann-Neiße, Max. *Kabarett: Schriften zum Kabarett und zur bildenden Kunst.* Edited by Klaus Völker. Frankfurt: Zweitausendeins, 1988.

Jelavich, Peter. *Berlin Cabaret.* Cambridge, MA.: Harvard UP, 1993.

Lareau, Alan. *The Wild Stage: Literary Cabarets of the Weimar Republic.* Columbia, SC: Camden House, 1995.

Mehring, Walter. *Einfach klassisch! Eine Orestie mit glücklichem Ausgang.* Berlin: Fürstner, 1919.

———. *Das politische Cabaret.* Dresden: Kaemmerer, 1920.

Panizza, Oskar. "Der Klassizismus und das Eindringen des Variété." *Die Gesellschaft: Monatsschrift für Litteratur, Kunst und Sozialpolitik* 12 (1896): 1252–74.

Reinhardt, Max. *Schall und Rauch*. Berlin: Schuster, 1901.

Rösler, Walter. *Das Chanson im deutschen Kabarett 1901–1933*. Berlin: Henschel, 1980.

Schutte, Jürgen, and Peter Sprengel, eds. *Die Berliner Moderne*. Stuttgart: Reclam, 1987.

Sprengel, Peter, ed. *Schall und Rauch: Erlaubtes und Verbotenes*. Berlin: Nicolai, 1991.

———. *Literatur im Kaiserreich: Studien zur Moderne*. Berlin: Erich Schmidt, 1993.

"Zur Feier des Krönungsjubiläums." [Unsigned] *Berliner Börsen-Courier*, 18 January 1901, 1.

Of Weimar's First and Last Things: Montage, Revolution, and Fascism in Alfred Döblin's November 1918 *and* Berlin Alexanderplatz

Michael W. Jennings

By the mid-1920s, montage had established itself as the dominant syntax in the formal language utilized by writers, artists, and architects on the left in the Weimar Republic. For the Berlin Dadaists, photomontage provided the technical means for the figurative destruction of the old order—the order of art as well as that of society—as well as for the construction of a series of figures of a new, sometimes utopian social space. The development of a montage-syntax soon began to have an effect on a broad range of cultural objects ranging from advertising and photojournalism in the popular press through the application of Dada techniques (often by the former Dadas themselves) to the staging of political theater pieces by Erwin Piscator. In the early twenties, a parallel instance of montage practices became evident at the Weimar Bauhaus; first the experimental houses and then the *Siedlungen* influenced by Gropius and his colleagues show the possibilities inherent in a combination of montage with new construction materials and techniques centering on prefabrication. In 1925, with the widespread showing of Eisenstein's *Battlecruiser Potemkin,* a second wave of montage fever swept through Germany. First evident in such films as Walter Ruttmann's *Berlin, Symphony of a Great City,* cinematic montage initially served mainly to replicate the frantic, discontinuous space and pace of the urban metropolis. But, often with film as a proximate example, montage soon began to exert a widespread influence in literature, where its uses were more diverse. Walter Benjamin's *One Way Street* invents a form of verbal montage derived in equal parts from photomontage and cinema. Benjamin's intricate interlacing of the erotic and the political in this text not only pushes the limits of the representation of things, but also draws on Dadaist visual techniques in an attempt to figure a new kind of social space. Montage served, in short, as the primary means to the figuration of a new, visionary social space in the 1920s.

Alfred Döblin's adaption of montage techniques in his novels was, if not the first, then certainly the most widely recognized such novelistic practice in Weimar. Beginning with the novel *Wallenstein* in 1919, Döblin had developed what he at first termed a "cinema style" *(Kinostil),* but gradually came to term montage. His great novel of 1928, *Berlin Alexanderplatz,* was only the best known of his novels to employ montage. Within five years of the feverish success of *Berlin Alexanderplatz,* however, Döblin's works were added to the lists of books banned in fascist Germany, and Döblin became part of the flood of German intellectuals forced to flee Hitler and seek refuge abroad. In exile in France and the United States, Döblin continued to write and publish, producing a series of works in which he attempted, among other things, to analyze the rise and final victory of fascism in Germany. After an attempt at the traditional form of the novel in *Pardon wird nicht gegeben* of 1934, Döblin in his next two works—a historical novel on the colonization of the Amazon, *Das Land ohne Tod* of 1937–38, and *November 1918: Eine deutsche Revolution*—returned to the formal vocabulary of modernism that had characterized his work in the 1920s, and especially to literary montage. The reasons for that return are complex and form the crux of the present essay.

Döblin's novel of the German revolution, *November 1918,* has a composition and publication history that bears painful testimony to the problems of exile and to the truncations of world history at the time. Döblin began work on the novel in 1937 in Paris and finished it in 1943 in Hollywood; the first volume was published in 1938, the last three only in 1948–50. Döblin's novel portrays the revolutionary events of the period from 10 November 1918 through 6 January 1918; in a sort of epilogue, the novel follows the fortunes of Friedrich Becker, one of its central figures, in the years after the revolution. The particular, and particularly complex, temporal relationship of the time of composition—the acceleration and seeming success of fascist war policy—and the narrated time—the revolution that marked the birth of the Weimar Republic itself—informs every aspect of Döblin's work. *November 1918* attempts to occupy both temporal and political extremes of Weimar. It is written as a history, critique, and eulogy of the German Revolution of 1918 and it explores the ways in which the hope and the failure of that revolution are related to and in part responsible for German fascism.[1] Döblin's novel, moreover, offers poignant testimony to the particular strains, fissures, and contradictions that the rapidly changing political formations, deformations, and allegiances that dominated the Republic and the antifascist exile produced in the self-understanding of a representative bourgeois novelist. More so than most works of fiction, it exists as a simultaneously symptomatic, critical, and transformative text.[2]

For many readers, the critical aspects—Döblin's excoriation of a failed revolution—will dominate their experience of the work. *November 1918* is in no way merely a eulogy for the nobility of the German revolution; more often than not, the narrative voices in the novel conspire to offer a withering critique of the conduct and course of that revolution. The uncompromisingly critical stance of *November 1918* vis-à-vis the events it represents stems in equal parts from Döblin's remembrance of the failure of Germany's one chance at social equity on the one hand and from the conviction on the other that the ground was laid for the victory of National Socialism by the majority Socialists when they put down the workers' revolt with the help of the General Staff. His intended priorities emerge clearly in a letter of November 1938, early in the composition process: "Hauptsächlich [bin] ich mit einer epischen Arbeit wie immer beschäftigt, mit der Schilderung der deutschen Zusammenbruchzeit und 'Revolution.'"[3] The first volume, in fact, of *November 1918,* entitled *Bürger und Soldaten,* is an intensive analysis of the conditions which prepared for the revolution; for Döblin, those conditions were wholly negative ones, defined by the "time of collapse."[4] Döblin sides here with those historians who have argued against the use of the word "revolution," stressing that the events of late 1918 and early 1919 were instead a spontaneous, fragmented, and largely local series of reactions to the demise of the imperial war machine.[5]

Even the geography of the novel serves as a figure for the negativity with which much of the revolution is presented. While the novel as a whole is set largely in Berlin as the site of the major workers' uprisings, the first volume, which analyzes the historical structures from which the revolution arose, takes place entirely in Alsace, mainly in a small provincial garrison town, and in Strasbourg. Döblin's motivations for the choice of Alsace were certainly in part biographical: he had been stationed as an army doctor in the small town of Hagenau, thirty kilometers from Strasbourg. More importantly, though, Döblin is able, through the juxtaposition of the return of the German army through Alsace and the events in Berlin, to trace the beginnings of the revolutionary actions to the Imperial war policies and especially to the situation which followed immediately upon the armistice. In choosing to represent the collapse of the old order on the battlefield in France rather than the events traditionally associated with the beginning of the revolution–the sailors' mutiny in Kiel–Döblin emphasizes the deeper structure of the historical situation, and especially that the Republic was born from defeat and failure, a fact relentlessly exploited by the National Socialists in particular and the antidemocratic right in general.

Döblin traces the spread of the negativity resulting from the initial collapse in Alsace to the rest of Germany through the device of a military hospital. Hospitals have by now certainly emerged as one of the century's favorite general figures for a society in collapse; Mann's *Berghof* in *Der Zauberberg,* Peter Weiss's asylum at Charenton in *Marat / Sade,* and Lindsay Anderson's *Britannia Hospital* come readily to mind. Döblin's metaphor distinguishes itself from these, though, through its mobility. After the defeat, the hospital moves onto a train and rolls slowly through most of Germany, spreading the sick and the broken throughout the interior. The internal collapse and resulting internal disease of a nation is figured most fully in the chief doctor, who dies during the journey of blood poisoning. Döblin's use of the "blood" rhetoric of the conservative revolution of the early twentieth century, with its prefascist emphasis on the purity and power of German blood, is subtle here.[6] The corruption and lethal character of the leader's blood, together with the slow withering of the hospital train, are symbolic of larger developments in the nation. "Das Lazarett, das sein Haupt verloren hatte, brauchte nicht mehr lange Zeit, um sich ganz aufzulösen" (*November 1918,* I, 183).

In *Bürger und Soldaten,* the reader experiences not merely the news of the Kaiser's abdication and the declaration of the Republic, but especially the ways in which internal decay had come to dominate the adherents of imperial ideology in all classes. This decay, exacerbated by class interest, reveals itself at all levels of the novel. The confrontation between the old and the as yet unformed is thematized in a astonishing variety of ways in the first volume. Red soldiers invade a military hospital; the first Council of Soldiers and Workers is formed in Strasbourg, only to flee before the French; while the soldiers in the little town abolish all officer ranks, a telegram arrives from Ebert acknowledging that the generals will retain command of the field troops; a loyalist major is forced to attend the burial of two revolutionary soldiers murdered by a loyalist officer; patrols of soldiers charged with keeping the peace clash with a similarly charged "citizen's militia"; a new, ethically tarnished entrepreneurial class arises as citizens loyal to France expropriate the property of their "old German" neighbors fleeing eastward. Döblin's novel reminds the reader in powerful ways of the microhistory of any revolutionary action. Such moments in the novel, all of which remain highly ambiguous in the first volume, come to bear a progressively negative charge as the novel grows–the resistance to change by the middle classes and the gradually reawakening confidence of capital are aided by confusion and human weakness within the revolution itself.

But it would be a mistake to overemphasize the critical aspects of Döblin's novel to the exclusion of its attempt to unearth and commemorate the positive, emancipatory contributions of the time. For all its ironic, often devastatingly naked assessments of the effects of the revolution, *November 1918* nonetheless clearly sets itself many of the challenges inherent in a commemorative or, in Walter Benjamin's terminology, redemptive historiography. For the dozens of prominent German novelists writing in exile, the historical novel was a privileged form. For most of them, the historical object was more distant, the political allegories more deeply embedded and less directly presented than is the case in *November 1918*.[7] Nevertheless, all these works reveal a common conviction that German culture in exile was concerned above all else to look backward, and an impulse to move not only the "treasures of German culture," but key moments of the German past itself above the foreseeable high-water mark of the fascist advances. Döblin's novel was of course not the only novelistic account of the revolution. The events of 1918–19 figure prominently in many novels of the period such as Joseph Roth's *Das Spinnennetz* and Bernhard Keltermann's *Der neunte November*. But Döblin's was the only text to combine a modernist technique fully adequate to the revolutionary events with the scope and consciousness of detail of a major history. Döblin proceeded, over large stretches of his novel, to conform to the Benjaminian assertion: "A chronicler who recites events without distinguishing between major and minor ones acts in accordance with the following truth: nothing that has ever happened should be regarded as lost for history" (*Illuminations* 254). As was his practice for most of his novels, Döblin compiled an enormous archive of historical data before beginning to write. The resultant historical sweep and specificity of *November 1918* establish it as one of the earliest histories of the events in question. The revolutionary days triggered a number of *immediate* reactions in works published between 1919 and 1922, the best-known of which is Eduard Bernstein's *The German Revolution* of 1921. Yet aside from memoirs of participants, the revolution then sank with astonishing rapidity into oblivion, recounted in no single historical study—either in Weimar or in exile—until Döblin's novel. It is surely not an exaggeration to claim, then, that the revolution was effectively suppressed as a valid moment in German history and in particular the history of the Republic. We cannot discount the historiographical significance of the mere act of remembering the revolutionary actions. And Döblin was clearly aware of the historiographical implications of his novel, as I will argue below; *November 1918,* in fact, is in many ways an attack on the generic boundaries between history and literature erected in the nineteenth century.

We must read Döblin's massive—and massively flawed—novel in a way that acknowledges its attempt to save from oblivion a historical constellation central to German history. This does not, of course, necessarily mean that Döblin offers "straight" historical fiction. Throughout the novel, the historical voice is tempered and even undercut through various narrative devices. Particularly in the first volume, *Bürger und Soldaten,* which bears an emancipatory content that will gradually diminish in the course of the novel, the omniscience of the traditional narrative-historian is supplemented, and balanced, finally called into question through the creation of a veritable polyphony of voices from every segment of German society; these voices are lent a specificity, gravity, and autonomy such that a kind of perspectivism comes to replace traditional historical narrative. In displacing the pulse of representation from the univocal perspective of an authorial narrator to the multiple viewpoints of representatives of every class and occupation in the early days of the revolution, Döblin implicitly questions the adequacy of a traditional narrative history to events such as the November days. Narrative, with its privileging of broad generalization over discrete facts and events, its constraints, and its production of a sense of inevitability conveys a kind of history at odds with Döblin's individualistic, idiosyncratic vision.[8]

For his primary means of representation in *Bürger und Soldaten,* then, Döblin makes extensive use not of narrative history writing, but of montage, the technique that had made him famous in *Berlin Alexanderplatz* in 1928. He builds some montages in *November 1918* out of many of the same materials prevalent in the earlier novel: excerpts from newspapers and diaries, political manifestos and flyers, posters, and dozens of found objects. This montage, what we might call a montage of concrete particulars, is in fact thematized directly in the first volume. A dead soldier's possessions, including at the express wish of his mother everything found in his pockets, had been sent home: books, military travel passes, theater tickets, war bonds, a receipt for a nightshirt, letters, empty postcards, even a dispatch from the Kaiser to his army. The narrator inventories the entire package, and inserts frequent excerpts from the textual materials. Like the Dadaists and Benjamin, Döblin was intensely aware of the status of the material in the montage: the disparate, forlorn nature of these personal effects speaks movingly of the historical situation, which is too often remembered through abstraction and narrative. The Dadaists and Benjamin, working in the early years of the Republic, could draw on new kinds of resources in order to construct figures of a new social space. Their selection of concrete material (represented in visual or textual form) from the detritus of Imperial and early Republican society is telling: they chose material that had been discarded by the powerful, material that could play no role in the old order. This ideologically untainted material was exploited for its emancipatory potential. Döblin, however, writing in exile and looking back on two decades from which the hope for change had gradually drained away, treats this same detritus simply as detritus, as the broken remnants of a wasted life.

This is not, however, the dominant use of montage in *November 1918*. Instead, the montages in the first volume in particular are made up primarily of bits and pieces of human voices. Montage in *November 1918* is more often than not a literary analogue to polyphony. Why, though, does Döblin favor a form of montage primarily concerned to bear the sound of human voices over one primarily concerned to represent the lived environment? The story of Döblin's changing conception of the nature and function of montage–and the ways in which his society determined those changes–is instructive.

In the essay of 1919, "An Romanautoren und ihre Kritiker," Döblin calls for the creation of a "Kinostil" capable of depicting the "entseelte Realität" which confronts the modern individual (*Schriften* 121). Döblin's conception of this reality is considerably broader than that propounded by the Futurists, upon whose representational techniques he clearly draws. In each of the novels that followed this essay in the early 1920s, Döblin struggled to find a technique that could represent not only the physical, but the spiritual, invisible, and irrational elements of the world as well. In his great novel of 1928, *Berlin Alexanderplatz: The Story of Franz Biberkopf,* Döblin achieved, if not a full realization of his early goals, then certainly a paradigm of the use of montage in the modernist novel. The full title of Döblin's novel is crucial. It makes explicit the antagonistic relationship between Biberkopf and the area of Berlin around the Alexanderplatz, then one of the main working-class areas of the city. *Berlin Alexanderplatz* does not, then, represent Berlin, as is often claimed; Döblin is rigorous in the exclusion of all aspects of the city alien to the specific class milieu around the Alexanderplatz, with its mixing of class types: proletarians, petit-bourgeois merchants (though no *Beamten,* or civil servants, a far more numerous and important component of the German bourgeoisie), and especially *Lumpenproletariar,* impoverished workers wholly without class consciousness.

For the depiction of this and the chaotic, explosive life it holds, Döblin exploits the full range of representational possibilities. His montage contains statistics, pictures of street signs, slang, dialect, excerpts from streetcar timetables, proclamations, the technical discourse of medicine, political jargon, headlines, posters, and, to some extent, voices: voices of conductors, of sugar daddies, passersby, newspaper sellers, disobedient sons, and fearful mothers.[9] And Döblin hardly limited himself to the prose adaptation of static pictorial montage; by the time he wrote his novel, Eisenstein's films, and especially *Battlecruiser Potemkin,* had had an enormous impact in Germany; Walter Ruttman's *Berlin, Symphony of a Great City* was only the first sign of Eisenstein's reception. The influence of cinematic montage is everywhere evident in Döblin's novel: in the cuts between "shots," in the changes in the order in which events are depicted, in juxtapositions of scenes. Cinematic montage in fact largely substitutes for linear narrative; we find contrast montage, parallel montage, and a form of montage which represents events occurring simultaneously.[10] The aim of all these techniques was immediacy.

Döblin's creation of a totalizing environment by use of the montage is brilliant. Better than any of his predecessors, he achieves in art the concrete objectivity of life in the metropolis. *Berlin Alexanderplatz* was immediately recognized as a breakthrough in the modern novel. As Brecht wrote to Döblin: "ich möchte die aufmerksamkeit möglichst vieler also auf meinen außerordentlichen fleiß lenken, mit dem ich Ihre literarischen werke studiert und die vielfachen neuerungen, die Sie in die betrachtungs und beschreibungsweise unserer umwelt und des zusammenlebens der menschen eingebracht haben, mir zu eigen gemacht habe."[11]

Problematically enough, however, the very brilliance and force of this evocation is the crux of the central difficulty in the novel: Biberkopf's role as human agent. It is the montage technique itself, with its inherent appearance of chaos and fragmentation, which most powerfully suggests to the reader the confusions inherent in Biberkopf's encounter with his world: the political, economic, and social subsystem within which he lives. One factor needs to be singled out here: unlike other Weimar artists such as the Dadaists in their photomontages, the followers of Eisenstein in the cinema, or even other pioneers in textual montage such as Walter Benjamin in his *One Way Street,* Döblin uses montage to focus in a concentrated way on the debris of the city in its singularity. There is no systematic will behind the individual evocations other than the effort to replicate mimetically the chaos and shock-character of the individual impressions in their cumulative effect. Had Döblin sought to evoke some such system or figure in the city's carpet, he would have had at his disposal either the optical or, in the case of prose, figuratively optical strategies employed in photomontage and the prose essay—the construction of associations and reverberations among the discrete elements in the montage—or, more directly, the intervention of an authorial narrator who could control the montage and mediate its effects. That Döblin does neither is significant. The discrete elements—street sign or proclamation—are most often simply inserted into the texture of the novel, suddenly interrupting the narrative flow, like a rock in a stream.

> Seine Nasenspitze vereiste, über seine Backe schwirrte es. "Zwölf Uhr Mittagszeitung", "B.Z.", "Die neuste Illustrirte", "Die Funkstunde neu"

"Noch jemand zugestiegen?" Die Schupos haben jetzt blaue Uniformen. (8–9)

In this description of Biberkopf on a street car, the rapid alternation of narrative modes—from authorial narration to direct quotation of the conductor's voice as Biberkopf hears it and further to the narrated monologue of Biberkopf's reaction (clearly signalled by the slang term "Bulle" or cop)—is punctuated by the unmediated insertion of the advertisements for newspapers and magazines displayed just below the streetcar's ceiling.

This combination of montage, narrated monologue, and neutral authorial narration is an accurate representation of Biberkopf's thought processes, which are limited throughout the novel to immediate association. The montage technique suggests to the reader the confusions inherent in Biberkopf's encounter with the world. It becomes visible and palpable that he is overcome by his world because he has nothing with which to counter it. In fact, so powerful is that evocation of environment, and so correspondingly weak are the resources given Biberkopf—and the other main characters as well—that the novel's characters are systematically determined by the represented world. They are little more than mirrors of external events, reacting to those events in their interiority.[12]

The forms of thought and feeling represented in *Berlin Alexanderplatz* are relentlessly tied to the chaos of the city. Since Döblin's portrait of that city is intensely critical, these thoughts and feelings are inevitably devalorized as denatured or sick. Biberkopf after his release from prison progressively loses the ability to distinguish exteriority and internal resolve, to distinguish the proper sequence and value of the manifestations of the world around him. "Bloß sind die Straßen da, da hört man und sieht man allerhand, fällt einem von früher wat ein, was man gar nicht will, und dann zieht sich das Leben so hin...(258). The tempo of this stream of associations, of Biberkopf's inner film, is determined solely by the varying pace with which external stimuli reach him. The sequence works both ways. In one case, Biberkopf encounters as an element of the montage a series of scenes from a pornographic movie; these images trigger not merely sexual desire, but also the memory of his crime, the rape and murder of his mistress. These reactions remain distinct until they are integrated in an action informed by repetition compulsion, the seduction/rape of the sister of his dead mistress. In a more complex manner, though, the environment as narrated can call up remembered associations which are themselves represented through montage.

Er wanderte die Rosenthaler Straße am Warenhaus Tietz vorbei, nach rechts bog er ein in die schmale Sophienstraße. Er dachte, diese Straße ist dunkler, wo es dunkel ist, wird es besser sein. Die Gefangenen werden in Einzelhaft, Zellenhaft und Gemeinschaftshaft untergebracht. Bei Einzelhaft wird der Gefangene bei Tag und Nacht unausgesetzt von andern Gefangenen gesondert gehalten. Bei Zellenhaft wird der Gefangene in einer Zelle untergebracht, jedoch bei Bewegung im Freien, beim Unterricht, Gottesdienst mit andern zusammengebracht. (9-10)

Here, Biberkopf instinctively seeks isolation in a dark street which seems to offer freedom from the demands placed upon him by contact with others, any capacity for which was taken from him in prison. The causal sequence is thus reversed; he has a dim sense of the causes for his actions, while those causes themselves are called up not through Biberkopf's memory of the prison, but through the montage of the text of the prison regulations in the novel.

So powerful is this evocation of a life lived as a series of shocks with concrete causes that the novel at times–the beginning of books two and four, for example–threatens to become little more than an archive of stimuli and associative processes. Döblin attempts to check this tendency through use of narrative voice. The authorial narrator's voice moves freely between a distanced reportage and that of a highly stylized, moralizing *Moritatensänger*. The introductions to each book evince with cumulative force the attempt on the part of the narrator to lend shape to the narrative, to direct the reader's understanding. This desire for form and control reveals itself, for example, in the increasing use of rhyme and meter in the prose introductions: "Er hebt gegen die dunkle Macht die Faust, er fühlt etwas gegen sich stehen, aber er kann es nicht sehen, es muß noch geschehen, daß der Hammer gegen ihn saust" (191). The localized effect of this narrator is Brechtian. The particular combination of neutral reporting and sententious evaluation which characterizes the authorial narrator, together with the unmediated, at times bestial immediacy of Biberkopf's responses, ensures that the reader is constantly distanced from the protagonist. Empathy for Biberkopf comes at a high price: to maintain empathy, the reader must in some sense become complicitous with a false subjectivity. Döblin sought more than this, however.

In attempting to chronicle Biberkopf's life, the narrator also attempts to make of him an exemplary figure, as seen in the increasing use of mythological references and tonality. In his principal attempt to construct a theory of the novel, "Der Bau des epischen Werks" of 1928, Döblin argues that the novel is concerned with a "super-real" sphere beyond the "historischen, aktenmäßig belegten Fakten," "eine wahre Sphäre" which can be achieved through the representation of "das Exemplarische des Vorgangs und der Figuren"; "diese menschlichen Ursituationen stehen sogar an Ursprünglichkeit, Wahrheit und Zeugungskraft über den zerlegten Tageswahrheiten" (106f). The dense symbol complexes, which include parables, individual symbols, and allegories; the complex web of foreshadowings and warnings, intertextual allusions, and symbolic exaggerations all contribute to this claim for exemplary stature.

Leaving aside the relative merit of this position, it is excessively clear in *Berlin Alexanderplatz* that Döblin could not achieve for Biberkopf the exemplarity he sought. The coercive effect of the montage discussed above militates strongly against this; moreover, the narrative voice, with which Döblin sought to claim for Biberkopf's life a paradigmatic quality, escapes his control. The novel is narrated not by one narrative voice, but by many. Aside from the sententious narrator discussed above, the first three pages of the novel alone hold the voices of a neutral, reportorial narrator, interior and narrated monologues associated with various characters, and a voice we might call the exemplary narrator whose tone and intentions vary consistently from those of the sententious narrator. The distinction between these narrators is clear in the contrast between statements such as the sententious narrator's "Damit ist unser guter Mann, der sich bis zuletzt stramm gehalten hat, zur Strecke gebracht," and the exemplary narrator's "Die Strafe beginnt" (4). The reader who is aware of these voices encounters a vexing number of assertions whose origin and perspective are simply indeterminate. As a technical achievement, Döblin's narrative has undeniable brilliance; the multiplicity and complexity of his voices compare favorably with the deconstructive irony of Musil's narrators or even the genius of Kafka's strategies for ensuring readerly complicity in his narratives of guilt. Yet, in the end, the narrative voices of *Berlin Alexanderplatz* are too many, their effects too diverse.

Compounded by the coerciveness of the montaged environment, these indeterminate perspectives culminate in the final political ambiguity of Döblin's novel. The sententious narrator claims that the ending–which finds a putatively rehabilitated Biberkopf observing, from his post as a nightwatchman, a political rally as it marches past–is unambiguous and that it brings with it a political enlightenment. "Wir"–that is, the readers of the novel–"sind eine dunkle Allee gegangen, keine Laterne brannte zuerst...allmählich wird es heller und heller, zuletzt hängt die Laterne, und dann liest man endlich unter ihr das Straßenschild" (409). Biberkopf, by contrast, was forced to run a gauntlet to reach that same state of illumination. "Mit zerlöcherten Kopf, kaum noch bei Sinnen, kam er schließlich doch an. Wie er hinfiel, machte er die Augen auf. Da brannte die Laterne hell über ihm, und das Schild was zu lesen" (409). Yet this costly enlightenment shows itself very soon to be nothing more than the deepest ambiguity. The final pages of the novel intersperse sententious authorial narration with large swatches of interior monologue, much of which is self-contradictory. "Viel Unglück kommt davon, wenn man allein geht," Biberkopf can assert in one paragraph, while in the next, "Wenn wir zwei sind, ist es schon schwerer, stärker zu sein als ich" (409). The issue of the integration of the individual into a larger social ensemble, which is the central issue of the novel and in many ways of Döblin's career, is resolved only in negative and even contradictory terms. The dominant impression– that the represented environment is a coercive force which determines absolutely the social, economic, and political shape of human lives–is reinforced by the book's ending. Its deliberate ambiguity mirrors the fragmentation of the narrative voice and of the ambient environment. The area around the Alexanderplatz (in the figure of the Whore of Babylon) has, to be sure, been banished from the narrative; there are relatively few montage effects in the final chapters. But the aftershocks remain: Biberkopf is deprived of rational choice and even volition. Far from imagining new social forms, the montage in *Berlin Alexanderplatz* figures social space as absolute negativity. This is the final paradox of the novel: Döblin's aesthetically most fully realized text is given its decisive shape by political uncertainty. How are we to approach this paradox from our much later vantage point?

Writing *November 1918* in the late 1930s, Döblin confronted not merely a changed audience and a changed historical situation but a new task for the montage form. The new conception of montage is immediately evident in the first volume of the tetralogy. In the first place, montage is less frequently employed as the unmediated insertion of elements of the experienced world. When objects, excerpts from texts, or other concrete manifestations do enter the novel, they consistently display their relation to their immediate context.[13] In an early episode, a newspaper enters the novel as a montage element. But we experience the newspaper from the perspective of a character reading; as the newspaper reader's eye strays from a serialized novel to the report of Max von Baden's relinquishment of the chancellorship, the reader of the novel receives a clear, even heavy-handed thematic message: for the average bourgeois reader in 1918, the momentous political events were marginal, even coincidental, coequal to the fictions of the popular novel. Insofar, then, as the sensuous detail of everyday life is evoked through the montage in *November 1918,* Döblin is careful to put that detail into perspective, avoiding the necessity of representing an environment—as he had in *Berlin Alexanderplatz*—that is coercive because of the contrast between the evocative brilliance of its technique and the pervasive passivity of the represented humans. In order that his characters retain some power of resistance, Döblin in *November 1918* resorts to an aesthetically conservative though politically stable form of montage.

More important than this strategy of contextualization, though, is a major rethinking of the concept of montage itself. The structure of *Bürger und Soldaten* derives in equal parts from Döblin's own experience with montage and from his study of the principles of Brecht's epic theater. The Brechtian influence in the novel is unmistakable. Like the scenes in Brecht's plays, each short section of the first volume of the tetralogy achieves a high degree of autonomy; although each section may eventually take its place in a larger narrative development, it is just as likely to function formally or thematically as a comparison or a counterpoint to another section from another plot strand.

Döblin's use of the epic technique, however, differs finally from that of Brecht. Where Brecht sought to create a distanced space in the theater for the sort of informed reflection which might lead to political action, Döblin adapts the main virtues of the technique to the achievement of a new diversity in the novel. Within each autonomous section, the human voice of the figures portrayed there also achieves a profile and autonomy otherwise impossible. The formal device of separating typographically each short section only enhances this effect. When, as is frequently the case, Döblin embeds within a short section the montage of many voices, this effect is intensified. This is nowhere clearer than in the representation of a meeting of the Strasbourg Workers' and Soldiers' Council. The sailors from Alsace who have just returned from the marine revolt at Kiel launch into the "International," but the narrator reports that many of the local insurgents do not know the words. For them it was "kein Klassengesang, sondern Kriegsende, Friede, menschliche Freiheit" (46).

Döblin was of course not the only European literary figure in the late 1930s interested in polyphony and diversity in the novel. Mikhail Bakhtin's ideas on heteroglossia figure here not so much as interpretive devices, but as exemplification of a utopian hope for the novel that parallels Döblin's own.

> What is involved here is a very important, in fact a radical revolution in the destinies of human discourse: the fundamental liberation of cultural-semantic and emotional intentions from the hegemony of a single and unitary language, and consequently the simultaneous loss of a feeling for language as myth, that is, as an absolute form of thought. (Bakhtin 366)

The rhetoric of this passage—with its use of terms such as liberation, revolution, and hegemony to describe a process occurring within the autonomous world of the genre of the novel—hints at the subterranean critique of totalitarianism intended by Bakhtin. And his is not an isolated theoretical endeavor. In exile in Paris in the 1930s, Walter Benjamin tried to construct what he thought of as a "primal history" of the nineteenth century that bore the working title "The Arcades Project" (*Das Passagen-Werk*). Just as Bakhtin's theories emphasize the polymorphous quality of the human voice in the novel, so Benjamin's theory, constructed through the montage, brings to the fore a vast array of French and other voices that had been suppressed from conventional histories of the era. Spoken discourse from all classes, popular song, political rhetoric, overheard conversations, and many other forms appear in order to give voice to those who had been forgotten.[14] Bakhtin, Benjamin, and Döblin clung to a leftist position that sought to counter the totalitarian regimes under which or against which they wrote. But Döblin's novel, like the theories of Bakhtin and Benjamin, has an ostensible countertheme: the failure of the socialist revolution, which was too German, too privatized, too theoretical, and could not sustain the tremendous weight of signification—and of hope—borne in each case by the human voice.

With astonishing frequency, the voices of the first volume remain anonymous or are tied to characters involved in tiny, transitory subplots within this massive text. And those voices are raised most often in a kind of counterpoint to the larger, historical movements in the novel. The German retreat, with its air of doom and resignation, plays against literally dozens of vignettes in which common soldiers, officers, bourgeoisie, workers, and farmers find opportunities for renewal on an individual level; when several of these individuals come together in loose networks, the effect is created of a potential break in the weave of seeming inevitability that is the history of the revolution. At times, Döblin goes so far as to attribute a consciousness of the mendacity of larger historical structures to the anonymous voices themselves:

> Lies, was sie schreiben über uns, wer wir sind. Das ist aus uns geworden.—Ja, und das ist wahr. Jetzt werden einem die Augen geöffnet. Wie man uns belogen hat. Die drüben. Ruinert haben sie uns.—Hätten wir's doch erkannt. Hätten wir's nicht mitgemacht. Hätten wir uns zur Wehr gesetzt.—Hätten, hätten. (I, 353)

From almost any conceivable later perspective, the modicum of resistance offered here must seem pathetic. Döblin's brilliant evocation of a concrete environment in *Berlin Alexanderplatz* was undercut, as we have seen, by an ultimately incoherent mix of narrative voices to lend to that novel at best a political ambiguity, at worst a social untenability. That novel was free, however, of the particular historical doubleness that shaped *November 1918*. Döblin's attempt to review the revolution as at once an important step toward fascism and a quarry for images and impulses that might allow for resistance makes for a difficult relationship between narrative and montage. At an important point in volume two, in fact, the narrator reflects on the tension between traditional historical explanation, with its emphasis on causality, and the sudden, spontaneous emergence of discrepancy and resistance.

> Es gibt eine Sorte von Erzählern und Geschichtsschreibern, die auf Logik, auf nichts als Logik schwören. Für sie folgt in der Welt eins aus dem andern, und die betrachten es als ihre Aufgabe, dies zu zeigen und die Dinge entsprechend auseinander zu entwickeln. Sie machen für jeden Vorgang der Geschichte einen andern ausfindig, aus dem er sich dann ergibt....Wir sind nicht von einer solchen logischen Strenge. Wir halten die Natur für viel leichtfertiger als die genannten Geschichts- und Geschichtenschreiber. (II, 385)

The montage of the human voice is very often that which breaks into and disrupts the seemingly inevitable narrative flow in *Bürger und Soldaten*. It remains the site of a lonely and perhaps unobtainable hope for Döblin. Through this device he does not so much figure a social space—the lived environments of the later novel, particularly in comparison to the 1928 evocation of the Alexanderplatz, remain almost abstract—as a disembodied society itself, a collection of voices that speak out of a no-place, a utopia, and toward another no-place, a hell on earth.

In the subsequent volumes, which depict the revolutionary events themselves, an unusually thoroughgoing analytic pessimism comes gradually to dominate, and that pessimism is borne primarily by a unified and highly intrusive narrative voice: the montage of voices characteristic of the first volume all but disappears. On the broad historical plane so important to the novel, Friedrich Ebert and the majority socialists bear the brunt of Döblin's scorn for their complicity with the generals, for their butchery of the workers in January, for the hypocrisy with which they understand socialism. But the SPD is by no means made the scapegoat for the more general failure of the revolution. No position, no party, no individual escapes the mixture of sarcasm, pity, and scorn which characterizes much of the narrative. Much of the analysis and criticism in *November 1918* was, in fact, common to the period immediately following the war. In his satirical depiction of war profiteers, of the mania for stability at any cost evinced by the *Großbürger,* of the poverty of effective leadership, of the mentality which formed and served in the *Freikorps,* of the allied peace policy, and of the impoverished theory and practical bumblings of the leftist leaders of the revolution, Döblin finally only echoes frequently-heard laments from 1919 on. He himself had in fact given voice to many of these sentiments in *Der deutsche Maskenball von Linke Poot* of 1921, a text based on occasional, pseudonymous cultural commentary which he had written for newspapers and journals in the period during and after the revolution.

The first sign of a new relationship between narrative voice, other voices in the novel, and the course of German history is immediately apparent on the first page of volume two, *Verratenes Volk.* The initial chapter, "Sturm auf das Polizeipräsidium," begins with a summary of what is to follow: "Ein junger Mensch kehrt aus dem Krieg zurück, gewinnt dem Leben in Berlin keinen Reiz ab und trifft andere, denen es ebenso geht. Einige aufgeregte Leute stürmen das Polizeipräsidium und können danach besser schlafen. Es ist der 22. November 1918" (9). Such summaries are wholly absent from the first volume of the novel. The narrative voice here demonstrates a personal investment in the events represented, as the colloquial tone and the final irony make clear; but far from the shifting perspectives characteristic of *Bürger und Soldaten,* this voice seeks to control and shape the events, guiding the reader through the material toward a predetermined evaluation. This shift from a localized to a purportedly global perspective is underscored by the narrator's adoption of a conspicuous, ironized first-person-plural perspective: the "we" that gradually emerges as a narrative voice claims a universality and a complicity in the desire for control that the narrative itself does not justify. The narrator in fact resorts to a myriad of narrative conventions in his desire to control and comment on events. In the course of the novel's second volume, montage of voices as a device is displaced by a series of vignettes that are so juxtaposed as to drive home a thematic point, as when a portrait of Ebert and his dealings with the military is bracketed by the story of a petty war profiteer. By the middle of the volume, the narrative voice has retreated into an archaic, sententious voice appropriated from eighteenth-century novels such as *Tristram Shandy.* In a section entitled "Der Verfasser geht mit sich zu Rate," the narrator has this to say:

> Überblicken wir an diesem Punkt die Ereignisse, die verflossen sind und uns unabwendbar überströmen, und bedenken wir, von einer erklärlichen plötzlichen Müdigkeit überfallen unter dem unaufhaltsamen Ansturm der Begebenheiten (und es sind erst zwanzig Tage der Revolution vorbei), was nun kommen wird, so ist uns schon einiges klar: Mit der Revolution wird es auf diese Weise nicht vorwärtsgehen. Es wird mit ihr

wahrscheinlich rückwärtsgehen. Bisher sind wirklich revolutionäre Massen nicht in unser Gesichtsfeld getreten. Man kann einem, wenn er eine Revolution beschreiben will, dies zum Vorwurf machen. Aber es liegt nicht an uns. Es ist eben eine deutsche Revolution. (242)

As the novel progresses, such devices become not only more frequent, but positively intrusive. In *Berlin Alexanderplatz* montage served not to figure a collective but to produce a new kind of realism in the novel, an evocation of the concrete reality of a part of Berlin; the narrative voices wove a complex pattern of indeterminacy around that represented environment. In *November 1918* the attempt to figure a collective gives way abruptly to a narrator who seeks an absolute control. Most tellingly, the montage is replaced in the last three volumes by a narrative device in which the narrator assumes the voices of a series of characters: now that of Becker, now that of an anonymous bourgeois supporter of Noske, Ebert's "bloodhound." D.H. Lawrence's injunction to trust the tale, not the teller is wholly appropriate to *November 1918*. The pretension to control and power demonstrated by the narrator of the last three volumes is symptomatic of a consciousness that is unwilling to allow historical events in their singularity to speak for themselves. It is the voice of a consciousness intent upon lacerating the historical past for its complicity in the historical present.

How do we account for the shift from the new uses of montage to a highly manipulative, even authoritarian narrative voice? This shift in tonality from the conflict between narrative history and the montage of voices characteristic of *Bürger und Soldaten* to the nearly pervasive bitterness of the remaining three volumes is of course a reflection twenty years after the fact on a failed revolution; the title of Helmuth Kiesel's study, *Literarische Trauerarbeit,* captures something of this. Some of Döblin's critics have ascribed differences in the last three volumes (without quite articulating the differences between them and the first volume) to Döblin's conversion to Christianity, which indeed occurred "between" the volumes. But this conversion itself, as much as the change in narrative pattern, seems less a cause than a symptom of a desperate search for control and significance in Döblin's life and writing.

For some understanding of this shift, it is necessary to trace, however briefly, Döblin's political path. The last three volumes make it quite clear that even a successful revolution such as the one envisioned by Karl Liebknecht and the Spartacists would have provoked a similarly negative reaction from Alfred Döblin in 1938. Much of the discussion of political theory in *November 1918* centers on internal debates on the course and goals of the revolution which take place between Liebknecht and Lenin's emissary to the German revolution, Karl Radek. Although the portraits which emerge of these historical figures are sympathetic, they also contain a marked amount of skepticism. This skepticism stems not so much from either an antirevolutionary or anticollectivist stance, nor yet from a kind of Christian resignation following Döblin's conversion, but rather from his rejection of the actual course of the revolution in favor of his own, revisionist political theory.

At the time of the revolution, Döblin had thrown his support to the USPD, the Independent Social Democrats who occupied a position between that of the political center and the active left. His experiences under the Republic gradually moved him leftwards: he joined the "Society of the Friends of the New Russia" in 1924, and became a founding member of the "Group 1925," an association of communist and left-liberal authors which included Brecht and Johannes R. Becher. Late in the decade, however, Döblin began to distance himself from an actively engaged politics. His election to the Prussian Academy of the Arts in 1928 occasioned a bitter debate and finally a split between left-liberal and communist authors; the latter finally seceded from Group 1925 and founded the German Union of Proletarian-Revolutionary Writers (Bund proletarisch-revolutionärer Schriftsteller Deutschlands or BPRSD).[15] The general movement in Döblin's thinking away from direct engagement culminated in the philosophical monograph *Unser Dasein* of 1933. This text is worth examining not only for the light it sheds on the novel, but in particular as a document symptomatic of the position of the exiled left-liberal Weimar intellectual.

Döblin's essential position proceeds from an assertion of the absolute priority of the individual: "Die Grundposition bleibt unerschüttert: daß wir uns auszuwirken und darzustellen suchen und dabei unsere Umwelt formen" (185). So strong, in fact, is the individualistic bias here that much of the latter part of the book is given over to an attack on all forms of collectivist organization. These sections stand under the sign of a strong reversion to the Nietzscheanism of Döblin's youth: "Und wir sind selber sehr zahm geworden, Gesellschaftstiere und Herdentiere" (348). Spontaneous collectivity is, to be sure, sanctioned in the book; it is apostrophized as the precondition for an intense awareness of individual existence. But organization in any form is subjected to a virulent, if hardly stringent critique. The public sphere is a "Moloch," organizations and collectives "unwahre Gebilde" which are "das Übel von heute" (418).

> Und die tausend Millionen armer Menschen, die in den Netzen hingen, was blieb ihnen weiter übrig, als mit zu schreien und zu stammeln: Krieg, Frieden, national, international, und verbrachten ihr Leben unter dem Netz wie eine grüne Pflanze unter dem Netz des Schimmelpilzes, der Pilz saugt sie aus, aber die Pflanze hat bald keinen anderen Ehrgeiz als zu sagen: sieh mal her, was gab ich dem Pilz für Kraft, was leiste ich, wie tüchtig ich bin. (423)

At the time these words were written in 1933, the identities of the plant and fungus were hardly clouded. Certainly from our present perspective, Döblin's skepticism as to the resiliency of leftist organizations and their ability to resist appropriation by fascism seems warranted.

It is worth noting that this idea of parasitic growth persists for Döblin: the careful mix in the novel's first volume of negativity and optimism is often expressed through organically-derived figurative language similar to that cited here. There are more than a few indications that something positive could be made to arise on the burned ground. In fact, this passage appears again, nearly word for word, in *Bürger und Soldaten,* where we find a long and botanically accurate description of the growth stages of the hops plant, followed by an equally lengthy disquisition on the varieties of pest which will feed on, infect, and finally suck the life from the new plants. The metaphors for new life—row after row of equal plants growing from newly arable ground—and the indigenous forces already in place to rob it of possibility and fruition sum up Döblin's pessimism in the first volume (*November 1918,* I, 89). But the remaining volumes of the novel cast not fascism itself, but rather an excessive, and excessively theoretical party organization in the role of the fungus that spreads over the workers' movement. In *Unser Dasein* Döblin offers an evaluation of the political party which finds its fictional counterpart in *November 1918:* parties can be positive forces insofar as they remain "flüssige Einrichtungen, bewegliche Organisationen." "Sie treten den eisernen Einrichtungen von Staat und Wirtschaft gegenüber als Feuer und Schmelztiegel auf. Schrecklicherweise verfestigen auch sie, erstarren, erlöschen. Nur eine Kraft bleibt Kraft, der lebende Mensch, der annimmt und verwirft....Wir sind weder für Individualismus noch Kollektivismus, sondern für das Ich" (*Unser Dasein* 435).[16]

In what collective shape, then, does the individual renewal called for by Döblin take place? In his political credo *Wissen und Verändern* of 1931, Döblin had called for an "protocommunist socialism" without, however, defining precisely what he meant. Much of *Unser Dasein* is given over precisely to a definition of this new political form. So strong is Döblin's resistance to theorized organization that his position becomes rigidly pragmatic: "Wir leisten, was wir für nötig halten, das genügt uns—die heutige Abwendung des Unheils, Beseitigung eines Übels, Schaffung neuer Lagen. Es ist nicht Sache der Menschen, Historie zu treiben, aber es ist ihre Sache, mit den Dingen um sich, in ihrer konkreten Lagerung, fertig zu werden....Daraus wächst Geschichte" (*Unser Dasein* 226). His primary example is Lenin, whom he praises not so much for his vision and theoretical power, but rather for his willingness to use violence against evil. Döblin's position thus rejects the sort of historical vision associated with all forms of scientific socialism. His is a Blanquist politics, a "ständige Auseinandersetzung allein mit den gegenwärtigen Zuständen" (230). The only human associations countenanced by Döblin are spontaneous, natural ones which answer to a concrete and present need; he offers the relationships between man and woman, parents and children, or common work such as communal erection of shelter, as examples. The search for a "wirklich flutende[s] Leben" (420) leads Döblin to the following statement, as close as he will come to a definitive statement of his politics after 1933:

> Die Menschen müssen deutlicher ihren Zustand und seine Ursachen erkennen und müssen von Gleichmütigkeit, Abstraktionen und Dogmen befreit und an die vernünftige Pflege ihrer Interessen geführt werden.

> Was Zusammenleben ist, müssen sie erst wieder lernen, und hier sind
> Keimzellen zu legen für die kleinen übersichtlichen Systeme, von denen
> ich sagte, daß sie allein imstande seien, menschliche Gesellschaftsor-
> ganismen zu bilden. (*Unser Dasein* 473)

Döblin's explicit model is the Greek city-state, with its reliance upon the collective decision-making capacity of all citizens. His model is more clearly derived, though, from the various political forms advocated and in some cases realized in the early days following the 1918 revolution. We should keep in mind the extraordinary possibility open to Germany in 1919. Every one of the literally hundreds of political associations in Germany—anarchists, syndicalists, anarchosyndicalists, monarchists, religious parties, socialists, utopian socialists, et cetera—had a particular vision of the new society. If history has chosen to remember that possibility along strictly dualistic lines—council republic or national assembly—then a multitude of other options, some of them radically new, some of them well-tested, and many of them hybrids, have been lost from memory. My point is that such historical oblivion has dulled the exhilaration and obscured those genuine attempts to imagine new possibilities that accompanied, briefly, the chance to form a new society. Döblin's is a form, then, of the sort of "basis-democracy" advocated later by the American New Left and by the Greens in contemporary Germany. It is too easy to dismiss Döblin's politics, to consign it to the dustbins reserved for utopias.

I have described, of course, the political vision that underlies only the first volume of the tetralogy. In the final three, Döblin's concern for the difficulties of the individual and in particular the difficulty of identity formation—after the war and under fascism—becomes dominant, indeed suffocating. In the final volumes, the chronicle function is balanced not by montages of voices, but by the traditional narration of the lives of Friedrich Becker and Erwin Stauffer. Döblin was equally attuned, then, to Benjamin's sense of how only the fullness of history can offer redemption: "To be sure, only a redeemed mankind receives the fullness of its past—which is to say, only for a redeemed mankind has its past become citable in all its moments" (*Illuminations* 254). Redemption, in fact, offers a note common to many discourses of the years immediately preceding the Second World War. Just as Benjamin's religiosity rises to the surface of his discourse in this period, so, too, does Döblin's novel increasingly organize itself around narratives devoted to figures in search of redemption: the war invalid Friedrich Becker and the dramatist Erwin Stauffer.[17] While Döblin never surrenders the historical sweep of the novel, and while the impressive multiplicity of characters and narrative situations is never wholly given up, these two narrative strands emerge as foci of attention. Each of these strands concerns above all else the intensely personal problem of the formation of identity after the war—and, by extension, in exile.[18] Ironically enough, then, the gradual emergence of a highly intrusive narrative voice in the last three volumes speaks not to Döblin's identification with and involvement in the events portrayed, but to his frustration with his and his country's failure to draw the consequences hinted at by the panoply of voices heard early in the novel. Friedrich Becker, impoverished and probably insane, is drowned in a sack at the novel's end. The apparent sovereignty of the narrative voice, weighted down with Döblin's fear and despair, sinks with it.

Notes

[1] The two major accounts of Döblin's production in exile are Helmut Kiesel, *Literarische Trauerarbeit: Das Exil- und Spätwerk Alfred Döblins* (Tübingen: Max Niemeyer, 1986) and Manfred Auer, *Das Exil vor der Vertreibung. Motivkontinuität und Quellenproblematik im späten Werk Alfred Döblins* (Bonn: Bouvier, 1977).

[2] On this terminology, see Dominick LaCapra, *History, Politics, and the Novel* (Ithaca: Cornell UP, 1987), 7.

[3] Alfred Döblin, *Briefe* (Olten: Walter, 1970), 228.

[4] The two volumes published in English as *A People Betrayed* and *Karl and Rosa* include in abridged form only the last three volumes of the tetralogy. *Bürger und Soldaten,* in many ways the most interesting and important of the volumes, was inexplicably discarded. *Karl and Rosa,* translated by John E. Woods (New York: Fromm International Pub. Corp., 1983); *A People Betrayed,* trans. John E. Woods (New York: Fromm International Pub. Corp., 1983).

[5] Detlev Peukert distinguishes between a long line of historians who date Weimar's troubles from the revolution itself, and others who see the revolutionary actions as unrealized possibilities. Peukert, *The Weimar Republic: The Crisis of Classical Modernity* (New York: Hill and Wang, 1993), xii.

[6] The best studies of the conservative revolution remain George Mosse, *The Crisis of German Ideology* (New York: 1964); Fritz Stern, *The Politics of Cultural Despair* (New York: 1961); and Kurt Sontheimer, *Antidemokratisches Denken in der Weimarer Republik* (Munich: 1968).

[7] Remarkably little systematic attention has been paid to the historical novels produced by the German exiles. Bruce Broermann, in his *The German Historical Novel in Exile after 1933: Calliope Contra Clio* (University Park: Pennsylvania State UP, 1986) makes a very tentative, almost exclusively thematic start.

[8] Here, too, Döblin's practice parallels that of Walter Benjamin. In folder "N" of *Das Passagen-Werke* Benjamin argues repeatedly for the existence of compelling parallels between narrative, bourgeois history writing, and the stories of domination that such narratives convey. Benjamin, *Das Passagen-Werk* (Frankfurt am Main: Suhrkamp, 1981), 571–611.

[9] Russell Berman has seen in *Berlin Alexanderplatz* a "vocalization of the collective," but the term seems misapplied, since anonymous voices play a minor role as compared to the evocation of the city as concrete environment; furthermore, these voices belong not to a class-conscious stratum of workers, i.e., a "collec-

Jennings: Of Weimar's First and Last Things   151

tive," but to *Lumpenproletarier.* Berman, *The Rise of the Modern German Novel* (Cambridge, MA: Harvard UP, 1985), 234.

[10] For a convincing articulation of Döblin's use of cinematic montage in his novel, see Ekkehard Kaemmerlin, "Die filmische Schreibweise," in Prangel, ed., *Materialien zu Alfred Döblins 'Berlin Alexanderplatz'* (Frankfurt am Main: Suhrkamp, 1975).

[11] Bertolt Brecht, 1932 letter to Döblin, cited in Roland Link, *Alfred Döblin* (Munich: Beck, 1981), 7.

[12] There is a considerable critical controversy on this point. Both Dollenmayer and Berman construe the city montage here as emancipatory, in that it allows the reader to construct the patterns of relation and significance; only Link argues for the denatured and denaturing effect of Döblin's use of montage here. Dollenmayer 131; Link 124–32; Berman 237.

[13] Dollenmayer simply refers to this practice as "conventional." David R. Dollenmayer, *The Berlin Novels of Alfred Döblin* (Berkeley: U of California P, 1988), 130.

[14] For a fascinating account of the role of the human voice in Benjamin's *Passagen-Werk,* see Lorenz Jöger, "Menschliche Artikulation in Benjamins Passagen-Werk," forthcoming in Klaus Garber, ed., *Internationaler Walter Benjamin Kolloquium* (Frankfurt: Piper, 1996).

[15] On Döblin's political affiliations, see Matthias Prangel, *Alfred Döblin* (Stuttgart: Metzler, 1973), 53–69.

[16] It is interesting to compare Döblin's position with that espoused retrospectively by Dagmar Barnouw in *Weimar Intellectuals and the Threat of Modernity* (Bloomington: Indiana UP, 1988). Barnouw argues in terms very similar to Döblin's, though they are derived from Karl Mannheim, that a kind of fluidity or adaptability was precisely the Weimar disease, and that political movements, or what she designates as "ideologies," were responsible for the failure to answer fascism's threat. It can come as no surprise that Ulrich, Musil's man without qualities, emerges as the hero of her study (Barnouw 11–43, 78–121).

[17] Benjamin's religiosity did not suddenly "return" in 1939 as a reaction to the Hitler-Stalin pact. On the status of religiosity as a subtext in Benjamin's "Marxist" phase, see my *Dialectical Images: Walter Benjamin's Theory of Literary Criticism* (Ithaca: Cornell UP, 1987), 5–7.

[18] The Stauffer strand, with its satirical characterization of the radical impotence of the German intelligentsia, constitutes one of the novel's glaring weaknesses. Stauffer finds even the ludicrous and pathetic efforts of the Berlin "Council of Intellectual Workers" too great and dangerous a commitment; he wanders through a series of erotic entanglements, each of which brings him further from the actions and decisions in Berlin which will shape his life. Döblin devotes hundreds of pages to Stauffer's ineffectuality, yet the mood of scorn and parody–

much of it self-directed—cannot carry the sheer number of pages devoted to Stauffer.

Works Cited

Bakhtin, Mikhail. *The Dialogic Imagination.* Austin: U of Texas P, 1981.

Benjamin, Walter. "Theses on the Philosophy of History." In *Illuminations.* New York: Schocken, 1969.

Döblin, Alfred. *November 1918: Eine deutsche Revolution.* Vol. 1, *Bürger und Soldaten.* Vol. 2, *Verratenes Volk.* Munich: Deutscher Taschenbuch Verlag, 1978.

———. *Schriften zu Aesthetik, Poetik und Literatur.* Olten: Walter, 1989.

———. *Berlin Alexanderplatz.* Munich: Deutscher Taschenbuch Verlag, 1969.

———. "Der Bau des epischen Werkes." In *Aufsätze zur Literatur.* Olten: Walter, 1963.

———. *Unser Dasein.* Olten: Walter, 1964.

———. "Wissen und Verändern." In *Der deutsche Maskenball von Linke Poot. Wissen und Verändern!* Olten: Walter, 1972.

Kiesel, Helmut. *Literarische Trauerarbeit: Das Exil- und Spätwerk Alfred Döblins.* Tübingen: Max Niemeyer, 1986.

"Wo gehörten sie hin?" The Berlin Autobiographies of Stephan Hermlin and Ludwig Greve

David Scrase

Politics and literature have always been bedfellows. The Greeks (whose language has given us the word "politics") certainly coupled them, as did the Romans; and German literature is full of political literature from the *Hildebrandslied* on. But one might be forgiven for thinking that no other nation or age has produced quite the quantity of politically-inspired literature as Germany in the twentieth century.

It is, to be sure, not easy to define political literature satisfactorily, and dangerous to try to do so narrowly. Indeed, it could be argued that, so long as politics are seen as an essential component of human existence, and so long as literature is understood to be a product of the interaction of author and society, then all literature is in some way political. But just as one might argue where the boundary between night and day is to be found yet nonetheless distinguish quite well between them, so, too, can one distinguish political literature from *poésie pure*, even if the degree of political content varies.

The variations in political content are directly related to sociohistorical trends. The rise of the working class, the urbanization following in the wake of the industrial revolution, and the resulting social problems all had their effect on the literature of Naturalism, for instance. In the twentieth century two world wars have left their marks on all European literatures. The second of these wars, involving as it did genocide, huge civilian losses, and large-scale destruction of cities, has left a different legacy from that of the first, the Great War. These factors and their effects on the victorious allies have resulted in a different literature from that of the vanquished—one need consider only *Die Blechtrommel* by Günter Grass and *Catch 22* by Joseph Heller to perceive just how different. Even within the vanquished nations—Germany, Italy, Japan—there are differences. Germany, blasted asunder through air raids, with substantial human losses of its own, has been obliged to come to terms with its guilt and culpability. Above all, it has had to come to terms with the policy it had embraced and put into action in regard to the Jews of Europe, the policy of ultimate destruction. Even in the 1990s its attempts to come to terms with this past, and particularly the destruction of the Jews, is continuing unabated.

If the politics of the "Jewish Question," which became and has henceforth remained a major focus of literature in the decades since 1945, has a very specific character, it has long been a German preoccupation in a more general sense. Gotthold Ephraim Lessing revealed it as a major concern in the eighteenth century, especially through his play *Nathan der Weise* (1779). Theodor Fontane, the chronicler of Berlin life in the second half of the nineteenth century, began to see the invaluable contribution Jews made to Germany's cultural life but could not shed his deep-seated anti-Semitism.[1] It was to Berlin that Samuel Fischer (1859–1934) came in 1879, leaving his native Slovakian corner of Austro-Hungary and determined to make a success of publishing. The Fischer Verlag soon attracted a significant group of authors which included Thomas Mann and Hermann Hesse, as well as Jewish writers such as Arthur Schnitzler, Alfred Döblin, and Jakob Wassermann.

Berlin, which Henry Adams called "a poor, keen-witted, provincial town, simple, dirty, uncivilized, and in most respects disgusting" (77), became towards the end of the nineteenth century the German city with the most vibrant community of Jews. About one-third of Germany's half a million or so Jews were living there when Hitler took power in 1933. By the time war broke out in September 1939 only about one half, eighty thousand, of that number remained. Berlin was also the city of the workers' movement, of the KPD and the SPD. It was a city that the Austrian *Führer* loved to hate, and it quickly became the city whose *Gauleiter*, Joseph Goebbels, identified as having a "Jewish Problem" of its own. He felt it was harboring Jews, hiding them, and not deporting them quickly enough in the early 1940s. In fact, the eighty thousand Jews still in Berlin in 1939 had been reduced to forty thousand by May 1942 and, by February 1943, had been eliminated to the point where Goebbels could pronounce his city "judenfrei." Two German Jews who experienced life in Berlin in the first years of the twelve-year Nazi Reich were Stephan Hermlin and Ludwig Greve. Both have written excellent autobiographical accounts dealing primarily with this time, accounts which bear careful scrutiny as survivor testimonies. Hermlin, always perceived as having become politicized during the ferment leading up to the Nazi takeover to the point of becoming a lifelong communist, in fact admits here to a position far closer to his bourgeois roots and upbringing. Greve, for his part, was jolted out of assimilation and into a Jewish identity which temporarily approached Zionist politicization during the growth of the Israeli state, only to return to Germany and reassume an identity close to that of the assimilated Jew he had been born.

Stephan Hermlin was born Rudolf Leder in Chemnitz in 1915, the son of a well-to-do Jewish textile merchant and an English mother. He grew up in Berlin. The pseudonym he took after the war is revealing: the common utilitarian quality suggested by the surname Leder (leather) is transformed into something far more rare, the elegant word for ermine. And the spelling of Stephan, with the *ph* rather than the common, everyday *f*, underlines poetic aspirations in the Symbolist tradition of Stéphane Mallarmé and Stephan George (as George for a time spelled his name).

As a boy Hermlin was raised in Berlin by governesses and educated at a boarding school in Switzerland and a Berlin Gymnasium. The highly assimilated Leder household was an upper-class cultured environment. The father collected art and was an accomplished musician. Artists and musicians were often invited, and the young Hermlin was an early initiate into the world of art, music, and literature as it thrived in the lively atmosphere of Berlin in the 1920s. Although his bond with his father was a close one, especially in artistic terms, Hermlin felt detached from his family roots and grew ever more so as he awakened politically. At the age of sixteen in 1931, at a time when the Nazis were in the ascendancy and when, with unemployment rampant, the left and right battled in the streets of Berlin, Hermlin joined the *Kommunistischen Jugendverband*. When the Nazis came to power, Hermlin, who had found work with a printer and became involved in illegal printing activities, was a marked man more because of his political leanings than because of his Jewish identity. Living underground, apart from his family, Hermlin continued his political work until 1936, when he left Germany. He thus avoided personal involvement in the intensification of anti-Semitic measures in the prewar years. Following *Kristallnacht*, in November 1938, however, Hermlin's father was caught in the general round-up and taken to Sachsenhausen where he apparently perished. Hermlin's grief and the depth of feeling for his father come out in muted form in an elegiac passage in his *Abendlicht*, as we shall see.

Just what, precisely, Hermlin did, and where, specifically, he did it from 1936 until he was interned in Switzerland in 1944 is subject to some conjecture. It has variously been written that Hermlin was in Egypt, Palestine, England, Spain, and France. There is some doubt that he was ever *in* Spain actively engaged in the Spanish Civil War; his activities on behalf of the Republic seem more likely to have taken place in France and to have been not at all martial. And the precise nature of the internment camps in France, where he spent most of the war years, is likewise unclear, as was his role in the French army, which he joined in 1940. On most of this period and especially his own activities therein, Hermlin is strangely silent. Smuggled into Switzerland by the French Maquis in 1944, Hermlin could cease his active resistance to and flight from the Nazis. He returned first to Frankfurt and then, in 1947, to Berlin in the Soviet Occupied Zone, where he has remained, in and out of favor, ever since.

Ludwig Greve, born in 1924, was nine years younger and consequently saw the rise of the Third Reich as a child, rather than through the eyes of a teenager. He, too, grew up in an assimilated family, although middle-class. His father was a salesman in a shirt factory. Greve's schooling, like that of all Jewish children, was interrupted in 1935, and he found himself removed from the public school to one of the many Jewish schools which sprang up at that time. Suddenly obliged to see themselves as Jewish rather than German, Greve's parents resolved that their children should in fact learn to be Jewish. There were religion and Hebrew lessons, and in 1938 a bar mitzvah. Christmas gave way to Hanukkah, much to the alarm of the children until they found a way to continue to celebrate Christmas in the kitchen with the Christian maid until she was dismissed, a victim of the Nürnberg Laws. This combined celebration of *Weihnachten* following Hanukkah the children called *Weihnukkah*. Greve's father, too, was rounded up after *Kristallnacht*, but spent only a month in Oranienburg, after which the parents intensified their efforts to emigrate, booking passage on the ill-fated *St. Louis*. Upon the ship's forced return to Europe, the Greves opted for France, where the children found themselves assigned to the school for Jewish refugee children at Montmorency. Then, as the Germans were poised to take Paris, the school was evacuated to Montintin not far from Limoges. Greve was now sixteen years old, separated from his parents and responsible for a short time for his sister, who was four years younger. The next four years Greve spent on the run, sometimes alone, sometimes united with his family as they fled south and eventually reached Italy. After incredible adventures and many close calls, Greve was able to reach Palestine and safety.

Each of these surviving Berlin Jewish writers wrote impressive autobiographies covering some of the years and some of the experiences of those years. Each is as interesting, almost, for what the writer chose to omit as for what he chose to include–although in the case of Greve, who drowned in the North Sea in 1991 before his account was finished, we shall never know what he might finally have included and what he might have excluded.[2] Neither Hermlin nor Greve described in any detail the more harrowing adventures experienced while on the run in France.

With regard to how each has chosen to describe his life, a brief examination of autobiographical writing is in place. Autobiography, it is widely believed, is a Western phenomenon and dates from St. Augustine's *Confessions*. It reached a peak in the German-speaking nations during the age of Goethe and declined during the second half of the nineteenth century (Fraser 15f). In our own century, and especially since the Second World War, however, it has increased in popularity—although, to be sure, it hardly approaches in quantity the considerable output in autobiographically-based fiction. This great increase in popularity in recent years, according to E.A.J. Honigmann, is due not least to changes in the law as well as in social attitudes. The contemporary reader is ready for and attracted to a greater openness on the part of the writer, whose willingness to provide veritable feasts composed of delectable morsels of bedroom gossip and salacious chit-chat is matched by vast hordes of readers ready to devour them.

In contemporary Germany there is the added factor of dealing with the catastrophic events of two world wars which I alluded to above. Whereas in the fictional accounts of autobiographical events, writers are free to distance themselves to a greater or lesser degree from their material, and whereas they may, if they so desire, avoid dealing with any personal development or maturation they underwent because of the events they describe, the autobiographer proper may not do so. Essential to true autobiography, says Bernd Neumann in words which might equally well describe the *Bildungsroman*, is a description of "das Leben des noch nicht sozialisierten Menschen, die Geschichte seines Werdens und seiner Bildung, seines Hineinwachsens in die Gesellschaft" (25). Neumann distinguishes between the autobiography, tracing the life of the writer until this point of integration into society, and memoirs, that is to say reminiscences of those who merely record events tangential to their lives but not essential to their development. The autobiography is accordingly very much concerned with inner events, the memoir depicts the external events touching upon a life. There is, then, a dichotomy involved in contemporary German autobiographical writing: on the one hand there is the goal of self-depiction, a superficial portrayal of the individual, who remembers and records significant events (the memoir); on the other hand there is a revelation of personal development in a historical and sociopolitical context where each impacts on the other (the true autobiography). The relationship of self and world is the critical distinguishing factor.

Self and world. Given the historical and sociopolitical events in the German-speaking realm in the twentieth century, it comes as no surprise that there are numerous personal accounts, genuine autobiographies in effect, which center on self and world: those of Ernst Toller, Stefan Zweig, and Carl Zuckmayer are among the better known of literary figures of Germany. In Stephan Hermlin's GDR, where literature had been programmatically *Wir*-oriented, the *auto*-biography, with some stress on the *Ich*, might seem to be in an ambivalent position—and perhaps it is. But as long as the individual element is connected with societal and political developments, it has general validity, and the GDR seems not to have fewer autobiographical tracts than the FRG. I would mention Johannes R. Becher's *Abschied* and Franz Fühmann's *22 Tage* as examples. Uwe Berger's *Weg in den Herbst* is a mere "Zhdanovist"[3] memoir. Stephan Hermlin's *Abendlicht* is a remarkable addition to GDR autobiographies. It is the life of an exemplary socialist. It is also the confession of a writer who recognizes that he can no longer reconcile art and politics. The irony is that, in writing the book, Hermlin does in fact reconcile them—*Abendlicht* is a *tour de force*, which, by combining art and politics, attempts to show how they cannot coexist.

Abendlicht was hailed on its publication in 1979 in the FRG as "Poesie und Traum, Schwärmen und Phantasie in Einklang mit einem politischen Gewissenskampf" (Auffermann). In the GDR it was described as "erlebte Geschichte...soziale und politische Erfahrung aus den Kämpfen unserer Epoche" (Richter). In a balanced and perceptive review by the former GDR critic and scholar Hans Mayer, it was called "ein Werk der lyrischen Prosa...[ein] dichterisches Monument für unauslöschliche Erinnerungen," and a work "das keinen Ehrgeiz hat, eine vollständige Lebensgeschichte zu bieten mit Privatem und Öffentlichem, mit Beweggründen und Postulaten," a work, Mayer continued, which has but two themes: "die Entscheidung für das Gedicht und die Entscheidung für den Kommunismus...," two themes which exist "als tief antagonistisches Spannungsverhältnis" (53). There were, to be sure, muted criticisms nestling among the laudatory comments: "Die Schilderung des Umbruchs von der Weimarer Republik zum Dritten Reich, sowohl in der privaten Sphäre wie in der Öffentlichkeit, gehört zu den Stärken dieses Buchs" said the *Stuttgarter Zeitung*, anonymously, but added, "Eine große Schwäche liegt freilich darin, daß Hermlin politische Entscheidungen von historischer Tragweite völlig unerwähnt oder doch unkommentiert läßt" (50). All these comments are largely true.

It is, perhaps, Hans Mayer's review which is the most challenging and illuminating. But, although he is correct in assessing the two major themes, he is misleading when he suggests that Hermlin has no desire to give us much in the way of private matters or public events. And the *Stuttgarter Zeitung* is also missing the point when it criticizes Hermlin's almost total omission of major historical events.

What Hermlin does in *Abendlicht* is to describe how he grew up in an affluent and cultured milieu, where a Kandinsky visited his father, where a portrait of his parents by Lovis Corinth graced the walls of his home, and where musical performance by family members was central to his own artistic development. His relationship with his father is portrayed primarily from this point of view—a sharing of cultural and artistic experience—because this was the essence of the relationship. For a child raised and educated by governesses, tutors, and in boarding schools, parents were experienced and viewed differently and not perceived in more mundane terms. Indeed, Hermlin's mother is hardly mentioned in the account except as a distant figure who enjoyed genteel living and refined social interaction. We accordingly see Hermlin's early cultural development rather clearly. His appreciation of music, his experience of great art in the original, his reading—all this figures prominently. His life in this milieu was so sheltered that he long believed that poor children existed only in books. Given this cultured upbringing, it is not surprising that the poet Hermlin's early writing consisted of an essay on Hölderlin, exquisitely crafted sonnets, and other formally perfected poems, as well as assured translations of such as Éluard and Neruda. Indeed, his development as a poet can be fully understood only through these aspects of his upbringing, unexciting though they may be.

In terms of its effect on Hermlin's political development, however, the lack of emotional warmth and attachment is intensified in the teenage Hermlin into distance, flight, and near repudiation as the adolescent threw himself into left-wing political commitment. Instead of returning home from Gymnasium, Hermlin would linger in the streets of Berlin listening to working-class Berliners, out of work as so many of them were. It was thus that he joined the Young Communists.

Not surprisingly, the writer Hermlin in his early years was capable of eulogizing Stalin in his poems—although, to be just, he subsequently subjected himself to a rigorous program of *Selbstkritik* and personal de-Stalinization in 1956. The courage needed to be a socialist in Hitler's Germany stood him in good stead at this time and again at various points in GDR cultural history. But there is relatively little about being a Jew in Germany between 1933 and 1936. He describes the vicious chatter of a group of Nazi sympathizers gathered in a bar as directed against "das jüdisch-bolschewistische Pack" (63), but he does not show himself as at all sensitive to such anti-Semitism. And when he is underground in France (primarily) in the later 1930s and 1940s, it is his socialism rather than his Jewish identity which is seen as a danger.

With regard to people, they are usually portrayed in terms of their politics rather than their human qualities. To be sure, he does allude to his father's imprisonment in Sachsenhausen in sympathetic terms. And we are left in no doubt as to his father's ultimate fate. He describes how similar father and son were, how they made music together; he speaks of his father's pacifism following his experiences as a soldier in the First World War, and he recounts in all brevity conversations in which the politically active son encouraged the father, in vain, to emigrate. He tells how his father resigned from his club before he was asked to do so, how he gave up collecting art and began to sell paintings, but how, for a while at least, business picked up under the Nazis. But again and again it is the political battle of the left against fascism which is central. The family is strangely distant and is portrayed accordingly—if, also, touchingly. When looking at the events of the twelve-year Reich leading up to the Holocaust proper, however, Hermlin can be insightful and astute. On those opportunists who sensed the Nazis were winning and who therefore joined them, for instance, he writes: "Unbezähmbar ist der Drang, bei den Stärkeren zu sein. Auf wie vielen Schlachtfeldern hatten die von der Niederlage Bedrohten die Fahne gewechselt" (49). And on a musically-gifted acquaintance, a pupil of the well-known concert pianist Wilhelm Kempff: "Er gehörte zu jenen zahlreichen hündischen Naturen, die nur im Rudel Mut schöpfen und gefährlich werden" (87). In another passage Hermlin describes how a couple of brewery workers sit on a bench marked "Nur für Juden" and defiantly eat their luncheon sandwiches there out of a sense of solidarity with the Jews (96–98). On the whole, however, Hermlin's *Abendlicht*, in which we become aware of his Jewish identity only on page seventy-seven, contains relatively little about the events which launched the Shoah.

Ludwig Greve's *Wo gehörte ich hin?* is quite different in this regard, although the poet also avoids or understates some of his worst experiences. Greve makes us aware of his Jewish identity at the very outset. At the same time he describes how the sudden awareness in the nine-year-old of this identity produced a crisis in him: "Wo gehörte ich hin?" (15). He informs us of the practical effects of discrimination, how friendships ended, how one's father needed to have served in the First World War *at the front* if one was to go to the Gymnasium. Soon, of course, Jewish children were to be excluded from all public schools. Greve describes how the family changed residences, was obliged to move again, how he felt as he saw his "friends" joining the HJ, as he saw the ubiquitous, grotesque, anti-Semitic caricatures displayed in the streets. He sees the family obliged to dismiss their forty-four-year-old Christian maid Mimi, who, however, remains true to them. He watches as his father loses his job, as he is arrested after *Kristallnacht* and returns home one month later, head shaven, his clothes hanging loosely on his starkly reduced body. We see the adolescent boy get into scrapes, become fanatically interested in football, go to the cinema illegally, take part in segregated athletics, but skate quite openly with Gentile children on the frozen park pond (seemingly this winter pastime escaped the notices of segregation routinely erected in all parks). As their situation worsened, as the composition of his class at school and the teaching staff changed daily, as the first *Kindertransporte* left, the Greves made their first attempts to emigrate. Aged fifteen, young Greve noted rather well what the acquisition of Cuban visas and return tickets on the *St. Louis* meant. His description of how he experienced this ill-fated voyage tells us much more than the history books do. Likewise, his description of life in the *Kinderheim* at Montmorency for the two years until this school and its sister schools are disbanded gives us information otherwise lacking in conventional histories.

It is at this point that Greve's account breaks off. Due to the painstaking research of Reinhard Tgahrt, who edited Greve's unfinished manuscript after his unexpected death, we know the bare outline of Greve's life from 1941 until 1943, when the whole reunited Greve family reached Italy. For a short while he was able to attend a French school, then he worked in a carpentry shop; he spent a short period living in the woods, then working on a farm. Meanwhile his false papers, in the name Louis Gabier, identified him as a Frenchman. On his way to his parents and sister, for whom he was to acquire false papers, he was arrested in Lyon but released three days later after he had convinced his German interrogators of his French identity! Now reunited, the family was able to reach Italy. Here, during a bombing raid on Italian partisans, Greve's mother was seriously injured. At this point Greve and his mother were separated from his father and sister. The latter were arrested, interned, then transported to Auschwitz, where they perished. Greve was able to save his mother's life and emigrate to Palestine upon liberation. He returned to West Germany in 1950.

Greve was unable, for whatever reason, to write about his adventures in France or to give many details of the year spent in Italy. In end-effect, then, his autobiography resembles Hermlin's, in that it omits many of the experiences made on the run. These omissions do not, however, detract from the autobiography, for we see the development of the child into the youth as the chronicle unfolds in response to a life in flight from the ever-present threat of destruction. Yet whereas Hermlin's development into an avid socialist and politically engaged and at the same time pronouncedly aesthetic artist is clearly articulated, the development of Greve as poet is less obvious.

Greve tells us very little, for example, of his reading or of his response, growing up, to art and music. Whereas Hermlin tells us of his first poetic attempts, Greve gives us hardly any information about his future métier. To have been able to do so, Greve would have had to continue his narrative at least into the 1950s, when his first poems, unpublished *and* published, showed to what extent his linguistic development had responded to life in flight from National Socialism. His French had become sufficiently good to save his life in France, but his German (a language which, had he been found speaking or writing it, would have meant his death) remained stunted.

Greve's education on the run seems to have been less in political matters than in his understanding of human nature, in tolerance, and in self-knowledge. As he becomes aware of his Jewish identity and knows how precarious his position is, the young Greve accepts the necessity to act out a new role. At school, at least, he felt a little more relaxed: "Ja, in der Schule lernte ich vergessen, was mich von den anderen Jungen unterschied" (19). But in other situations, in which his school comrades were free to go to the bakeshop or the candy store, he had to remain aware "daß ich eine Rolle spielte.... Mir blieb...nichts übrig, als jeden Morgen...mich von neuem zu erfinden" (20). He watched how non-Jews lived, and grew envious. "Begreifst du," he asks his imagined reader, "warum ich in die Gojim vernarrt war, so wenig sie auch von mir wissen wollten? Sie lebten aus dem Vollen, arm oder reich, wir aus zweiter Hand" (46).

But it is *Kristallnacht,* experienced by the fourteen-year-old, which has its most telling effect. With his bar mitzvah not long behind him, young Ludwig Greve was obliged to watch his father led away without his being able to do anything for him. Then he saw his father return, a changed, almost broken man. As he went through his rebellious teens he noticed how little his father was able to respond to his son's behavior with anything resembling control or discipline. His enforced independence during the years in France and Italy up to the time his father was detained once again and deported led to a rift between father and son which bordered on contempt on Ludwig's part. His father's fate then induced and intensified the typical survivor's guilt syndrome. It was not until the 1970s, as we shall see, that Greve, now the father of teenagers, was able to resolve his guilt and the tortured relationship he had not been able to work through fully earlier on—the mark of a true autobiography.

The two autobiographies resemble one another most obviously in that each omits the more harrowing facets of life on the run. Neither pays great attention to the major developments and events of the Third Reich – though each, in its quiet way, gives us more than is at first apparent. *Abendlicht* seems to provide for the most part information pertaining to Hermlin's political and poetic development; *Wo gehörte ich hin?* would seem to dwell mainly on Greve's development as a person. Both books leave only a shadowy picture of the mother; both give a fuller portrayal of the father.

It is in this latter resemblance—the father treatment—that the two works in the end event prove most interesting. And it is the pivotal event of *Kristallnacht* which points up the greatest similarity in the two works. Although Hermlin had separated himself from his family long before *Kristallnacht* and had, moreover, left Germany in 1936, contact with his father was maintained, and Hermlin continued to urge his father to leave Germany. The real separation, with all its finality, occurred in November 1938. In recollecting the time and the event, Hermlin is necessarily brief in terms of his father's fate:

> Von dem, was meinem Vater später widerfuhr, weiß ich nur wenig, von wenigen Zeugen. Einer meiner Freunde, ein junger Metallarbeiter, hatte ihn in Sachsenhausen gesehen, wie er, gegen Ende des Jahres, in dünnem Drillich Steine klopfte. Er habe gewußt, sagte mein Freund, daß mein Vater niemals zuvor körperlich gearbeitet hatte; er habe ihn auch ohne Klage schwere Lasten tragen sehen, nach seiner Einlieferung, die besonders furchtbar gewesen sei. Er habe der SS gegenüber bis zuletzt eine merkwürdige Haltung gewahrt, die Disziplin, Höflichkeit und Verachtung ausdrückte. (108-09)

Following this brief, sober passage, Hermlin is more expansive in his memories of his father. The events from his childhood that he chooses to relate show a deeply loving and caring father, a pacifist who had never shared in the blind patriotic fervor of the year 1914, and a cultured man who immersed himself ever more in music as he looked resignedly towards the impending catastrophe. The bitter irony: a man so intimately caught up in German culture that he could not leave the country that had marked him for destruction. Hermlin remembers the art in his father's collection; he remembers calling to him, and remembers how his father ignored him. In 1978-79, as Hermlin recalls his childhood, it is these aspects—art, pacifism, love, and separation—that are uppermost. It is in *Abendlicht* that Hermlin comes to terms with them.

In addition to this personal coming-to-terms, it is important to stress that *Abendlicht* also depicts Hermlin's resolution of the two apparent incompatibles, the two themes named by Hans Mayer: the choice of poetry and the choice of communism. In showing how, through his father and his cultured upbringing, he came to poetry and art in general, and how, in conscious repudiation of his father and this legacy, he came to communism, Hermlin seems to be emphasizing their incompatibility. He had in effect done so much earlier when he gave up writing poetry in the late 1950s. Now, in 1978-79, it appears as if he is reaffirming the role of art and poetry. Indeed, as was pointed out in *Der Spiegel*, Hermlin quite specifically confirmed his identity as a poet in provocative and unequivocal terms in May 1978 at the GDR *Schriftsteller-Kongress*: "Ich bin ein spätbürgerlicher Schriftsteller—was könnte ich als Schriftsteller auch anderes sein."[4] Clearly, Hermlin is now fully cognizant of his debt to his father and his cultured, bourgeois heritage. Equally clearly, since this statement came in response to official sanction of the Biermann signatories—Hermlin was first among them—Hermlin was then questioning his own affiliation to the communism of the GDR. *Abendlicht*, in resolving heritage and politics as they had earlier developed in parallel fashion, was then also resolving them in the present (1978-79) context of the GDR. If it might seem that all that is needed is for Hermlin to begin to write poems again, he has in effect already begun to do so, for his autobiography is, as Mayer called it, "ein Werk der lyrischen Prosa"—a prose poem.

With regard to Ludwig Greve, fourteen years old at the time, the effect of *Kristallnacht* was also to induce a physical separation between father and son. In this case, however, it served to emphasize the emotional separation which had developed quite naturally as the rebellious teenager sought independence. For this separation to continue to develop *naturally* in the following months as the Greves set off on the odyssey of what they initially thought was emigration, would have needed a continuation of something approaching "normal" family life. The next five years, as we have seen, produced nothing remotely resembling normalcy, and we can only speculate as to how the separation, which was initially emotional, then both emotional and physical, and then from 1944 on total and final, developed, and what tensions arose.

That there were tensions and that they were powerful and lasting, there can be no doubt. Greve's poem "Mein Vater," written in 1966, reveals the presence of these tensions and demonstrates their resolution some two decades after his father's death.[5] "Mein Vater" portrays the quest of the rebellious son for his lost father. It is a quest fraught with, and growing out of, guilt. Greve describes in an essay entitled "Warum schreibe ich anders?" how he watched his father and sister leave to obtain Italian papers from the authorities in Cuneo while he remained with his injured mother: "Als [Vater und Schwester] sich in einiger Entfernung noch einmal umdrehten, hob ich den Arm und rief: 'Bis heute Abend!' Ich rief sie nicht zurück" (329). In fact, as Reinhard Tgahrt reveals in his postscript to *Wo gehörte ich hin?*, both were arrested and taken to the camp at San Borgo Dalmazzo. Here Greve was able to visit them–his papers did not identify him as the son–with plans for their escape. Unfortunately, before he was able to set the plans in action, his father and sister were removed to Turin, and thence to a death camp. Greve continues his account: "So schwer es mir fällt, glaube ich doch, diese Schuld eingestehen zu müssen; erst mit ihr brach die Kindheit ab. Ich konnte meine Mutter in Sicherheit bringen" (329).

"Mein Vater" enables Greve, at the time of writing the poem himself a father, to assuage his guilt. The poem, which had begun with the statement "Spät komme ich zu dir" ends with the terse confirmation of this fact: "Ich komme, Vater." Some of Greve's guilt is the guilt of the survivor. But some, if not most, is the guilt of a son who realizes late, but not too late, that his willful and recalcitrant behavior was unjust and improper, and that a simple apology is not possible.

Written at various stages at least a decade after "Mein Vater," Greve's *Wo gehörte ich hin?* has less need to come to terms with the past. The episode of the final leave-taking is not mentioned, in fact. Instead Greve shows his early development, and concentrates poignantly on the critical point of *Kristallnacht* and his changed view of his father.

"Wo gehörten sie hin," these two Jewish Berliners forcibly uprooted because of the Shoah? Quite clearly in the land of their fathers, is the brief answer. Despite the differences in the autobiographical approach by each author, despite their choice of a different Germany to settle in after the war was over and as they became aware of a need to choose where to live after so many years deprived of choice, each author in effect returned to his roots. Hermlin came to a realization that he was, in essence, a bourgeois poet with all the baggage which that entails. Greve returned to being an assimilated Jew in Germany—albeit in Stuttgart rather than Berlin. Hermlin's long life as a socialist did not obliterate his childhood. Greve's life blending into France, Italy, and his choice of over five years in Eretz Israel, did not cut him off from his early roots. In part by means of their literary autobiographies they retraced lives formed by the extreme political events of mid-twentieth-century German life, and in so doing found themselves. Like Ludwig Greve, Stephan Hermlin might well have said: "Ich komme, Vater."

Notes

[1] See *New York Review of Books*, 18 April 1996, 4.

[2] In fact, since the publication of *Wo gehörte ich hin?* in 1994, its editor, Reinhard Tgahrt, has found a further complete chapter describing a visit Greve made while still underground in 1944 to a cultivated Italian gentleman not far from Lucca. This chapter will be published with other short prose pieces in the near future.

[3] Wesley Blomster's felicitous description. See *World Literature Today* 59 (1985): 426.

[4] Reported in *Der Spiegel*, 3 December 1979, 240.

[5] For a full interpretation of this important poem, see my article "Correcting Emotion: The Poetry of Ludwig Greve within the Context of West German Trends," *German Life and Letters*, n.s. 41 (July 1988): 494–503.

Works Cited

Adams, Henry. *The Education of Henry Adams: An Autobiography.* Boston: Houghton Mifflin, 1961.

Auffermann, Verena. "Fragen–Antworten–Fragen." *Rhein-Neckar Zeitung*, 19–20 January 1980, 6.

Fraser, Catherine C. *Problems in a New Medium: Autobiographies by Three Artists.* New York, Berne, Frankfurt am Main: Peter Lang, 1984.

Greve, Ludwig. "Warum schreibe ich anders?" *Neue Deutsche Hefte* 27 (1980): 328–36.

———. *Wo gehörte ich hin?* Frankfurt am Main: S. Fischer, 1994.

———. "Mein Vater." In *Sie lacht,* by Ludwig Greve. Frankfurt am Main: S. Fischer, 1991.

Hermlin, Stephan. *Abendlicht.* Berlin: Klaus Wagenbach, 1979.

Honigmann, E.A.J. "Me, Myself, and I." *New York Review*, 7 December 1989, 16–18.

Mayer, Hans. "Lyrik der Hoffnung: Stephan Hermlin's *Gesammelte Gedichte* und *Abendlicht*." *Die Zeit*, 21 September 1979, 53.

Neumann, Bernd. *Identität und Rollenzwang: Zur Theorie der Autobiographie*. Frankfurt am Main: Athenäum, 1970.

Richter, Hans. "Bekenntnis und Rückschau in poetischer Geschlossenheit." *Neues Deutschland*, 21 November 1979, 4.

"Stalin—ganz unbestechlich. Glanz und Elend eines Kommunisten: Stephan Hermlin." *Stuttgarter Zeitung*, 1 December 1979, 50.

Excalibur: *Film Reception and Political Distance*

Ray Wakefield

When John Boorman's film *Excalibur* appeared in spring 1981, Ronald Reagan was only a few months into his first term as president, Klaus Theweleit's two-volume study of the nexus between fascism and sex, *Männerphantasien,* was still much discussed in German intellectual circles, and the films of Leni Riefenstahl persisted in the memories of movie audiences even across the distance of two generations' remove. As this investigation into the German reception of *Excalibur* will show, these seemingly disparate phenomena—Reagan's election, Theweleit's *Männerphantasien,* Riefenstahl's films—all played major roles in the problematic reaction to Boorman's film by German audiences. Though the documentation on the film's genesis and development reveals no overtly political agenda on Boorman's part, the way he prepared the Arthurian material for his filmic text, including a deliberate decision to depict Arthur as charismatic leader *par excellence,* a Jungian focus on the masculinity in Malory's *Morte D'Arthur,* and a penchant for undisguised borrowing from other films, literature, and the visual arts, had repercussions for German audiences and film critics which were unique among film audiences in the West. The issue I wish to explore is how Boorman's aesthetic choices came to be rejected on political grounds by German audiences who found in the valorization of a charismatic male leader of mythical proportions unacceptable reminders of their own recent and troubled history. The fact that this English-language film appeared hard on the heels of America's election of a charismatic Cold Warrior brought history into the present for German viewers. After all, they could not easily forget the Hollywood actor who promised in his presidential campaign to make Germany a nuclear battlefield, if necessary, in reaction to Soviet aggression. In one of his seminal works on literary reception, Hans Robert Jauss characterizes the disparity between the audience's horizon of expectations and the "newness" of a piece of literature as "aesthetic distance" (25–28); in the reception of *Excalibur,* a different dynamic of reception is at work—the German audience was distanced from the film politically rather than aesthetically.

Boorman and Malory

Among the credits in *Excalibur* is the indication that the film is adapted from Sir Thomas Malory's *Morte D'Arthur,* and it is undeniable that Boorman follows in a general way Malory's early Renaissance retelling of the cycles of Arthurian romances. Lovers of Malory, however, find little to admire in this film, if faithfulness to the source is an important criterion. Boorman takes great liberty with the Malory telling of the story and does so without even a hint of apology. Asked in one interview about his opinion of Malory, Boorman responded: "Malory was really the first hack writer" (Kennedy 33). This is not Boorman's way of showing disrespect for his source; indeed, it proves to be a very revealing statement about the way in which Boorman assimilates and transforms Malory, while at the same time remaining true to Malory's own approach to the *materie de Bretagne*. Malory's approach is straightforward and typical of premodern concepts of authorship: gather the best sources available to you and use them to tell the tale according to your own best talents. Malory scholarship traditionally claims that one can discretely discern, beneath the surface of Malory's prose, whether he is depending at that moment on the French prose, the English alliterative verse, or, the English stanzaic verse of his primary sources (Lawlor xxiii).

In his numerous interviews following *Excalibur's* debut, Boorman talked at some length about his lifelong obsession with Arthuriana. He recalled in one interview spending hours with his parents' illustrated edition of *Morte D'Arthur* when he was only about five years old (Allen 1). From this early beginning, Boorman retained an interest in Arthurian literature, film, and illustration; he told Henry Allen, "I've been trying to make this film for 20 years" (2). Perhaps more interesting than Boorman's preoccupation with Arthuriana is the way he incorporates a wide variety of sources into his work and deliberately makes each source transparent. He is adopting Malory's own approach: take whatever you can use from whatever sources are available and let the sources be seen clearly by viewers just beneath the surface of your own filmic text. Since every scene in *Excalibur* may well have come from somewhere else, Boorman invites casual viewers and film critics alike to join him in a gigantic game of Arthurian trivial pursuit. In his early *Washington Post* interview with Henry Allen he revealed three of his favorite borrowings to set this game in play: 1) the sword emerging from the water in the hand of the Lady of the Lake is a filmic copy of an illustration by Aubrey Beardsley in an edition of *Morte D'Arthur*; 2) Lancelot's self-inflicted wound is intended to refer both to Adam's rib and to the wound in Christ's side; and 3) the scene depicting the simultaneous death blows delivered by Arthur to Mordred and Mordred to Arthur is taken directly from a favorite Arthur Rackham illustration in an edition of *Morte D'Arthur*. With Boorman himself urging them on, it is not surprising that film critics joined the game and identified a host of other sources: for example, Vincent Canby traced Merlin's initial appearance walking through a mysterious mist to George Stevens's *The Greatest Story Ever Told,* where Jesus makes a similar appearance, and he saw many of the gory battle scenes as similar to those in *Monty Python and the Holy Grail.* Jean Markale found the scene with the "Minnegrotto" and the sword between the lovers reminiscent of Gottfried's *Tristan.* The audience of course is also invited to play, and as the film acquired cult status in the United States, viewers would come equipped with notebooks for second and third screenings. But beyond the sense of play and the delight afforded in discovery lies Boorman's serious intent to follow Malory's method with relation to his medieval sources rather than to swallow whole Malory's version of the Arthurian story.

The Critical Reception: America and Germany

Among the very first American journals or newspapers to comment on *Excalibur* was the film trade journal *Variety*, which picked Boorman's film to be a big winner with audiences and with critics, praising it as "exquisite, a near-perfect blend of action, romance, fantasy and philosophy, finely acted and beautifully filmed by director John Boorman and cinematographer Alex Thomson" (8 April 1981). Although other major newspapers and magazines joined *Variety* with positive reviews, Vincent Canby of the *New York Times* found the film tedious: "one longs to be able to laugh, if only to be able to establish the fact that one is, after all, awake."

The most extensive early review was by the aforementioned Henry Allen, who places his critique in the context of a personal interview with the director. Allen reviews the initial critical reception of *Excalibur* in terms of near polar opposition of opinion, a "violent mix of reviews ...from outraged scorn to tones of wonder." What is striking, however, in reading the English-language reviews and articles is not just how mixed they are, but rather how numerous they become. In the six years following the film's appearance (1981–87), the *Film Literature Index* lists thirty-five reviews and feature articles in English. In Western Europe, the numbers are equally impressive during these years for magazines and journals in French, Italian, and Dutch: twenty in French; seven in Italian; and six in Dutch.

The critical nonreception of *Excalibur* in Germany is thus all the more puzzling against the backdrop of the considerable attention it received in other Western cultures. There is not one serious critical review or feature article in German. In 1982 a West German educational magazine, *Medien und Erziehung*, warned parents that *Excalibur* is much too violent to be viewed by children. In 1987 an East German magazine, *Film und Fernsehen*, issued a similar warning. An article in the *Spiegel* issue of 26 October 1981, features two large photos of scenes from *Excalibur*, but it turns out that the focus in this seven-page feature by Urs Jenny is on the renewed German interest for things Arthurian in general (228–35). *Excalibur* is granted a scant two paragraphs in this extensive feature and is dismissed summarily as a film whose director lacks imagination, a failure which Boorman, according to Jenny, attempts to finesse with an overly dramatic soundtrack (Wagner and Orff) and with strikingly colored visuals. The two film scenes illustrating the *Spiegel* feature may tell us more about the reason for Jenny's rejection of *Excalibur*. He carefully selected two of the most grotesque and violent scenes in the filmic text. The first shows Mordred in full armor on horseback, his helm wrought to a glowering likeness of his own features; he is pursuing a helpless and unhorsed King Uriens. The landscape is sullen, bleak, and barren; one can sense the cold-blooded murder which is about to occur. The second scene is from the concluding cataclysmic battle in the film. Mordred and Arthur are at the center surrounded by death and destruction in a setting-sun landscape that looks very much like the end of the world. In the midst of this filmic Armageddon, Arthur is deliberately impaling himself ever more deeply on Mordred's lance so that he can get close enough to strike a fatal blow with his sword, *Excalibur*. These three brief references–two parental warnings and one quick rejection illustrated by two grisly film scenes calculated to frighten off all but the most stout of heart–are the total extent of *Excalibur's* "critical reception" in Germany. If we look for a common thread in these three abbreviated reviews, it might be the negative reaction to the film's violence. But, given the overall lack of critical attention, this would have to be the most slender of common threads. Perhaps, in the context of such extensive critical reception elsewhere in Western Europe as well as in America, we should avoid the urge to read between the lines and accept the fact that there is no meaningful critical reception of the film *Excalibur* in Germany.

The Audience Reception: America and Germany

Though *Variety's* optimism concerning appeal to the critics was not universally realized, its prediction of success with American audiences was accurate. Beginning with the film's first appearance in the reporting of box-office earnings (22 April 1981), *Excalibur* vaulted immediately to the number two ranking. For the next two weeks, 29 April and 6 May, the film climbed to number one at the box office. Overall, *Excalibur* spent nine consecutive weeks among the top ten money-making films in America, grossing more than $25 million in the first five weeks alone. However mixed the American critical reception of Boorman's film, the audience reception is nothing short of spectacular. Filmgoers flocked to see this film, and thus it is not surprising that American film critics felt obliged to write about it frequently and at length.

In Germany in the early 1980s, there was nothing comparable to the film trade journal *Variety* to take the pulse of audience interest in films. We have to depend on indirect and anecdotal evidence. From the observation that German film critics virtually ignored *Excalibur*, one is tempted to the presumption that audience interest was also low. Anecdotal reports from acquaintances interested in film or in the reception of Arthuriana in contemporary cultures support this presumption. All of these reports in personal communications indicate that *Excalibur* had a short run and tiny audiences in German-speaking Europe. In the absence of a better critical apparatus, it is difficult if not impossible to determine whether disinterest among German critics was the underlying cause of the lack of audience interest or its product. In either case, we have established that German film critics ignored the film, and it is difficult to imagine that this could have occurred if *Excalibur* had been a smashing success with German film audiences. Based on the information available at this point, we can conclude preliminarily that *Excalibur*, which experienced considerable, though mixed, critical reception and huge audiences in America, was almost totally ignored both by German critics and German audiences.

The Unifying Metaphor

In Boorman's Arthurian world, we are treated to a play of multiple surfaces. At the most fundamental level, we have the example of Malory's prose–a surface beneath which we can identify his French and English source texts. By analogy, Boorman informs us that the surface of his filmic text is equally transparent; he invites us to gaze beneath this surface and identify his multiple sources, both verbal and visual. This multiplicity of surfaces is extended, however, to the level of metaphor in Boorman's depiction of the masculine and the feminine in *Excalibur*. We are alerted to this unconventional vision early in the film when Merlin, as in Malory's story, transforms an erotically aroused Uther Pendragon into his enemy, the Duke of Cornwall, so that Uther, in the Duke's absence, may enter his castle undetected and satisfy his erotic obsession by making love to the Duchess Igraine. At least, "making love" is the point in Malory's version. As Boorman constructs this scene, Uther rides upon the mists to the castle, and, as he rides, we observe the outer transformation of his horse, armor, and face into those of the Duke. Upon entering the castle, Uther proceeds directly to Igraine's bed chamber, tears away her gown, and, while still in full armor, sexually assaults the Duchess.

This is Boorman's first signal to us that armor in this film is much more than utilitarian protection or medieval decoration for the male body. The knights of the Round Table are rarely seen without their armor, often polished to a highly reflective silvery sheen so that these knights walk about bathed in an eerie metallic light. And, unlike real knights in the Middle Ages, these knights wear their armor for all occasions: indoors, outdoors, while dining, napping, et cetera. After Uther's armored sexual assault, we understand that Boorman's knights also wear their armor while sleeping and in ladies' chambers. Lest we miss the importance of this knight-always-in-armor motif, Boorman has Lancelot swear fealty to Arthur with the following words: "I live within this metal skin." This then is the surface for males in *Excalibur:* a metal skin. They live in this metal skin so long as it preserves them whole in their masculinity, and they die in this metal skin when it is penetrated, as with the Duke of Cornwall and later even with Arthur, when we can actually see the fleshy softness and blood beneath the surface of the armor.

The women in *Excalibur* are represented with distinctly opposite surfaces. As with Igraine, we see the few female figures in soft flowing gowns, or, more often than Malory's plot would dictate, they appear nude and bathed in gentle, warm light to emphasize their softness and vulnerability. This female softness is also subject to penetration by male bodies, but when this happens, Boorman does not show us humanity and mortality beneath the surface; his women are either barren or able to produce only male children who soon appear in their knightly metal skins. Igraine becomes pregnant and produces Arthur. Guinover, on the other hand, is loved by the greatest knights, Arthur and Lancelot, and is unable to produce a child. Morgana, who uses her dark magic to seduce her half-brother Arthur, gives birth to the monster Mordred. Morgana is also the only woman in the film who dares to wear armor, the result of which is the immediate loss of her feminine guile and her death at the hands of her own son. Within this metaphor of surfaces, Boorman's women are portrayed as men turned inside-out: the surface is soft, but beneath it lies a hardness: sterility, an icy ambition, or the limited capability of producing only future warriors.

Boorman and his Agenda: A Troubling Silence

In his various interviews, Boorman insisted that *Excalibur* has everything to do with myth and Jungian archetypes and nothing to do with politics. The following statement is fairly typical of his explanations regarding his fundamental approach:

> Jung said that every myth is about having a turning point in consciousness. The movie starts out with men as primeval animals, dinosaurs really (with snoutlike visors on their armor as they thunder around in a hellish mist), man struggling from the slime. But as he emerges, what he loses is his harmony with nature and his sense of magic. (Allen 1)

As convincing as such statements may appear upon first glance, one must remain skeptical. Given the emergence of gender studies in the 1960s and 1970s, it is difficult to imagine a film which supposedly has no political agenda and, at the same time, transforms traditional, entertaining narratives into a focus on masculinity and the charismatic male leader. We can perhaps be even more skeptical in this case because the late 1970s saw the publication of seminal gender studies by men about men. One such book with wide, popular distribution is Marc Fasteau's *The Male Machine*. Here the reader encounters as early as page one masculinity problematized in images linked to knights, battle, and armor:

> The male machine is a special kind of being, different from women, children, and men who don't measure up. He is functional, designed mainly for work. He is programmed to tackle jobs, override obstacles, attack problems, overcome difficulties, and always seize the offensive.... He has armor plating which is virtually impregnable. (1)

The fact that such knightly images relating to the problematics of contemporary masculinity were current at the time Boorman commenced work on *Excalibur* suggests that his own characterizations of the film are disingenuous and/or incomplete.

Some film critics attempt to address these issues in their interviews with Boorman; it is clear that he is given opportunities to talk about the potential problems associated with his representation of masculinity and the charismatic male leader. Dan Yakir asked Boorman about the domination of *Excalibur* by males who are mostly given violent and macho personalities. The response amounts to an evasion of the question, which is then followed by Boorman changing the subject:

> My whole life I've been surrounded by women, and perhaps I try to escape from that in my films.... So in this film I tried to explore the world of men. (51)

Henry Allen confronted Boorman with the danger of mythologizing the great, charismatic leader. Here also, Boorman's answer is less than helpful before he pointedly moved on to another topic:

> It's dangerous, terribly dangerous territory.... The Nazis used myths, but in a distorted way. (2)

We can speculate, probably without any satisfactory conclusions, on the level of Boorman's awareness of gender-based issues or the valorization of male charismatic leaders. What we know for certain is that others brought these difficult matters to his attention, and he chose to maintain a troubling silence.

Excalibur's Nonreception in Germany: Other Silences

Boorman's silences are matched on the German side. As indicated above, both critics and audiences avoided serious engagement with *Excalibur*. I do not mean to suggest that German audiences and critics were obliged to like this film or to praise it in print. As we have seen, many American film critics met *Excalibur* with scathing condemnation. The uniqueness in Germany has to do with the silence of film critics who are not normally shy when it comes to lambasting Anglo-American films. If *Excalibur* had also been ignored in other West European cultures or in America, this German silence would be unremarkable. As matters stand, the singularity of the silence in Germany invites attempts at explanation, even if mostly in the realm of speculation.

As indicated earlier, the few, scanty comments which are in print on this film reveal that German film reviewers were made extremely uncomfortable by Boorman's depiction of male violence and the charismatic male leader. The reasons for this discomfort may have their origins in Germany's disastrous twentieth-century experiences with charismatic male leaders, an unfortunate history which undergirds Theweleit's 1977–78 study of post-First World War, protofascist Germans. In large public gatherings during the 1930s, German fascists organized, choreographed (and sometimes filmed) mass formations of male bodies. The way Theweleit describes the individuals in these mass public displays could also serve as film-scene descriptions for Boorman's hard-bodied males:

Hubert Lanzinger: Hitler as Flagbearer
Courtesy US Army Center of Military History

> Men themselves were now split into a (female) interior and a (male) exterior—the body armor. And as we know, the interior and the exterior were mortal enemies. What we see being portrayed...are the armor's separation from, and superiority over the interior: the interior was allowed to flow, but only within the masculine boundaries of the mass formations. (I, 434)

As has become widely known by now in both the United States and in Germany through the circulation of confiscated art such as Hubert Lanzinger's striking painting of Hitler as medieval knight (Figure 1),[1] the fascist aesthetic made eager use of images glorifying struggle, commemorating past battles to prepare the way for future conflict and celebrating charismatic leaders of the real or mythic past.[2] Theweleit's massive study helps to explain why a contemporary German audience would be profoundly uncomfortable with a return of these images, especially in a film with graphic violence and a pair of charismatic males at its center.

There is another element in Boorman's film which must have struck a similarly negative chord in German filmgoers when its source was identified. One can put it in the terms of trivial pursuit which Boorman himself encourages. The category is "History of German Cinema". Name the German film which is about mythologizing the charismatic male leader and his faithful chieftains, which features a soundtrack drawn extensively from Richard Wagner's music and whose director wins international acclaim. To anyone, German or not, familiar with German cinema, the obvious answer is Leni Riefenstahl's *Triumph des Willen*. And yet, if we keep the clues and change only the category to "English-Language Cinema of the 1980s," Boorman's *Excalibur* is the response most likely to come to mind. It should not be surprising, then, that many German critics and audiences found little they wanted to talk about in Boorman's film.

As if the connections to early German fascism and Nazi propaganda were not sufficient to account for the nonreception of *Excalibur* in Germany, we must also include the shock of Ronald Reagan's election to the presidency of the USA in 1980. Reagan's style and Cold War rhetoric caused widespread anger and resistance in the German public. He was billed as America's new charismatic leader, the cowboy who threatened the Soviet Union with nuclear attack if it did not cease its policies of aggression against the West. Not only did this former Hollywood actor refuse to guarantee that nuclear weapons would be used only for defensive purposes, he calmed his American supporters by volunteering Germany as the probable nuclear battlefield, should he decide to launch a nuclear strike against the Soviets. It was in the same year of Reagan's swearing-in as America's commander-in-chief that *Excalibur* made its appearance in German movie theaters. We must imagine the impact of an English-language film glorifying King Arthur as the charismatic leader who engages in violent clashes with his enemies and launches battles which eventually result in the bloody destruction of his court, his son, his knights, his culture, and himself. This is not a film destined to be received, critically or popularly, by Germans in October 1981.

Notes

[1] The perfectly transparent iconography of this painting has made it a symbol for the entire corpus of art produced under National Socialism. The painting was confiscated by the United States Army following World War II and stored with hundreds of others in the U.S. Army Historical Collection before being eventually repatriated to Germany. For a color reproduction, see Rhodes 43.

[2] Lanzinger was of course not the only artist to invoke the motif of the knight in armor. Rudolf Otto's *Kampfbereit,* reproduced in Hinz (203), is for instance striking in the similarity of its glowing green coloration of the knight's sword to Boorman's luminous solution for the depiction of the sword, Excalibur. Hinz features additional examples by Werner Peiner, Wilhelm Petersen, Wilhelm Sauter, and Albert Burkart. I am grateful to Mark Cory for bringing this to my attention.

Works Cited

Allen, Henry. "Return of the Hero." *Washington Post,* 12 April 1981, 1–2.

Beardsley, Aubrey, illus. *Le Morte D'Arthur.* By Sir Thomas Malory. 2 vols. London: J. M. Dent, 1893–94.

Canby, Vincent. Review of *Excalibur,* by John Boorman. *New York Times,* 10 April 1981, 11.

Caxton, William, ed. *Le Morte D'Arthur.* By Sir Thomas Malory. London, 1485.

Excalibur. Directed by John Boorman. Orion Pictures, 1981.

Fasteau, Marc. *The Male Machine.* New York: Dell, 1976.

Film Literature Index. Albany: Filmdex, 1973–present.

Hinz, Berthold. *Die Malerei im deutschen Faschismus: Kunst und Konterrevolution.* Munich: Karl Hanser, 1974.

Jauss, Hans Robert. *Toward an Aesthetic of Reception.* Translated by Timothy Bahti. Minneapolis: U of Minnesota P, 1982.

Jenny, Urs. "MacGuffin und der Märchenkönig." *Der Spiegel,* 26 October 1981, 228–35.

Kennedy, Harlan. "The World of King Arthur According to John Boorman." *American Film* 5 (1981): 30–37.

Lawlor, John. Introduction to *Le Morte D'Arthur*. By Sir Thomas Malory. 1, vii–xxxi. London: Penguin, 1969.

Malory, Sir Thomas. *Le Morte D'Arthur*. 2 vols. London: Penguin, 1969.

Markale, Jean. "*Excalibur* ou l'impossible grand-oeuvre." *Positif* 242 (1981): 38–43.

Pietsch, Ingeborg. "Gewalt für Jugend zugelassen?" *Film und Fernsehen* 14 (1986): 24.

Rackham, Arthur, illus. *The Romance of King Arthur*. Abridged from Sir Thomas Malory. New York: Macmillan, 1917.

Rhodes, Anthony. *Propaganda: The Art of Persuasion: World War II*. New York and London: Chelsea, 1976.

Schmidt, K. "Excalibur." *Medien und Erziehung* 26 (1982): 19–22.

Theweleit, Klaus. *Male Fantasies*. Translated by Stephen Conway. 2 vols. Minneapolis: U of Minnesota P, 1987–89.

_____. *Männerphantasien*. 2 vols. Frankfurt: Roter Stern, 1977–78.

Triumph des Willen. Directed by Leni Riefenstahl. Ufa, 1935.

Variety. 18 April 1981, 18.

Yakir, Dan. "The Sorcerer." *Film Comment* 17.3 (1981): 49–53.

Ein weites Feld: *The Aesthetization of German Unification in Recent Works by Günter Grass*

Mark E. Cory

In contradistinction to the surprising event itself, Günter Grass's 1995 novel about German unification, *Ein weites Feld,* was long anticipated and broadly advertised in its coming.[1] Very like unification, however, the novel since its arrival has been more criticized than celebrated. There is at least a double irony in this. First, many of those who have criticized the novel betray the same inflated expectations that made German unification a cultural happening before it could logically aspire to become a political and economic reality; and second, inflated expectations are part of what this novel is about. Those who hungered for a celebratory novel, an "Ode to Joy" as it were, chose to ignore the series of works leading up to *Ein weites Feld,* works which are not only internally consistent but which are superbly complemented by this latest novel. This essay examines the series, beginning with *Totes Holz* (1990), continuing with *Unkenrufe* (1992) and *Novemberland* (1993), and culminating with *Ein weites Feld,* both to construct a context for this latest novel and to lay the foundation for what is to date the most developed aesthetization of the unification by a single writer in German letters.

Totes Holz (1990)

From his earliest work on, Grass has reminded his readers that contemporary German culture is more than just West German culture. The ostinato of this reminder pulses softly in some of the works, becomes strident in others, but never falls completely silent. We hear it in the Polish-Kashubian-German cadences of Oskar's tin drum, we hear it in the various dialects of the poets gathered in Telgte, in the staccato Es-Pe-De of *Aus dem Tagebuch einer Schnecke,* in the more muted hymn to a single *Kulturnation* sung in *Kopfgeburten,* we hear it in the utopian and dystopian songs of fishes and rats.

At its most powerful moments, this refrain has seemed almost an appeal to a reunified Germany. Both in Grass's active political campaigning for Willy Brandt's *Ostpolitik* and in his literary campaigning for a German *Nationalstiftung,* the fact of two German states seemed in constant tension with the passionate ideal of a single cultural union. Given this, it is small wonder that Grass surprised and disappointed legions of readers (and, one suspects, still greater legions of nonreaders) by his outspoken opposition to German economic and political unification when it suddenly became possible, even inevitable. Grass in turn seemed surprised at the reaction his opposition provoked. In a short essay published in March of 1990, he relates being denounced by a young man in Hamburg as a traitor.[2] Admitting his fundamental opposition to a unified Germany, Grass asserted that in fact he had been outspoken in this opposition since the mid-sixties, extolling instead his idea of a German *confederation*. It now seems reasonably clear, however, that the distinction Grass tried to draw between a unified Germany and a political confederation with a common cultural tradition was too subtle to dam the emotional flood released by the collapse of the Berlin Wall in the fall of 1989. Stung by charges of "traitor," Grass and his publisher Luchterhand nevertheless went to considerable trouble to articulate and defend the intellectual consistency of his views on the German question, most notably by publishing under the title *Deutscher Lastenausgleich: Wider das dumpfe Einheitsgebot* a collection of his essays, poems, and excerpts from the novels to that point. While this collection reveals Grass's shortcomings as a prophet ("Es wird keine Vereinigung der DDR und der Bundesrepublik unter westdeutschem Vorzeichen geben," 1970), it does document the emergence of a coherent vision of Germany as "zwei Staaten–eine Nation."

By February of 1990, Grass had apparently reconciled himself to the ineluctability of political union. His lecture at the University of Frankfurt, repeated a week later in East Berlin and published in June, is still somewhat defensive and self-serving, but "Schreiben nach Auschwitz," his theme and title, gives a new and extraordinarily provocative challenge to the legitimacy of unification:

> Nichts, kein noch so idyllisch koloriertes Nationalgefühl, auch keine Beteuerung nachgeborener Gutwilligkeit können diese Erfahrung, die wir als Täter, die Opfer mit uns als geeinte Deutsche gemacht haben, relativieren oder gar leichtfertig aufheben. Wir kommen an Auschwitz nicht vorbei. (41f)

Despite this kind of provocation, events washed over these protests with scarcely a pause. Polls of contemporary authors in the *Stuttgarter Zeitung* (2 October 1990) and *Die Zeit* (5 October 1990) attempted to keep something of an intellectual debate alive, with Grass representing one extreme and Martin Walser the other, but attention gradually shifted to the juicier issue of how writers from the former GDR like Christa Wolf and Hermann Kant should now be regarded.

The process of aestheticizing his passionate involvement with issues of unification began for Grass at the very height of the intellectual debate during the summer of 1990 with the publication of a volume of sketches entitled *Totes Holz*. Critically praised,[3] *Totes Holz* most resembles Grass's sketchbook from his Calcutta experience, *Zunge zeigen*. Like the latter, it consists primarily of annotated charcoal and ink drawings, but in this instance the theme on every page is *Waldsterben*. Viewed superficially, the images convey a lifeless sameness, a stark and wintry landscape of black on white. These are not all winter scenes, however, and the unnatural death of the forest is what arrests the viewer and draws us to look more deeply into each frame. Even before reading the accompanying texts, we notice the quirky suppleness of some of the fallen and twisted trees, an anthropomorphic quality to trunk and limb that evokes a battlefield or the human victims of some natural disaster.

From the captions we learn that this barren wood stretches from Denmark along the German *Märchenstraße,* Erzgebirge, Oberharz, thence along the German-German border towards Prague. This was the route Grass wandered from the summer of 1988 through the fall of 1989, sketchbook in hand, revisiting some of the places in the venerable arbor of German culture made special by Goethe, Heine, and the Brothers Grimm.

The texts are actually of three types: verbatim quotations from the 1989 annual report of the Federal Ministry for Agriculture and Forestry; succinct, often lyrical captions by Grass to the individual sketches, sometimes only slightly embellished over what appears handwritten on the sketches themselves; and a seven-page afterword with the title "Die Wolke als Faust überm Wald: Ein Nachruf."

This "Nachruf," which pulls together and elaborates on the themes of the individual captions, is both an obituary for the German forest as fallen friend and an ambivalent testimonial to the way this friend has been preserved in German culture. The causes for and extent of the destruction are so widely known and well documented that Grass need spend little time reviewing them. The dry quotations from the annual W*aldzustandsbericht* accompanying nearly every drawing are sufficiently eloquent. As Grass sketched his way in the footsteps of Caspar David Friedrich from Rügen to Dresden, he observed the roughly parallel phenomena of the dying forests and the crumbling of the GDR: "Dann zerfiel von Tag zu Tag die Staatsmacht der Deutschen Demokratischen Republik, während ich zwangsläufig Blatt nach Blatt totes Holz zeichnete. Das färbte auf Untertitel ab" (106). Gradually, in fact, the arrangement of the sketches reflects a shifting of emphasis away from the ecological subplots of the 1986 novel *Die Rättin* towards a thematic complex specifically rooted in the issue of German reunification: for instance, "Wenn man im Oberharz von Deutschland nach Deutschland schaut, sind die Waldschäden verwandt und ist die Wiedervereinigung schon vollzogen. Mit Glasnost in den Wäldern beginnen!" (106), or "Als das Volk in Leipzig, Dresden, Berlin rief: 'Wir sind das Volk!', stand auf einem der Transparente: 'Sägt die Bonzen ab, schützt die Bäume!' " (107).

Sometimes his criticism is more complicated, as for instance when charcoal becomes simultaneously a self-reference to the artist ("Ich zeichnete sie allseits mit Blei, stinkender Tintenfischtinte, mit Kohle") and a satirical comment on the cavalier attitude of the Federal Republic's chancellor towards trees, and by extension towards the human victims of reunification ("Hier gilt noch immer der alte Köhlerglaube: Es ist ja genug da"). These victims are those other Germans, "die drüben." None of these human victims figures in the drawings, only "totes Holz." Yet the anthropomorphic quality of some of the images of fallen trees acquires its specifically political dimension from the accompanying texts, which either remind the reader of a gradual dying away, "Von Montag zu Montag," "schon lange vor Leipzig," or suggest that the trees, like Macbeth's Birnam Wood, and like so many people in the East, were ready to move on: "auswandern, doch wohin?"

Here again, as in so many of his earlier works, Grass can argue simultaneously for two seemingly contradictory points. First, that just as the *Märchenwald* is a part of a common German culture, the destruction of the forests knows no political boundaries, and second, that the solution to saving what may be salvageable does not lie in a buyout of East Germany by the Federal Republic.

The first point, though hardly original with Grass, is convincingly and movingly illustrated in this slender volume. The title of the afterword, "Die Wolke als Faust überm Wald," is taken from the caption to one of the last sketches in the series. It in turn derives from two earlier drawings, one of a dark cloud over dying trees and the other of a dead owl hovering, cloud-like, over a yet more sterile landscape. The cloud contains acid rain and in Grass's iconography signifies the hole in the ozone layer, "dieser gänzlich humorlose Spielverderber" which respects no political boundary. The owl, another in the long list of animal totems in Grass, carries both mythical attributes of wisdom and natural attributes as a forest creature whose soft song is stilled in the dying wood. "Silbenschwund, Lautverfall," reasons enough for an artist better known for long novels to turn to these spare strokes of pen and charcoal in order to express his indignation and his latest vision of our common future. That dark vision is the pair of blackened fists clenched ominously over a desolate hillside denuded of all life, littered with the skeletal corpses of *totes Holz*. Just as this work, unique in the Grass corpus, adds the owl to the incredible bestiary of dogs, snails, bats, blackbirds, flounders, and rats, so, too, does it add this cloud-fist to his catalog of apocalyptic images.

Why then the palpable resistance in ecological terms to German unification? From references to Chernobyl and to the reliance upon sulfur-rich brown coal in the GDR, it is clear that Grass is under no illusion about the ecological conditions in the East. But the prospect of a Germany dominated by the Western ethos is just as environmentally risky. With slogans extending from the ADAC's "Freie Fahrt für freie Bürger" to advertisements for the leading German export to the tropical rain forest, the "umweltfreundliche" Stihl chainsaw ("mit Katalysator"!), the West German consumer economy is unmasked as the more crippling partner of the two in crimes against our environment.

The oft-repeated observation that Günter Grass as writer is indistinguishable from Grass as graphic artist is confirmed perhaps more by *Totes Holz* than by any previous work. There is evidence enough in this volume that Grass knew the eventual outcome of the political events of 1989, and feared it. His invocations here of Buchenwald and Waldheim prefigure the position of "Schreiben nach Auschwitz," yet in the drawings and poetic texts there is the stubborn refusal to abandon all hope, a refusal that in the essays sometimes is drowned out by the shrillness of Grass's polemic.

Irmgard Hunt has perfectly described this refusal as the tension between hope and skepticism, an "Ästhetik des Schwebens." Here the ecological and cultural threats hover over Germany in the related forms of cloud, owl, and clenched fists. The tension is still there; outcomes are suspended; protest still possible.

Unkenrufe (1992)

In an interview conducted during the annual Frankfurt Book Fair in October of 1990 on the publication of *Totes Holz,* Grass was asked about his next novel. He replied, "Ich habe ein Thema im Kopf, das kann ich aber erst zu Papier bringen, wenn wir in historisch ruhigeres Fahrwasser kommen. Ich hoffe, dies wird nächstes Jahr der Fall sein."[4] The product of the calmer days that eventually followed German unification was *Unkenrufe.* This short novel, or *Erzählung* as the author calls it, is the first narrative in the Grass canon to thematize German unification, and so functions as a kind of prelude to the more fully orchestrated *Ein weites Feld* coming three years hence.

The narrative posture is familiar: a former classmate relates events in the life of a German native of Danzig, now sixty-two and a professor of art history in Germany. The skewed optic which has become one of the hallmarks of Grass's style creates a predictable uncertainty about the faithfulness of the chronicle of the protagonist Alexander Reschke, and the fluid time dimension now well known to Grass readers as the "Vergegenkunft" again provides just enough slippage to the historical events against which this chronicle occurs to preserve a future orientation to details of Germany's recent past. The major difference is the age of protagonist and narrator: when Pilenz described the cat and mouse adventures of his schoolmate Mahlke, both were teenagers; when Eddi Amsel took us into the complicated world of Walter Matern in *Hundejahre,* both narrator and subject were in their thirties. Now the history of that oft-bloodied city at the mouth of the Vistula is revisited by a sixty-two year old German scholar and widower, who returns in the fall of 1989 to the city of his youth and discovers both a new love and a novel idea for the genuine dismantling of the tensions between Poles and Germans characteristic of this and so many previous centuries.

The idea has to do with death. Death in fact saturates this novel to an extent unequaled in even the most apocalyptic of Grass's earlier fiction. Alexander Reschke is something of a specialist in death. As a scholar of baroque emblems and iconography, he has come to Danzig in part to deepen his knowledge of tombs, gravestones, sarcophagi, charnel houses, and their inscriptions and representations in art. While not really morbid by nature, he earned the nickname "Unke" among his students because his general nature coincides with the pessimism attributed in German folklore to the orange-speckled toad. In compiling his chronicle, the narrator interviews one of Reschke's students at the University of Bochum, who remembers him: "Eigentlich mochten wir ihn. Was soll ich noch sagen?

Manchmal stand er wie abgemeldet rum, und ständig hat er ziemlich negativ rumgefuchtelt, na, über die Zukunft, das Wetter und das Verkehrschaos, über die Wiedervereinigung und so. Hat ja mehr oder weniger recht gehabt–oder?" (104f).

With characteristically impish irony, Grass hatches the central and funereal idea of reconciliation through a German-Polish Cemetery Society at the very moment a new romantic love between the protagonist Reschke and a fifty-nine year old Polish art restorer named Alexandra Piatkowska comes to life. The fact that they meet on All Souls' Day, 2 November, just days before the fall of the Berlin Wall, is the first tip that this story of love and death is an allegory of European relations at the close of our century. But what occurs to both Alexander and Alexandra as they stand in a Polish cemetery from which prewar German graves have been ruthlessly stripped and contemplate the grave of her Lithuanian-born parents is simply that the time has come literally to bury old animosities and allow people to be interred in the soil they call home, regardless of present arbitrary political boundaries.

Despite criticism from Reschke's own daughters ("necrophiler Revanchismus"), the simple idea finds ready acceptance by church and civil authorities in Poland and Germany, with Lithuania reserving participation until its relationship with Russia has been clarified. A corporate board is constituted, an office opened, and Professor Reschke must turn his attention to the unpracticed details of managing a small business specializing in the acquisition of burial plots in Danzig for displaced Germans wishing to return "home."

After many frustrations–for example, the economical coffins obtained from the VEB Erdmöbel are found to be unsuitable, their low quality appropriate only for cremation–the plan rapidly attracts a long list of "Beerdigungswilligen"–a sign, Reschke excitedly reports, of a pent-up desire, an unexpressed hope for just the kind of solution that their plan offers. Having survived finally all the irritating delays accompanying events triggered by the fall of the Wall, the Deutsch-Polnische-Friedhofsgesellschaft conducts its first burials on 21 June 1990–the same day as the Oder-Neiße border is jointly recognized by the respective governments of East and West Germany.

On the personal side, the romantic love between widow and widower grows ever more intimate, so that we are not surprised by the marriage when it occurs near the end of the novel. On the commercial side, too, the positive energies unleashed by the initial vision of international reconciliation grow, and even compound. The idea spreads beyond Danzig to Silesia and Pomerania. By the conclusion of the tale, more than a hundred Polish cemeteries have been opened to Germans yearning to return home. But like two sorcerer's apprentices, Alexandra and Alexander find they have unleashed an idea whose power they had not anticipated and cannot control. Sensing the profits to be made, the German-Polish corporate board extends the original idea by establishing "Seniorenheime" (a euphemism for "Sterbehäuser") in the proximity of the Polish cemeteries.

Dilapidated villas, vacant warehouses, and decaying hotels slowly going broke under the changing economic conditions are elaborately renovated and leased (with an option to buy) to enthusiastic Germans "Unter dem Motto 'den Lebensabend in der Heimat verbringen'" (191). This first escalation seems a benign extension of the original, humane and spontaneous vision, but by the spring of 1991 a further escalation brings dissension to the board. Not content to profit from the sentimental hunger of the displaced elderly, some board members (and not exclusively from the German side) conceive of the idea of "Umbettung." The notion of massive repatriation of already deceased Germans who came originally from what is now officially accepted as Polish territory produces anxiety among other board members, scornful laughter from Alexandra, and resentment on the part of Alexander that his scholarly expertise on the subject of charnel houses is being misused. In the Polish press one begins to read uncomfortable sentiments: "Eine Armee deutscher Leichen tritt zur Eroberung unserer Westprovinzen" (197).

Of course, these objections are inadequate to forestall further commercial exploitation of what originally was a good and simple idea. When the smooth arguments about reducing unemployment and attracting western capital fail to placate suspicious members of the board, the idea designed to foster reconciliation leads ironically to open dissension. But the first resignations merely allow the introduction of new board members, younger and more aggressive still. To the expanding scope of Reschke's original idea of a "Versöhnungsfriedhof," which mutated into "Seniorenheime" and "Umbettungen," comes the even more profitable scheme of "Bungagolf," a series of luxury bungalows on the links for the active senior set and their affluent German offspring. An air charter service is added to accommodate the flood of subscribers, and when Polish authorities finally begin to resist further land sales, the market pressures lead to clandestine burials at sea in the Danziger Bucht, "wilde Seebestattungen" (236).

It is at the point of this grotesque deformation of their original idea that Alexander and Alexandra quit the board. What was conceived as a hopeful gesture of reconciliation between peoples long separated by suspicion and conflict had become little more than "eine deutsche Landnahme" (236). Reschke resigns with these words: "Die hinlänglich bekannte Vergnügungssucht der Enkel- und Urenkelgeneration will man...zur Kasse bitten. Das Ganze verschönt mit versöhnendem Wortgeklingel, als wären Golfplätze erweiterte Friedhöfe nur. Nein! Das ist nicht mehr unsere Idee. Hier wird, was durch Krieg verlorenging, mit Wirtschaftskraft wieder eingeheimst" (246).

It should be clear to readers by this time that *Unkenrufe* is only in part a novel about German-Polish relations. Andrzej Szczypiorski, reviewing the work solely from the Polish perspective in *Der Spiegel* (4 May 1992), made the mistake of assuming that the main point had to do with Poland. *Unkenrufe* is just as much a novel of German-German relations, and just as much a novel of the role of a united Germany in European relations. It is, of course, Grass himself who has played the part of Unke in connection with

German unification, and the commercial exploitation stretched here in fictional form to seemingly grotesque limits becomes less and less grotesque as the historical process of unification unfolds. As Grass has detailed in the essays mentioned earlier, the simple and thoroughly understandable emotional appeal of unification can be all too easily corrupted by nationalistic excess, political opportunism, and economic greed, to the end result of a virtual occupation of one country by another. As a more desirable alternative Grass has consistently held out a vision of separate countries with a shared cultural heritage. In *Unkenrufe* he refers briefly to the eighteenth-century Polish-German engraver Daniel Chodowiecki, a figure to whom he devoted an entire address on the occasion of the Evangelischen Kirchentag in Dortmund in June of 1991. His point then, and his major point in this novel, are one and the same: "Was Deutsche und Polen gerne beteuern zu sein, Chodowiecki war es: ein Europäer." Instead of composing his novel about an eighteenth-century Polish-German engraver, however, Grass unites late twentieth-century figures—both of whom have to do with art—in marriage. Theirs is a union of genuine affection, strong enough to withstand the petty annoyances of idiosyncratic behavior and irritating mannerisms, strong enough to hold against even philosophical differences over art—Alexander as an art historian prizes authenticity, Alexandra as an art restorer knows to value a good counterfeit. In their attraction for each another, and in their differences, these figures act out the kind of union Grass seems to crave for his Germanies, and for Germany and her neighbors. To be sure, the narrative closes with the deaths of Alexandra and Alexander on their honeymoon, but even here Grass makes his point. Killed in an auto accident somewhere between Rome and Naples, the couple lies buried neither in Germany, nor in Poland, but in an Italian village situated longitudinally almost exactly halfway between their respective countries.

However, Grass's ambitions for a positive European vision are even larger in *Unkenrufe* than the subtle reference to Chodowiecki and the marriage between Alexander and Alexandra can carry. Intertwined with the twin narratives of romantic love and nationalistic expansionism is the lightly sketched tale of Mr. Chatterjee, Bengali entrepreneur. Reschke and Chatterjee meet in the bar of the former's hotel on the same day Alexander and Alexandra make their fateful acquaintance. Chatterjee, whose common name figures also in *Zunge zeigen,* confronts Reschke's anxious vision of a Europe dominated by a unified Germany with a contrasting vision of a more pluralistic Europe created by population pressures from India, Pakistan, and Bangladesh. The 1,000,000,000 living souls he represents put the several hundred thousand displaced and deceased Germans in perspective. But Chatterjee's intentions are not hostile. On the contrary, with his system of bicycle rickshaws, he offers a simple and environmentally effective solution to one of Europe's most acute problems: urban traffic congestion. Wiry and fit at age forty-two, he can ferry passengers comfortably and swiftly through cities threatened by auto gridlock. By the end of the novel, which projects us years into the future to the end of the century, Chatterjee's solution has spread throughout Europe, even to the once totally choked streets of Rome.

At its height, the bicycle rickshaw becomes the counterexample to the German-Polish Cemetery Corporation as a model for a rational solution to many post-Cold War problems. Like the cemeteries and their extensions, the bicycle rickshaws are "seniorenfreundlich." But in this case, the strong market demand produces an environmentally friendly product in the factories formerly devoted to military armament and solves a problem of mass transportation that otherwise threatens every developed society. Moreover, instead of triggering old habits of nationalistic thinking and chauvinistic emotions, the explosion of Bengali-pedaled rickshaws stands as a metaphor for nothing less than "die Vitalisierung Europas durch asiatische Zuwächse" (59).

Why then does Mr. Chatterjee's bicycle bell sound the mournful cry of the toad? In none of his utopian glimpses does Grass grant a purely radiant vision, any more than he gives an unrelentingly dark vision in his dystopian, apocalyptic scenarios. His talent has always lain in the tease: a little of this, but a little of that as well, *mal ja, mal nein*. In satirizing German unification by having it roll back, as it were, the mass deportations of our century, Grass shows how a simple and intuitively sound idea can be corrupted by base instincts of greed and nationalism. The two people whose linked past, different cultures, and present affection promise so much become emblematic for a utopia for which Europe at the close of the twentieth century is still not ready—in order to preserve their relationship, Alexander and Alexandra must flee. In like measure, Mr. Chatterjee—himself a cultural and ethnic mixture of Indian and Pakistani—represents a measure of rejuvenation and cultural diversity for which Europe is also not ready.

In general, however, Grass is much gentler in *Unkenrufe* than in his other satires. This has distressed some reviewers and critics who evidently prefer the earlier and more volatile narratives.[5] Known for so long as the quintessential *Schwarzseher*, Grass seems uncharacteristically mild-mannered in this tale, his toad a rather dull addition to an otherwise colorful bestiary. I would argue that such reactions underestimate the extent to which *Unkenrufe* shows a mature artist responding with both consistency and freshness to a very challenging point in his career. As Grass has aged, so logically have his narrative personae. To object to the general sense of fatigue that spills over from the fictional characters in *Unkenrufe* to the reader is to miss the point that this novel is in part about an aging culture at the end of a wearying century. In beginning his story in the autumn with a couple choosing among the last available asters, by then projecting the close of the story to the year 1999, Grass in fact evokes unmistakable *fin-de-siècle* echoes. The imaginative construct of a German-Polish Cemetery Corporation relentlessly turning all of Poland into a trendy necropolis gives away nothing in terms of satirical bite to Oskar Matzerath's onion cellar, Eddi Amsel's bauxite cavern, or the *papier-mâché* replica of the Grimm Brothers' magical forest in *Die Rättin*. But in giving us more positive elements than we are used to, Grass reminds us that the call of the toad is both a folk warning and a sound of nature. Typically, Grass novels leave the reader poised between *ja* and *nein*, between utopian and apocalyptic visions. *Unkenrufe* gives more encouragement than any earlier work to affirm the good and humane aspects of various cultures, while continuing to resist those forces which can make the union of two individuals, or two peoples, something to fear rather than celebrate. It is as if the graying of Günter Grass and his characters is accompanied by a blending of the black and white dichotomies of his younger fiction. Within this context, the moderation of novelistic flamboyance and the substitution of the toad for the wise flounder and the cunning rat seem appropriate markers in the maturation of his art.

Novemberland (1993)

The narrative patterns of *Unkenrufe* will be resumed in *Ein weites Feld,* but filling in the period between it and the publication of *Unkenrufe* is a slim volume of thirteen sonnets accompanying an equal number of sepia drawings called *Novemberland* (1993). As in *Totes Holz,* this cycle, too, offers both dense formal and thematic congruity between text and drawings. Each of the thirteen drawings is dominated by an inked Arabic numeral from one to thirteen superimposed upon a fragment of hand-lettered text, and then flanked on the opposite page by that text as printed sonnet. The resulting nexus of number, inked image, verbal imagery, and content is often very rich and very subtle. Grass, however, rejects a simple correlation between the sonnet number and an historically or culturally significant day in November. For instance, the sonnet titled "Allerseelen" is not the second in the cycle and hence does not correspond in that simple way to All Souls' Day, but rather comes fourth in the cycle. Nevertheless, the bold "4" inked on the facing page fades unmistakably to an endless double row of cemetery crosses. The eighth sonnet, perhaps the most melancholy of the entire cycle, bears the title "Andauernder Regen," and accompanies a large fluid "8" like intersecting puddles across which a gusting wind drives droplets of text. This sonnet is followed by one lamenting the renewal of a fortress mentality in Germany, with repeated "9s" linked so that their crowns resemble concertina wire across the top of a wall. The penultimate sonnet, given the ironic title "Bei klarer Sicht," begins "Komm, Nebel, komm! und mach uns anonym." In its drawing, the "12" swims through a murky curtain of text.

The title "Novemberland" occurs in the first sonnet and is then repeated at intervals in the sixth, ninth, and thirteenth poems. *Novemberland* thus becomes a metaphor for *Deutschland,* a word which never appears, draping Germany with a cold, gray mantle of melancholy pierced only occasionally by flashes of anger. Reminiscent both in form and diction of Gryphius's sonnets from the Thirty Years' War, these thirteen poems lament a land ravaged not by war, but by "verkehrte Konjunktur," a people suffering not hunger, but overindulgence, the return of the plague in the form of drug addiction and the epidemic of AIDS, conniving politicians ready to exploit xenophobia ("Skins mit Schlips und Scheitel") now taking the place of Gryphius's "frecher Völker Schar." As metaphor, *Novemberland* is also the locus of dates that resonate powerfully in Germany's more recent history, obviously the fall of the Berlin Wall in November of 1989 which triggered the formal unification a scant year later, but also the abortive putsch by Hitler in November of 1923, and *Kristallnacht* in November of 1938.[6]

November was also the month in which, in 1992, Grass was invited to speak in the series "Reden über Deutschland," organized by the publishing house of Bertelsmann. His "Rede vom Verlust" carries the subtitle "Über den Niedergang der politischen Kultur im geeinten Deutschland" and functions as a kind of gloss to *Novemberland*, incorporating many of the themes and even some of the language of the poems and drawings. Still angry over the 1989 charge of "traitor," Grass makes explicit his higher allegiance to the German constitution, that is, to a promised *new* constitution, and of course his dismay over the watering down of asylum rights in the present Basic Law. It was specifically that summer's reports of violence against asylum seekers in Hoyerswerda, Rostock, and other German cities, Grass writes, that interrupted his writing (presumably the work on *Ein weites Feld*) and triggered the autumnal musings about the loss of a political culture of civility in Germany.[7] Loss is the key signature of this lament, a sense of loss Grass remembers experiencing over Danzig and chronicling in the famous early novels, a sense now rekindled over Germany itself:

> Wie ich dieses Land nicht loslassen wollte.
> Wie dieses Land mir abhanden gekommen ist.
> Was mir fehlt, und was ich vermisse. Auch
> was mir gestohlen bleiben kann. ("Rede vom Verlust" 40)

Of the four works that thus far constitute Grass's attempts to come to terms with unification, *Novemberland* is the most unrelieved in its pessimism. The playful twists of language in *Totes Holz*, the likeness of Grass himself peering impishly through the forest in one sketch, the mischievous humor in the exaggerations of *Unkenrufe*, the charming awkwardness of flirtation between people long out of practice as lovers, the upbeat energy of Mr. Chaterjee—nothing of that survives in the leaden spirit of these poems, of which the opening quatrain of sonnet number eight, "Andauernder Regen," is an example:

> Die Angst geht um, November droht zu bleiben.
> Nie wieder langer Tage Heiterkeit.
> Die letzten Fliegen fallen von den Scheiben,
> und Stillstand folgt dem Schnellimbiß der Zeit.

Ein Weites Feld (1995)

The gloomy mood of *Novemberland* carries over into Grass's latest, and longest novel (781 pages). *Ein weites Feld* opens, in fact, in deepest winter and closes with the renunciation of a country where a profound sense of loss has overshadowed any benefits of staying. As noted earlier, Grass had already established a clear pattern of allowing his subjects to age synchronously with their author. So whereas Alexander was sixty-two when *Unkenrufe* opens in Grass's sixty-second year, Theo Wuttke, alias Fonty, is seventy in that same fateful year (1989). By the time of publication Grass had turned sixty-seven. Those readers who looked to the leading novelist in what had now become pan-Germany for youthful enthusiasm for the prospects of unification were blind both to this pattern and to the evidence of disquiet manifest in the other postunification works. What makes Wuttke an especially interesting focal point for Grass in this, his major literary statement on German unification, is his capacity simultaneously to juxtapose two turning points in German political history: the *Gründerjahre* of the nineteenth century and the late twentieth-century collapse of the GDR into the expanded Federal Republic. Fonty manages this by virtue of his double identity as retired civil servant in the Theodor Fontane archives of the former GDR and expert on, impersonator, and cultural soulmate of Fontane himself.

This doubling, already suggested by the borrowing of the closing words of Fontane's 1895 novel *Effi Briest* for its title, has received well-orchestrated attention.[8] By creating a subject (Wuttke) whose life has been absorbed by his own subject (Fontane), Grass deliberately invokes a comparison of the state of German political culture now and at the end of the previous century. Fontane, as moderately subversive commentator on the period of German restoration after the unification of 1871 under Bismarck, is a genial vehicle. His contrast between the old and the new, between progress and tradition, and his fascination with those whose personal lives and fortunes are sacrificed on the anvil of these changes, make him highly instructive. Both Wuttke and Fontane attended the same Gymnasium in Ruppin. The inscription over the portal reads in Latin, "to the citizens of the future" *(civibus aevi futuri)*, which Wuttke now reads with different eyes from those when he was a student in 1938. Such snapshots are the technical innovation of this novel. By giving his protagonist a double life, and then having him retrace, in the critical period of late twentieth-century German unification, both the stages of his own life under National Socialism and the German Democratic Republic and the stages of Fontane's wartime service and disaffection from Wilhelmine Germany, Grass creates an extraordinarily dense set of palimpsests, a text with multiple impressions, none quite erased, each still faintly visible as a reminder of past efforts and past failures to serve the German citizens of the future.[9]

Wuttke is accompanied throughout the novel by a shadowy figure named Hoftaller, a former Stasi agent borrowed from the 1986 novel by

Hans Joachim Schädlich, *Tallhover*. Hoftaller is the symbol of the ubiquitous State apparatus synonymous with the GDR. Assigned to Wuttke because of the latter's quietly subversive activities (for example, Wuttke has used Fontane to criticize the GDR as he used him to criticize the Nazis, he stubbornly refuses to join the Party, he opposed the 1968 invasion of Czechoslovakia, and came out in support of fellow GDR dissident Wolf Biermann), Hoftaller is omnipresent, omniscient, and even in his retirement apparently omnipotent, at least as far as the individual fortunes of Wuttke and his family are concerned. When, in the early chapters of the novel, Wuttke attempts to break out of a collapsing system and a deteriorating family situation and flee, like Fontane, to Scotland, it is Hoftaller who intercepts him on the train and "persuades" him to remain. Later, after Wuttke's Jewish friend Professor Freundlich has committed suicide in the wake of university political reforms following unification, and after the Treuhand has taken away Wutttke's office in the Fontane archives, a despondent Wuttke plans again to flee, only to be intercepted once more by Hoftaller. It had been Hoftaller who forced Wuttke and his wife Emmi to break off contact with the Freundlichs on a vacation trip and return with him in his Trabant, Hoftaller who exploited Wuttke's daughter Martha when she was a Young Pioneer, inviting her to write about what was discussed by the people her father invited to their home, and Hoftaller who threatens to reveal that Wuttke's son had been a spy.

Referred to throughout the novel as Wuttke's "Tagundnachtschatten," Hoftaller is a figure who has fascinated Grass ever since he encountered Schädlich's original on the flight to Calcutta. In *Zunge zeigen* Grass invokes both Fontane, whose novels were then being read by his wife Ute, and Tallhover, an agent first of the Kaiser, then of the Weimar Republic, then of National Socialist Germany, and finally of the young GDR, as examples of a German-English-Indian colonial nexus. Fontane, who in *Zunge zeigen* appears as a subtle suggestion of marital tension between travelers Günter and Ute,[10] becomes the central means by which Grass personifies the unification in *Ein weites Feld*, but Hoftaller is no less important. Significantly, there is an act of generosity for every hostile act Hoftaller commits against Wuttke and his family. We learn, for instance, that Wuttke was marginally involved in the Resistance during the war while serving in France. His resistance consisted on the one hand of reading aloud from Fontane's work, readings which were taped and secretly circulated, and on the other of serving as a courier for the internal Resistance group Rote Kapelle once he was posted again to Berlin. In both instances, the omniscient Hoftaller protected Wuttke, hence his sobriquets, "heilender Arzt" (229) and "Schutzengel" (236). Later, when Wuttke speaks out too openly against Walter Ulbricht, it is again Hoftaller who saves him from prison. At the marriage of Wuttke's daughter, Hoftaller appears, an uninvited guest, to present as his wedding gift Martha's Stasi file, tastefully bound in leather. And still later, as the novel nears its end, Hoftaller and Wuttke ride the giant Ferris wheel above Berlin together and shred incriminating evidence against Wuttke's son, Teddy.

Hoftaller's greatest service to his quarry consists of helping Madeleine, Wuttke's issue from a wartime love affair, locate her grandfather. The considerable irony here is that Madeleine is the product of Wuttke's illegitimate child and independent enough in her thinking to cut through the constricted emotions which divide Wuttke from his French and German offspring, effecting a relationship of warmth and tenderness not seen in Grass since Oskar sought refuge beneath the wide skirts of his Kashubian grandmother. There was a time when Hoftaller used Wuttke's affair and illegitimate offspring to blackmail him into becoming one of the many, many casual informants for the Stasi. This explains some of the stranglehold Hoftaller is able to exert on Wuttke, alert as he is to the latter's desire to leave Germany. The motif of submerging, *untertauchen*, introduced in the earliest works such as *Blechtrommel* and *Katz und Maus*, becomes once again crucially important, and the novel ends with Fonty and Madeleine successfully slipping away from Germany, presumably to Fontane's Scotland.

It is, however, not only Wuttke, alias Fonty, who slips away from a Germany whose unification has created domestic tensions, has resulted in the death of his friend Professor Freundlich, has involved him in the economic spectacle of the Treuhand, and has threatened the Fontane archive which has indulged his identification with Fontane for decades. Hoftaller, too, finds his existence threatened by unification. Known as "der Spezialist für Systemwechsel" because, like his prototype Tallhover, he can finesse every political crisis to his own advantage, Hoftaller adopts a baseball cap and sneakers as his postunification uniform. In the central chapter of the novel, significantly called "Platzwechsel," he gleefully confides to Wuttke an alternative reading of German unification as a carefully orchestrated coup by the Stasi to avoid the Third Way of democratic socialism! The opening of the Berlin Wall was thus a Stasi plan to allow the West to swallow the weakened East, in order that a unified but doubly weakened Germany might then be forced, through inevitably resulting chaos, to reestablish law and order by reinstating the Stasi on its own terms. In his interpretation, the agent of this chaos is the state fiduciary commissioned to oversee the enormously difficult task of privatization, the Treuhand. The central metaphor for the persistence of old structures such as the Stasi under political systems whose newness may only mask the continuation of deeply entrenched ways of thinking is the venerable elevator in the building into which the Treuhand moves, a building which was once home to the Third Reich's Air Ministry, then functioned as Haus der Ministerien in the GDR. Affectionately named the Paternoster, this endlessly rising and descending series of open two-person cabinets into which passengers nimbly step has served equally well to transport Goebbels, Walter Ulbricht, Erich Honecker, and now the chief of the Treuhand. "Hübsch das Bild mit dem Paternoster, der unter jedem System seinen Dienst leistet" (577), Hoftaller comments, believing that, in one capacity or another, he, too, will be indispensable as governments come and go.[11]

Enough attention in the novel is devoted to the insensitivity of the Treuhand and—through the marriage of Martha and the ambitious West German developer Grundmann—to the crass commercial exploitation of the former East German states by the West to generate considerable sympathy for Hoftaller's position. Indeed, in what is surely the greatest exculpatory gesture of his fictionalization of German unification, Grass deliberately constructs so tight and sympathetic a pairing between agent and victim that it becomes impossible to tell who ultimately is more subversive. We can, however, say which of these two old men is ultimately more deserving of our sympathy, because only Wuttke is given the charming company of a bright, witty, enthusiastic, and above all loving granddaughter named Madeleine for his emigration. Hoftaller, since he has exhausted his supply of good cigars, is assumed to be emigrating to Cuba (or perhaps to Miami!), but he must do so alone. Nevertheless, at their parting, the two old men embrace.

Conclusion

Grass's long occupation with German unification[12] extends over a time when his notion of two states sharing a common cultural roof (*Das Treffen in Telgte*) has been supplanted by the reality of a unified country in which culture has an uncertain future (*Ein weites Feld*). In coming to terms with this changed political and cultural landscape, Grass has used his narrative, poetic, and graphic talents to record, where possible to retard, and always to contextualize and problematize a process many in Germany have been content to accept uncritically as a natural, even inevitable phenomenon. This process constitutes a remarkably consistent and at the same time remarkably inventive aesthetization of one of the stunning political reversals of the twentieth century. Aesthetization is, of course, sometimes taken to mean the systematic rendering of political events in a way that strips them of their context, makes them universal, immunizes them from questions of guilt and responsibility, in other words a process of depoliticization. With Grass, the aesthetization of German unification operates on several levels, but its purpose is never to depoliticize.

On one level, Grass as visual and verbal artist aestheticizes simply by illustrating these events of high political and cultural significance. On a second level, Grass uses fictional artists as narrative vehicles. As Thomas Mann aestheticized the demonic aspects of National Socialism through the fictionalized persona of a composer in his 1947 novel *Dr. Faustus*, so Grass gives us an art historian (Alexander) and a writer (Wuttke) as the principal lenses through which unification is viewed. And on yet a third level, Grass deliberately invokes a large number of actual artists, both living and deceased, to populate and indirectly to comment upon the changing cultural landscape of Germany. Thus in *Totes Holz* we are conscious of the influence of the painter Caspar David Friedrich, in *Unkenrufe* of the engraver Daniel Chodowiecki, in *Novemberland* of Andreas Gryphius and Simon

Dach implicitly, and of Hölderlin explicitly, and finally in *Ein weites Feld* of Fontane, but also of Christa Wolf, Wolf Biermann, and Uwe Johnson.

On all these levels of aesthetization, what has irritated so many readers is Grass's refusal simply to venerate unification and its associated phenomena. Instead, he teases out of every image or encounter as many conflicts as he can, thus problematizing the Treuhand, the Stasi, a market economy or a constitutional capitulation to xenophobia. His dogged persistence, in the face of a generally hostile reception to both the ideas contained in his work and the shaping of that work as art, is remarkable. Clues as to what motivates this persistence are of course scattered throughout most of his work, yet because they reside in the diaphanous layer of optimism often overshadowed by a more strident pessimism, they tend to be missed. One such clue is the union of Alexander and Alexandra in *Unkenrufe*, another the union of Wuttke and Madeleine in *Ein weites Feld*. Significantly, these interpersonal stories link Germans with representative neighbors to the east and to the west. Also significant is the fact that both unions take the German protagonists, the figures most readily identified with the author, out of Germany at the conclusion of these two narratives of unification. The pessimistic interpretation, entirely consistent with the dark mood of *Novemberland,* is expressed by Fonty in his last letter to his daughter: "In Deutschland ist keine Bleibe mehr" (674f). But a more subtly optimistic dimension lies in the achievement of an integration of Germany into Europe. It is towards this vision that both narratives point, a utopian vision that Grass dares to assemble out of all his disappointments over the defeat of democratic socialism. These unions are, of course, not the kind of union which occurred in Germany, which Grass regards as the swallowing up of one people by another. One is a marriage of two equal and independent persons, the other is a "union" which bridges an entire generation. In each such union, the differences between the partners are as important to the success of the bond as the elements held in common. The latest version of his stubbornly hopeful vision is the *summa* of Grass's aesthetization of unification and allows Fonty to say, in the final lines of the novel, "Übrigens täuschte sich Briest; ich jedenfalls sehe dem Feld ein Ende ab..." (781).

Notes

[1] For a summary of German reviews, see *Fachdienst Germanistik* 10 (1995): 14ff. See also note 8 below.

[2] Grass, "Kurze Rede eines vaterlandslosen Gesellen," in *"Nichts wird mehr so sein, wie es war": Zur Zukunft der beiden deutschen Republiken*, ed. Frank Blohm and Wolfgang Herzberg (Frankfurt: Luchterhand, 1990), 226–31.

[3] See summary of reviews in *Fachdienst Germanistik* 1 (1991): 17.

[4] Sabine Karradt, "Gegen den deutsch-deutschen Kahlschlag," *Der Morgen,* 9 October 1990.

[5] For a summary of German reviews, see *Fachdienst Germanistik* 7 (1992): 16ff.

[6] Michael Hamburger, in a footnote to his translation of these sonnets, points out the loaded references to 9 November.

[7] As Irmgard Elsner Hunt points out in her review of *Novemberland* and "Rede vom Verlust," the latter is dedicated to three Turkish women killed in anti-foreigner violence in Mölln.

[8] As indicated in the introduction to this article, *Ein weites Feld* was anticipated with an intensity unparalleled in the history of Grass criticism. Not only was the appearance of the novel an infamous cover story for *Der Spiegel* (21 August 1995), but *Stern* devoted a lavishly illustrated twenty-four page photo article on Grass, his novel, and its setting (17 August 1995). Michael Hamburger's review in English (*The European MagAZine* of 24–30 August 1995) is accompanied by the note that a new English translation of *Effi Briest* (Angel Books) was timed to coincide with the publicity surrounding *Ein weites Feld*.

[9] I am indebted to J.M. Coetzee for introducing me to the notion of palimpsests, which he discusses in his review of Salman Rushdie's latest novel, *The Moor's Last Sigh*, but which seems splendidly applicable to *Ein weites Feld*. See Coetzee, "Palimpsest Regained," *The New York Review of Books*, 21 March 1996, 13–16.

[10] Grass relates a dream in which Ute and Fontane have an affair. See Monika Shafi, "'Dir hat es die Sprache verschlagen': Günter Grass' *Zunge zeigen* als postmoderner Reisebericht," *The German Quarterly* 66 (1993): 339–49, for early mention of the suggestion of marital tension between Grass and his wife on this stressful voyage to India.

[11] Ironically, although Fontane is celebrated and referred to throughout the novel by the plural narrator (members of the Fontane archive) as "der Unsterbliche," it is the Stasi agent Hoftaller who emerges as immortal. Grass reveals his intentions in this regard already in *Zunge zeigen* when he protests Schädlich's original end for Tallhover, "Ich werde Schädlich schreiben: nein, Tallhover kann nicht sterben" (*Zunge zeigen* 26f).

[12] The earliest phases of Grass's fictionalization of German unification are nicely reviewed in Thomas W. Kniesche, "Grenzen und Grenzüberschreitungen: Die Problematik der deutschen Einheit bei Günter Grass," *German Studies Review* 16 (1993): 61–76.

Works Cited

Grass, Günter. "Chodowiecki zum Beispiel." *Die Zeit,* 14 June 1991, 51f.

_____. *Das Treffen in Telgte.* Darmstadt and Neuwied: Luchterhand, 1979.

_____. *Deutscher Lastenausgleich: Wider das dumpfe Einheitsgebot.* Frankfurt: Luchterhand, 1990.

———. *Ein weites Feld.* Göttingen: Steidl, 1995.

———. "Kurze Rede eines vaterlandslosen Gesellen." In *Nichts wird mehr so sein, wie es war: Zur Zukunft der beiden deutschen Republiken,* edited by Frank Blohm and Wolfgang Herzberg, 226–31. Frankfurt: Luchterhand, 1990.

———. *Novemberland: 13 Sonette.* Göttingen: Steidl, 1993.

———. *Novemberland.* Translated by Michael Hamburger. New York: Harcourt Brace & Company, 1996.

———. *Rede vom Verlust: Über den Niedergang der politischen Kultur im geeinten Deutschland.* Göttingen: Steidl, 1992.

———. *Schreiben nach Auschwitz.* Frankfurt: Luchterhand, 1990.

———. *Totes Holz.* Göttingen: Steidl, 1990.

———. *Unkenrufe: Eine Erzählung.* Göttingen: Steidl, 1992.

———. *Zunge zeigen.* Darmstadt: Luchterhand, 1988.

Gryphius, Andreas. "Tränen des Vaterlandes / Anno 1636." In *Das Zeitalter des Barock: Texte und Zeugnisse,* edited by Albrecht Schöne, 244. Munich: CH Beck'sche Verlagsbuchhandlung, 1963.

Hunt, Irmgard Elsner. Review of *Novemberland* and *Rede vom Verlust,* by Günter Grass. *World Literature Today* 68 (1994): 559f.

———. "Zur Ästhetik des Schwebens: Utopieentwurf und Utopieverwurf in Günter Grass' *Die Rättin.*" *Monatshefte* 81 (1989): 286–97.

Szcypiorski, Andrzej. "Froschegequak und Krähengekrächz." *Der Spiegel,* 4 May 1992, 263–65.

Contemporary Theory and the German Tradition: Some Stages in the Emergence of Critical Realism

Michael Morton

In section six of the *Discourse on Metaphysics* (1686) Leibniz asserts the principle that "everything is in conformity with respect to the universal order" (Leibniz, *Philosophical Essays* 39). This is a thought familiar to all readers of Leibniz, and in itself it may appear to express little more than a kind of pious hope. It as yet says nothing about why anyone should believe that what it claims to be so really is so. With this in mind, Leibniz's continuation of the passage assumes particular interest. "This is true to such an extent," he says, "that not only does nothing completely irregular occur in the world, but"—and this is the part of the passage that I think should commend itself most especially to our attention—"*we would not even be able to imagine such a thing*" (39, emphasis added). Nearly two and a half centuries after this was written, essentially the same key insight was expressed by Wittgenstein in his first (and almost only) published work, the *Tractatus Logico-Philosophicus*. There he writes: "It used to be said that God could create anything except what would be contrary to the laws of logic.—The truth is that we could not *say* what an 'illogical' world would look like" (Wittgenstein 3.031). In other words, as Wittgenstein puts it still more tersely later in the text, "What makes logic a priori is the *impossibility* of illogical thought" (5.4731).

From Leibniz to Wittgenstein a revolution is accomplished in ways of thinking about what is and is not the case—about what it *means* for something to be or not to be the case. It is difficult to overstate the magnitude of this revolution, upsetting as it did a fundamental assumption regarding human knowledge that had gone effectively unchallenged for over two millennia. And yet there is a striking disproportion to be noted between the magnitude of the revolution itself and its resonance in contemporary critical theory. There are a variety of reasons for this disproportion, but in order to see them in proper perspective it is necessary first to say something about the key epistemological assumption itself of which I just spoke.

Almost from its beginnings, Western philosophy is both animated and frustrated by an unresolved tension between ontology and epistemology, between the theory of what there *is* and the theory of what we *know*. Already on the part of some of the pre-Socratics, notably Parmenides and Heraclitus, there is at least a nascent tendency to interpret ontological questions as, in effect, epistemological ones. The same problematic duality then appears for the first time in sharp outline in what is often regarded as the founding corpus of philosophy proper in the West, the works of Plato. For some, indeed, these writings virtually define philosophy. In our century, Whitehead famously maintained that all philosophy is merely a series of footnotes to Plato. And though for a very long time after Plato there was a certain rough plausibility to this claim, for my purposes here it is crucial that we recognize the point in our history at which it ceases to be valid. This is the point at which the unresolved tension between the ontological and the epistemological is finally addressed and the first attempts at a resolution of that tension made.

The roots of Platonic metaphysics are, of course, to be found in the practice of Socratic inquiry—both in the objects of that inquiry and, even more importantly, in its distinctive forms and methods. And although this is all quite familiar terrain, it is nonetheless useful to remind ourselves of just what Socrates was after and how he typically went about trying to get it. In a word—and this is especially characteristic of the earlier dialogues, those in which the figure of Socrates appears to be speaking most nearly in the voice of the actual historical Socrates—he is seeking what we can call unity of definition. Rather than ask, as his more cosmologically inclined predecessors had done, what is the basic stuff of which the universe and all its particular phenomena ultimately consist, he asks instead, what do we truly *mean* when we use terms such as *knowledge, virtue, justice,* and a host of other familiar examples. This is a momentous shift, and it marks a watershed in the history of thought. Its effect is to make the outcome of inquiry dependent not on more or less unconstrained speculation, but rather on conceptual analysis and logical inference—the two principal components of the Socratic method.

On this basis Plato then erects the first great metaphysical system of the West. It is a system in which the linkage of metaphysics and logic is drawn more tightly than at any time previous and considerably more so than on most occasions since. And yet, the grounding of that linkage in specifically *human* forms of conceptualization and linguistic interchange, which is still evident in Socrates, is elided. Instead the ultimate objects of our knowledge, the true elements of reality, are removed to a plane beyond that of mere human commerce—the realm of the forms—from which we are supposed to have come originally and to which we aspire to return. For Heidegger, the Platonic inauguration of the tradition of Western metaphysics coincides with what he calls the "oblivion of the question of Being" *(Vergessenheit der Seinsfrage).* By this he means the moment in our history at which Being ceases to be experienced (and so articulated) in ontologically primordial fashion and is instead reduced to the status of one being, one entity among others. In Plato, for Heidegger, this reduction yields ideas; in Aristotle, essences; in Descartes, and for the most part thereafter, the subject; in Nietzsche, finally, the will to power. Another way of viewing this crucial juncture, not altogether at odds with Heidegger, is as follows.

Plato sets firmly in place the epistemological model that the medieval Scholastics would later term the *adaequatio intellectus ad rem*, the correspondence, or adequation, of the intellect to the thing. On this view, the attainment of knowledge consists in bringing the mind, via its representations, or images, or ideas, or some other sort of mental material, however construed, into conformity with an object of knowledge, which is itself understood to exist prior to, and wholly independently of, the act of cognition and the epistemic relationship thereby established. Already in antiquity, of course, there were challenges to this view, for which the famous assertion of Protagoras that "man is the measure of all things" may stand as an early paradigmatic instance. It is pivotally important, however, to be clear on just what it is to which Protagoras and his brethren among the Sophists are objecting. For on closer inspection it appears that, precisely in seeking to undermine the Platonic epistemological model, they have in fact already conceded the field to it in the one respect that really matters. The Sophists' project of relativizing cognition to particular forms of human perception and conceptualization is, in a sense, simply a radicalization of the approach taken by Socrates as described a moment ago (and in this connection it is worth recalling that Socrates was in fact viewed by many of his contemporaries as himself merely one among the Sophists). Yet, at the same time, the Sophists have already tacitly accepted the Platonic model of the *adaequatio intellectus ad rem* as the *only* possible way of conceiving knowledge under any circumstances. Thus rather than *reanalyzing* the concept of knowledge *in terms of* human perception and conceptualization, the Sophists insist on (merely) relativizing cognition to such forms. This insistence and the denial of the realizability of the epistemological ideal expressed in the *adaequatio* that naturally follows lead them to deny the possibility of knowledge as such.

With this the battle lines are drawn in what would become a centuries-long struggle for dominance between metaphysical dogmatists and skeptics. The story of the shifting fortunes of the two positions is a rich and fascinating one; to a large extent, it is the story of Western intellectual history at large. One of its striking features is just how little ever changes in all the time that the battle has been raging. As historians of skepticism such as Richard Popkin make clear,[1] the standard arguments for skepticism in almost all its variants were already well developed in antiquity and in fact brought to a level of refinement and sophistication rarely if ever surpassed since then. Nor should we find anything surprising in this. For just as the epistemological structure of metaphysical dogmatism undergoes no fundamental change over time—it is always that of the *adaequatio intellectus ad rem*—so, for precisely the same reason, skepticism remains, and must remain, in essence the same position it has always been. For, again, as we have seen, the skeptic denies only what the dogmatist asserts. The two are committed in precisely equal measure to the metaphysical model of the *adaequatio*. Dividing them is nothing more than a difference of opinion as to whether or not the epistemological aspiration contained in that model is capable of fulfillment. The model itself is never called into question.

The other notable thing revealed by the history of the dogmatism-skepticism wars is that neither side is ever able to gain a definitive victory. And, again, there is nothing surprising in this. The dogmatist will always be vulnerable to the skeptic's objection that the epistemic linkage of knower and known presupposed in the *adaequatio* is in the end a wholly arbitrary assumption, grounded (and groundable) in nothing more than a leap of faith. The skeptic, on the other hand, has in the end no response to the dogmatist's contention that he (the skeptic) does not truly believe his own arguments—that his entire life, including in particular his *discursive* relationships with his environment, human and otherwise, shows him to be perfectly certain of a vast number of things, great and small. Thus he cannot avoid lapsing at every turn into what today is often called performative contradiction.

Many contemporary skeptics compound matters by, in effect, rendering their existentially implicit performative contradiction altogether explicit. This occurs in the following way. The persons in question advance the standard arguments for one version or another of relativism, perspectivism, particularism, antifoundationalism, or (to use an umbrella-term for such outlooks that has been gaining favor for a while now) constructivism. These arguments are intended to establish the familiar skeptical conclusions *vis-à-vis* claims to objective reality and the possibility of its being known with certainty. Yet many who advance such arguments also evidently wish to make one or more exceptions to the otherwise all-consuming skeptical sweep of their position. These essentialist exceptions appear in numerous forms. Familiar examples include the oft-cited triad of race, gender, and class. Somewhat more recently, in part in conjunction with the emergence of both the new historicism and what is now widely termed postcolonial criticism, so-called national or cultural "identities" have similarly become candidates for this type of essentialist privileging. Other examples could be cited as well. For present purposes, however, I am less interested in the details of the phenomenon than I am in what all its particular manifestations have in common. This is the remarkable ability—and *remarkable* does not seem too strong a word here—of what are for all intents and purposes metaphysically dogmatic views to coexist with otherwise thoroughly skeptical outlooks in the minds of individual critics. I would venture to say that there is probably no more characteristic feature of current critical theory than this rather singular combination.

In a well-known, highly critical discussion of Derrida in *The New York Review of Books* a number of years ago, John Searle offered what might be taken as at least a partial diagnosis of this phenomenon (Searle "Word").[2] Searle noted his initial astonishment that a position as philosophically primitive as Derrida's could ever have attracted a serious following in the first place. But he noted as well that this following was primarily among literary critics, not philosophers (as, indeed, it has largely remained, though more recently with some slippage on the side of the philosophers). Searle felt constrained to observe that the literary folk who had flocked to the deconstructionist banner were for the most part simply far out of their depth when it came to actually assessing the claims advanced by Derrida (to the extent that those claims could be given intelligible content at all). And while this may not be the most charitable way to speak of one's colleagues in the academy, it is a largely accurate assessment. Until very recently people trained as literary scholars and critics received little or no training in either the history of philosophy or in techniques of philosophical analysis. Even today the situation has not changed as much in either of these respects as is sometimes supposed. Thus it was natural that many should miss altogether the extent to which Derrida's ostensible innovations in critical theory, beginning in 1966 and 1967, were in fact merely restatements of classical *topoi*, long familiar through centuries of repetition. Many to whom these arguments seemed so strikingly new were also not in the best position to detect the fundamental flaws in them—the same flaws that have always rendered skepticism an untenable position, untenable, because ultimately self-contradictory. Yet Derrida himself, no less than many of his followers, shows himself in several crucial respects remarkably unfamiliar with the history of thought; and in his case, as someone trained in academic philosophy, the lapse is far less excusable. The lacuna in his thinking—the lacuna that to a great extent makes deconstruction possible at all—can be shown in a number of different ways. One of these is by looking more closely at the point from which the deconstructionist enterprise takes its start. This is Derrida's encounter with, and attempt at a critical analysis of, the philosophy of Husserl.

For Derrida, as for most thinkers in the French tradition since the seventeenth century, the nature of the philosophical project and the path to its resolution (if any) are established by Descartes. Thus it is not surprising that some of Derrida's earliest work should have taken the form of a critical engagement with perhaps the most Cartesian of non-French philosophers, Husserl. Husserl himself frequently acknowledged the Cartesian provenance of his philosophy, perhaps most conspicuously in the title of his penultimate major work, the *Cartesian Meditations* of 1931. Long before this, however, Husserl was already pursuing an essentially Cartesian goal by essentially Cartesian means as he labored to define and give explicit content to the sort of philosophizing that he termed "phenomenology." Like Descartes, Husserl is seeking an absolutely firm, indubitable foundation for human knowledge, a once-and-for-all unassailable basis on which the entire edifice of philosophical science can be erected in reliable fashion. And like Descartes, the quest for this epistemological philosopher's stone leads him inexorably into the interior of the self, in an effort to lay bare the structure of what he calls "pure consciousness." Though Husserl often proclaimed as his motto the principle "zu den Sachen selbst" (to the things themselves), he might with equal justice have adopted the words of Novalis: "nach Innen geht der geheimnisvolle Weg" (inward leads the mysterious path).

For Descartes, once the putative ground of certainty has been located in the soul's encounter with its own intellective activity, there remains the problem of how to demonstrate conclusively that these movements of the spirit actually do link up with the things of the external world in such a way as to yield genuine knowledge of them. Indeed, the realms of spirit and matter are so defined by Descartes that, notoriously, he is unable even to account for the union of soul and body in the individual human being. Though he continued to grapple with the issue, in letters written in the last decade of his life he was obliged to acknowledge that the mind-body problem (as it has come to be known) remains perhaps the principal unresolved difficulty in his philosophy (Descartes 274-82). But the mind-body problem is merely one instance of the general epistemological problem that Descartes creates for himself. Starting from *within* the self, conceived in isolation from everything else, there will never be a way of getting back outside and establishing firm connections with the world. The only recourse is, ultimately, a leap of faith that those connections just do after all somehow get made. Descartes' position, in other words, is in classic fashion that of the metaphysical dogmatist, and, as is always the case with metaphysical dogmatism, it positively invites skeptical challenge (an invitation that was not long in being taken up by his contemporaries and successors).

The corresponding version of this Cartesian problem in Husserl arises one step earlier in the overall process. Whereas for Descartes the difficulty is how to get back outside to the world, for Husserl the real and persistent difficulty is how to get all the way inside in the first place. Husserl does not doubt, as Descartes before him did not, that the locus of certainty, the "Archimedean point" capable of grounding all else, lies within us. Where Descartes, however, is content to appeal in fairly straightforward fashion to the (again, supposedly) unimpeachable certainty of the *cogito*, for Husserl the picture is a decidedly more complicated one with respect to both the ultimate source—what he calls the "transcendental ego"—and the means of access to it, a process that he terms "eidetic intuition." And it is at this level that Husserl creates for himself a metaphysical bind directly analogous to the Cartesian one seen a moment ago. In his determination to find an absolutely presuppositionless ground for our knowledge of reality—for reality itself insofar as it can be experienced—Husserl seeks to "bracket out" everything that is in any way part of our "natural attitude" toward things, including in particular any assumption as to their real existence. The aim is to build in from the outset methodological safeguards against prejudicing the outcome of inquiry through covert or unreflected reliance in our explanations on the very things that need to be explained in their own right. This has the consequences, however, first, of opening a gulf between the empirical and the transcendental self, and, secondly, of thereby rendering access to the latter an almost wholly mysterious, even mystical, process of preconceptual appropriation. Again we find ourselves forced in the direction of an ultimately arbitrary leap of faith, this time even to set the machinery of inquiry into motion to begin with.

It must not be supposed, however, that the problem is merely one of execution on the part of the thinkers in question. The quest for ultimate foundations, not merely as *pursued*, but already as *conceived* in the Husserlian-Cartesian manner, can lead to no other conclusion. But Derrida (like many others today) believes that the only alternative to a dogmatic postulation of foundations of this sort is a skeptical denial of such foundationalism. And it is this (as Searle observes in the essay noted earlier) that marks him unmistakably as the classical metaphysician he is. As we have seen, the skeptic, accepting unquestioningly the model of the *adaequatio*, merely denies what the dogmatist asserts. He is committed to the necessity of a metaphysically conceived foundation as the ultimate guarantor of the certainty of knowledge and the determinacy of signification—the necessity, that is, of an "Archimedean point," or, as in Derridean idiom, an *archè*–he merely despairs of the possibility of ever discovering such a point. One thinks of Heine's characterization of himself as a "defrocked Romantic." Like Heine, who can no longer believe in the realizability of the Romantic program but who is in equal measure unable to conceive of salvation in any other terms, the skeptic refuses to honor the check offered by the dogmatist in payment of the epistemological bill, but at the same time he continues to carry the check with him as a permanently unredeemed and unredeemable IOU.

The key mistake here—and with this we return to the great lacuna in Derrida's knowledge of the history of thought—is to suppose that there is any bill to be paid, any debt to be redeemed. As Searle says of Derrida, Derrida sees that there is no possibility of providing metaphysical foundations for knowledge and signification, but he mistakenly supposes that with the discovery of that impossibility something basic and important is lost. Yet it is only when one assumes the inevitability of the *adaequatio*-model that that conclusion follows. And there is in fact nothing at all inevitable about that model. In some of his later writings, notably in the *Cartesian Meditations* and also in *The Crisis of European Science*, Husserl, too, begins to move away from that model. Though the exposition still remains hampered by the foundationalist assumptions that dominated his earlier writings, Husserl also gives clear evidence of a fundamental change in outlook regarding both the nature of the basic problems of philosophy and the path to their resolution. A passage from one of the shorter companion pieces to *The Crisis of European Science*, published independently in 1939 after Husserl's death under the title *On the Origin of Geometry*, illustrates this pivotal shift in his thinking:

> The objective world is from the beginning (*von vorneherein*) a world for all, the world that "everyone" has as world-horizon. Its objective being presupposes human beings, in their humanity, as creatures of a common language. Language, in turn, as a function and learned capacity, is correlative with the world, linked to the universe of objects as linguistically expressible in their being and being-as-such. Thus human beings qua human, the human community at large (*Mitmenschheit*), the world—the world of which we can speak at all—and, finally, language are all inseparably bound up with one another; the certainty of each is always already given with and in this reciprocal referential unity. (Husserl 370; my translation)

Husserl enunciates here the principle that I call the *co-originality thesis*. The term *co-originality* is borrowed from Husserl's (sometimes wayward) student Heidegger, who, notwithstanding numerous and serious lapses in both judgment and conduct in his own life, nonetheless also developed a brilliantly original interpretation of the principle in question, chiefly in the early sections of *Being and Time*. Heidegger's word is *Gleichursprünglichkeit*. The key insight here is that human beings, the world of human experience, and the linguistic-conceptual framework in which alone that experience has form and content are so thoroughly and inseparably bound up with one another from the outset that no account of any of them can possibly be adequate if it is not at the same time an account of them all. This, in turn, has the immediate (and salutary) consequence of permitting us—indeed, requiring us—to jettison the epistemological model of the *adaequatio*. It can no longer even make sense to ask how the mind, conceived of in pristine isolation from the correspondingly conceived objects of knowledge, bridges the gap between it and them. For there is no gap to begin with, nor could there be. There is no "us" at all except as always already immersed in the vast world of lived experience—what Husserl calls the *Lebenswelt*—just as there is no "world" that is not already (again, always already) thoroughly informed and determined by the linguistic-conceptual structures that render it *our* world, the world of human beings.

As the supposed gap between mind and world vanishes, so there vanishes as well both the possibility and the need for metaphysical foundations. And thus we are able to profess ourselves philosophical realists, both in accordance with common sense and also with an epistemologically clear conscience. But the realism for which I am arguing here no longer has much besides the name in common with the traditional realism of the *adaequatio*. Thus it seems useful to keep the two terminologically separate. My way of doing so is to speak of precritical realism, on the one hand—the realism that expresses the never fulfillable aspiration of the metaphysical dogmatist—and *critical* realism, on the other, the realism to which each of us always and unavoidably attests, if only tacitly, simply by living. The choice of idiom once again reflects a philosophical borrowing, this time from Kant. Kant's contribution to the theory of critical realism is immense. But it is not the only such contribution. There is a large and multifaceted genealogy of this outlook, much of which still remains to be traced by intellectual historians. It is also, in particular, a chapter in our history of which Derrida seems altogether unaware.

Before proceeding further I want to say a couple of things by way of terminological clarification. First, many philosophers today distinguish between realism and antirealism. The position I am here calling critical realism is often regarded as a species of antirealism. I confess I have always found this puzzling. Perhaps it reflects an unstated assumption that *realism*, if it means anything, must mean what I am calling precritical realism. It is central to my argument, however, that realism, so construed, remains, and must remain, a doomed project. Expressed positively, I am urging that the only realism we are capable, not only of understanding, but actually of defending against skeptical challenge, is critical realism. Secondly, with regard to the term *critical realism* itself, in the interests of full disclosure and especially in view of the fact that I am accusing Derrida of a certain culpable negligence in his reading, it must be acknowledged that I am to some extent open to a similar criticism. When I first adopted the term *critical realism* as a convenient shorthand designation for the standpoint I was seeking to expound, I failed to inquire sufficiently into previous uses of the term. Two of these, one going back a number of years, the other quite contemporary, are by Roy Wood Sellars and Roy Bhaskar. So far as I can tell—and the actual answer must await a more thorough study—there seem to be both relevant similarities and important differences in these three notions of critical realism: Sellars's, Bhaskar's, and my own.[3]

To return, then, to my own exposition of critical realism in historical perspective, one of the fascinating things about this story is the way in which critical realism emerges, as it were, a piece or two at a time. Prior to the twentieth century, I know of no really comprehensive statement of the position; even its most able exponent in this century, Wittgenstein, left work for his successors to do. For the beginning of the story, however, as I suggested at the outset, we do best to look to the emergence of modern German thought at the turn of the seventeenth to the eighteenth century in the work of Leibniz. Among the many important contributions to philosophy made by Leibniz, there are two in particular that I want to single out for emphasis. Their joint effect is to establish a context and direction of thought that in succeeding years would make possible the emergence of a gradually, but steadily, more articulated theory of critical realism. Leibniz begins, in effect, to conceive of logic not as a theory of thoughts but rather as a theory of statements, and then to conceive of metaphysics on the model of the logic so construed. (I say "in effect" so as to leave to one side the question of how Leibniz himself may have viewed the relationships among the logical, linguistic, and metaphysical aspects of his philosophy. Leibnizian scholars are themselves not altogether of one mind on this issue. For present purposes, I am interested only in what I think may plausibly be read out of Leibniz for a larger genealogy in the history of thought, that of critical realism.)

To encounter Leibniz's philosophy is to experience an extraordinary combination of what seems, on the one hand, resolutely down-to-earth, almost commonsensically obvious plain-speaking with, on the other hand, what may well strike us as utterly fantastic, almost otherworldly speculation. (This is the sort of thing I was getting at a moment ago in suggesting that the theory of critical realism emerges historically a piece or two at a time. The various components of the theory are formulated only incrementally, and the relationships among them perhaps even more so. Thus at any stage in the overall genesis of the theory we should not be surprised to find what may seem in retrospect rather odd combinations of views, which on closer inspection reveal insights that prove to have been of enduring value, having been subsequently developed, reformulated, and recombined with later advances.) On numerous occasions Leibniz declares his "chief principle" to be what is usually known as the *in-esse* principle (Leibniz, *Philosophical Writings* 62). This asserts that the truth of a proposition is, and can only be, a matter of the predicate of the proposition being *contained in* the subject. At the same time, he comes very close to asserting that this is simply what *truth* means. In the short piece generally known as *Primary Truths,* he seems to leave no doubt whatsoever as to his opinion: "The predicate or consequent, therefore, is always in the subject or antecedent, and this constitutes the nature of truth in general, or, the connexion between the terms of a proposition" (*Writings* 87). In the somewhat later piece *On the Principle of Indiscernibles,* he again accords this principle a position of primary importance: "All that we have said here," he writes, "arises from that great principle, that the predicate is in the subject" (*Writings* 135).

The question then naturally arises: what does it mean for the predicate to be contained in the subject? Leibniz makes quite clear that he understands this relationship above all as a matter of conceptual analysis: the predicate of a proposition is said to be contained in the subject when analysis of the concept, or notion, of the subject reveals that the corresponding concept, or notion, of the predicate is in fact nothing different from it, but rather already from the outset part of its complete definition. Thus the subject-predicate form of the proposition is simultaneously the model of truth and, for the same reason, the form of reality itself. Such truths are referable in turn to what Leibniz calls substances (later, monads), each of which, he maintains, "expresses" the entirety of the universe in its own way, that is, from its own unique perspective and with the degree of clarity, distinctness, and adequacy appropriate to it. Exactly what Leibniz understands by *expression* here already perplexed some of his contemporaries. Responding to Arnauld on this score, he writes: "One thing *expresses* another (in my language) when there is a constant and ordered relation between what can be asserted of the one and what can be asserted of the other" (*Writings* 71).

In the probably fairly late *Metaphysical Consequences of the Principle of Reason* he returns to the question and glosses the notion of *expression* again in basically the same terms: "It is sufficient for the expression of one thing in another that there should be a certain constant relational law, by which particulars in the one can be referred to corresponding particulars in the other" (*Writings* 176–77).

In both cases it is instructive to consider the examples that Leibniz offers to illustrate this relation of "expression." On both occasions he refers to the use of mathematical figures as *projections* of other figures, shapes, or models. What the expression has in common with the thing expressed, that which makes the relation of expression possible at all, is thus evidently what Wittgenstein, in the *Tractatus*, would call their "logical form." And it is interesting to recall that Wittgenstein, too, makes use of illustrations of much the same sort, pointing out, for example, that there must be some feature in common linking the notes of a musical score, the grooves of a phonograph record, and the acoustic vibrations of the music itself. Again, it is a matter of a rule-governed, structural isomorphism among three superficially quite distinct sorts of phenomena. Indeed, for Leibniz, as for Wittgenstein, the ubiquity of expressive relationships of this sort, taken together with the fact that they are at every point correlative with the forms of human intellection itself, yields the conclusion that absolute *dis*order or *in*comprehensibility in the world is at once impossible and inconceivable, and this for precisely the same reason. As Leibniz puts it in *A Specimen of Discoveries About Marvellous Secrets of Nature in General*, "just as no line can be drawn, with however casual a hand, which is not geometrical and has a certain constant nature, common to all its points, so also no possible series of things and no way of creating the world can be conceived which is so disordered that it does not have its fixed and determinate order and its laws of progression" (*Writings* 78–79).[4]

The difficulty with Leibniz's system is that it seems to prove too much. This is at once the advantage and the disadvantage of the *in-esse* principle. By means of it Leibniz is able to develop a kind of partial or protoversion of critical realism; the linkage that he establishes connecting individual substances (in particular, human souls) with the logical forms of conceptualization and thereby also the phenomena of experience is sufficiently tight for us to recognize at least an anticipation of the co-originality thesis. Yet, at the same time, the logic of the argument pushes us in the direction of wholly isolated, windowless monads, bearing no real relationship to one another save that of a divinely ordained pre-established harmony. It is at least questionable how much such a system truly enables us to make sense of experience. Both the attractions and the drawbacks of the Leibnizian approach appear in sharp outline in his analysis of causality. As numerous passages in his writings make clear, for Leibniz what are commonly called cause-and-effect relations are nothing other than matters of rational explanation. "A *cause*," he says in *A Resumé of Metaphysics*, "is simply a real reason" (*Writings* 145). More specifically, in the *New System of the Nature and Communication of Substances*, although there neither is nor can be, in Leibniz's view, any actual contact (causal or otherwise) between substances, "it may fairly be said that when the particular disposition of a given substance is the explanation of a change taking place in an intelligible manner, so that we can infer that it is to this substance that the others have been adjusted in this regard from the beginning...then that substance ought to be conceived as in that respect *acting* upon the others" (*Writings* 124–25). In short, as he puts it in the *Specimen of Discoveries*, "causes are assumed, not from a real influx, but from the need to give a reason" (*Writings* 79).

In thus reducing causality, in effect, to logical entailment, Leibniz blocks any possibility of a skeptical challenge of the sort that Hume would later mount; but he does so only at the cost of emptying the concept of causality of the content normally felt to inhere in it. The problem, I would suggest, is that for all the advance he represents over Cartesian metaphysics, Leibniz nonetheless remains in the end trapped within the subject, endeavoring to get outside and link up with the rest of reality. And thus he, too, must in the end fall back on an ultimately dogmatic leap of faith, appealing finally (not altogether unlike Descartes) to the assumed providential omnipotence of God to anchor the entire system. To put it another way, he has not yet taken the crucial step from a traditional deductive method—philosophy *more geometrico*— to a method of *transcendental* deduction. Or, perhaps more accurately, he has not yet completed that step. For there is a great deal in his thinking that clearly anticipates developments in the eighteenth century and thereafter. We think, for example, of Leibniz's repeated insistence that, whereas most created substances merely express the world, it is the preeminent privilege of human souls to express God. The human soul, in other words, is a kind of microcosmic image of divine creative *activity*. The activity of perception in the soul is time and again spoken of by Leibniz as a process of *synthesis*. And this activity is closely linked to the other defining property of the soul, which Leibniz terms *appetition*. This is the expression of the soul's inherent dynamism, its spontaneous tendency to undergo a ceaseless process of progressive change and development. This is, moreover, a process to which, in accordance with the active, quasiconstitutive nature of perception just noted, the sequence of changes in the universe at large must of necessity be correlative.

It would be the task of another study to show in detail the extent to which these Leibnizian motifs are picked up and expanded in the writings of Kant, Herder, Hegel, and numerous others down to our own day. I do want to suggest at least something, however, of how critical realism after Leibniz continues to emerge in the eighteenth century as the way of avoiding the precritical alternatives of dogmatism and skepticism. The key figures here are Kant and Herder. Each introduces important advances in the theory; the problem is simply that there are two of them. A single Kant-Herder could perhaps have completed the theory, or at least have brought it as far as it has come to date. As it was, however, each merely provided what the other was not able to; and for a variety of reasons (some of them having to do with the strained personal relations between the two) a meeting of the minds never took place. Both Kant and Herder are, in basic philosophical intent, critical realists; both, that is, are seeking an adequate formulation of the co-originality thesis. Kant's strength is in the systematic rigor of his exposition, reflected above all in his invention of the type of argument known as the transcendental deduction. Yet, in part due to his adoption of the faculty-psychology vocabulary of Wolff, Kant remains largely trapped within the subject, like Leibniz, and this would subsequently leave his arguments open both to criticism and to misappropriation by his successors.

Herder, on the other hand, though possessing little of Kant's talent for architectonic (and still less of his inclination for it), nonetheless senses clearly the missing piece in the Kantian puzzle: *language*. Again, language had already figured prominently in Leibniz's deliberations, for example, in his dream of a *characteristica universalis*, a universal symbolism capable of being employed (within the limits of human finitude) as an all-disclosing calculus of thought. Yet it is Herder who first takes the step of grounding this central role of language in the concrete, lived world of human linguistic commerce. He is, in other words, the first to recognize that the co-originality thesis can never be established on the basis of pure consciousness alone. Rather than beginning *in here*, in the head, it is crucial to start *out there*, in the public, communal sphere that Husserl terms the *Lebenswelt*. Moreover, this is no merely arbitrary decision on Herder's (or Husserl's) part. If it were, it would be open to skeptical challenge in its own right. But skeptical challenges, no less than any other form of human activity, must themselves be situated—in particular, *linguistically* situated—if they are to be anything at all for human beings. And thus, precisely to the extent that they can even be formulated in (apparently) intelligible fashion, skeptical challenges to objectivity and coherence cannot help bearing witness to the very thing they would undermine. Skepticism cannot shake our faith in ultimate grounds or foundations of knowledge and signification, for there *are* no such grounds, hence nothing to lose faith in.

Derrida, surprisingly perhaps, comes very close to this recognition with his famous assertion *il n'y a pas de hors-texte*. If by *text* we understand the co-original triad of human beings, the world of experience, and the linguistic-conceptual structures in which both of these are mediated and communicated, then of course there is no "outside" of this. But Derrida seems not to believe (or not to grasp the true import of) his own thesis. His inveterate skepticism depends on a persistent positing of the very thing he would deny: an ultimate, but never attainable, foundation of the very "textuality" that in the same breath he wants to claim is all there is. From the standpoint of the history of critical realism as it has unfolded, chiefly in Germany since the eighteenth century, much of contemporary theory, literary and otherwise, cannot help but appear rather shopworn, endlessly ensnarled in the same, long-since obsolete aporias of dogmatism and skepticism. If there is to be a genuine revitalization of criticism, as we approach the turn of the millennium, it will surely have to begin with a renewed recognition of the reality of the critical triad. If literature (not to speak of culture at large) is something worth taking seriously, and if its critical elucidation is something on which it is worth expending our effort, then this must ultimately be because it speaks to both the reality and the possibility of human experience. It can be supposed to do so, however, only if the language in which it speaks is first recognized as a reality in its own right and not a perpetual misfiring at a never discernible target. We do not need to be, and should not aspire to be, either hyperessentialists, as in the later Heidegger, or negative essentialists like Derrida. The task is rather to translate the *non*essentialism of critical realism into an interpretive idiom capable of doing justice to the texts themselves, and that is to say: to the world of lived experience from which they come and to which in the end they always return us, however much in the meantime we may have gone astray.

Coda: The Post-Postmodern Condition

One of the distinctive features of the German intellectual tradition is that *idealism*, which has been for the most part in one form or another the dominant strain in that tradition, typically manifests a twofold sense not generally reflected in the idealist philosophies of other nations. We can call these two senses—not always clearly or sharply demarcated from one another—the *descriptive* and the *projective*. In accordance with the first of these, idealism characteristically finds the ultimate locus or source of reality in the realm of what is variously called the intelligible, the mental, the spiritual, the ideational, or some such similar designation. The domain of the material (or corporeal), on the other hand, is a kind of second-order or derivative sphere, not necessarily devoid of reality, but also not primarily, or ultimately, real. This much is more or less standard fare for all versions of idealism, true for Plato no less than for Hegel. It is with the second of these two senses, and the various possible combinations with the first of which it admits, that the distinctively German versions of idealism come into view. Here the relationship between the ultimately real and the not-quite-as-real is construed in *temporal* terms, projected onto a *historical* axis, and so becomes a relationship between the fully real*ized* on the one hand and that which is still underway toward that goal on the other. The latter is comprehended in a (possibly endless) process of *development* by which the merely potential, or latent, or virtually existent in it is rendered actual.

From the standpoint of epistemology this has the consequence that the object of our endeavors is removed from its previous position "behind," or prior to, us to a (possibly indeterminate) location out in front of us: the ideal objects of knowledge, rather than being eternal, *a priori* existents with which we seek to bring our cognitive faculties into alignment (as, for example, in Plato), *acquire* that very status. They *become* the ideal objects which in prospect they are, only insofar as they are brought into being–constructed, constituted as such–by us. Or, most interestingly of all, *both* these points of view may be combined in a single philosophical perspective, in such a way that while both remain discernibly active, each is also modified to some extent precisely by virtue of the relationship it is now seen as entertaining to the other. Such, I think, is clearly the case with Leibniz. Both the element of descriptive reflection (or expression) of reality and that of projective (indeed, explicitly teleological) realization of the design of Creation are built into the Leibnizian metaphysics at the most basic level in the form of what are for him the two (and only two) defining properties of each substance (or monad): perception and appetition. But this twofold pattern–a kind of mutually implicative relationship of *is* and *ought*–is not confined merely to the realm of abstract theory in Leibniz's work. It has altogether down-to-earth, real-world implications for him as well. One way to see this is by considering the leading role played in his thought by the idea of universal harmony.

Commentators are generally at one in noting that if there is a single overarching principle informing all of Leibniz's work, it is surely that of universal harmony. The view of things as constituting a rationally ordered totality, each of whose elements is coordinated with all the others in accordance with the rule of maximum possible perfection, is attested to repeatedly and in numerous ways throughout his writings. And at the level of abstract theory, it incorporates the dual aspect of description and projection that tends to be characteristic of German idealism. That same dual aspect, however, also appears in connection with the idea of universal harmony in another fashion. The Europe of Leibniz's time was still riven by factional, and especially confessional, division. As a German, Leibniz was particularly well positioned to appreciate just how serious the consequences of such division could be. The level of violence and the extent of the devastation wrought by the Thirty Years' War, for which the German-speaking regions of central Europe had provided most of the principal battlefields and theaters of operations, would not be equalled for another three centuries. In this circumstance it is not surprising that thoughts of how–or whether–at least some minimal degree of concord might be achieved among potential (perhaps permanently potential[5]) adversaries should loom large in Leibniz's deliberations. The idea of universal harmony thus functions in his work not merely as the centerpiece of a metaphysically guaranteed, comprehensive *account* of the nature of reality at large. It is at the same time for him an entirely concrete and specific *aspiration* for the organization and conduct of human affairs in society—in short, the key to a Leibnizian theory of, and program for, political dealings among individuals and groups.

In effect, Leibniz lays the foundation for the development of a politics in critical realist perspective. The epistemology of critical realism, as we have seen, seeks not so much to refute skepticism (along with its mirror image, dogmatism) as to dissolve it. It does so by bringing to light, in Wittgensteinian fashion, the confusions on which skepticism of necessity always rests; in that way it deprives the skeptic of the possibility of even a coherent formulation of his position, much less an actual defense of it. The critical politics that we can see emerging, at least implicitly, in Leibniz attempts something analogous in the realm of human commerce and the decisions by which it is governed. In each case the pivotal question to be asked is: how fundamental is difference? how fundamental *can* it be, even in principle? And in each case the answer is, as it must be: not fundamental at all. It is important to recognize that the force of this "must" is logical, not merely hortatory. For once it is granted that difference is (or even that it might conceivably be) fundamental, as between, say, perspectives on the world or discursive regimes in terms of which it is discussed, there will no longer be any way of blocking a slide into precisely the sort of skeptical incommensurabilism that is in fact the hallmark of so much of contemporary theory. And once the door is left open even to the possibility of truly fundamental (and global) differences in interests and experiences among people—such differences being referred to incommensurably different "identities," whether national, racial, ethnic, sexual, or however construed[6]—again the slide can no longer be halted. The slide in that case would be from politics as a process of rational deliberation and adjudication into the sort of permanent agonistics and war of all against all that is not merely pointed to but in fact celebrated by many writers today as the true and ineluctable human condition.

In attempting to counter this sort of epistemological and political incommensurabilism, it is no use appealing in any sense to "the better angels of our nature"—simply repeating the plaintive wish, "can't we all just get along?" For on the view in question there are no such "better angels," because there is no such (common) "nature" to begin with. Such an appeal amounts in the end to nothing more than the dogmatist's leap of faith in the face of the skeptic's challenge, and of course that is no more effective now as an actual counter-*argument* to skepticism than it has ever been. The need, as always, is to show not simply the error but the incoherence—the literal unintelligibility—of the skeptical position. Or, in other words, to show that there is in fact *no such thing* as a skeptical position to begin with, and hence nothing that even requires refutation in either the epistemological or the political sphere. Showing this involves two demonstrations in particular. One (the fairly easy one) consists in showing that would-be skeptics are always unavoidably in performative contradiction with themselves, that they cannot so much as begin to formulate their position without immediately (if only tacitly) committing themselves to its opposite: even the attempt to articulate skepticism entails a pragmatic acknowledgment of the very realism it would deny. Making good on this claim also requires that *realism* itself be reinterpreted as *critical* realism, that is, in the terms provided by the co-originality thesis. This is the key step by which the overcoming of skepticism secures itself precisely *as* an overcoming—and not merely a protest—and so avoids lapsing back into mere dogmatism.

The second of the two demonstrations in question is the somewhat more challenging one. It consists, in essence, in extending the gains achieved with the first of these from the epistemological to the political realm. And that means collapsing the difference between the two domains by reanalyzing the latter fundamentally in terms of the former. The very nature of political contestation, including the terms of its resolution, thus comes to be construed in its own right along the lines implicit in the co-originality thesis. The result (to the extent that the argument is carried through successfully) is what might be thought of as a transcendental deduction of human civilization at large. I am suggesting that we can find at least the starting point for such a deduction in the protoversion of critical realism presented by Leibniz. The same line of thought receives a much more explicit formulation and development in some of Kant's historical and political writings.[7] And among contemporary thinkers it is probably most prominently and influentially represented in Habermas's ongoing project of articulating and defending a theory of what he calls discourse ethics.[8]

It is well to remind ourselves that philosophical argument, no matter how cogent, can carry us only so far in circumstances such as these. One need not subscribe to Schiller's gloomy assessment, "gegen die Dummheit kämpfen sogar die Götter vergebens," to recognize that if such argument were sufficient to deal with the absurdities and excesses of contemporary skepticism, it would long since have vanished from the scene. In this situation one should not underestimate the value of ridicule. By now there can be few if any of those interested in such things who are still unaware of physicist Alan Sokal's recent *tour de force:* In an inspired combination of satire, criticism, and performance art, Sokal in effect induced several of the panjandrums of High Theory to stage a revival of *The Emperor's New Clothes* with themselves in the title role.[9] This is in the finest tradition of guerilla theater. The weaknesses of postmodernist theory—the amateurishness of its attempts at philosophical argument together with its vast ignorance of history, economics, linguistics, and other branches of learning, including in particular (the principal object of Sokal's demonstration) natural science—have long been obvious to many; yet those same weaknesses, turned outward in a kind of programmatic irrationalism, have also long served (at least to the satisfaction of the practitioners of the theory and their disciples) to buttress it against rational analysis and critique. The brilliance of Sokal's strategy consists in having found a way to draw the postmodernists out of their cover. The key was to offer them an opportunity *to take upon themselves* the task of demolishing their own position—not by arguing against it, but rather precisely by continuing to exhibit it in all its flagrant illogic and incomprehension of reality. And, of course, it was an offer they could not refuse. Now there is no going back. To continue, post-Sokal, to assert the tenability of postmodernism, the hollowness of which he has so adroitly exposed, is merely to call attention to the extent of the confusion, or denial, or some combination of the two in which one is still trapped.

There is (or may be[10]) an at once striking and amusing parallel to Sokal's stratagem in Leibniz's career, albeit lacking the satirical and polemical intent that was Sokal's primary motivation. In his early twenties Leibniz moved from the University of Leipzig to the University of Altdorf in order to receive his doctor of law degree. But, always a man of the most wide-ranging and diverse interests, Leibniz took the occasion to pursue inquiries into a very different field. As Roger Ariew recounts the story:

> While he was at Altdorf, Leibniz went to Nuremberg to see some scholars who told him about a secret society of alchemists seeking the philosopher's stone. Leibniz decided to profit from this opportunity and learn alchemy, but it was difficult to become initiated into its mysteries. He proceeded to read some alchemical books and put together the more obscure expressions—those he understood the least. He then composed a letter that was unintelligible to himself and addressed it to the director of the secret society, asking that he be admitted on the basis of his great knowledge, of which the letter was proof. According to the story, no one doubted that the author of the letter was an adept alchemist or almost one; he was received with honor into the laboratory and was asked to take over the functions of secretary. He was even offered a pension. (Ariew 21)

At this relatively early stage in life, Leibniz appears to have been persuaded, or at least open to the possibility, that alchemical lore either included genuine scientific knowledge or at any rate could function as a propaedeutic to such learning. In later years his view of alchemy changed and as Ariew suggests, it was in light of that change that he would himself repeat the above story in a spirit of mockery of the object of his youthful interest.

Leibniz's experience with the alchemists invites speculation that the parallel with Sokal's case could well have been extended further. For had Sokal been inclined *not* to reveal the hoax, it seems scarcely far fetched, given the reception of his "article" by his hapless victims, to imagine him as by now occupying a place of honor on the editorial board of *Social Text*. At the same time that we enjoy the joke, however, we should not lose sight of the ultimately quite serious issues that gave rise to it. Irrationalism and obdurately maintained ignorance are not, finally, laughing matters. In a host of ways they are corrosive and at least potentially destructive of the edifice of civilization itself (as no one who has lived through any substantial portion of the twentieth century should need to be reminded). Steven Weinberg, in the essay cited above, sums up with admirable concision what is at stake here:

> Sokal was not the first to address these issues,[11] but he has done a great service in raising them so dramatically. They are not entirely academic issues, in any sense of the word "academic." If we think that scientific laws are flexible enough to be affected by the social setting of their discovery, then some may be tempted to press scientists to discover laws that are more proletarian or feminine or American or religious or Aryan or whatever else it is they want. This is a dangerous path, and more is at stake in the controversy over it than just the health of science.... Our civilization has been powerfully affected by the discovery that nature is strictly governed by impersonal laws. As an example I like to quote the remark of Hugh Trevor-Roper that one of the early effects of this discovery was to reduce the enthusiasm for burning witches. We will need to confirm and strengthen the vision of a rationally understandable world if we are to protect ourselves from the irrational tendencies that still beset humanity. (Weinberg 15)

Notes

[1] See Popkin, "Skepticism," in *The Encyclopedia of Philosophy*, VII, 449–61; and "Skepticism in Modern Thought," in *Dictionary of the History of Ideas*, IV, 240–51.

[2] The essay was ostensibly a review of Jonathan Culler's *On Deconstruction*, but that merely provided Searle with the occasion. He was after bigger game, in effect returning to and reenacting in summary form his deconstruction of Derrida in the *Glyph*-exchange of several years earlier. See Searle, "Reiterating the Differences."

[3] More recently still, the term *critical realism* has appeared in the title of a study by Dagmar Barnouw of the film critic and theoretician Siegfried Kracauer.

[4] This same fundamental insight is a recurrent theme in Lewis White Beck's classic *Early German Philosophy*. With regard to Leibniz and Nicholas of Cusa he notes: "For each, the world is isotropic, both geometrically and intellectually. It does not matter where one begins, for each part reflects the whole, as a mirror or a microcosm, and the intellectual and cosmological bonds which connect each part with all the others and with the whole are organic or mathematical, or both" (Beck 58).

[5] A thought reflected, for example, in the darkly brooding opening question of the late Emmanuel Levinas's *Totality and Infinity*: "Does not lucidity, the mind's openness upon the true, consist in catching sight of the permanent possibility of war?" (Levinas 21).

[6] The various loci of "identity," on this view, are themselves of course not subject to skeptical challenge but are rather simply posited as, in effect, unassailable metaphysical essences. We see here, again, the characteristic combination of dogmatism and skepticism in contemporary theory.

[7] See, for example, the pieces collected in the volume Kant, *On History*, in particular the essay "Perpetual Peace."

[8] Among relatively recent publications in this vein, see, for example, Habermas, *Moral Consciousness and Communicative Action* and *Justification and Application*.

[9] For details of the story—again, in the unlikely event that anyone reading this needs to be apprised of them—see Sokal, "A Physicist Experiments with Cultural Studies," and Weinberg, "Sokal's Hoax." The parallel to the classic fairy tale is, of course, too obvious not to have struck numerous other readers as well. See, for example, David Layton's comment on the "Sokal Affair," *Lingua Franca* (July/August 1996): 62.

[10] Aiton raises at least some question as to the reliability of the story (23–24).

[11] Weinberg mentions here Holton, *Science and Anti-Science*, as well as Gross and Levitt, *Higher Superstition*.

Works Cited

Aiton, E. J. *Leibniz: A Biography*. Bristol and Boston: Hilger, 1985.

Ariew, Roger. "G. W. Leibniz, Life and Works." In *The Cambridge Companion to Leibniz*, edited by N. Jolley. Cambridge: Cambridge UP, 1995.

Barnouw, Dagmar. *Critical Realism: History, Photography, and the Work of Siegfried Kracauer*. Baltimore: Johns Hopkins UP, 1994.

Beck, Lewis White. *Early German Philosophy: Kant and His Predecessors*. Cambridge, MA: Harvard UP, 1969; Reprint. Bristol, England: Thoemmes Press, 1996.

Culler, Jonathan. *On Deconstruction: Theory and Criticism after Structuralism*. Ithaca: Cornell UP, 1982.

Descartes. *Philosophical Writings*. Translated and edited by E. Anscombe and P. T. Geach. Indianapolis and New York: Bobbs-Merrill, 1971.

Gross, Paul R., and Norman Levitt. *Higher Superstition: The Academic Left and Its Quarrels with Science*. Baltimore: Johns Hopkins UP, 1995.

Habermas, Jürgen. *Justification and Application*. Cambridge, MA: MIT Press, 1993.

———. *Moral Consciousness and Communicative Action.* Cambridge, MA: MIT Press, 1990.

Holton, Gerald. *Science and Anti-Science.* Cambridge, MA: Harvard UP, 1993.

Husserl, Edmund. *Die Krisis der europäischen Wissenschaften und die transzendentale Phänomenologie.* Edited by W. Biemel. The Hague: Martinus Nijhoff, 1954.

Kant, Immanuel. *On History.* Edited by L. W. Beck. Indianapolis and New York: Bobbs-Merrill, 1963.

Leibniz, G. W. *Philosophical Essays.* Edited and translated R. Ariew and D. Garber. Indianapolis and Cambridge: Hackett, 1989.

———. *Philosophical Writings.* Edited by G. H. R. Parkinson. London: Dent, 1973.

Levinas, Emmanuel. *Totality and Infinity: An Essay on Exteriority.* Translated by A. Lingis. Pittsburgh: Duquesne UP, 1969.

Popkin, Richard H. "Skepticism." In *The Encyclopedia of Philosophy*, edited by Paul Edwards. New York: Macmillan, 1967.

———. "Skepticism in Modern Thought." In *Dictionary of the History of Ideas*, edited by Philip P. Wiener. New York: Scribner's, 1973.

Searle, John R. "Reiterating the Differences: A Reply to Derrida." *Glyph I* (1977): 198–208.

———. "The Word Turned Upside Down." *The New York Review of Books*, 27 August 1983, 74–79.

Sokal, Alan D. "A Physicist Experiments with Cultural Studies." *Lingua Franca* (May/June 1996): 62–64.

Weinberg, Steven. "Sokal's Hoax." *The New York Review of Books*, 8 August 1996, 11–15.

Wittgenstein, Ludwig. *Tractatus Logico-Philosophicus.* Translated by D. F. Pears and B. F. McGuinness. 2nd ed. London: Routledge and Kegan Paul, 1972.

Afterword

Beth Bjorklund and Mark E. Cory

The news that Frank G. Ryder, Kenan Professor of German *emeritus* at the University of Virginia, had died on 28 August 1996, changed the nature of this volume. What had been conceived as a collection of essays by established American Germanists, all of whom had studied with or learned from one of the great contemporary interpreters of German literature in this country, was nearing completion. Its title, *Politics in German Literature*, had been borrowed from a project in which Frank Ryder himself had been engaged. Its focus reflected a concern for the nexus between art and life that had been a hallmark of his teaching and writing, and consequently a great influence on his students. None of that has changed; what was intended as gift to our profession and to a general audience of readers interested in German letters on the occasion of our teacher's eightieth birthday merely acquires additional significance as a memorial to his legacy.

Frank Ryder's interest in the sociopolitical dimension of literature is evident in many of his essays, for example in his seminal work on Goethe's *Götz von Berlichingen,* as well as *Hermann und Dorothea*, on Lessing's *Emilia Galotti*, Schiller's *Wilhelm Tell,* and Kleist's *Der Findling*. His attention was drawn especially to issues of social justice and personal liberty in relation to the competing claims of authority in late eighteenth and early nineteenth-century German literature. In these essays and in his graduate seminars, he inquired into the ways political and ideological issues consciously or unconsciously affect literary technique. His detection of discrepancies between the deep structure and surface structure of a text perhaps prefigured the critical movement of deconstruction, yet Ryder declined to take that step. Rather than abstract theory, Ryder stressed an empirical approach and remained committed to practical criticism. It was a touchstone of his careful textual analyses that any unilateral reading unable to assign precise cause or responsibility in crucial areas of meaning must be called into question.

Intrigued as he was by issues of social justice and political authority, Ryder also questioned a too facile pairing of politics and literature. In a marvelous essay entitled "Literature as Truth" (1969), Ryder contrasts the certainties of political language with the ambiguities of poetic language. "For the conviction that life is meaningless, the appropriate mode of utterance would seem to be philosophy—or silence. For insights in the domain of possible certainty, the prose of the social scientist. For the claims of certainty, propaganda. None of these is art" (1969: 7). In delicate balance among those modes of thought lies literature, which "offers a distillation of experience....For certain perceptions about life it is the only adequate and relevant vehicle" (1969: 6).

For other examples of literature as vehicle for "certain perceptions about life," one turns to Ryder's work of poetic language. He wrote essays on the sound and meaning of poetry, its rhyme, rhythm, and meter; and he engaged in the great debates of the 1960s and 1970s on issues of prosody. If that is seemingly apolitical, it only demonstrates Ryder's conviction that "form is meaning"; and "the very being of a poem or a play argues against the interpretation of life as randomness" (1969: 6). In a Keatsian state of mind, in which the "irritable reaching after fact and reason" vanishes, Ryder finds the truth of literature in its form (1975: 433). That truth has then none of the pretentiousness inherent in most assertions of "truth" but affirms rather the indeterminacy of any truth.

Realizing that "this ambiguity, this absence of finality, is uncomfortable" to many (1969: 7), Ryder yet sought to impart it to his students. For, as young people must invariably learn, "we have more than one Scylla-Charybdis course before us" (1967: 121). Ryder's textbooks for German literary instruction, such as *Lebendige Literatur*, *Zehn Jahrzehnte*, and *Die Novelle*, are known by virtually every student of German in the United States. There was no getting around Ryder, and the popularity of his textbooks demonstrates that he had put his finger on something. That "something" is, besides his judicious selection of texts, his keenly insightful questions. Rather than asserting a certain, dogmatic truth and telling students what a literary text means, he leads them to the ambiguities of literary statement, the very ambiguities he demonstrated so well in his advanced research. Although some of his textbooks are now no longer in print, well-worn copies or photocopies of copies are among the most treasured tools in many teachers' professional kits. Thus Ryder's mode of thought outlives the vagaries of the marketplace.

Continuing to act both on his conviction about the value of literature and on his desire to impart it to a wider audience, Ryder turned to translation. After official retirement from the University of Virginia, he published many volumes of German literature in translation, making Goethe, Keller, and the Romantics available to an English-speaking audience. Although his concentration was German, Ryder was interested in language and literature per se, and in his later years he began work on a popular history of the English language. That was a rather large project for retirement, yet the courage and sense of curiosity Ryder demonstrated was an inspiration to all who knew him.

Despite his focus on the language of literature, no one could accuse Ryder of being *weltfremd*. He chaired large and complex academic units; and the German departments at Dartmouth, Indiana, and Virginia owe their current stature in great measure to Ryder's excellence as an administrator and program builder. Ryder was influential also in academic associations such as the Modern Language Association, the American Association of Teachers of German, the Association of Departments of Foreign Languages, and *The German Quarterly*. If this involved academic 'high' politics, Ryder was active also on the other end of the scale, as he taught English to the Spanish-speaking laborers in the fruit orchards near his home.

All of this Ryder accomplished, from politics and poetics in literature to politics in academia and linguistics in migrant-worker camps. Yet he left work for his students to do. Responding to Ryder's encouragement and mentoring, many of his students went on to become teacher-scholars who have themselves spawned a new generation of students, thus transmitting the Ryder legacy. That the editors of the present volume are in the profession today is directly attributable to Frank Ryder. And from his example we share an ethic of service that we hope to pass on to others. In the fractious, sometimes demoralized climate of contemporary literary studies, it is more important than ever that we recall a career such as Ryder's and draw encouragement and inspiration from the example he set. Already honored in 1970 by the Goethe-Medaille in Gold, Frank G. Ryder received the American Association of Teachers of German Outstanding Educator Award in 1996 upon the belated nomination of his students. The present book grew out of that project, as the editors and contributors all realized anew how great were the contributions of our teacher.

Frank G. Ryder
Selected List of Publications

1940 "Variant [γ] in the Aklan Dialect of Bisayan." *Papers of the Michigan Academy* 26: 573–83.

1941 "Modes of Connection in the Aklan Dialect." *Papers of the Michigan Academy* 27: 671–80.

1949 "George Ticknor's *Sorrows of Young Werter*." *Comparative Literature* 1: 360–72.

1950 "A Suggestion for Elementary German." *Language Learning* 3 (January): 3–13.

1951 "Syntax of Gothic Compound Verbs." *JEGP* 50: 200–17.

1952 "George Ticknor and Goethe–Boston and Göttingen." *PMLA* 67: 960–72.

George Ticknor's The Sorrows of Young Werter, edited and introduced. UNC Studies in Comparative Literature, no. 4. Chapel Hill, NC.

1953 "First American Commentary on Faust." *American-German Review* 19 (February): 9–11.

"George Ticknor and Goethe: Europe and Harvard." *Modern Language Quarterly* 14: 413–24.

1954 "'Proseminar' for German Two." *German Quarterly* 27: 48–50.

1958 Carl Zuckmayer's *Das kalte Licht*, edited. New York: Appleton-Century-Crofts, 1958; London: Methuen, 1960.

1959 "An American View of Germany–1817." *American-German Review* 25 (February-March): 16–19.

"The Design of Hofmannswaldau's 'Vergänglichkeit der Schönheit.'" *Monatshefte* 51: 97–102.

"George Ticknor on the German Scene." *American-German Review* 25 (April-May): 28–30.

Zehn Jahrzehnte, edited and compiled. New York: Henry Holt, 1959. Revised Edition, 1966.

1960 *Lebendige Literatur*, edited, with E. Allen McCormick. Boston: Houghton Mifflin, 1960. Second Edition, Revised, 1974. Third Edition, 1986.

"'Der römische Brunnen': Sound Pattern and Content." *Monatshefte* 52: 235-41.

1962 "Individualization in Baroque Dramatic Verse." *JEGP* 61: 604-15.

The Song of the Nibelungs: A Verse Translation from the Middle High German Nibelungenlied. Detroit: Wayne State UP, 1962. Reprinted in *German Epic Poetry*, edited by Francis G. Gentry and James K. Walter, 9-294. The German Library, vol. 1. New York: Continuum, 1995.

"Toward a Revaluation of Goethe's *Götz:* The Protagonist." *PMLA* 77: 58-78.

1963 "How Rhymed is a Poem?" *Word* 19: 310-21.

"Off-Rhymes and Consonantal Confusion Groups." *Lingua* 12: 190-98.

1964 "Season, Day, and Hour: Time as Metaphor in Goethe's *Werther*." *JEGP* 63: 389-407.

"Toward a Revaluation of Goethe's *Götz*: Features of Recurrence." *PMLA* 79: 58-66.

1965 "Literature in High School: A College Point of View." *German Quarterly* 38: 469-79.

1967 Articles on Fleming, Anton Ulrich von Braunschweig, Rist, Lohenstein, Hofmannswaldau, Reuter, Moscherosch, Harsdörffer, Rollenhagen, Weckherlin, Weise, Zesen, Spee, and Zinkgref. In *European Authors, 1000-1900: A Biographical Dictionary of European Literature*, edited by Stanley J. Kunitz and Vineta Colby. New York: H.W. Wilson.

"Realism: A Symposium." *Monatshefte* 59: 118-25.

"Vowels and Consonants as Features of Style: Some Poems of Goethe and Klopstock." *Linguistics* 37: 89-110.

1969 "Perspective: Literature as Truth." *Dimension* 2: 6-7.

"A Call to Action." *Bulletin of the Association of Departments of Foreign Languages* 1: 3.

1970 "The Study of English Prosody," with Karl Magnuson. *College English* 31:789–820.

1971 *Die Novelle*, edited and compiled. New York: Holt, Rinehart and Winston.

"Second Thoughts on English Prosody," with Karl Magnuson. *College English* 33: 198–216.

1972 "Hölderlin's Spondee–True or False?" In *Essays on European Literature: In Honor of Liselotte Dieckmann*, edited by Peter Uwe Hohendahl, Herbert Lindenberger, and Egon Schwarz, 133–46. St. Louis: Washington UP.

"*Emilia Galotti*." *German Quarterly* 45: 329–47.

1973 "The Ebbing of Style: Hölderlin's Late Poetry in the Perspective of Meter." In *Texte und Kontexte: Studien zur deutschen und vergleichenden Literaturwissenschaft. Festschrift für Norbert Fuerst zum 65. Geburtstag*, edited by Manfred Durzak, Eberhard Reichmann, and Ulrich Weisstein, 161–76. Bern: Franke.

"*Emilia Galotti* and the Algebra of Ambivalence." In *Husbanding the Golden Grain: Studies in Honor of Henry W. Nordmeyer*, edited by Luanne T. Frank and Emery E. George, 279–94. Ann Arbor: Department of Germanic Languages and Literatures, U of Michigan.

"German in High School: Some Reflections and Proposals." *Die Unterrichtspraxis* 6 (Fall): 11–18.

"A Matter of Image." *Bulletin of the Association of Departments of Foreign Languages* 5 (November): 5–11.

1975 "Changes in Graduate Training: 'Pittious Worke of Mutabilitie'?" *Bulletin of the Association of Departments of Foreign Languages* 7 (November): 3–8.

"The Irony of Goethe's *Hermann und Dorothea*: Its Form and Function," with Benjamin Bennett. *PMLA* 90: 433–46.

"Schiller's *Tell* and the Cause of Freedom." *German Quarterly* 48: 487–504.

1976 "*Emilia Galotti* and the Limits of Psychological Criticism." *University of Dayton Review* 12 (Spring): 99–110.

1976 "The Organizational Structure of the Profession." In *German Studies in the United States: Assessment and Outlook*, edited by Walter F. W. Lohnes and Valters Nollendorfs, 258-63. Madison: U of Wisconsin P.

"The Present and Future Shape of Graduate Programs." In *German Studies in the United States: Assessment and Outlook*, edited by Walter F. W. Lohnes and Valters Nollendorfs, 121-27. Madison: U of Wisconsin P.

"Some Declarations for 1976." *Bulletin of the Association of Departments of Foreign Languages* and *Bulletin of the Association of Departments of English,* Special Joint Issue (September): 33-37.

1977 "Kleist's *Findling*: Oedipus *manqué?*" *MLN* 92: 509-24.

"Lessing on Liberty: The Literary Work as Autobiography." In *Studies in Eighteenth-Century Culture*, edited by Ronald C. Rosbottom, 6: 229-44. Madison: U of Wisconsin P.

1979 "The Uses—or Uselessness?—of Adversity." *Bulletin of the Association of Departments of Foreign Languages* 11 (September): 5-9.

1980 "Foreign Language Study at the Postsecondary Level." In *Learning a Second Language*, edited by Frank M. Grittner, II: 128-49. Seventy-ninth Yearbook of the National Society for the Study of Education, edited by Kenneth J. Rehage. Chicago: U of Chicago P.

1981 "How Joseph Got Tenure in Less Than Seven Years" (SAMLA Presidential Address). *South Atlantic Review* 46.2: 9-16.

1982 Gottfried Keller. *Stories,* edited. The German Library, vol. 44. New York: Continuum.

1983 *German Literary Fairy Tales,* edited with Robert M. Browning. The German Library, vol. 30. New York: Continuum.

"Kafka's Language >Poetic<?" In *Probleme der Moderne: Studien zur deutschen Literatur von Nietzsche bis Brecht. Festschrift für Walter Sokel,* edited by Benjamin Bennett, Anton Kaes, and William J. Lillyman, 319-30. Tübingen: Max Niemeyer.

1984 "The Study and Teaching of Foreign Languages" (MLA Centennial Forum address). *PMLA* 99: 985-90.

1985 *German Romantic Novellas,* edited with Robert M. Browning. The German Library, vol. 34. New York: Continuum.

1987 Johann Wolfgang von Goethe. *Verse Plays and Epic*, edited with Cyrus Hamlin. Goethe's Collected Works, vol. 8. New York: Suhrkamp. Reprint. Princeton, NJ: Princeton UP, 1995.

"Goethe's *Natürliche Tochter*: A Paradox of Politics." In *Antipodische Aufklärungen: Antipodean Enlightenments. Festschrift für Leslie Bodi*, edited by Walter Veit, 423–37. Frankfurt a.M.

"Poetic Prose: A Suggested Approach by Way of Goethe's *Werther*," *Style* 21: 427–38.

1988 Johann Wolfgang von Goethe. *Early Verse Drama and Prose Plays*, edited with Cyrus Hamlin. Goethe's Collected Works, vol. 7. New York: Suhrkamp. Reprint. Princeton, NJ: Princeton UP, 1995.

German Romantic Stories, edited. The German Library, vol. 35. New York: Continuum.

1993 Johann Wolfgang von Goethe. *Plays*, edited. The German Library, vol. 20. New York: Continuum.

1995 "The Political and Psychological Burden of *Kabale und Liebe*: In *Literary and Musical Notes: A Festschrift for William A. Little*, edited by Geoffrey C. Orth, 153–68. Bern: Peter Lang.

List of Contributors

Beth Bjorklund is Associate Professor of German at the University of Virginia. She took her Ph.D. at Indiana University, where she studied with Frank Ryder before later becoming his colleague at Virginia. Her research interests include contemporary Austrian literature, eighteenth-century aesthetics, prosody, and modernism. Her book-length studies on comparative prosody and contemporary Austrian poetry are accompanied by articles on poetic form, narrative strategies, Klopstock, Horváth, Bachmann, and Mayröcker, among others.

Mark E. Cory is Professor of German and Director of Humanities at the University of Arkansas. One of the earliest disciples of Frank Ryder, he studied with Ryder at Dartmouth College for the BA, then again at Indiana University for the M.A. and Ph.D. His research includes experimental forms in twentieth-century German literature and postwar literature in general. His monograph on the experimental *Hörspiel* is accompanied by articles on Böll, Grass, Eich, Gomringer, Dürrenmatt, and the literature of the Holocaust.

David H. Chisholm is Professor of German Studies at the University of Arizona. He received his Ph.D. from Indiana University, where his worked with Frank Ryder. His research includes linguistic and computational approaches to literature, German poetry and prosody, music and German literature, and German cabaret. His books—a study of Goethe's *Knittelvers*, and concordances to *Faust* and to C. F. Meyer's poetry—are accompanied by articles on phonological and prosodic aspects of German literature and other topics.

Richard T. Gray is Professor of German and Chair of the Department of Germanics at the University of Washington. He studied under Frank Ryder at the University of Virginia, where he took the Ph.D. His research spans German literature and intellectual history from the eighteenth to the twentieth centuries, with special emphasis on political and sociological questions. His most recent book is entitled *Stations of the Divided Subject: Contestation and Ideological Legitimation in German Bourgeois Literature, 1770–1914.*

Ronald Horwege is Professor of German at Sweet Briar College. He took the M.A. and Ph.D. at Indiana University during Frank Ryder's tenure as chair, moving to Sweet Briar in 1971, the same year in which Ryder became Kenan Professor of German at the University of Virginia, which facilitated their continued professional contact. His research interests lie in literature and nationalism, Romanticism, Early New High German literature, and Scandinavian literatures.

Michael W. Jennings is Professor of Germanic Languages and Literatures at Princeton University. He took his M.A. and Ph.D. at the University of Virginia, where the political orientation of his work found its inspiration in Ryder's seminars. He is the author of a study of Walter Benjamin's literary theory, *Dialectical Images*, and general editor of Benjamin's *Selected Writings*. His forthcoming book, *In Spite of All That*, examines cultural objects from diverse media and genres in their interaction with political, economic and social forces in the Weimar Republic.

Horst Joachim Lange is Assistant Professor of German at the University of Nevada, Reno. He studied philosophy and German literature at Tübingen before taking the Ph.D. at the University of Virginia, where he developed his association with Frank Ryder, who was by then already *emeritus*. He is the author of a book on Kant and is currently working on a book-length study entitled *Gewalt und Geselligkeit: Die Relevanz des Politischen bei Goethe*.

Paul Michael Lützeler is Rosa May Distinguished University Professor in the Humanities at Washington University in St. Louis and Director of the European Studies Program and the Center for Contemporary German Literature. He took his M.A. and Ph.D. degrees from Indiana University, where he worked with Frank Ryder. His research interests include Hermann Broch, exile literature, German and European Romanticism, and German Studies. His most recent books include *Europäische Identität und Multikultur* and *Klio oder Kalliope? Literatur und Geschichte*. Last year he was elected an Honorary Member of the AATG.

Michael M. Morton is Associate Professor of German at Duke University. He took his Ph.D. at the University of Virginia with a dissertation on Herder under the direction of Frank Ryder. His research interests include intellectual history from the eighteenth to the twentieth century, as well as literary and critical theory. His books, *Herder and the Poetics of Thought* and *The Critical Turn*, are accompanied by articles on Herder, literary theory and the philosophy of language, Lessing, Lenz, Wittgenstein, and Hofmannsthal, among others.

David A. Scrase is Professor of German and Director of the Center for Holocaust Studies at the University of Vermont. He took the B.A. in German from Bristol University before coming to Indiana University for the Ph.D., where he worked with Frank Ryder. His research interests encompass lyric poetry, the literature of the GDR, Holocaust studies, and translation. He has published monographs of Bobrowski and Lehmann and edited volumes on Lehmann and on approaches to the teaching of the Holocaust.

Ray M. Wakefield is Associate Professor of German at the University of Minnesota. The earliest student of Frank Ryder here represented, he studied with Ryder at Dartmouth College for the B.A., then followed him to Indiana University for the M.A. and Ph.D. His current fields of specialization include medieval German literature, medieval Dutch literature, and second language acquisition. He has published a monograph on the prosody of the *Nibelungenlied.*

Margaret E. Ward is William R. Kenan, Jr. Professor of German at Wellesley College. She took her M.A. and Ph.D. at Indiana University during Frank Ryder's tenure as chair. Her areas of specialization include political drama, Berlin in the 1920s, and nineteenth- and twentieth-century German women writers. Author of a monograph on Rolf Hochhuth, she has also published on political drama of the 1960s and 1970s, Bertolt Brecht, theater in the GDR, Ingeborg Drewitz, and Fanny Lewald.

Index

a priori 195, 209
adaequatio intellectus ad rem 197–98, 201–02
Adams, Henry 154, 164
Adams, John Quincy 2, 28–30
aesthetic distance 166
aesthetization 6, 111, 177–78, 191–92
Allen, Henry 167–68, 171–72, 175
Anderson, Lindsay 134
  Britannia Hospital 134
Anneke, Mathilde Franziska 67, 77
antifoundationalism 198
antirealism 202
anti-Semitism 2, 24, 99, 154, 158; anti-Semite, anti-Semitic 85, 155, 159
antiquarian historian 37
Aristotle 196
armor 6, 168, 170–71, 174–75
Arnauld, Antoine 204
Arndt, Karl J. R. 28, 35
art nouveau 119, 122
Aston, Louise 67, 77
Auffermann, Verena 157, 164
Auschwitz 6, 160, 178, 180, 194
Austro-Fascism 113
autobiography 4–5, 62, 65, 80, 103–07, 112–13, 156–57, 160–62, 164
"auto-geographical" 60, 62, 67, 82
autonomy 8–9, 24, 26, 36, 42, 55, 70, 136, 142
Bacheracht, Therese von (Lützow) 67, 70–71, 74, 79–80, 82
Baader, Johannes 129
Bakhtin, Mikhail 143, 152
Ball, Hugo 128
Bartels, Adolf 85, 99, 100
Barthes, Roland 108, 115
Bauernroman 98, 102
Bauhaus, Weimar 132
Bavarian Monarchy 129
Beardsley, Aubrey 167, 175
Becher, Johannes R. 147, 157

Benjamin, Walter 55–58, 132, 135–38, 143, 149–52
  One Way Street 132, 138
  Das Passagen-Werk 143, 150
Berger, Uwe 157
Berlin 4–5, 27, 35, 61–62, 66–67, 69–73, 78–80, 89, 92, 96, 117–20, 122–23, 127–32, 134, 137, 145–46, 151, 153–56, 158, 163–64, 178–79, 189
Berlin Wall 6, 178, 182, 187, 190
Bernauer, Rudolf 125, 130
Bernstein, Eduard 136
  The German Revolution 136
Bhaskar, Roy 203
Biedermeier 121–22
Bierbaum, Otto Julius 118–21, 130
  "Der lustige Ehemann" 121–22
  Deutsche Chansons (Brettl-Lieder) 119
  Stilpe 119–20, 130
Biermann, Wolf 162, 189, 192
Bildungsroman 112
Bismarck, Otto von 24, 188
Blass, Ernst 127
Blomster, Wesley 164
Bolzano, Bernhard 28
Boorman, John 1, 6, 166–72, 174–75
  Excalibur 1, 166–72, 174–76
Börne, Ludwig 28
bourgeois literature 4, 6, 103–04, 112, 133, 142, 146, 150, 164
bourgeoisie 37, 71, 84, 104, 108–09, 112, 114, 122–23, 137, 143, 146, 154, 162
Brahm, Otto 123, 125, 130
Brecht, Bertolt 138, 140, 142, 147, 151; Brecht-Archiv 129
Brennert, Hans 122
  "Das Überlied" 122–23
Broch, Hermann 113
Brontë, Charlotte 66, 79; Brontë sisters, 78
Bruant, Aristide 117, 127–28
  "A la Rocquette" 127

Buchenwald 180
Bund proletarisch-revolutionärer Schriftsteller Deutschlands 147
Buntes Theater (Motley Theater) 5, 120, 122–23, 126
Busch, Adolphus 27
cabaret *chanson* 121; *chanson* 117, 119, 127, 129, 131,
Cabaret Voltaire 128
Canby, Vincent 167–68, 175
capitalism 45, 55–56, 98–99
Carlyle, Jane and Thomas 73–74, 79
Cartesian; see Descartes
Caxton, William 175
censorship 4–5, 33–34, 62, 70, 113, 118, 127, 129
chanson; see cabaret *chanson*
characteristica universalis 207
charismatic leader 6, 166, 171–72, 174
Chat Noir (Berlin) 127
Chat Noir (Paris) 117
Chernobyl 180
Chodowiecki, Daniel 184, 191, 193
church-state relationship 9, 19
cinema, cinematic 5, 132, 138, 151, 159, 174
class (economic, social, political) 2–5, 40, 55, 61, 63, 71, 75–78, 83–84, 86, 95–97, 99, 107–13, 115–17, 123–24, 134–37, 143, 150, 153–55, 158, 198
co-originality thesis 202, 205–07, 210
coffeehouse 106–07, 110, 114
commerce, commercialism 3, 36–37, 39–57
commodity aesthetics 40, 52
communist 147–48, 154, 158
competition (economic) 2, 36, 44–45, 47–48
constancy, law of 36
constructivism 198
consumerism 40, 114
contingency 54–55
Corinth, Lovis 158
couplet 107, 117–18, 121
critical realism 1, 195, 202–03, 205–07, 209–10, 213–14
Culler, Jonathan 213–14
Dach, Simon 192

Dada 128–29, 132, 136–38
death 5–6, 9–12, 18, 24, 40, 51, 54, 61–62, 65, 79, 85–87, 98, 104, 106, 114, 160–61, 163, 169, 171, 178, 181–82, 184, 190, 201
Debussy, Claude 128
deconstruction 141, 198–99, 213–14, 216
deferred gratification 45
democracy, democratic 2, 5, 29, 30, 32, 38, 44, 70, 72, 80, 123, 134, 149; see also social democracy/democrat
depoliticization 191
Der blaue Reiter 128
Der neue Club 127
Der Sturm 127–28
Derrida, Jacques 1, 198–203, 207, 213–14
Descartes, René 196, 199–200, 206, 214; Cartesian 199–201, 205
Detjen, David W. 27, 35
Deutsches Theater 123–26, 130
Die Aktion 127
Die bösen Buben 125–26
Die silberne Punschterrine 127
discourse ethics 211
division of labor 51–52
Döblin, Alfred 5, 132–52, 154
  "An Romanautoren und ihre Kritiker" 137
  Berlin Alexanderplatz 136–42, 144, 146, 150–52
  Das Land ohne Tod 133
  "Der Bau des epischen Werks" 140, 152
  Der deutsche Maskenball von Linke Poot 145, 152
  November 1918: Eine deutsche Revolution 5, 133–37, 142, 144–46, 148, 152
  Pardon wird nicht gegeben 133
  Unser Dasein 147–49, 152
  Wallenstein 132
dogmatism 6, 197, 200, 206–07, 209–10, 213
Drachmann, Holger 120
Droste-Hülshoff, Annette von 84
ecotourism 42, 54
economic transformation 36, 48, 55–56

Index 229

education, educational 19, 23, 32–34, 38, 44, 61, 69–70, 75, 78–79, 108, 113, 161, 164, 168; see also women's issues
Eichhorn, Maria ("Dolorosa") 127
Eisenstein, Sergei 132, 138
  Battlecruiser Potemkin 132, 138
Eisner, Kurt 129
Eliot, George 66, 78
Éluard, Paul 158
emancipation 4, 8, 25, 61–62, 74, 77, 112; emancipate, emancipatory 3, 9, 60, 62, 77, 79, 135–37, 151; see also women's issues
Enlightenment 2, 8–9, 16, 18, 21, 25, 28, 31, 44
epistemology, epistemological 6, 195–97, 199–202, 208–10
essences 196, 213
Europe, European 2, 4, 8, 16–18, 27–35, 37, 63, 65, 69, 72, 79, 100, 118, 143, 153, 168–69, 172, 182–85, 192–93, 201, 209
Ewers, Hanns Heinz 120
exchange 3, 37, 39–40, 42–43, 48–50, 52–53
exchange-value 51
expression 204, 206, 208, 211
Expressionism, Expressionist 127–28
Eysler, Robert 120
"family values" 49, 56
fascism 5, 132–33, 144, 147–49, 151, 159, 166, 174; fascist 113, 132–35, 172, 174
Fasteau, Marc 171, 175
  The Male Machine 171, 175
feminism 35, 67–68, 82; feminist criticism 60, 62, 70, 82
Film Literature Index 168, 172
Fischer, Samuel 154
Fontane, Theodor 6, 85, 153, 188–90, 192–93
Forms 196–97
Frankfurt am Main 70–72, 155, 178, 181
Frankfurt Parliament 70, 72
Franz I 30
Franz Joseph 72
Fraser, Catherine C. 156, 164
Freytag, Gustav 85

Soll und Haben 85
Friedrich, Caspar David 179, 191
Fühmann, Franz 157
Fulton, Robert 27
Ganghofer, Ludwig 84
Gaskell, Elizabeth 66, 78
gender 60, 63, 71, 114, 171–72, 198
George, Stefan 109, 154
German confederation 6, 178
German Democratic Republic (GDR) 5, 98–99, 157–58, 162, 178–80, 188–90
German unification/reunification 6, 177–81, 184–85, 187–93
Goebbels, Joseph 154, 190
Goethe, Johann Wolfgang von 1–2, 7–9, 15–16, 19, 22–26, 32, 62–63, 66, 75, 156, 179, 216; Goethe-Medaille 218
  Iphigenie auf Tauris 1, 8–16, 19–24, 26
Goethe, Ottilie von 3, 61
Gorky, Maxim 126
  Nachtasyl 126
Görres, Joseph 31, 34–35
Gottfried von Strassburg 167
  Tristan 167
Grass, Günter 6–7, 153, 177–89, 191–94
  Aus dem Tagebuch einer Schnecke 177
  Das Treffen in Telgte 191, 193; Telgte 177
  Deutscher Lastenausgleich: Wider das dumpfe Einheitsgebot 178, 193
  Die Blechtrommel 153, 190
  Die Rättin 179, 185, 194
  Ein weites Feld 6, 177, 181, 186–89, 191–94
  Hundejahre 181
  Katz und Maus 190
  Kopfgeburten: oder, Die Deutschen sterben aus 177
  Novemberland 177, 186–88, 191–94
  "Rede vom Verlust" 187, 193–94
  "Schreiben nach Auschwitz" 6, 178, 180, 194
  Totes Holz 177–81, 186–87, 191, 194
  Unkenrufe 181, 184–85, 187
  Waldsterben 178
  Zunge zeigen 178, 184, 189, 193–94

230 Politics in German Literature

Greul, Heinz 118, 128–30
Greve, Ludwig 5–6, 153–56, 159–64
  "Mein Vater" 163–64
  Wo gehörte ich hin? 5, 159, 161, 163–64
Grillparzer, Franz 33
  Medea 33
Gropius, Walter 132
Grosz, George 128
Group 1925 147
Gründerjahre 188
Gryphius, Andreas 186–87, 191, 194
Guilbert, Yvette 117–18
Guinover 171
Gutzkow, Karl 71, 74, 79–80, 82
Habermas, Jürgen 6, 211, 214–15
Habsburg Monarchy 28, 38
Hahn-Hahn, Ida 60, 66–67, 79
Halbe, Max 126, 130
Hardekopf, Ferdinand 127
Hauptmann, Gerhart 84–85, 109, 123–25
  Die Weber 124
Hegel, G. W. Friedrich 206, 208
Heidegger, Martin 196, 202, 207
Heimatkunst 85, 98, 102
Heine, Carl 118
Heine, Heinrich 32, 34–35, 66, 68, 73, 80, 179, 201
Heller, Joseph 153
  Catch 22 153
Heller, Otto 27–28, 35
Henning, Hans 85, 102
Hennings, Emmy 128
Heraclitus 195
Herder, Johann Gottfried 32, 206–07
hermeneutics of divine signs 2, 11–14, 16–17, 22–25
hermeneutics of suspicion 2, 14–17
Hermlin, Stephan 5–6, 153–62, 164–65
  Abendlicht 5, 155, 157–59, 161–62, 164–65
Herrmann-Neisse, Max 127, 130
Hesse, Hermann 154
Heym, Georg 127
Hildebrandslied 153
Hille, Peter 127

Hiller, Kurt 127
Hitler, Adolf 85, 132, 151, 154, 158, 173-74, 187
Hobbes, Thomas 2, 9, 16–20, 26, 29, 58
  Leviathan 16, 26
Hoddis, Jakob von 127–28
Hofmannsthal, Hugo von 4, 103, 109, 111, 115, 126
  "Age of Innocence" 111
  "Chandos-Brief" 111
  Elektra 126
  "Gabriele d'Annunzio" 111
Hölderlin, Friedrich 158, 192
Holl, Gussy 127
Hollaender, Victor 120
Holocaust 159; see also Shoah
Honigmann, E.A.J. 156, 165
horizon of expectations 166
Huelsenbeck, Richard 128
Hugo, Victor 28
Humanität 8, 22
Hume, David 49, 58, 206
Hunt, Irmgard Elsner 181, 193–94
Husserl, Edmund 199–202, 207, 215
Hyan, Hans 127
Ibsen, Henrik 123, 125
  A Doll's House 125
idealism 107, 208–09
Ideas (philosophical) 196–97
identity 1, 9, 25, 60, 67, 83, 88, 103, 107, 149, 154, 159, 160–62, 188, 213
Igraine 170
in-esse principle 204–05
incommensurabilism 209–10
individual 8–9, 16–17, 19, 29, 31, 39, 44, 83, 87, 112, 123, 137, 141, 143, 147–49, 157, 186, 200, 205, 209
individualism 43–46, 48, 52–53, 57–58, 112, 148
industrial economy 2, 36–37, 47, 49–50, 52, 56, 75, 84, 95, 104
industrial revolution 83, 104, 153
industrialization 37, 42–43, 83, 92–93, 118
intercalated tale 62, 64–66, 70, 74
Jackson, Andrew 2, 30
Jakob, Max 128

Index 231

Jacoby, Johann 70, 72, 80, 82
Jauss, Hans Robert 166, 175
Jefferson, Thomas 9, 18, 24
  Bill for Establishing Religious Freedom 18
Jelavich, Peter 121, 130
Jenny, Urs 168, 175
Jew, Jewish 5–6, 24, 60–61, 63–64, 74, 76, 80, 84–85, 88–89, 91–92, 113, 153–56, 158–59, 161, 163–64, 189
Jewish Question 153
Jewsbury, Geraldine 73–74, 77–80
Johnson, Uwe 192
Joseph II 2, 28–30, 32
Jungian archetypes 166, 171
Kandinsky, Wassily 128, 158
Kant, Immanuel 6, 202, 206, 210, 213–14
Kaszynski, Stefan H. 84, 98, 100–01
Kauflust 39–40, 47
Kayßler, Friedrich 124
Keller, Gottfried 84–85, 217
Keltermann, Bernhard 135
  Der neunte November 135
Kempff, Wilhelm 159
Kennedy, Harlan 167, 175
Kerr, Alfred 121
Kindertransport 160
King Arthur 166–67, 169–71, 174–76
Kinkel, Gottfried and Johanna 67, 78
Klee, Paul 128
Kleines Theater 126
Kneipenbrettl 126
Königsberg 3, 60
Kristallnacht 155, 159, 161–63, 187
Kuh, Emil 50
Kulturkampf 24
Kummer, Friederich 84, 101
Lancelot 167, 170–71
Langenbucher, Helmuth 85, 101
Lanzinger, Hubert 173–75
  "Hitler as Flagbearer" 173
Lareau, Alan 122, 129–30
Lasker-Schüler, Else 128
Lauff, Josef 121, 125
  Adlerflug 121
Lausitz 86
Lawlor, John 167, 175

Lebenswelt 202, 207
Leibniz, Gottfried Wilhelm 1, 6–7, 195, 203–06, 209–14
Lenin, Vladimir Ilyich 84, 98–101, 146, 148
Lessing, Gotthold Ephraim 23–24, 153, 216
  Emilia Galotti 216
  Nathan der Weise 24, 153
Lévi-Strauss, Claude 103, 108, 115
Levinas, Emmanuel 213–14
Lewald, Fanny 3, 60–82
  "Die Frauen und das allgemeine Wahlrecht" 70, 81
  Dünen- und Berggeschichte 76, 81
  England und Schottland 62, 74, 81
  Erinnerungen aus dem Jahre 1848 62, 67, 81
  Gefühltes und Gedachtes 73, 81
  Italienisches Bilderbuch 62, 66, 74, 81
  Meine Lebensgeschichte 1860–61 61–62, 64, 79, 82
  Römisches Tagebuch 1845/46 62–63, 65, 82
Lichtenstein, Alfred 128
Liebknecht, Karl 129, 146
Liliencron, Detlev von 85, 121
Linden, Walter 85, 101
Locke, John 9, 18, 26, 58
  Letter Concerning Toleration 18, 26
Loewenson, Erwin 127
logic, logical 1, 13, 24, 44, 195–96, 203, 205, 209, 215
London 30, 73–77
Louis Napoleon 72
Luther, Martin 16
Luxemburg, Rosa 129
Madison, James 9, 18–19, 23–26
  Memorial and Remonstrance against Religious Assessments 19
Maeterlinck, Maurice 125
Mallarmé, Stéphane 109, 154
Malory, Sir Thomas 166–68, 170, 175–76
  Le Morte D'Arthur 166–67, 175–76
Manchester 73–74, 77–78
Mann, Heinrich 118
  Professor Unrat 118
Mann, Thomas 84, 134, 154, 191
  Der Zauberberg 134
  Dr. Faustus 191

Maquis 155
Marc, Franz 128
Markale, Jean 167, 176
market 34, 39, 48, 114, 183, 185, 217
market economy 37, 39–40, 55, 192
Marx, Karl 40–42, 58, 95, 100–01
Marxism, Marxist 83, 151
masculinity 166, 170–71, 174
materie de Bretagne 167
Mayer, Hans 157–58, 162, 165
Mehring, Walter 129–30
  Das politische Cabaret 129–30
Meinhard, Carl 125
memoir, memoirs 72–73, 136, 156–57
memory 18, 57, 62, 71, 103, 139–40, 149, 162, 166
Merlin 167, 170
metal skin 170
metaphors of the self 62, 65
metaphysics, metaphysical 6, 195–98, 200–206, 208–209, 213
Metternich, Klemens Wenzel Fürst 2, 28–34, 69
Milton, John 32
mind-body problem 200
Mitterer, Felix 114–15
modernism, modernist 4–5, 36, 117–19, 123, 133, 135, 137
Moeller van den Bruck, Artur 118
monads 204–205, 208
money 18, 39–40, 45, 49, 58, 88, 90–97, 104–06, 108–09; money-lenders 84
Monroe, James 31
Montesquieu, Charles-Louis Baron de 9, 18, 32
Montintin 156
Montmorency 156, 160
Monty Python and the Holy Grail 167
Mordred 167–69, 171
Morgana 171
Morgenstern, Christian 120–21, 128
  "Der Lauffgraf" 121
Mosse, George L. 85, 99, 101, 150
Mühsam, Erich 127–28
Münchner Kammerspiele 128

myth 56, 99, 108, 143, 171–72; mythic, mythical 6, 63, 85, 166, 174, 180
mythology, mythological 52–53, 115, 140, 172; mythologizing 10, 172, 174
Nadler, Josef 85, 101
Napoleon 30, 34
National Socialism/ Socialists 5–6, 24, 83, 85, 133–34, 160, 175, 188–89, 191; see also Nazi
Nationalstiftung 177
natural economy 41, 44, 46, 50, 52, 54–56
naturalism 84–85, 123, 153
Nazi propaganda films 174
Nazi, Nazis 99, 101, 113, 154–55, 158–59, 172, 189; see also National Socialism
Nelson, Rudolf 127
Neopathetisches Cabaret 127
Neruda, Pablo 158
Neues Theater (am Schiffbauerdamm) 126
Neumann, Bernd 156, 165
Niboyet, Eugene 68–69, 80
Nicholas of Cusa 213
Nietzsche, Friedrich 37, 58, 109, 120, 123, 130, 147, 196
nobility 84, 86, 89, 92, 133
Novalis 200
Nürnberg Laws 155
objectivity 5, 138, 207
Oldenburg 61, 64, 66–67, 72
ontology, ontological 195–96
Oranienburg 155
Orff, Carl 168
Ostpolitik 177
Panizza, Oskar 118, 131
Paris 30, 66–71, 73, 79–80, 117–18, 120, 126, 133, 143, 156
Parmenides 195
particularism 198
peace, religious 2, 16–17, 19, 21–23
performative contradiction 198, 210
perspectivism 136, 198
Petzold, Alfons 4, 103–15
  Das rauhe Leben 103, 113, 115
Pfemfert, Franz 127
phenomenology 199
Piscator, Erwin 132

Plato, Platonic 195–97, 208
Polenz, Wilhelm von 3–4, 83–88, 90, 97–101
  Die Büttnerbauer 3–4, 83–86, 98–101
  Sachsengänger 93, 100
political stability 3, 39, 52, 142
Popkin, Richard 197, 213, 215
possessive individualism 43–46, 48, 52–53, 57–58
Postl, Karl; see Charles Sealsfield
postmodernism, postmodernist 211
precritical 202, 206
pre-established harmony 205
Prinzip des Individualismus 112
proletarian literature 4, 103, 109, 112–13
property 32, 34, 41, 43–45, 53, 55, 57, 86, 89, 135; property of the soul 206
propertyless class 44
prosperity 27, 38–40, 43, 47–49, 52, 54–56, 76
Protagoras 197
race 99, 114, 198
Rackham, Arthur 167, 176
Rasch, Wolfdietrich 1, 8–11, 15, 22, 24–25
  Goethes "Iphigenie auf Tauris" als Drama der Autonomie 8, 25–26
rationalization (of industry) 47–48
raw and cooked 103, 108, 115
Reagan, Ronald 166, 174
realism 1, 78, 85, 108, 146, 195, 202–03, 205–07, 210, 213–14; realist, realistic 28, 99, 114, 202, 206, 209
reception aesthetics 166, 168, 170, 174
reconciliation 182–83
Reformation 9, 16, 112
Reinhardt, Max 5, 123–24, 126, 128–31
relativism 198
religion 8, 15–19, 23–25, 29, 32, 34, 63, 106–107, 155; religious 1–2, 8–10, 16–19, 21–25, 32, 113, 149, 212; religious beliefs 15–16, 24, 55, 87
Resistance 189

revolution 2, 5–6, 18, 29, 31–32, 35, 63, 68–69, 72, 83, 94–95, 98, 124, 129, 132–36, 143–47, 149–50, 152, 175, 195
Revolution of 1848 3, 6, 38–40, 43, 52, 56, 58–59, 67–69, 76–77, 80
Richter, Hans 157, 165
Riefenstahl, Leni 166, 174, 176
  Triumph des Willen 174, 176
Riehl, Wilhelm Heinrich 83, 102
Rilke, Rainer Maria 4, 103, 109, 111, 115
Romanismus 87
romanticism, romantic 78, 83, 201, 217
Rome 16, 61, 64–65, 184–85
Rosegger, Peter 84, 101
Rösler, Walter 120, 131
Roth, Joseph 135
  Das Spinnennetz 135
Rothstein, James 120
Rousseau, Jean-Jacques 18, 32
rural community 42, 55–56
Ruttmann, Walter 132, 138
  Berlin, Symphony of a Great City 132, 138
Sachsenhausen 155, 159, 162
Salis, Rudophe 117
Salus, Hugo 120
Sand, George 66, 86, 93–94, 104, 107
sanftes Gesetz 3, 40, 59
Saxony 69, 86, 93–94, 104, 107
Schädlich, Hans Joachim 189, 193
Schall und Rauch 5, 123–26, 129, 131
Schanzer, Rudolf 121
Scheidemann, Philipp 129
Scherer, Wilhelm 84, 102
Schiller, Friedrich von 32, 75, 107, 119, 211, 216
  Wilhelm Tell 216
Schnitzler, Arthur 4, 103, 108–10, 115, 120, 154
  Jugend in Wien 103, 115
Scholastics 17, 197
Schönberg, Arnold 128
Schulz, Erich 85, 102
Schulz, Georg David 127
Schutte, Jürgen 123, 131
Scriabin, Alexander 128

234 Politics in German Literature

Sealsfield, Charles (Karl Postl) 2, 7, 27–35
- *Austria as it is* 2, 28–29, 35
- *Die Vereinigten Staaten von Nordamerika* 2, 28, 35

Searle, John 198, 201, 213–14
Secessionsbühne 120
self-sufficiency (economic) 40, 42, 44, 52, 54–55
Sellars, Roy Wood 203
sexuality 106–07, 110
Shakespeare, William 32, 126
- *A Midsummer Night's Dream* 126

Shoah 159, 163
Simplizissimus 124
skepticism (philosophical) 6, 197–201, 203, 205–07, 209–14
Sloterdijk, Peter 112–13, 115
Social Democrats 107, 147; see also SPD
social democratic 67; democratic socialism 190, 192
social realism 85
Socialism, Socialist 83, 113, 133
socialism, socialist 68, 76–77, 94, 113, 123, 144–45, 148–49, 157–60, 164, 190, 192
Society of Friends of the New Russia 147
Socrates 196–97
Sokal, Alan 211–13, 215
Sophists 197
Spartacists 146
SPD 145, 154, 177; see also Social Democrats
Spinoza, Baruch de 9, 18–19
Sprengel, Peter 26, 123, 131
St. Augustine 156
St. Louis (Missouri) 27
St. Louis 156, 160
Staël-Holstein, Anne Louise Germaine de 34
Stahr, Adolf 3, 61–62, 64–67, 69–76, 79–81
Stalin, Joseph 151, 158, 165
Stasi 33, 188–90, 192–93
Stein, Heinrich Friedrich Karl Reichsfreiherr vom und zum 32
Stevens, George 167
The Greatest Story Ever Told 167

Stifter, Adalbert 2–3, 36–48, 50–59, 84; logical gaps in narrative 53; structural center 37
- *Bergkristall* 3, 36–37, 40–44, 46, 48–53, 55–59
- *Bunte Steine* 3, 37–38, 40, 44, 46, 55, 58–59
- *Der heilige Abend* 38, 43, 46, 50–51, 53–54
- "Die oktroyierte Verfassung" 38, 59
- *Kalkstein* 54, 59
- *Kulturpolitische Aufsätze* 44, 59
- "Waarenauslagen und Ankündigungen" 39, 47, 52, 59
- *Zwei Schwestern* 51, 54–55, 59

Straus, Oscar 120–21; see also Bierbaum
Strindberg, August 109, 126
Stutz, Ludwig 121
subject 53, 108, 181, 188, 196, 204, 206
sublimation 46
substances 204–06
Szczypiorski, Andrzej 183
Tgahrt, Reinhard 160, 163–64
theater 4–5, 107–09, 118–28, 130, 132, 136, 142; see also cinema
Theweleit, Klaus 6, 166, 172, 174, 176
- *Männerphantasien* 6, 166, 176

Third Reich 83, 85, 155, 161, 190
Thirty Years' War 7, 9, 16, 87, 186, 209
Thoma, Ludwig 120
"Zur Dichtkunst abkommandiert" 120–21
Thomson, Alex 168
Tilke, Max 127
Tingeltangel 4, 117–20
Tocqueville, Alexis de 34
Toller, Ernst 157
Tolstoy, Leo 84, 98–99, 107
transcendental deduction 206, 210
travel literature 3, 60, 62, 66–67, 74–75
Treuhand 189–92
Tucholsky, Kurt 127, 129
Tzara, Tristan 128
Überbrettl 5, 120, 122–23, 126–27, 130

underground 106, 114, 155, 158, 164
unemployment 96, 106, 155, 183
use-value 51
Uther Pendragon 170
utopia, utopian 28, 37, 55, 132, 143–44, 149, 177, 185–86, 192
utopianism 37
Variété (Variety Theater) 118–20, 131
Vergegenkunft 6, 181
Viebig, Clara 84
Vienna, Viennese 4–5, 27, 33, 36, 38–39, 69, 71, 103–05, 114–16; Wien, Wiener 39, 103, 106, 109, 115–16
violence, religious 1–2, 9–10, 14–19, 21–24, 209
völkisch 3, 83–85, 87, 89
Vormärz 66, 78
Wagner, Richard 168, 174
Walden, Herwarth 127
Waldheim, Kurt 180
Walser, Martin 178
Walzel, Oskar 84, 102
wars, religious 9, 16; see also Thirty Years' War
Washington, George 2, 29–30
Washington University 27
Wassermann, Jakob 154
Wedekind, Frank 118, 125, 128
Weimar Classicism 8
Weimar Republic 4–5, 117, 129–30, 132–33, 136, 138, 147, 150–51, 157, 189
Weinberg, Steven 213–15
Weiss, Peter 134
Marat/Sade 134
Werfel, Franz 128
Whitehead, Alfred 196
Wien; see Vienna
Wilde, Oscar 126
Salome 126
Wilhelm II 121, 124–25, 129–30
Wilhelmine 117, 121, 123, 129–30, 180
will to power 196
Wittgenstein, Ludwig 6, 195, 203–05, 209, 215
Wohlbrück, Olga 120
Wolf, Christa 178, 192

Wolff, Christian 207
Wolzogen, Ernst von 5, 118, 120, 122–23, 126–27, 130
"Das Laufmädel" 120
"Madame Adèle" 120–21
women's issues
  education 33, 66, 68–69, 75, 78–79
  emancipation 61–62, 77
  right to vote 68, 70
  right to work 66, 68
workers 44, 46–47, 70, 77–78, 93–96, 107, 123, 133–35, 137, 143–44, 148, 150–51, 154, 159, 218
working class 78
Yakir, Dan 172, 176
Zepler, Bogumil 120
Zola, Émile 84, 109
Zuckmayer, Carl 157
Zum hungrigen Pegasus 127
Zweig, Stefan 4, 103, 108–111, 116, 157
  Die Welt von Gestern 103, 116